a theory and procedure of scale analysis

methods and models
in the social sciences

1

MOUTON · THE HAGUE · PARIS

a theory and procedure of scale analysis

With applications in political research

by R. J. MOKKEN

University of Amsterdam

MOUTON · THE HAGUE · PARIS

This book was published with the aid of the Netherlands Organisation for the Advancement of Pure Research (Z.W.O)

Voor Thelma, Wiebe, Marc en Fleur

Contents

vii

PART II. APPLICATIONS IN POLITICAL RESEARCH

Acknowledgements

This study is a result of my activities at three academic institutes in Amsterdam: the Department of Mathematical Statistics of the Mathematical Centre and the Institutes of Mass Communications and for Political Science of the University of Amsterdam. It served as a dissertation in the Faculty of Social Sciences of the University of Amsterdam.

Much gratitude is owed by me to my nearest colleagues and numerous former colleagues for their kind cooperation and assistance as well as for the opportunities they have given me.

I benefited much from the critical comments and general guidance of Professor H. Daudt of the Institute for Political Science during the preparation of the manuscript.

Special thanks are due to Drs. W. van Nooten of the Mathematical Centre for our thorough and frequent discussions about chapters 3 and 4 which led to many improvements.

With pleasure I also acknowledge the collaboration with Drs. F. Bergsma and Drs. F. N. Stokman in the research, some results of which are reported in chapters 6 and 9, and that with Drs. Constance E. van der Maesen and O. Schmidt in the research, reported in chapters 7, 8 and 9.

For the typing of the manuscript I owe much to the concerted efforts of Miss Anke Faddegon, Miss N. Kool and, last but not least, of my wife Thelma. The author's English was corrected skilfully by Mrs. C. M. van Staalen.

I also wish to thank the Netherlands Organization for the Advancement of Pure Research (Z.W.O.) for their contribution in the costs of publication.

Robert J. Mokken

Badhoevedorp, November 1970

CHAPTER 1

The scope of the study

1.1 INTRODUCTION

The rapid development throughout the 1950's of the behavioral
approach in political science from a "protest movement" (Dahl,
1961a) into a fully-fledged empirical wing of the discipline in the
1960's has brought about the increasing application of a growing fund
of research techniques in a widening field of problems. In his review
of this development, Dahl remarked that

"One consequence of the behavioral protest has been to restore
some unity within the social sciences by bringing political studies
into closer affiliation with theories, methods, findings, and outlooks
in modern psychology, sociology, anthropology and economics"
(Dahl 1961a, 770).

In this process, political scientists have been and still are profitably
borrowing measurement techniques and other analytic methods from
these sister sciences, besides developing some methods of their own.

The channeling of the available opportunities for survey research
into the study of voting behavior stimulated this process of adoption,
which during its accelerated course reflected and still is reflecting the
same problems that confronted the other related disciplines in their
struggle to find adequate techniques.

In the field of measurement techniques, the main area of investigation of this study, the early days were marked by the almost exclusive
use of relatively simple procedures. Single questions or other behavioral items were mainly used as indicators of relevant variables without
taking much account of the possibility that a number of these items
may be measuring essentially the same variable. On the other hand, in
other cases indices were constructed from sets of indicators by a
purposive but possibly arbitrary combination of single indicators

1

without much conscious consideration of the possible effects of the heterogeneity of the separate components.

In one of the pioneering works of this early period, *The People's Choice*, the index of political predisposition (Lazarsfeld, Berelson and Gaudet, 1948) is a good example of this type of index. It had some success in its day due to its relation to the theory of cross pressures as a determinant of voting behavior, which in that context was based on just this heterogeneity of the index components: urbanism, wealth and religion (Daudt, 1961, 105–22).

Another example is the index of political self-confidence used by Janowitz and Marvick (1956, 116–7), which, as we shall see later in this study (section 7.1.5), can be shown to form a scale.

It was not the simplicity of these methods of measurement and classification that led to the introduction of other techniques in the search for more efficient methods of measurement. The main disadvantage of the simple indices of this early type was that their rules of construction were not derived from a relation of the index components to the variable which the index was supposed to measure. Instead, these rules were imposed on the data for more or less intuitive and often not clearly stated reasons. Consequently the resulting indices were frequently of a rather arbitrary nature.

It was the lack of any clear-cut explanatory relation of the data to the variable to be measured that inspired the search for other techniques by means of which the observations might be linked explicitly to a postulated, underlying variable in such a way that they would be open to empirical confirmation. After sufficient empirical verification of the appropriateness of the postulated relations, the underlying, explanatory variable might then be measured in terms of the inference provided by observations.

These developments are based on the realization that the assumption that one behavioral item (*e.g.* the answers to one given question in a survey) forms an indicator of a given variable, implies the existence of a broader set of similar behavioral items that can also be chosen as indicators of that same variable. Thus, for instance, Lazarsfeld postulated the interchangeability of indices (Lazarsfeld, 1959b, 113–7), a phenomenon that has had ample empirical verification.

Assuming the existence of a set of items that are homogeneous in this sense, we may devise ways of combining such a set of items into a single measurement of a variable of greater reliability or, for that matter, greater precision than the single-item measurements. For instance, early standard results of psychometric test theory produced sufficient empirical and mathematical foundations for such combination procedures, of which the scaling methods, the main subject of this study, are a special type.

For these reasons, the available techniques of scaling were applied in the field of voting studies at an early stage. One of the earliest examples is the well-known scale called "sense of political efficacy" which has been used in the Michigan voting studies since 1952 (Campbell, Gurin and Miller, 1954, 187–94) and which has proved to be useful in other studies as well. In this study we shall pay more attention to this particular scale.

Recently we have seen an increasing application of scaling techniques in those fields of political research which are based on survey research. To mention just a few examples: they have been used in cross-national comparative studies (Almond and Verba, 1963, 231–6), some of the consequences of which will be touched upon in this study, in community studies (Agger *et al.*, 1964, 755), and in recent studies of political opinion aiming at finding a more penetrating means of analysing public opinion (Verba *et al.*, 1967).

In the major part of these applications, Guttman-type methods of scaling have been used predominantly. The pragmatic nature of these methods and the relative simplicity of the scaling model itself, which is certainly one of the merits of these procedures, may well have been related to their success. For these same reasons a further investigation of Guttmann-type scaling methods will form the main part of this study.

The more striking developments in the study of political behavior were not restricted to the observation of behavior by survey methods alone. Students engaged in the investigation of other areas of policital behavior succeeded in re-defining their problems and re-casting their observations into other forms of data, which lent themselves to the more general application of formal models such as those of scale analysis, factor analysis and other multivariate techniques, thus leading the way to new and often more penetrating methods of measurement and analysis.

As an early example we may mention the discovery that in the United States of America the states could be scaled on the basis of their legislative structure along a dimension measuring legal discrimination against negroes (Shapiro, 1948). In the study of legislative behavior, methods of roll-call analysis used scaling methods to scale legislators or items of legislation. In the same problem area, methods of cluster analysis and factor analysis were tried out with some success in identifying homogeneous groups, clusters or voting-blocs in legislative institutions (MacRae, 1958; Anderson, Watts and

Wilcox, 1966). In the same way, in the field of international relations scaling methods were advocated and used to study behavior in international organizations (Rieselbach, 1960), while methods of factor analysis have been applied recently to the study of voting behavior in the General Assembly of the United Nations, in an effort to detect voting blocs in terms of the results of votes cast on a set of issues (Alker, 1964; Alker and Russett, 1965).

Recent efforts to accumulate evidence from the observed behavior of national representatives in public committees of international organizations may well point the way to other data amenable to the types of analysis and measurements mentioned above (Alger, 1966). Even in the behavioral analysis of historical data, methods like these have been used with some success (Ulmer, 1966).

Although we do not attempt to give even a cursory enumeration, these examples may suffice to illustrate the successful application of well-known techniques in a broadening field of political analysis. The adoption of techniques by another discipline and their fruitful application in empirical areas and situations often strongly different from those in which they originated, has been and sometimes still is a source of bewilderment and raising of eyebrows. This widening field of application is, of course, the result of the general applicability of the formal measurement model on which these methods of analysis rely. In general this applicability has proved to be much wider than it was generally thought to be in the particular discipline in which the procedures originated.

In the meantime the various branches of "empirical social science", with the aid of the many-sided services of modern mathematics, have been a continuous source of technical and analytical innovation. The modern electronic computer has made it possible to apply more complicated and faster techniques of analysis. The development of modern mathematical statistics and probability theory has inspired new insights and developments in the field of measurement and analysis which have still not reached the stage of a more or less definite formulation. The application of such statistical and probabilistic procedures may help us in at least two respects.

On the one hand, it may make possible a reappraisal of the existing pragmatic and simple scaling procedures of the Guttman type. On the other hand, it may indicate ways of formulating other more adequate, though not necessarily more simple, measurement models.

This study gives a summary of some of the author's researches in both respects.

1.2 DATA MODELS

Measurement implies the assignment of numbers to the objects of empirical inquiry. This aspect is common to most of the current definitions of measurement. In its broadest sense measurement consists in the establishment of a correspondence between mathematical objects, such as real numbers or vectors, and empirical objects such as forces, colours, and particular classes of behavior. This correspondence can be constructed by the detection of an isomorphism between the observable formal properties of the empirical objects and the operations performed on them, and the formal properties and the corresponding operations characterizing the mathematical objects (Krantz, 1967, 1).

One of the weakest forms of measurement, very commonly used in the social sciences, has been called *measurement by definition* or *measurement by fiat* (Torgerson, 1958, 22). The observations are simply combined into numerical indicators or indices more or less arbitrarily. The combination procedures do not refer explicitly or clearly to the variables that are to be represented, nor are they suggested by a specified relation of the observations to such variables. The indices and indicators that often figure in political research can mostly be classified under this heading. The *index of political predisposition* that we have mentioned before is an example of this type of measurement. Other, more recent examples of indices of this type can be found in Dahl's study of the influence structure of New Haven (Dahl, 1961 b, 342–3). In this study he defines an *index of campaign participation* based firstly on the distinction between "voters" and "non-voters", the "non-voters" forming the lowest level of the scale, and secondly on the division of the "voters" into four levels, according to the number of certain campaign activities reported by them. This resulted in a five-point scale. In a similar way he defines an *index of non-campaign participation in local affairs* by counting the number of activities reported by respondents on a list of four (talking about politics with friends, getting in touch with local officials or politicians about an issue, taking an active part in a local issue or problem, and any contact they might have had with political or governmental officials in the past year or so). The two indices were then combined into an *index of local action* by assigning numerical weights (0–5) to the various combinations of the two indices.

The possible dangers of the heterogeneity of the two index components in the last example can be illustrated by the subsequent analysis in Dahl's study, which gives some indication that the two basic indices may measure different types or, for that matter, different dimensions of political activity (Dahl, 1961 b, 285) (see our section 9.4.). It should be stressed, however, that despite the unkind names – "measurement by fiat" or "measurement by definition" – given to these methods, there is nothing inherently wrong, invalid or illogical in these types of measurement.

The essential difference, however, between such methods of measurement by definition and the other methods of measurement that form a contrast to them, is that the latter relate the observations to one or more underlying variables by means of a model. Such a model enables us to predict the existence of a set of specific inter-relations between the observations, as an internal consistency imposed on them by these underlying variables. If these interrelations can be verified empirically, this is evidence that a common variable does indeed exist and may be measured by the observations. Only if this specific internal consistency is observed may we try to measure the variable in what is probably a more reliable way and, it is hoped or believed, with better chances of validity.

As for general validity, however, all types of measurement will have to stand the ultimate test of construct validity: their satisfactory performance within the theoretical and operational context to which they refer (Cronbach and Meehl, 1955; De Groot, 1961, 271–8).

Other general types of measurement have been distinguished. Those forming part of what has been called "the classical view of measurement" are well-known and have been highly influential (Stevens, 1959, 21–3). This classical view produced what was mainly a reconstruction of the measurement procedures commonly used in the physical sciences in the form of a measurement theory (Krantz, 1967, 12). This theory has had great impact in the social sciences, although there measurement procedures as common and obvious in the light of everyday experience as those used in physics do not occur.

A well-known typology of measurement used in this classical theory is that of Campbell, who distinguished *fundamental measurement* and *derived measurement* (Campbell, 1928, 14). Fundamental measurement is direct in the sense that no prior measurements are involved, whereas derived measurement is based on other measurements, as in the classical example of temperature and density. Fundamental measurement is performed directly on the observations and in this respect resembles measurement by fiat, except for the fact that in its original formulation as a measurement procedure Campbell restricted it to the measurement of *quantities*, *i.e.* empirical properties admitting an empirical operation equivalent (or rather isomorph) to the mathematical operation of addition. The classical example is the measurement of mass in which the "additive" operation consists of putting weights together in a balance.

Therefore, in the classical exposition referred to, the procedures of fundamental measurement and necessarily those of derived measurement, as they were ultimately based on the former, resulted in ratio or interval scales. This narrow definition of measurement was broadened considerably as further developments of the measurement theory took place in the social sciences. S.S. Stevens took the first step by taking into consideration the range of transformations under which a particular scale was invariant and introducing his well-known classification of scales of measurement (Stevens, 1951). A later axiomatic treatment of measurement theories (Scott and Suppes, 1958) in a more recent version introduced a method of fundamental and derived measurement in which no special value is attached to the existence of an additive operation, which in the social sciences is a very rare phenomenon (Suppes and Zinnes, 1963). In this system the various models giving rise to Coombs' unfolding technique (Coombs, 1950) are regarded as examples of the extended concepts of fundamental measurement, whereas both the Bradley–Terry–Luce models and the Thurstone models for paired comparisons data (Bradley and Terry, 1952; Luce, 1959; Thurstone, 1927) are seen as examples of derived measurement, because a first operation of measurement, the introduction and estimation of probabilities for pairs, is necessary before the ultimate scale values can be derived.

We shall see that in this study a first step of measurement is postulated by introducing probabilities of a positive response to items as functions of the unknown scale values of subjects. The models dealt with in this study can therefore be classified most appropriately as derived measurement models, if we follow the foregoing reasoning.*

Apart from what has been said about the development of a formal measurement theory, it has also rightly been stated that

"... at the present stage of development of quantitative theory in social science, it is impossible to separate the search for interesting empirical laws from the discovery and refinement of measurement procedures" (Krantz, 1967, 13).

Indeed, significant break-throughs in the social sciences have often

---

*Pfanzagl (1968, 173–4), however, treats paired comparison as fundamental measurement. He puts up a rather convincing argument that "derived measurement" should not be considered measurement at all (Pfanzagl, 1968, 31).

been associated with new methods of observation, data construction and finally measurement. The development of factor analysis is just one well-known example of this process. Such developments lead to a continuing increase of the observational possibilities and a multitude of data configurations, which almost defies classification.

The development of modern probability theory and mathematical statistics has opened up further perspectives, making it possible to formulate and test probabilistic models which formalize behavioral theories in terms of a great variety of data. For a particular set of data we may derive from a plausible theory such a probabilistic model, which explains the data partially in term of parameters that are defined within the model. One might argue that as soon as values of parameters are estimated for such models from the data, a problem of measurement is in question. This would lead to a very broad definition of measurement indeed. For the purposes of our study, at least, we shall use a more narrow one. In fact, we shall distinguish data models in general from measurement models in particular.

Coombs (1964, 4–6) has pointed out that the term *data* is commonly used in the behavioral sciences in a double meaning. In the first place it is used to denote the original recorded observations, the "raw" empirical items that are first collected as part of the process of inquiry. The voting record of legislators in a particular session of a legislature, the votes cast by members of the United Nations General Assembly, the answers of a respondent to a set of questions in a questionnaire are examples of *data* in this first meaning.

According to another usage, the term *data* is used to denote only those observational elements that enter into the models used for analysis. These observational elements are not necessarily identical to the original recorded observations. Thus a number of roll-calls concerning a group of legislative items may form the recorded observations. The matrix of correlations between pairs of legislative items, taken over legislators after a proper scoring of votes, may form the set of data for a factor analysis or a multidimensional scaling model.

Another example that corresponds more closely to the type of problems in this study is that in which, after a proper dichotomous scoring of the answers to a set of questions, the set of (2×2)-tables between questions and taken over respondents, forms the data that are entered into a scale analysis.

Coombs particularized the term *data* to denote only observational elements according to this second meaning, indicating the class of restructured observations that enter into the analytic models used for inference and distinguishing them from the original recorded observations. The merit of this specialized definition of the term *data* is that it helps us keep in mind that these original recorded observations can be converted into a plurality of different types of data corresponding to different types of models.

Following Coombs's argument, three phases of scientific activity may be discerned in the inferential process.

The first phase covers the recording of the primary observations from the "real world" as a universe of potential observations.

In the second phase these recorded observations are converted into data by a creative effort of interpretation on the part of the scientist. In this second phase the observations are mapped onto data, so to speak. This entails the identification and interrelation of individuals and stimuli, subjects and objects or whatever different classes of observational units are brought in relation to each other in a particular form of data.

The third phase, finally, involves the detection of relations, order and structure that follow from the data and the model chosen for analysis, leading to a classification of *e.g.* individuals and stimuli.

For instance, applying our model to the data, we may estimate parameters or other quantities that we require in the context of our research. In the case of measurement this third phase leads to the determination of scale values for individuals. For this type of model, one that reflects the data and is used to analyze them in order to obtain inferential evidence, the name *data model* has been used (Stouthard, 1965).

Thus Coombs' view of the process of inquiry may be summarized as follows: observations are recorded, the *recorded observations* are converted into a *set of data* which then by means of a *data model* is analyzed for inferential evidence or classification.

1.3 MEASUREMENT MODELS

It will be clear from the discussion in the last section that – leaving out of account the trivial fact that there are an infinity of ways of collecting and recording observations – given a certain set of observations, there are many different ways of converting these into data. Again, given a particular set of data, there will usually be numerous possibilities of constructing models to describe and analyse these data.

Stouthard (1965, 59–75) has stressed the point that data models form a much larger class than measurement models. In this study we shall also consider measurement models as a sub-class of the data models, distinguished from the other types by the special purpose for which they are used. This purpose is not in the first place to seek an adequate unidimensional or multidimensional representation of our set of data, as is the case in, for instance, the analysis of the structure of party preferences in electoral research (Converse, 1966). The purpose is primarily the derivation of numerical values for a variable that may be used as valid measurements to relate such a variable to other quantitative attributes in research.

For the purpose of this study, we may therefore define a measurement model as a data model applied with the intention of inferring from the postulated or verified fit of the data to the model the values of the model variable, as determined by the data, to be used as measurements in a wider research context. The insistence on the intention of actual use of the variable in research, though admittedly rather pragmatic, is not in disagreement with the traditional views on measurement and is intended to exclude to a certain degree models that are of limited use. It should incline us to select the simplest models with which the data are in agreement. Henceforth we shall use the term *scaling model* in a sense more or less synonymous with measurement model.

All data models are based on theories that are partly imposed and partly tested on the data models, and this is therefore true of measurement or scaling models as well.

As Coombs has remarked:
"This illustrates the general principle that all knowledge is the result of theory – we buy information with assumptions – "facts" are inferences, and so also are data and measurements and scales" (1964, 5).

In addition to this we want to stress once again the fact that different data models, that is, different behavioral theories, can be used to describe the same set of data even in the case of measurement models. This whole study, for instance, may be regarded as an illustration of the fact that many different models can be used to explain or describe dichotomous data of a particular kind.

From the multitude of possible models for a given set of data, we may prefer to choose for our measurement models only those that are relatively simple in their behavioral assumptions, as are some of those which we will discuss in later chapters. In a sense this is simply another application of Thurstone's "principle of parsimony".

Despite the narrowing of our definition of a measurement model, the variety of types of data and corresponding models appropriate to the construction of measurement procedures is still very great. In Coombs' theory of data, which is concerned with behavioral theory at the level that forms the basis for measurement and scaling as practised in the social sciences, a formal classification of data types is attempted on the basis of a triple dichotomy, superseding an older classification (1964, 3–31, 561–5; 1953, 491–4).

One important basis for classification in Coombs' system may be mentioned here to locate the major part of the research reported in this study. This is a distinction based on the sets of observational elements that are brought into relation with each other in data and model. In a general formal context, two different sets may be involved: a set of *subjects*, *individuals*, or respondents and a set of *items* or *stimuli*. The classification of data involved here is based on the way the two types of sets are dealt with in the data. Either both sets or only one of them may be distinguished in the model.

For instance, a large class of psychological scaling data is based on experiments in which stimuli are compared. Pair comparison data form an example here. In the corresponding scaling models, the individuals involved are not distinguished, but seen as replications of the same comparison experiment. In the models for these *stimulus comparison data* (or B data; Coombs, 1964, 27–8) only one set, the set of stimuli, is specified. In multiparty systems, for instance, we may ask a sample of the electorate to judge all possible pairs that can be formed from the relevant parties and to indicate their relative preference for each pair presented.

In models for this type of data it is sometimes assumed that the preference judgements are determined mainly by the relative position of the parties with respect to each other irrespective of the individual differences between subjects. In that case only the values and positions of the stimuli (parties) enter into the data model.

In the type of scaling problems with which we are concerned in this study, a different situation prevails. In this case the respondents may be thought of as comparing *themselves* (*i.e.* their attitudes) to stimuli or items one at a time. A typical case is the situation where respondents compare their dispositions and the contents of certain questions when trying to answer them.

Let us consider the case of a respondent determining his response to an interview question related to a concept such as the "sense of political efficacy" (see chapters 7 and 8). First of all we may assume that as a stimulus the content and meaning of that particular question require a certain minimum amount of efficacy for respondents to give an affirmative response. That minimum amount is considered a quality of the question which may be conceptualized as its "efficacy"-value. As such, this value is perceived by the respondent, who measures his own feelings of efficacy against it when replying. According to this reasoning, therefore, subject values are related to stimulus values in the model. The same situation is involved in the case of a legislator considering his vote on a particular legislative issue.

In models for data of this type we may want to distinguish individuals as well as items or stimuli. Therefore, in models designed for such *individual-stimulus comparison* data (also called *single stimulus* or A data; Coombs, 1964, 27–8), two sets are distinguished: a set of individuals and a set of stimuli, the elements of *both* of which are to be scaled on the basis of a response relation that is defined for pairs consisting of elements of each of the two different sets.

The three approaches to scaling put forward by Torgerson (1958, 45–60) are closely related to the classification described above. He first mentions the *subject-centered approach*. Stimuli are seen as replications of the same experiment and combined solely with the purpose of differentiating between subjects. As examples Torgerson mentions the Likert-type procedures and most of the methods in the field of mental testing. Following Coombs' terminology, one might call them *individual comparison data* (if one is prepared to include stimuli comparing individuals), as only the set of individuals is involved in these procedures, which Torgerson somewhat casually regards as belonging to the domain of measurement by definition. Methods of this type, which belong chiefly to the field of mental testing, are not discussed by Torgerson, who refers the reader to standard texts in this field (*e.g.* Gulliksen, 1950). In this study no very important place is given to them either.

As a second approach Torgerson mentions the *stimulus-centered* or *judgement approach*, which is essentially based on Coombs' previously mentioned stimulus comparison data or B-data, whereas Torgerson's *response approach*, in which the variability of reactions to stimuli is ascribed to differences in the subjects as well as in the stimuli, corresponds to the individual-stimulus comparison data or A-data of Coombs. As has been said before, the major part of the research reported here has been carried out on the basis of this response approach. Another important distinction is that between *unidimensional* and *multidimensional* scaling methods.

In our discussion we have mentioned the two basic sets that can be considered in measurement models. In the unidimensional measurement models, the sets involved are mostly represented as sub-sets of the real line, "the single continuum" as it is traditionally called. The position of an individual is reduced to one value, which indicates his position (score) on the single dimension, the interpretation of which again depends on the problem behind the data.

In the more general models that have been developed, these sets are sub-sets of n-dimensional Euclidean space. In the case of the set of individuals, for instance, the individual is considered as a point in this space, the nature and interpretation of which depend on the problem at hand. If the space can be interpreted as an attitude space, the individual's position (attitude) as a point in that space will be given by the coordinates of that point, *i.e.* the collection of values of that particular individual on each of the relevant attitude dimensions that are spanning the space. Factor analysis is one of the early methods used to generate metric multidimensional representations.

We shall mention just one recent example. Alker represented the nations participating in the Sixteenth General Assembly of the United Nations on the basis of a factor analysis of seventy votes from this session in terms of their positions in a two-dimensional space spanned by and "East-West" and a "North-South" conflict dimension (Alker, 1964). Besides the methods of metric multidimensional scale analysis based on an observed distance metric (Torgerson, 1958, 247–97), methods of non-metric multidimensional scaling have been developed which seem very promising indeed.

As examples of more recent developments we may mention Shepard (1962a; 1962b) and the improvements of his model by Kruskal (1964a; 1964b) and Guttman (1968). (See also Roskam, 1968). Stokes (1963) has been studying the use of spatial models to explain party competition. Converse (1966) suggested that non-metric multidimensional scaling methods be used to analyse perceived party distances in multiparty systems for the analysis of voting change.

The research that is reported here is for the most part restricted to unidimensional scaling methods. Despite the increasing importance of multidimensional measurement procedures, at least two arguments can be put forward in support of the continuing investigation and application of unidimensional scaling models.

In the first place, many of the uses that have been made of multi-dimensional techniques fall outside the field of measurement as defined in this study. Then the problem is primarily to *detect* relevant dimensions and not to *measure* them. For instance, the major part of the applications of factor analysis falls into this class. In the same way, multidimensional scaling models, apart from providing possibilities for genuine multidimensional measurement, may continue to serve to a considerable extent the purpose not so much of measurement, but of the reduction of data structures in search of simple and useful dimensions.

Once these facts have been realized and relevant dimensions have been found, further application of these results in research may very often call for adequate *unidimensional* scaling models based on observations ("pure items") which are constructed especially for the purpose of measuring each of the dimensions concerned (for an example see section 6.6.). Therefore adequate unidimensional techniques are still needed as well as multidimensional techniques.

Another argument in favour of the use of adequate unidimensional scales stems from the increasing use of more advanced multivariate techniques. A recent trend is the application of linear models for purposes of causal analysis (Blalock, 1961; Boudon, 1967, 30–202; Alker 1966). One of the earlier examples of this approach in the field of political research is the analysis by Miller and Stokes (1963) of the influence of constituency opinion on roll call behavior of Congressmen. Other examples followed: Cnudde and McCrone (1966), in the same field as the last-mentioned study, and Tanter (1967), in the field of political development. Goldberg in a similar analysis of data on voting behavior even expects that such procedures will become a part of statistical orthodoxy (Goldberg, 1966). The fact that models of this type are rather demanding as regards the levels of measurement of the data that form their input suggests a second argument in favour of the development of more appropriate unidimensional scaling techniques.

Another distinction that plays an important role in this study is that between *deterministic* and *stochastic* or *probabilistic* scaling models.

In the case of the individual-stimulus comparison data or response models that are mainly dealt with in our study, *deterministic* models are used when, given the position of the individual on the attitude continuum (the subject set) and given the place of the stimulus (item) on a related continuum (the item set or stimulus set), the subject's response to that particular item is completely determined: the subject can respond in only one manner, or in terms of probabilistic models, he will give a particular response with probability one. Alternative responses are not open to the subject: the probability that one of these responses will be given by this subject is zero in deterministic models.

Most of the models that are associated with the approach of

Coombs are deterministic in nature. For the types of measurement models considered in this study, the Guttman model is the well-known example. This model will be the subject of chapter 2.

In *stochastic* or *probabilistic* models *all* the possible responses open to the individual will in general be given with non-zero probability. This probability will again depend on the position of the subjects and items on their continua.

In chapter 4 we shall consider models in which, for instance, the probability that any given subject will respond positively to a certain item increases as his attitude increases. These positions of subjects and items on a given attitude continuum may enter into the measurement model as separate parameters, the estimation of which forms the measurement problem. In chapter 3 we shall consider a very general model of this type and some specific cases that are designed for dichotomous data. The advantage of such models is that they take into account the possibility of the "response-error" that deterministic models have to cope with when they are applied to actual data. Whenever measurements have been made in any branch of empirical investigation, scientists have been faced with the necessity of incorporating a theory of error in relation to their measurements. In this process, we shall see, many of the niceties of deterministic models may be lost. Coombs (1964, 81–2), in discussing this point, has remarked:

"The effect of strengthening a technique as a scaling method is to reduce its capability as a scaling criterion. When we are interested in scaling from the point of view of a scaling criterion we are interested in psychological theory; when we are interested in scaling from the point of view of a scaling technique we have already adopted some theory (that which led to the data and their conversion to measurements) and are interested in constructing tools for further research."

It is exactly this last focus of interest that dominates the research reported here.

1.4 OUTLINE OF THE STUDY

We may summarize our introduction by saying that this study is mainly concerned with unidimensional measurement models based on data of the individual-stimulus comparison type (A-data in Coombs' first typology) and the response approach (Torgerson, 1958). Our analysis will be further restricted to stimuli or items with dichotomized response alternatives. Both deterministic and probabilistic measurement models will be investigated.

The major part of our study will, however, be devoted to models of the latter type, the former, deterministic, models serving mainly as a good starting point from which the analysis can proceed. The well-known Guttman scale will serve as the deterministic example because of its pragmatic value in research, demonstrated by the many scaling procedures it has fathered. In fact a major purpose of these probabilistic models will be to find a better methodological basis for the procedures of cumulative scaling that have proved so useful in many fields of social research. Yet these models have been given relatively little attention in the more comprehensive monographs that have been published up to now. Coombs, commenting on the individual-stimulus comparison data, the data which form the chief basis of our study (QIIa or b data in his later system of classification, 1964, 211–83), remarks that they are the most prevalent in psychology. Nevertheless he treats these models only summarily, referring for a more elaborate treatment to Torgerson's study (1958). The major part of the latter work is, however, devoted to Thurstonean models based on the judgement or stimulus-comparison approach which originated in the problems of psychophysical scaling. Compared to the elaborate treatment of this subject, the discussion in the Torgerson monograph of the measurement models that are the object of our study is but a cursory one. It provides a good though not complete survey of the techniques of Guttman scaling, but does not give much information about probabilistic versions; this is due to the fact that such stochastic scaling models are comparatively new developments in the behavioral sciences.

Our study will consist of two parts. In the first part (chapters 2-5) the *theory and method* of scaling proposed by us will be dealt with. In the second part (chapters 6-9) we shall consider a number of *applications*.

In *chapter 2* (part I) we shall investigate the relevant characteristics and practices of the conventional methods of Guttman scaling for dichotomous data. It is not our purpose to give a complete survey of all the varieties of practical methods and techniques that are commonly used in social research. We are interested mainly in an analysis of the common deterministic assumptions from which they were derived. We shall end our analysis with a discussion of the conclusion that this deterministic framework led to cumbersome procedures frequently containing fallacious elements. The admission of "error", which is necessary in order to arrive at practical procedures that can be used in research, and the corresponding concept of a "quasi-scale", underline the necessity of incorporating a theory of error in the model itself. Consequently, probabilistic response models should be analyzed and used to evaluate or set up scaling methods instead of deterministic response models. The survey of chapter 2 therefore suggests the framework of the next two chapters and the problems that will be investigated in these chapters.

Chapters 3 and 4 are unabashedly mathematical and contain analyses of a type which will probably be beyond the range of interest to be expected from many readers concerned with social measurement and its applications. Instead of relegating his mathematical analyses to appendices, the author preferred to develop them in the context of his study in separate chapters.

The reader who is not sufficiently interested in these mathematical details may skip chapters 3 and 4 and will find in the first section of chapter 5 a summary of the main results of these chapters.

We begin the analysis in *chapter 3* with a mathematical scaling model of extreme generality which allows of multidimensional subject and item representation. This model is presented as a generalization of the "latent structure" model suggested by Lazarsfeld (1950). It includes as special cases not only all the models proposed under this heading but also models such as factor analysis. This model gives us the opportunity of mentioning the types of problems involved in probabilistic models and dealing with a specific sub-class of latent structure models which can be derived through the application of an interesting new theory of measurement proposed by Rasch. In the second part of chapter 3 the latent structure model is specialized for dichotomous data and one-dimensional subject representation. As an illustration of the theory developed in the first part, specific parametric models based on the cumulative normal (normal ogive) and the logistic curves are considered.

In *chapter 4* we continue our mathematical analysis of models for dichotomous data with a general class of models with one-dimensional subject and item representation and without a specification of their parametric or functional form. These non-parametric models, which are called *monotonely homogeneous* and *holomorph* or *doubly monotone* seem fairly natural probabilistic counterparts of the Guttman model. They give us the opportunity of deriving a number of properties which serve to evaluate prevalent usages in conventional Guttman scaling methods and of arriving at new scaling methods not containing the fallacious elements of the first.

This derivation of a class of scaling methods and procedures based on a clear definition of a scale is undertaken in *chapter 5*. The chapter begins with a summary and recapitulation of the main results of chapters 3 and 4. Using these results, a new, simple definition of a scale is given in terms of which a class of scaling procedures can be developed and actually were subsequently developed in a system of programs as the Mathematical Centre in Amsterdam. Chapter 5 concludes Part I and the discussion of our scaling theory.

Part II (chapters 6–9) is devoted to a number of applications of our methods. Apart from the fact that these applications may serve as illustrations of several methods suggested in this study, the author hopes that these chapters will have a substantial interest of their own. They are based on results obtained in the fields of local politics, electoral research and mass communication research at the Institute for Policital Science and the Institute for Mass Communication at the University of Amsterdam. The investigations whose results are reported here were not just constructed as particular examples of scales but were carried out in the context of current research in accordance with the author's conviction that the development of theory and measurement should go firmly hand in hand.

The first two *chapters (6 and 7)* of Part II contain the results of some cross-national comparative investigations in the framework of cross-cultural methodology. The general validity of variables measured in terms of measurement models such as scales attains a special significance when we investigate the common existence of the dimensions concerned in a cross-cultural or cross-national context. We hope to demonstrate that our models and methods supply us with the means of developing a methodological and conceptual framework on the basis of which such problems may be analyzed with profit.

Chapter 6 gives an introduction to the subject with a comparative study of factor analyses of readership interest in the contents of newspapers. The chapter concludes with some evidence that in certain cases dimensions found by factor analysis may subsequently be scalable.

In *chapter 7* the cross-cultural existence of common dimensions is investigated in terms of the concept of the "robustness" of scales. The discussion is based on a comparative analysis of the scale of the "sense of political efficacy" for the United States and the Netherlands.

In *chapter 8* we report our results concerning the development of a scale of the "sense of political efficacy" in the Netherlands as an extension of the original scale. After an additional scale concerning the sense of efficacy with respect to local politics had been set up, the analysis produced evidence of a more general dimension of "local" and "national" political efficacy.

In *chapter 9*, finally, we report the results of a number of analyses in which our procedure of multiple scaling was applied with varying degrees of success. The results concern scales of the type of informal communication behavior associated with opinion leadership, of the sense of civic competence (compared with the sense of political efficacy), and of two dimensions of influence stereotypes. The chapter concludes with our findings concerning the scalability of political participation. In *chapter 10*, our final chapter, we summarize our main conclusions.

Some final remarks must be made with respect to the *numerical references* to sections, tables, figures and theorems in the text. Sections and sub-sections are numbered lexicographically within the chapters or sections. For instance, section 8.1. denotes the first section of chapter 8 and section 8.1.2. the second sub-section of section 8.1. Figures and tables are numbered consecutively according to the chapter, so that table 9.3 denotes the third table of chapter 9. In order to keep numerical references relatively simple, theorems, lemmas and corollaries will be numbered according to the sections and sub-sections only, without reference to the number of the chapter. In chapter 4, therefore, the second theorem of sub-section 1.4. is theorem 1.4.2.

PART I

Theory and method

CHAPTER 2

The deterministic model: the Guttman scale

2.1 INTRODUCTION

Having developed his technique of scalogram analysis throughout the 1940's in several articles, Guttman published the final and well-known version of his method in *Measurement and Prediction*, the fourth volume of the *Studies in Social Psychology in World War II* (Stouffer *et al.*, 1950). Since then the method has had an enormous success, despite the many difficulties that were encountered in its application. The clear-cut model behind the procedures that made them compare favorably with apparently more arbitrary techniques of item analysis such as those of the Likert type, must have contributed a great deal towards this success. In addition the model did not exclude relatively easy and pragmatic methods of analysis that could be used to define variables in research. The increasing availability of mechanical equipment in the early fifties and the subsequent advent of high-speed electronic computors enlarged these possibilities.

The literature on the many variants of this model that have been developed is highly dispersed. Good reviews available at the moment are those of Green (1954), Edwards (1957), Torgerson (1958, 298–345). Matalon (1965) and Sixtl (1967). Most general reviews such as these give a good survey of existing procedures and methods of Guttman scaling. Yet a critical analysis and evaluation of the several types of coefficients of reproducibility or scalability, which are central to these methods, seem to be lacking in these reviews, as is an investigation of the interrelation of these coefficients as criteria of scalability.

Then again, a number of problems are virtually neglected in the literature, although they have been recently solved, or may be solved with the help of a stochastic model, instead of the deterministic one originally given by Guttman.

One such class of problems concerns the statistical theory of sample coefficients of scalability: their sampling distribution and their utility as estimates and criteria for statistical tests concerning scalability coefficients defined for populations. The deterministic theory of the Guttman scale has led to quite a number of rules of thumb, meant to refine practical methods of scaling. In chapter 4 we shall attempt to evaluate a number of such rules with the help of a stochastic scaling model. We may prepare the way for such an analysis by an appraisal of the Guttman model and the procedures that have prevailed in practice.

Still another reason for reviewing this simple model is that it displays in a rudimentary form virtually all the major properties and problems that characterize the more general scaling models which we shall consider in chapters 3 and 4 and of which it will prove to be a special case. As such the model is a good introduction to the general problem of scaling. In fact, when re-reading Guttman's original text, one is struck by the fact that almost all these aspects were seen or surmised by Guttman at that time (Guttman 1950 a, b).

In our review we will not attempt to give a complete survey of all the techniques and problems that have been treated under the heading of the Guttman method. For this we may refer the reader to the well-known reviews mentioned above. We shall restrict ourselves to the properties, problems and criteria that seem relevant in trying to evaluate and develop scaling procedures based on a non-deterministic theory.

Moreover, we will consider only dichotomized items. As this type of data very much prevails in practical applications, this restriction does not seem too narrow. Nor shall we deal with the metric solution and the related problem of the principal components of scalable attitudes, intensity analysis and the determination of a zero point, for which we may refer the reader to Torgerson (1958, 336–46).

2.2   THE PERFECT SCALE

We saw in chapter 1 that in the case of individual-stimulus comparison data, two different types of sets may be distinguished. Guttman (1950a, 80) already referred to a set of objects and a set of attributes, remarking that "*scale analysis is a formal analysis, and hence applies to any universe of qualitative data of any science, obtained by any manner of observation"* (1950a, 88).

We shall specialize this general form to suit the type of empirical research reported in this study, as follows. In the first place there will be one set of individuals or respondents. We shall refer to this set mostly as the *set of subjects*. The second set consists of stimuli presented to these subjects, such as a number of items presented in the context of a survey questionnaire. We shall refer to this set as the *set of items*. It is assumed that each subject responds to each item as a single stimulus, that is, that he measures himself against the items one at a time and does not measure the items against each other.

2.2.1   Dichotomous data

A subject may respond in many ways to the stimuli that are presented to him. As a result we can usually discern for any stimulus or item a number of different possible responses or categories in the raw recorded observations. In the data models which we shall consider in this study, these numerous possible responses are reduced through an appropriate combination to just two responses, the same for each subject. In fact, we select one response category, or combine a number of important response alternatives into one category, and then consider all other response alternatives as the second, complementary response category. We may therefore think of this reduction as a one-sided dichotomization of the original response alternatives. The adjective "one-sided" is used mainly to stress a certain point of view with respect to an interpretation of the resulting dichotomous response categories. We may clarify this point as follows.

One-sided dichotomization occurs when we isolate from the possible response alternatives that alternative which is considered on the basis of item content to be related most significantly or meaningfully to the underlying continuum that is being measured. In this sense we may consider that alternative as containing the information most relevant for the measurement of the underlying variable. We shall call this alternative in the resulting dichotomy the *scale alternative* or *scale response* and occasionally, when no confusion seems possible, the *positive alternative* or *response*. The information in all the other alternatives is disregarded, for these alternatives are lumped together in the second complementary alternative of the dichotomy. The meaning of this second alternative is derived solely from the scale alternative in that the former is the negation of the latter.

Two examples borrowed from *Measurement and Prediction* (Suchman, 1950a, 125) are given to illustrate the procedure. They concern two items from a scale measuring "Satisfaction with One's Army Job". First an item of the Yes-No variety.

"Would you change to some other Army job if given a chance?"
  1 – Yes
  2 – No
  3 – Undecided

In this case 2: "No" may be considered to be the scale alternative (the "positive" answer), "Yes" and "Undecided" forming the complementary alternative.

Next a multicategory item:

"Which of the following would you say best applies to your job?"
  1 – Time always passes quickly.
  2 – Time passes quickly most of the time.
  3 – Enjoy working part of the time, but it drags at other times.
  4 – Time drags most of the time.
  5 – Time always drags.
("No answers" were all coded 0).

Here alternative 1 may be the scale alternative. However, one might also combine several alternatives to form the scale alternative, *e.g.* alternatives 1 and 2. The other alternatives together form the second complementary alternative.

Guttman's original method was also designed to scale multicategory items without dichotomizing them. We shall not consider these items in this study, and again refer the reader to Torgerson (1958) or Matalon (1965). This restriction does not seem too severe when we consider that dichotomized data are used very frequently in measurement and analysis in the behavioral sciences.

2.2.2   *Monotone items and trace lines*

It has been said that each subject "measures" himself against each item in terms of the variable we want to measure, his response giving the result of this comparison. The content of the item determines this response behavior.

Now this response behavior can be partially classified into two types, leading to a classification of items that is very important in scaling models. We can illustrate this with the usual example of tallness. When investigating the heights of people we might formulate two types of questions or items that lead to totally different forms of response behavior.

1. "Are you   1.73 m. tall?"
2. "Are you over 1.73 m. tall?"

The hypothetical results are shown in figure 2.1.

The variable that we are measuring and that may be thought to generate the responses of the subjects to the items, can be represented as the "single continuum" along the horizontal axis. In our example this "underlying" variable is the "unknown" length of the respondents. In our model each subject compares his own position on this continuum with the item content as related to the attribute. Let us take as scale alternative in both questions the answer "yes". We can imagine respondents of all possible heights distributed along the horizontal axis. A respondent of a certain height (the degree, quantity or value of the attribute) will give the "positive" answer (scale alternative) with a probability depending on that degree or value. Assuming that with all subjects of the same height, the same probability exists that they will do so, we can measure the probability of a positive answer (scale alternative) and plot this probability as a function of the "underlying" or "latent" attribute of height.

This method of representation, very common in stochastic scaling models, introduces the probabilities of a positive response as curves. In both cases these curves will range along a P-axis between the values zero and one.

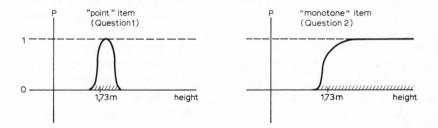

Figure 2.1   The probability of the scale alternative for two types of questions. The shaded area indicates the interval with non-zero probability of positive response.

These curves have been called *item trace lines* in latent structure analysis (Lazarsfeld, 1950), *item operating characteristics* (Green, 1954) or *item characteristic curves* (I.C.C.'s) in mental test construction (Lord and Novick, 1968, 366).

Following Lazarsfeld we will mainly use the term *trace lines*. To return to our example: we first note a striking dissimilarity in the trace lines of items 1 and 2. Of course that difference is based on the different content of the items. In question 1 only respondents whose height is around 1.73 m. will be inclined to say "yes" to item 1. By doing so they identify their height with the *proximity* of the point 1.73 m.

With subjects that are either much taller or much shorter than 1.73 m., there is a high probability that they will not give the scale answer "yes". Items that elicit this behavior have been called *point items* (Mosteller, 1949) or *differential items* (Loevinger, 1948).

On the other hand, the trace line of item 2 indicates quite another type of behavior. This again is due to the wording of the question, which makes the subject compare his own height with that mentioned in the question and which admits of the answer "yes" only when the subject rates himself at least as tall as the item states. The respondent orders himself in comparison to the item.

These two types of behavior, one indicating *proximity* to the stimuli and the other indicating the *order relationship* of subjects to items, has been made one of the three basic dimensions in Coombs' most recent typology of data (1964, 19).

With regard to the trace line of question 2 we may make two remarks. In the first place, as a function it is monotonic (weakly, non-decreasing): the probability of the scale alternative "yes" does not decrease with an increase in tallness.

Items of this type have for this reason been called *monotone* by Coombs, who contrasted them with *non-monotone* items in an older typology of data (1953, 493–4; 1964, 561–3). Loevinger (1948) called these items *cumulative*.

Secondly, we may notice in figure 2.1 that the trace line of question 2 virtually bisects the underlying continuum of "tallness" at the point 1.73 m. Practically all the subjects with values greater than 1.73 m. will choose the scale alternative "yes". Practically all the subjects shorter than 1.73 m. will not choose that scale alternative and answer "no". There is virtually a 1–1 correspondence between the two alternatives and the two intervals into which the item divides the continuum of "tallness". This behavior is characteristic for the perfect Guttman item, as we shall see. In figure 2.1 this pattern is due to the steepness of the trace line of question 2. In our example, as people in general are well aware of their own height as a stable attribute and as the item clearly embodies a well-defined value of the attribute of tallness, we may expect a trace line like this, though in the neighborhood of the value 1.73 m. some erroneous answers may be possible, as indicated by the slopes in figure 2.1.

For items related to vaguer and less stable attributes such as, let us say, attitudes, we have less reason to expect steep trace lines like those for question 2. For these attributes the items might be more like those given by Ford (1950), such as "Are you taller than a table?",, "Are you taller than the head of a pony?" and "Are you taller than a good-sized bookcase?"

In this study we will consider only items with monotone trace lines. For methods of analyzing point items we refer the reader to Mosteller (1949) and Torgerson (1958, 312–7). Again this restriction does not seem too severe to us, because by far the greater part of scaling practice based on the measurement models that we shall consider shows at least an implicit use of monotone items.

2.2.3   *Properties of the perfect scale*

In general we shall consider the case of n subjects, each answering to the same set of k items, each item being scored dichotomously. According to conventional statistical practice each item will receive a score of 1 when the scale response is given and 0 when it is not.

For each subject the resulting response pattern can be represented by a row vector:

$$x = \{x_1, x_2, \ldots, x_i, \ldots, x_k\}; \qquad x_i = 1, 0; i = 1, 2, \ldots, k, \qquad (1.1)$$

where x_i is the score for item i.

There are theoretically 2^k different response patterns.

We shall further suppose that each subject has a given, but unknown numerical value on the variable (*e.g.* attitude). Let that unknown value be θ. Our measurement problem amounts to getting information about θ from the observable response vector **x**.

In our discussion of the trace lines of items we noted that they represented the probability of a scale answer (score 1) as a function of this unknown value θ. We might formulate this probability as*

$$P\{\underline{x}_i = 1 | \theta\} \qquad (1.2)$$

*Stochastic variables will be underlined in this study.

A perfect scale is based on perfect items. A perfect item is character-
ized by a trace line as shown in figure 2.2, where $P\{\underline{x}_i = 1|\theta\}$ is
plotted as a function of θ. One of its properties is that there is a
certain unknown, critical value, δ_i, on the θ-axis. Subjects with
θ-values lower than δ_i will never choose the scale alternative for item
i. They will always score zero on that item. Subjects with θ-values
as high as or higher than δ_i, on the other hand, will certainly score 1
on item *i*, as they will always choose the scale alternative.

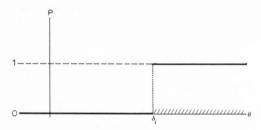

Figure 2.2　Trace line of G-item *i*. The shaded area indicates the interval with non-
zero probability of item score 1.

A subject's response to any item is entirely determined by his
own value on the variable (θ) and by that of the item (δ_i). Hence the
term *deterministic* model.

We see therefore that a subject will score 1 on item *i* either with
probability one or with probability zero, depending on his own
θ-value and on the value δ_i of that item. This unknown value δ_i we
may call the *item difficulty* of item *i*. To express this dependence on
δ_i, we may formulate the definition of the trace line for a perfect item
(Guttman-item or G-item as we shall call it for short) as follows:

$$P\{\underline{x}_i = 1|\theta, \delta_i\} = 0 \quad \text{if} \quad \theta < \delta_i$$
$$= 1 \quad \text{if} \quad \theta \geqslant \delta_i. \tag{1.3}$$

In other words, when a subject responds positively to an item if and
only if he has a value on the latent variable (*e.g.* attitude) that is at least
equal to the item difficulty, the item is a perfect item (G-item). In this
case the respondent indicates by a positive answer that his attitudinal
value is equal to or exceeds that indicated by the item difficulty.

A set of k G-items forms a perfect Guttman scale.

We shall throughout this study adopt the convention by which items
are numbered according to the order of their item difficulty, the most

difficult one being given 1, the least difficult one k. The same numbering will hold good for the components of the response vector given in (1.1).

We can now summarize the well-known properties of the perfect scale. In figure 2.3 we have given a version of the usual picture for a four-item scale adapted to our purposes. This illustration gives us a simultaneous view of the trace lines for four (perfect) G-items. Each of these trace lines follows the course given in figure 2.2.

For instance, the trace line of item 3, which indicates the probability of a positive response (the scale alternative), has the value zero for all θ-values to the left of value δ_3. At point δ_3, this probability jumps to one, which is the value for the trace line for all θ-values to the right of (*i.e.* greater than) δ_3.

The breaking point δ_3 therefore represents the item difficulty of item 3. Items can be represented by their difficulties (δ_i). In figure 2.3 we can see that item 2 is more difficult than item 3 ($\delta_2 > \delta_3$) and that the convention of item numbering mentioned above has been followed, item 1 being the most difficult item and item 4 the "easiest" one. In figure 2.3, furthermore, five subjects have been introduced. They are identified by their θ-values, given as encircled points.

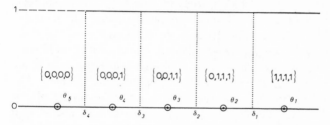

Figure 2.3   Trace lines of four G-items forming a perfect scale. Subject positions encircled.

A subject with a θ-value exceeding the difficulty of an item, and who therefore answers that item positively, must necessarily answer positively all the items with smaller item difficulties. For instance, a subject with the value θ_2 will score 1 on items 4, 3 and 2, and 0 on item 1, thus producing the pattern $\{0, 1, 1, 1\}$. As a matter of fact any subject with a θ-value in the interval (δ_2, δ_1) will do this. The four G-items therefore divide the θ-axis into five intervals, to each of which one and only one possible response pattern corresponds:

$$\delta_1 \leqslant \theta \qquad : \{1, 1, 1, 1\}; (\text{see } \theta_1);$$
$$\delta_2 \leqslant \theta < \delta_1 : \{0, 1, 1, 1\}; (\text{see } \theta_2);$$

$\delta_3 \leqslant \theta < \delta_2 : \{0, 0, 1, 1\}$; (see θ_3);
$\delta_4 \leqslant \theta < \delta_3 : \{0, 0, 0, 1\}$; (see θ_4);
$\theta < \delta_4 : \{0, 0, 0, 0\}$; (see θ_5).

These are the "perfect" response patterns.

The only information the respondent gives about his θ-value is that it is within one of these intervals: he indicates by his answer, which must necessarily be a perfect pattern, to which interval he belongs.

In general, with a perfect scale of k items, only $k+1$ "perfect" response patterns can occur out of 2^k possible patterns.

Although not only the θ-values but also the δ_i-values and therefore the locations of the intervals are unknown, an ordering of the n subjects and the k items must always be possible in the case of a perfect scale, and will lead to something like table 2.1. Only perfect patterns occur.

The arrangement of table 2.1, which corresponds to the situation of figure 2.3, is such that the items are ordered according to the number of subjects that scored 1 on them. The number of subjects giving that scale response on item i is denoted as n_i.

In a total sample of n subjects, the fraction $p_i = n_i/n$ of subjects doing this for item i may be called the *sample difficulty*, which should be distinguished from item difficulty as defined above. In most applications of scale analysis, the former is called *item popularity* or *difficulty*. We shall see that we can also define a *population difficulty* for the population from which our sample of n subjects was selected. The sample difficulty of an item may be regarded as an estimate of this population difficulty. We shall also see in chapters 3 and 4 that whereas the item difficulty (δ_i) is defined as a characteristic value of the item independent of the distribution of the population of subjects over the θ-axis (*e.g.* attitude axis), the population difficulty of an item, and hence its sample difficulty, is mainly determined by that distribution.

From table 2.1 it can easily be seen that:
1. the items are perfectly ordered by their sample difficulties: $i < j$ implies $p_i < p_j$;
2. the ordering of the p_i is exactly the same as that of the unknown δ_i.

An item i, with an item difficulty δ_i *larger* than that of another item, δ_j, $(i < j)$ will in general also have a sample difficulty p_i *smaller* than

Table 2.1 *The ordering of items and subjects in a perfect scale*

Subjects*		Items 1	2	3	4		Scale score(s)
1		1	1	1	1	:	4
2		1	1	1	1	:	4
.		.	.	.	.	.	.
n_1-------	1	1	1	1	:	4
n_1+1	0	1	1	1	:	3
n_1+2	0	1	1	1	:	3
.		.	.	.	.	.
n_2-------	0----	1	1	1	:	3
n_2+1	0	0	1	1	:	2
n_2+2	0	0	1	1	:	2
.		.	.	.	.	.
n_3-------	0----	0---	1	1	:	2
n_3+1	0	0	0	1	:	1
n_3+2	0	0	0	1	:	1
.		.	.	.	.	.
n_4-------	0----	0----	0---	1	:	1
n_4+1	0	0	0	0	:	0
n_4+2	0	0	0	0	:	0
.		.	.	.	.	.
n	0	0	0	0	:	0
Total number of positive score (n_i)		n_1	n_2	n_3	n_4		

*Total sample of n subjects

p_j. In the case of the perfect scale the reasons are clear: if $i < j$, that is, according to our convention, if $\delta_i > \delta_j$ and item i is therefore more difficult than item j, then all the subjects scoring one on item i will have the same score on item j, but there will be subjects scoring zero on item i and one on item j, therefore $p_i < p_j$.

A glance at table 2.1 will show that the subjects are also ordered according to their attitudes (θ-values), but less perfectly. The attitudes form a system of ordered classes (a quasi-series) (Suppes and Zinnes, 1963, 23), that correspond one to one with the $k+1$ perfect scale patterns. To every class belongs one perfect scale pattern as the only possible response pattern.

The subjects are ordered *between* the classes, but the scale gives no information about the order of the θ-values *within* a class. This apparent asymmetry of our model as regards the degree to which it orders items and subjects is inherent not to the model, but to the empirical content in which we use it. As can be seen in figure 2.3, where items as well as subjects are perfectly ordered by the response patterns, two subjects (*e.g.* θ_3 and θ_4) can be ordered as soon as we have an item with an item difficulty (*e.g.* δ_3) dividing the interval (θ_3, θ_4) between these subjects. The same holds good for any two items: they can only be ordered according to their δ-values when there are subjects which fall between them.

In the empirical context under consideration, there are typically many possible subjects (n large) and limited possibilities for the use of many items (small k). Therefore, although the formal model is perfectly symmetrical as regards the two sets of subjects and items, in this empirical context we shall have to cope with this asymmetry of a large n relative to k.

If we define the *scale score(s)* of a subject as the number of scale alternatives chosen by a subject from the set of items (the number of ones a subject scores in his response to the k items), we shall see that the subjects are ordered by their scale score, and that this scale score (running from 0 to k) identifies the $k+1$ classes. One score belongs to each class. This last fact in our perfect scale results in the property that has been stressed most in the analysis of the perfect Guttman scale: the property of *reproducibility*. From his scale score not only is the class to which a subject belongs identified, but his exact response behavior will also be known; *e.g.* to a scale score of 3 only one response pattern, $\{0, 1, 1, 1\}$, is possible out of the total number of four response patterns.

In table 2.1, for instance, all subjects with this score (number $n_1 + 1$ to n_2) have this response pattern in common. If any subject with this score had as response pattern $\{1, 0, 1, 1\}$, that pattern would be in "error" in terms of the deterministic model, as the most difficult item 1 would have received a positive answer (1) and the easier item 2 a negative answer (0). In a perfect scale, the scale score therefore contains all the information about the respondent's position. This property reminds us of the property of *sufficiency* of the scale score as a statistic in some of the stochastic models that we shall consider in chapters 3 and 4.

Let us consider for any two items i and j, ordered according to our convention ($i < j$: $\delta_i > \delta_j$; $p_i \leq p_j$; $n_i \leq n_j$), the (2×2)-table giving the simultaneous distribution of the answers of all the subjects to the two items. Table 2.2 represents such an arrangement. Under the conditions of the perfect scale, it is clearly impossible for any subject to score 1 on the more difficult item i and 0 on the less difficult item j. The corresponding cell in table 2.2 therefore shows zero frequency.

Table 2.2   Two perfect items

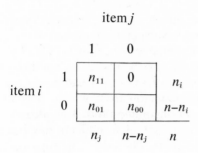

$i < j : n_i \leqslant n_j$

Given the ordering of the k items, this cell, the *zero-cell* or *error-cell*, is uniquely defined for every item pair. For a set of n subjects and a set of k items, the items will form a perfect scale if and only if for every pair of items from the set, the error-cell has zero frequency.

2.3   THE TWO SETS AS POPULATIONS

The two fundamental sets were treated above as finite collections of n subjects and k items, which is the usual practice. However, our theoretical interest usually goes a great deal further than that, because we want to generalize beyond the particular realizations of the sets we are dealing with. In the first place the set of subjects in the analysis is seldom interesting in itself. We shall usually want to generalize from that set to other sets of subjects. If k items scale for a sample of subjects, we shall want these items also to scale for the population of subjects from which the sample in hand has been taken, because we generally want to measure a much wider variety of subjects.

Secondly, we do not want to see a particular set of k items as the only behavioral items tapping the unidimensional attitude or whatever other conschuct we hope they measure. In general we want to postulate a larger spectrum of behavioral items of all sorts, all related to our underlying variable in the way our model describes.

A solution is to consider both sets as sub-sets chosen from larger sets, and to consider them representative of these sets. They are then in a way samples from broader populations. This is exactly what Guttman proposed (1950a).

2.3.1   *The population of subjects*

The idea of considering the set of n subjects used in an analysis as a sample from a broader population of subjects, distributed through space (and time), is a familiar one to behavioral scientists. This goes without saying for the specialists in survey research, but in the experimental disciplines, where there is a less direct relation between the subjects and the well-defined population from which they are "sampled", the sampling model is not uncommon too. This idea of a population of subjects from which the set of n subjects has been sampled has some interesting implications. The most important ones follow from the fact that it implies a *population distribution*, a distribution of subjects, or rather θ-values, that is characteristic for a given population in a given space and at a given time. Here already arises the problem of finding out which scale properties are preserved for different distributions and which are dependent on a particular distribution. From figure 2.4, for instance, we can see the influence that a population distribution will have on what we will call the *population difficulty* of an item. It is the population equivalent of the *sample difficulty* of an item and should again be distinguished from the item difficulty δ. We shall denote* the population difficulty of item i by π_i. This population difficulty π_i may be interpreted as that fraction of the *population* of subjects that will respond positively (will give the scale response) to item i. It may be estimated with the *sample* difficulty p_i that was defined in section 2.2.3.

Figures 2.4 and 2.5 illustrate the effect of different population distributions in the case of (perfect) G-items.

In figure 2.4, for instance, π_i, the fraction of the population which passes δ_i along the θ-axis, is represented by the shaded area under the distribution curve to the right of the point δ_i. For the one population the value for $\pi_i = 0.50$, for the other one it is much lower than that, because the latter population, though identical in form, has a lower average value for θ than the former.

---

*In conformance with common practice in mathematical statistics, Greek symbols will be used for the (unknown) parameters of stochastic models.

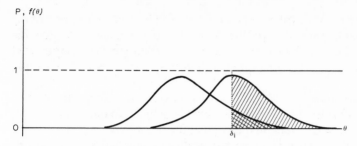

Figure 2.4   G-item with two differently located populations. The shaded areas indicate the population difficulties (π_i) of item i.

Even for populations with the same average attitude position (θ-value) the population difficulties may differ for one and the same item, as can be seen in figure 2.5, where G-item 2 has for both populations difficulty $\pi_2 = 0.50$, but where G-item 1 has different values for π_1. We also see that it is for this reason that the relative position of the π_i can vary from population to population.

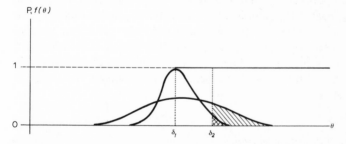

Figure 2.5   G-items with two identically located populations of a different spread. The shaded areas indicate the population difficulties (π_i) of item i.

The problem then arises of which properties are invariant in spite of changes in the population distribution or, what may amount to the same thing, which properties are roughly preserved with different samples of subjects. We may call such properties *population free* (Rasch, 1960). Some of these problems will be investigated in a more general context in chapters 3 and 4.

It will be seen that the properties of a perfect scale will be preserved when the k items form a set of G-items for the population.
1. The scale scores will still reproduce the perfect pattern which corresponds to it, as the other patterns are not possible (their probability is zero).

2. The order of the item difficulties (δ_i) will be reflected by that of the population difficulties of the items (π_i). That is, if $\delta_i > \delta_j$ (item i is more difficult than item j), then $\pi_i < \pi_j$ (a smaller fraction will answer positively to G-item i than to G-item j. See also section 4.1.3).
3. The system of the ordered classes is essentially determined by the item difficulties δ_i. The proportions of subjects in these classes are, however, dependent on the population distribution.
4. A set of k items forms a perfect scale for a population if and only if, given the ordering of the items, the error cell in the corresponding (2×2)-table has zero probability for every pair in the set, that is, if it is impossible for any subject drawn from the population to score 1 on any item and 0 on any less difficult item in the set. (See also section 4.1.4, proposition 1.3.9).

If we want to regard our set of n subjects as a sample from a population, we are immediately confronted with the problem of inference. We will return to this subject later in this chapter, and will limit ourselves here to indicating one theoretical, but nevertheless major problem of inference: even if a set of k items proves to form a *perfect* scale for a particular sample of n subjects, it need not necessarily form a perfect scale for the whole population. One can imagine sub-sets of the population, covered by that sample, for which the items do not scale at all. These remarks may be extended to the particular sets of items used in research. These will be the subject of the next section.

2.3.2.   The population of items

Apart from the familiar notion of a population of subjects, Guttman introduced with great emphasis that of a population of items (1950a, 80–90), although he preferred the term "universe" to distinguish it from the population of subjects. (1950a, 80, note 10). He introduces this concept as a universe of attributes or a universe of content from which k items are sampled. Remarking that in the case of a scalable universe (in which all possible questions of the same content form G-items), a person ranking higher than another on a sample of items will rank higher in the universe also, he goes on to say without further proof:
"This is an important property of scales, that *from a sample of attributes we can draw inferences about the universe of attributes*" (1950a, 81).

Now as common as is the notion of a population of subjects, as uncommon proved to be this idea of a universe of content, from which items are chosen. Perhaps it was the somewhat literal interpretation of Guttman's idea of sampling items, inspired by his own straight-forward exposition of it, that led to much criticism of this concept (Torgerson, 1958, 332–6; Matalon, 1965, 29; Campbell and Kerckhoff, 1957).

Campbell and Kerckhoff point out in their criticism of the concept that the fact that a sample of items proves to be a perfect scale does not necessarily mean that the population of items is scalable. This, it must be said, is hardly a valid criticism of the concept of a population of items, because, as we saw at the conclusion of 2.3.1, the same argument can be used against the concept of a population of subjects. In fact, the argument implies a criticism of the perfect scale as a usable construct.

Campbell and Kerckhoff also point out, and with more reason, that there is no genuine sampling procedure for the items, because the boundaries of the population of items are not known. Consequently statements about the universe of items based on a set of items must be made within unknown probability limits. They conclude that therefore, beyond the items used in a scale, no meaningful construction of a wider universe is possible. Although we have our objections to this evaluation of the utility of the concept of a wider population of items, their concluding appraisal of scale analysis itself is much to the point. They remark that scale analysis enables us to judge whether the set of items used possesses "a single central core of meaning". If the set forms a scale we can say that respondents behaved as if these items had a single core of meaning. If not, then either the items lack *uniformity of meaning* for the respondents, or they have no *unidimensional* meaning for the respondents.

It is certainly true that the careful and purposeful methods of item selection and construction do not bear the faintest resemblance to the procedures of random selection in the sampling of respondents. Therefore the traditional sampling theory based on these last pro-cedures cannot adequately be used for inferences about a wider population of items. But in the experimental branches of the behavior-al sciences, the methods of subject selection are often as far removed from the survey sampling procedures. In other disciplines, such as biometric research, where models highly akin to those treated in chapters 3 and 4, are used in experiments to estimate the toxicity of medicines (bio-assay), guinea pigs and other animals are selected by procedures much farther removed from such sampling methods.

Yet the results of such experiments are being used for generalizations about other (*e.g.* human) populations. In all these cases statistical models form an attempt at providing a basis for the generalization, apparently with some claim to success.

The concept of a wider population of behavioral items relevant to a construct we wish to measure is well in agreement with intuition. As anyone knows who has tried to construct an attitude scale or has studied items as indicators of other types of behavior, in spite of the carefulness with which one works, one ends up with the feeling that other items might have done just as well. The whole empirically founded idea of *the interchangeability of indices* presupposes something like a population or universe in which they are embedded. Lazarsfeld put up a convincing argument for the introduction of this concept:

"In the formation of indices of broad social and psychological concepts, we typically select a relatively small number of items from a large number of possible ones suggested by the concept and its attendant imagery. It is one of the notable features of such indices that their correlation with outside variables will usually be about the same, regardless of the specific 'sampling' of items which goes into them from the broader group associated with the concept. This rather startling phenomenon has been labeled 'the changeability of indices'" (Lazarsfeld, 1959b, 113).

We shall in due course investigate models incorporating the idea of a population of items from which a given set of k items were "selected". We shall see in chapters 3 and 4 that the formalization of such models enables us to gain some general insight into the effects of item selection and the properties that are invariant for variations in procedures of item selection (or the "distribution" of the population of items).

Many properties can be derived from a certain symmetry in the roles of the subject parameters, (θ), and the roles of the items, (δ). Formally the roles of the two sets are often identical. For instance, we may use this symmetry of the perfect Guttman model to reverse the roles of items and subjects and repeat our argument of section 2.3.1. This is illustrated in figure 2.6, which is similar to figure 2.5. The roles of items and subjects have, however, been reversed. In figure 2.6 we have introduced two subjects with values θ_1 and θ_2. Just as we postulated a trace line for a given item in figure 2.5, which gives at a certain point on the θ-axis the probability that a subject with that value will pass that item, we may, inversely, introduce in figure 2.6 a trace line for subject θ_1. This "subject trace line" gives for any point δ on the δ-axis the probability that an item with that value will be passed by subject θ_1. For perfect scales this probability is zero to the right of point θ_1 (item difficulty δ larger than subject value θ_1) and one elsewhere.

Figure 2.6 shows the two trace lines of subjects θ_1 and θ_2. The population distribution of item values δ (density $g(\delta)$) is given along

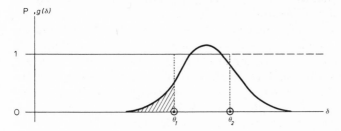

Figure 2.6   The distribution of G-items and two "subject trace lines"

the δ-axis. In the case of verbal items, where the item difficulty is strongly determined by the meaning of the item, we may interpret this as a sort of semantic distribution. In figure 2.6 the shaded area indicates the proportion of the item universe that is passed by θ_1. It is a measure of his ability, attitude, or whatever variable is measured by θ, in the sense that for perfect scales these proportions, though dependent on the particular item distribution, will reflect perfectly the order of the θ_i: for θ_1 that proportion is smaller than that for θ_2 because $\theta_1 < \theta_2$.

For a "sample" of k subjects these proportions may be roughly estimated by means of the formula s_i/k: the scale score of subject i divided by the number of items. Apart from the fact that the quality of our sampling from the universe is unknown, the estimate must be a very rough one because k, the number of items, is generally rather small in the types of research under consideration. It is a virtue of the model that it teaches us to be modest concerning the precision of the measurements which we base on scales.

In chapters 3 and 4 we shall investigate such properties for probabilistic models.

2.4   THE IMPERFECT SCALE: THE PROBLEM OF "ERROR"

When we try to apply this Guttman model of a perfect scale to empirical data, its deterministic features will lead to imperfections. Perfect scales and perfect items rarely exist in practice. One has to face the fact that the ideal, as usual, can only be approximated. Scaling procedures that are aimed at a rearrangement of the data, subjects and items, in order to arrive at a pattern like that in table 2.1, will be obstructed by the fact that once the order of the items has been established and the perfect patterns have therefore been ascertained, numerous "imperfect" patterns will occur, due to responses that are "in error".

Let us consider, for instance, the situation in figure 2.3 and the corresponding table 2.1. The occurrence of a response pattern such as $\{0, 1, 0, 1\}$ is contradictory to the deterministic model, according to which only the "perfect" pattern $\{0, 0, 1, 1\}$ consistent with the scale score of 2 is possible. This pattern is "imperfect": the second item has a positive response whereas the third and "easier" item is answered negatively. From a deterministic viewpoint there must be an "error" somewhere. Yet in actual practice such deviations from the deterministic model may well occur. What do these "errors" lead to?

2.4.1   *The failure of determinism: some consequences*

One of the immediate consequences of deviations from the deterministic model in practical applications is, of course, the loss of the property of *reproducibility*. No longer does the scale score of any subject predict his response pattern exactly: other "imperfect" patterns with the same score may occur.

Still other problems have to be coped with when the deterministic model is used as a guide line for the construction of practical instruments for measurement. The basic one is that of error. If the ordering of the items is given, the perfect patterns can be established. In all applications, patterns deviating from these perfect patterns are considered "imperfect" and held to contain some error. In order to arrive at some objective basis of judgement from which the seriousness of such deviations may be evaluated it is necessary to determine clearly what an "error" is. This problem of the *definition of error* will be the subject of section 2.4.2. The other sections of this chapter contain a discussion of some of the remaining problems and the ways in which they have been solved in most practical applications. For instance, if a certain definition of error has been set up, we must find a way of ascertaining how serious the deviation of a set of items is from the ideal of the perfect scale for a given population of subjects. This is the problem of determining the *scalability* of a set of items: the degrees to which a set of items may be said to fit the model of a perfect scale. We must therefore devise *criteria of scalability* in terms of which sets of items may be evaluated, and we must design *procedures* to find and construct scales from sets of items in terms of such criteria.

Finally, in the literature on the subject of scales, much attention has been paid to the problem of determining the proper score for subjects with imperfect response patterns. This *scoring problem* has generally led to the allocation of a perfect pattern to subjects with imperfect ones.

2.4.2   *The definition of "error"*

The main purpose of procedures of scale analysis is, as we have seen, to establish the order of the items and that of the subjects. Once the order of the items has been established, the perfect scale patterns corresponding to that order, are known and so therefore are the imperfect patterns, the "wrong" ones. We have to decide how "wrong" they are, that is, we have to define error.

This definition of error is important because in all scaling procedures it determines the criteria by which the scalability of a set is judged. Much of the confusion and many of the difficulties that have often hindered a clear assessment of the many criteria of scalability that have been put forward, are simply the result of a lack of an insight into the concept of error, as we hope to demonstrate.

In fact, the early standard works on the subject do not give an unambiguous definition of error. This has led to a rather unfortunate formulation of coefficients of scalabiltiy, as will be shown in section 2.5.

One of the simplest definitions of error gives equal weight to every imperfect *pattern*: they all count as one error. This simple method of defining error has hardly been actually put into practice. In most definitions of error that are actually used, however, some imperfect patterns are judged "more wrong that others", as we shall see.

First there is the definition by Guttman himself. It is clear enough. Defining a coefficient of reproducibility, he states:
"It is secured by counting up the number of responses which would have been predicted wrongly for each person on the basis of his scale score, dividing these errors by the total number of responses and subtracting the resulting fraction from 1" (1950a, 77).
The first part of this quotation gives a precise definition of error in terms of the principle of reproducibility which states that for a perfect

scale the scale score of any subject will be the result of one and only one response pattern: the perfect pattern corresponding to that score. Keeping in mind our method (see section 2.2.3) of ordering and numbering the item scores in the response vector according to their difficulty from left to right with *decreasing* δ_i; $i = 1, 2, \ldots, k$; (or *increasing* "easiness"), we may consider the following examples from table 2.3, which is designed in the form of table 2.1.

Table 2.3   Imperfect patterns

	Items						
Patterns	1	2	3	4	5	6	Scale score(s)
1	1	1	1	1	1	1	6
2	0	1	1	1	1	1	5
3	0	0	1	1	1	1	4
4	0	0	0	1	1	1	3
5*	1	1	0	1	0	0	3
6*	0	0	1	1	0	1	3
7	0	0	0	0	1	1	2
8	0	0	0	0	0	1	1
9	0	0	0	0	0	0	0

*Imperfect patterns.

In table 2.3 we see enumerated for a six-item scale all the possible perfect response patterns, together with two "imperfect" patterns (patterns 5 and 6 with a score $s = 3$). This enables us to predict, from the reproducibility property of a perfect scale, the pattern $\{0, 0, 0, 1, 1, 1\}$ (pattern 4). Counting the errors in reproducibility per item, the imperfect pattern 5, $\{1, 1, 0, 1, 0, 0\}$, contains 4 errors according to this definition. Because this definition was used by Goodenough (1944), we shall henceforth call it the Guttman–Goodenough definition. The fact that according to this definition "imperfect" patterns are weighed differently according to their number of errors, will become clear when the definition is applied to the imperfect pattern 6, $\{0, 0, 1, 1, 0, 1\}$, which also has a score of 3. In this pattern there are two errors.

In *Measurement and Prediction*, however, a second definition is used which leads to a definition of error and hence of scalability differing from the Guttman–Goodenough definition.* This definition is contained in Suchman's discussion of the scalogram board technique:

"We define 'scale type' for the purpose of scalogram analysis as that perfect scale type which the given individual most closely approaches with the least number of errors. If there is more than one perfect scale type to which the given individual approaches most closely, he is classified as belonging to that scale type which best maintains the 'solid streaks'" (Suchman, 1950, note 8, 106).

In this procedure of defining error, therefore, the principle of reproducibility from the scale score is partially disregarded. First a "nearest" perfect pattern is sought, that is, a perfect pattern in comparison with which the imperfect one shows the least number of items in error. This number forms the number of errors of our imperfect pattern. In our example of table 2.3, a comparison of the *imperfect* pattern 5, $\{1, 1, 0, 1, 0, 0\}$, with all the perfect response patterns that are given in that table, will show that the "nearest" perfect patterns are both pattern 1, $\{1, 1, 1, 1, 1, 1\}$, and pattern 9, $\{0, 0, 0, 0, 0, 0\}$. We have to change more than three "error"-items to convert this pattern into any one of the other possible perfect response patterns. Three is therefore the minimum number of "error"-items needed to convert this imperfect response pattern into one of the possible perfect response patterns. Here the related perfect pattern is not the one predicted by the principle of reproducibility from the score, but another perfect pattern leading to fewer errors. We shall see in section 2.6.2 that this approach led to the fallacious procedure of allocating a new score on the basis of the pattern which most closely resembled it. It is clear that this second definition will result in a lower number of errors than the Guttman–Goodenough definition and may therefore lead to a less stringent criterion of scalability. This definition, which for the sake of convenience we shall call the Guttman –Suchman definition, has formed the basis of by far the greater part of the scaling procedures that have been used since.

Green (1956, 83–4) gives a procedure of determining scalability that amounts to an algorithm of counting errors in a pattern which is identical to the Guttman–Suchman definition. We shall briefly describe it here because we have to return to it later. Green's algorithm for counting errors in a pattern consists of several steps. It may have been noticed that, given the ordering of the items according to our system, we would not detect adjacent item pairs of the type $\{1, 0\}$

---

*Torgerson seems to confuse these two definitions, as many others did (Torgerson, 1958, 318–9).

in scanning a pattern from left to right. In such a pair the responses are in "error", because a more difficult item has been scored one and a less difficult item zero. Hence we may call such a pair of item responses an adjacent error pair. According to Green's first step, one counts and eliminates from the pattern all adjacent error pairs met with in scanning a response pattern from left to right. These are called *first* order error pairs. As these item pairs are not considered in the steps that follow, their elimination from the original pattern results in a reduced pattern. In the second step we repeat the whole procedure with this reduced pattern, and count and eliminate the *second* order adjacent pairs. We repeat this procedure in counting and eliminating *third* and higher order error pairs, until we are left with an errorless pattern.

Every *error pair* which is counted by this procedure in any of the successive steps contains at least one *error item* which would have to be changed in order to bring about a conversion of the imperfect pattern into the "nearest" perfect one. Consequently, the total number of error pairs counted by means of Green's algorithm for an imperfect pattern gives a lower bound for the total number of errors. This total number of errors is defined by Green as the number of item corrections needed to transform the imperfect pattern into one of the possible perfect patterns. It can be proved that any pattern can be converted into a perfect pattern by correcting exactly the number of errors that was counted with Green's algorithm. This procedure therefore gives us the minimum number of errors which forms the basis of the Guttman–Suchman procedure and proves to be identical to the latter procedure for a given item ordering.

As an example we may apply Green's algorithm to our imperfect pattern 5, $\{1, 1, 0, 1, 0, 0\}$, from table 2.3. We count three errors: two first order errors (indicated by the arcs) and one second order error.[*]

As Goodman (1959, 34–5) points out, any definition of error generally implies a special method of allocating numbers (of errors) to patterns. Each definition, as will be seen later, implies the construction of a different criterion of scalability with, probably, different consequences of interpretation. Sagi, for instance, used a different definition of error for an imperfect pattern. His number of errors for

---

[*]Green's analysis (and consequently that of Torgerson too) seems to contradict his own statement of the algorithm. He suggests that the only possibility for second order errors is in a sub-pattern such as $\{1, 1, 0, 0\}$, whereas in our example we encounter a different type of second order error, which Green, in analyzing exactly the same example calls a third order error (Green, 1956, 84; Torgerson, 1958, 226–7).

any pattern is simply the number of first order errors in terms of Green's algorithm. He would describe our example $\{1, 1, 0, 1, 0, 0\}$ as having two errors (Sagi, 1959, 20). Loevinger, who developed a theory of scaling parallel to Guttman's, uses yet another definiton of error. For a given pattern she counts the number of error pairs $\{1, 0\}$ considering all possible item pairs. Our example would have eight errors according to this procedure (Loevinger, 1947; 1948).

Up to now we have counted errors over item responses within a given response pattern for one subject. Adding up the errors for all the subjects in the sample gives us the total number of errors for all the subjects and items. We shall see in section 2.5 that this total number is used to define a coefficient of scalability for the whole set of items. We can also count the number of times one item was answered wrongly by the subjects. This might enable us to devise a criterion for the scalability of this particular item with respect to the other items. This presupposes that for the item in question it is clearly established for each subject whether his response to that item is "in error" or not. Sometimes (depending on the definition of error used) this may be difficult, because we may not be able to do this in such a way that no further assumptions are involved.

For instance, in the case of the Guttman–Goodenough definition it will always be possible to ascertain for any item and any subject whether the item response is in error or not. This is not the case with the Guttman-Suchman definition. In our example $\{1, 1, 0, 1, 0, 0\}$, we saw that with this method three errors were counted which would have to be "corrected" in order to convert the pattern into one of the two possible "nearest"-perfect patterns: $\{1, 1, 1, 1, 1, 1\}$ or $\{0, 0, 0, 0, 0, 0\}$. As a result it is not *a priori* clear which item responses are in error. For the determination of item scalability this problem was supposedly solved in the Guttman–Suchman procedure and other methods based on it by means of a prior allocation of the imperfect pattern to one of the possible "nearest" perfect patterns. We shall return to this method in section 2.6.2.

All the known theories and procedures of Guttman scaling have focussed on the *imperfect* patterns only for the sake of the definition and estimation of error. The implicit suggestion is that for perfect scales and perfect patterns the problem of response error does not exist. We may observe, however, that as soon as the possibility of response error is admitted, this situation will be seen in a different light.

Let us consider the situation given in figure 2.3. Consider, for instance, subject θ_3, who in the case of the perfect pattern will produce the response vector $\{0, 0, 1, 1\}$. Once we have admitted the possibility of error and an imperfect response from θ_3, e.g. $\{0, 1, 0, 1\}$, there is no reason why we should not expect "errors" like $\{0, 0, 0, 1\}$ or $\{0, 1, 1, 1\}$, patterns which, though perfect, are in contradiction to the position of θ_3. Although, of course, only the imperfect patterns manifast error, we may conclude *that of every perfect pattern an (unobservable) fraction may be in "error" with regard to the perfect scale.*

Torgerson (1958, 334–5) remarks that under certain circumstances a scale may be perfect without the items being perfect (G-items) at all, as can be seen from figure 2.7, borrowed from Torgerson (1958, 334). It contains three items that are not G-items, because the

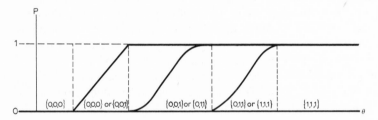

Figure 2.7   Three imperfect items forming a perfect scale

probability of a scale response is positive but smaller than one over a certain interval on the θ-continuum. However, the trace lines of the items are such that this probability reaches the value 1 for any item before the point where the corresponding probability departs from zero for the more difficult items. Hence, the responses to such items correspond to those expected in a perfect scale. Torgerson remarks that this effect might partly account for the fact that orthodox scaling procedures usually end up with only a few (four or five) items forming a reasonable scale. This might be the result of a spacing of imperfect items according to their difficulty.

2.5   COEFFICIENTS OF SCALABILITY

In the behavioral sciences extensive use is made of a great variety of coefficients which often serve more or less the same purpose. In their review of the measures of association for cross classifications, Goodman and Kruskal (1954, 735; 1959; 1963) put forward strong arguments that such coefficients should be derived from clear theoretical and analytical premises in terms of which they get a definite operational meaning which facilitates their interpretation. Occasionally, however, such principles do not seem to serve as guide lines in the construction and evaluation of indices and coefficients. They are sometimes applied rather uncritically, their use apparently being based on such considerations as the authority of their designer or their general curiosity value. The use of coefficients as criteria of scalability in general is an illustration of these uncritical methods. From the very beginning, the finding of a good coefficient as the main criterion of scalability has presented some difficulties.

This proved to be true especially for Guttman's own *coefficient of reproducibility* which, following the convention, we shall denote by Rep. The principle on which it was constructed was given in Guttman's definition of reproducibility as quoted in section 2.4.2. As this coefficient, and similar ones, were designed primarily to measure the scalability of a set of items, we prefer to give them the general name of "*coefficients of scalability*". (See also Goodman, 1959, 36). Guttman's Rep and its relatives have been used widely as the main criterion in determining scalability despite some serious drawbacks. On the other hand, the many attempts to provide better coefficients, which did lead to real improvements, have often only added to the confusion. It therefore seems worthwhile to investigate more closely a number of coefficients without attempting a complete review of the many different varieties.

We shall consider three types of coefficients: Rep, and two other classes of coefficients which we shall call types S_1 and S_2.

2.5.1 Coefficients of reproducibility (Rep)

All the various coefficients that were designed depended on the particular definition of error used. The prototype was the Rep based on the Guttman–Goodenough definition. Applying the formula contained in our quotation of section 2.4.2, we have to count, for each subject and per item, all the errors his response pattern contains. This will be done in the Guttman–Goodenough way. First the order of the items is established from the sample difficulties. (See table 2.1). In what follows we shall assume that the items are numbered according to our convention, the first item being the most difficult and the last (k^{th} item) the least difficult of the set of k items. The errors are then counted in the Guttman–Goodenough way: by comparing the response pattern for any subject with the perfect pattern expected from his scale score on the basis of reproducibility and the difficulty ordering of the items. Adding up all the errors over all n subjects (and over all k items) will give us the total number of errors over all the subjects (and items). Let us denote this total number of errors in the sample as E_{GG}, the last two initials referring to the particular definition of error used. As we have n subjects responding to k items, we have a total number of nk responses. Applying Guttman's formula, we can therefore define* the well-known (Guttman-Goodenough) Rep as:

$$\text{Rep}_{GG} \overset{d}{=} 1 - E_{GG}/nk \tag{5.1}$$

In a similar way we can define the Guttman–Suchman Rep:

$$\text{Rep}_{GS} \overset{d}{=} 1 - E_{GS}/nk \tag{5.2}$$

using the Guttman–Suchman definition and applying, on the basis of the difficulty order of the items, Green's algorithm to count the total number of errors, E_{GS}.

Given the total number of errors (E) according to the particular definition of error used, the class of Reps in general can be defined by means of the general formula

$$\text{Rep} \overset{d}{=} 1 - \frac{E}{nk}.^{**} \tag{5.3}$$

The coefficient of Sagi (Type III, Sagi, 1959, 20) is of this type, as is Green's Rep_A (1956, 81). Scalability coefficients of this type have encountered severe attacks almost from the very beginning (Festinger, 1947). The criticism was mainly directed at the fact that the Rep could be spuriously high. This is due to two different causes.

The *first* cause has to do with the normalizing of the coefficients by

---

*In this chapter all coefficients are simply defined on the basis of samples of subjects. According to modern mathematical statistical practice, these coefficients should be defined as parameters on populations. This will be done in chapter 4.

**By a similar procedure, a criterion of *item* scalability may be defined as

$$\text{Rep}_i \overset{d}{=} 1 - \frac{E_i}{n}; \quad i = 1, 2, \ldots, k \tag{5.4}$$

in which E_i is the total number of errors over all the subjects for item i. This presupposes that the uniqueness problem of item error which was mentioned in section 2.4.2 has been solved.

the denominator nk. The Rep coefficient might easily be interpreted by the average behavioral scientist as having values between zero and one. As a criterion of scalability, a value of at least 0.90 was suggested by Guttman as a reasonable requirement for a set of items to scale (Guttman, 1950a, 77), a suggestion that has generally been followed. The value of coefficients of the Rep class will be one if the k items form a perfect scale over the n subjects, E being zero in that case. The difficulty is however, that these coefficients will not in general attain the minimum value of zero. We shall demonstrate that the minimum value of Rep coefficients (Rep_{min}) can only be larger than zero. For some coefficients of the Rep type these minimum values are often much higher than 0.50. Although this circumstance is the main source of the "spurious" inflation of the Rep, it has only occasionally been recognized explicitly in the literature. White and Saltz (1957) mention a lower bound of 0.50, and in Goodman's review (1959) this fact is merely implicit in his exposition. Only very recently has Galtung (1967, 267–9) dealt with this problem explicitly for the Rep_{GG}.

The numerator nk in coefficients of this class stands for the maximum number of errors that can be made. As such it is only valid when the order of the items is known *independently* of the sample. In that case every subject can answer all the k items wrong, that is, contrary to this order.* But in actual practice we have to depend on the information of samples in estimating the order of the items, and then the number nk is no longer valid as the maximum number of errors.

Let us first consider the Guttman–Goodenough method following Galtung's exposition in a changed notation. Let us suppose the difficulty order of the items to be established from the sample of n subjects. It can then be shown that for any response pattern the maximum number of errors it may contain depends on its scale score, which we shall denote by s ($s = 0, 1, \ldots, k$).

Let us consider the case where k is *even* and a score of s. Let $s \leq k/2$. We can determine the perfect pattern from the score s and the difficulty ordering of the items. Therefore we can distribute the s item scores with value 1 in such a way that a score of 1 is placed where it does not belong, given the scale score of the pattern. By doing so we generate two errors in the Guttman–Goodenough sense: one by placing a 1 where there should be a 0 and one by leaving a zero

---

*In that case, however, we might as well consider an unknown fraction of every "perfect" pattern as in error, as we remarked in section 2.4.2.

where a 1 should have been placed. Distributing s item scores of 1 "erroneously" we therefore created $2s$ errors. In our case ($s \leq k/2$; k even) the maximum number of errors which a pattern can contain is therefore k.

For scores $s > k/2$ we can distribute zeros in a way contrary to the perfect pattern that is determined by reproducibility and by the difficulty order of the items and the score s.
We can then create at most

$2(k-s) < k$ errors.

In the case where k is *uneven*, this reasoning again leads to a maximum score of $2s$ when $s \leq \frac{1}{2}(k-1)$ and $2(k-s)$ when $s \geq \frac{1}{2}(k+1)$, with a maximum number of $k-1$ errors with a score of $\frac{1}{2}(k-1)$ or $\frac{1}{2}(k+1)$.

The upper bound for $E_{GG_{max}}$ will therefore be:

k even : nk

k uneven : $n(k-1)$

This, however, would mean that *all* the subjects are assumed to score the value $s = k/2$ (k even) or $s = \frac{1}{2}(k-1), \frac{1}{2}(k+1)$ (k uneven) in a way completely contrary to the item ordering, which is possible only if the difficulty ordering is established independently of the sample.

Galtung gives a sharper estimate of the lower bound for $E_{GG_{max}}$ by considering the distribution of the subjects over the scores. These values are

k even $: 2 \sum_{s=0}^{\frac{1}{2}k-1} s(m_s + m_{k-s}) + k \cdot m_{\frac{1}{2}k}$

*k uneven** $: 2 \sum_{s=0}^{\frac{1}{2}(k-1)} s(m_s + m_{k-s});$

where m_s is the number of subjects with score s.

These limits are, of course, lower than nk. But Galtung's exposition does not indicate that the exact value of $E_{GG_{max}}$ may be still lower. The values he gives will be reached when every subject with a particular

*Galtung's formula contains a misprint: the upper limit of summation is erroneously given as $k-1$.

score achieves the maximum number of errors. But usually the maximum number of errors is defined with the aid of the difficulty order of the items as estimated from the sample difficulties from the same sample. In other words: the maximum number of errors is defined as the worst possible distribution of responses to items which will nevertheless result in the same sample difficulties (n_i/n; see table 2.1). This requirement imposes k restrictions on the possible distributions of the subjects over the patterns with a given score s: these distributions should be such that adding up the responses for any item over all the subjects should result in the given sample difficulty for that item. Because of these restrictions it may well be impossible to achieve a distribution of subjects which is such that every subject is allotted the response pattern that contains the maximum number of errors possible with his score. Hence $E_{GG_{max}}$ may be correspondingly smaller and $\text{Rep}_{GG_{max}}$ correspondingly larger than zero, because obviously

$$\text{Rep}_{min} = 1 - \frac{E_{max}}{nk}$$

Still worse is the situation with the Rep coefficient that has in fact been used in by far the greater part of the applications of scale analysis: the Guttman-Suchman method, Rep_{GS}. The easiest way to explain this is by referring to Green's algorithm (see section 2.4.2). For any pattern the number of errors is given by the number of error pairs that are eliminated step by step. The maximum number of errors must therefore necessarily be $k/2$ when k is *even* and $\frac{1}{2}(k-1)$ when k is *uneven*.

Therefore:

$$k \, even \quad : \text{Rep}_{GS_{min}} \geq 1 - \frac{1}{2} \, nk/nk = 0.50$$

$$k \, uneven \quad : \text{Rep}_{GS_{min}} \geq 1 - \frac{1}{2} n(k-1)/nk = 0.50 + \frac{1}{2k};$$

(*e.g.* 0.60 for a 5-item scale).

But the situation may be still worse than this, because in the construction of a set of items with the same sample difficulties, and with the maximum number of errors, we have to satisfy the condition that the summation of all the errors over all the subjects should produce for every item the given sample difficulties (same item marginals).

The determination of the exact value of $E_{GS_{max}}$, given the sample difficulties of the items, is therefore a rather complicated problem. But enough has been said to stress the point that the exact value of $Rep_{GS_{min}}$ may very well be much higher than 0.50, depending on the item marginals n_i. The determination of $E_{GS_{max}}$ will not be treated here, because there is another bound which worries us more.

This problem brings us to the *second* cause of an inflated interpretation of Rep, which has been given a great deal of attention. If we start from the (null) hypothesis that a set of k items, given the sample marginals (n_i) of the k items, is answered randomly by a sample of n subjects, the values of Rep expected under that null hypothesis can be very high, especially when k is small (*e.g.* $k = 4$ or $k = 5$). There are many examples in the literature (Festinger, 1947; Green, 1954; Guttman, 1950 b; Torgerson, 1958). Guttman (1950 b, 288–91) gives an elaborate example of four independently answered items with population marginals of 0.20, 0.40, 0.60 and 0.80, and therefore an expected reproducibility of 0.90, which would classify the set of items as a scale.

This second cause of spuriously high Reps should not surprise us after the discussion of the first cause: if the Rep_{min} is already very high (for $Rep_{GS_{min}}$ above 0.50), the value of the Rep expected under the null hypothesis must necessarily be higher and sometimes much higher than Rep_{min}.

To summarize our argument: Rep coefficients may be too high due to two related causes:
–their lower bounds were higher than zero;
–consequently the values of Rep coefficients expected under conditions of random response were also higher than zero.
Efforts to improve analysis by the construction of better coefficients were essentially focussed on either of these two causes, thus leading to two classes of coefficients. As these two causes and therefore the resulting two classes of coefficients have not been distinguished clearly in any review known to the author, it seems worthwhile to analyse them. The various disadvantages were in fact seen by the authors of *Measurement and Prediction* themselves. We shall return to this point in section 2.6.2, which is about criteria of scalability.

2.5.2   *Coefficients of type S_1 and S_2*

It will be clear from our discussion in the last section that we need some guide lines to evaluate coefficients of scalability. Three condi-

tions have been implicit in our review. They are the following:
1. the theoretical maximum of the coefficients should be invariant over scales;
2. their theoretical minimum should be invariant over scales;
3. it should be possible to evaluate scales for the set of items as a whole as well as for the individual items.

Similar conditions were given by White and Saltz (1957, 82), who added a fourth condition:
4. it should be possible to test sample values against the null hypothesis. This fourth condition concerns the statistical theory of *sample* coefficients of scalability, but only with respect to a very specific problem of statistical interference: testing the null hypothesis of random response.

We propose to add a more general condition of this type:
5. It should be possible to estimate the population values for the scale coefficients, determine the confidence intervals for these population values and test the values between populations.

Condition 3 will usually be fulfilled automatically, because, as we have seen above, given a particular definition of error, an item coefficient of scalability may be defined. Conditions 4 and 5 will be the subject of section 2.5.4.

Faced with the difficulties mentioned above, various authors have put forward coefficients which focus on either one of the causes of inflation of Rep. Before we mention some of them, it seems appropriate first to indicate the two general types of coefficients that may result from such efforts. In this section our treatment of these two general types of coefficients will be mainly in terms of conditions 1 and 2.

The *first* type of coefficient, type S_1, tackled the first and major cause of the inflation of Rep. It has the following form:

$$S_1 \overset{d}{=} 1 - \frac{E}{E_{max}} = \frac{Rep - Rep_{min}}{1 - Rep_{min}} \tag{5.5}$$

The last equality follows from simple numerical calculation and can be seen as a transformation of Rep as illustrated by figure 2.8.

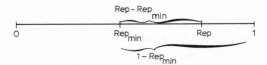

Figure 2.8   Relation of S_1, Rep and Rep_{min}

We see in figure 2.8 that S_1 is just the proportion of the two line segments. This type of coefficient is mentioned by Galtung (1967, 269).*

Condition 1 will always be fulfilled: in the case of a perfect scale S_1 will assume the value 1 for any test.

For condition 2 to be fulfilled, however, it will be necessary to calculate the exact values of Rep_{min}, which, as we have seen, is no simple problem in most cases.

We prefer the *second* type of coefficient, S_2, which is intended to correct the second cause of the inflation of Rep as well. Let us proceed not from Rep but from coefficients of type S_1, in which the first cause of inflation has been eliminated. The second cause of a "spurious" indication of high values will still exist in coefficients of type S_1, as can be judged from figure 2.9. There the point S_{10} represents the value for S_1 expected under the null hypothesis of independent response to the set of k items.

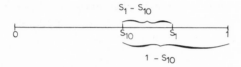

Figure 2.9   Relation of S_2 and S_1

Of course a value for S_1 equal to S_{10} does not necessarily mean that the items are answered independently by our sample of n subjects. Nevertheless we may want our set of items to scale much better than that. In our opinion, this constitutes a convincing argument in favour of transforming the coefficients S_1 in a similar way as was done with the Rep: as the ratio of the line segments of figure 2.9.

We therefore define S_2 as:

$$S_2 \overset{d}{=} \frac{S_1 - S_{10}}{1 - S_{10}} = 1 - \frac{E}{E_0}; \qquad (5.6)$$

in which E_0 denotes the total number of errors expected under the null hypothesis of independence, given the particular definition of error and the ordering of the items: ($S_{10} = 1 - E_0/E_{max}$).

We prefer this type of coefficient of scalability S_2 to S_1 because *both* causes of a spuriously high value of Rep have been eliminated.

---

*He does not, however, consider our second type of coefficient, type S_2.

In how far does this coefficient fulfil the conditions mentioned above?

As with S_1, condition 1 will be fulfilled for every set of items if it forms a perfect scale for the sample of n subjects, the value of S_2 being 1 in that case. The fulfilment of condition 2 requires some specification. According to our convention that only scales with better results than would be expected under the null hypothesis of independent subject response will be accepted, the *admissible* range of values for S_2 is between zero and one. Negative values for S_2 are possible but inadmissible in the sense that the scale hypothesis will then be rejected.

With this restriction of the admissible values of S_2 for the interval $(0, 1]$, we may say that condition 2 is also fulfilled.

2.5.3 *Various coefficients used in actual practice*

The types of coefficients discussed in the last two sections in a fairly general form may be used for the classification of some of the coefficients that are frequently mentioned in the literature. Of all the coefficients that have been put forward as better solutions to scaling problems, we shall just mention a few, mainly with the purpose of classifying them as one of the three types Rep, S_1 or S_2.

Rep-type coefficients: Green (1956) put forward three coefficients of which two belonged to this type and the third to type S_2.

The first, called Rep_A, was based on a counting of errors according to his algorithm. However, only first order and specific second order errors of the $\{1, 0\}$ and $\{1, 1, 0, 0\}$ sub-pattern type were counted in the total E and then a coefficient of the Rep type was computed. This gave an overestimated Rep_{GS} due to a different ordering of items and the neglection of higher order errors.

A second coefficient, Rep_B, was designed for the purpose of estimating Rep_A by estimating the frequency of second order error patterns on the basis of a certain hypothesis of independence within these patterns (Green, 1965, 85). This coefficient was easier to calculate, because it was based on an analysis of the (2×2)-tables for the items (see section 2.2.3, table 2.2). We have seen that for a perfect scale, given the ordering of the items according to increasing sample marginals (diminishing sample difficulties), the error cell is uniquely defined. (When the sample difficulties are equal we may arbitrarily define one of the equally filled $\{0, 1\}$ or $\{1, 0\}$ cells as the error cell.)

Let the frequency in the error cell be n_{ij}, $(i < j)$, and let n_i and n_j be defined as above.
Then Rep_B may be defined as:

$$\text{Rep}_B \stackrel{d}{=} 1 - \frac{1}{nk} \left(\sum_{i=1}^{k-1} n_{i+1} + \frac{1}{n} \sum_{i=1}^{k-3} n_{i,i+2} n_{i+1,i+3} \right). \tag{5.7}$$

Both Rep_A and Rep_B proved to be good approximations to Rep_{GS} in a few comparisons that Green made with some examples from *Measurement and Prediction* (Green, 1956, 85). From the foregoing discussion, this should not surprise us too much, because we have seen that they were related through Green's algorithm for counting errors.

S_1-*type coefficients*: Jackson (1949) designed a coefficient called Plus Percentage Ratio. Menzel (1953) introduced a Coefficient of Scalability. Pearson (1957) noted that these coefficients were essentially the same as regards their empirical results; this is not surprising because both use the same definition of error and are of type S_1.
Boudon (1966), on the basis of graph-theoretical considerations, designed a coefficient *indice de transitivité*, which is also of type S_1.
S_2-*type coefficients*: Coefficients of this type have also been put forward, sometimes disguised as another type. In addition to Rep_A and Rep_B, Green (1956, 81) introduced a third coefficient.* This was his *index of consistence*, which was to serve the explicit purpose of compensating for the defects of Rep coefficients due to our second cause: independent (or random) response behavior, given the item marginals. It was defined thus:

$$I = \frac{\text{Rep} - \text{Rep}_1}{1 - \text{Rep}_1}; \tag{5.8}$$

where for Rep either Rep_A or Rep_B may be used, and Rep_1 is the value for the chosen Rep coefficient expected under the null hypothesis of random response behavior (chance Rep). When Rep_B is used, for instance, the chance Rep becomes

$$\text{Rep}_1 = 1 - \frac{1}{n^2 k} \left(\sum_{i=1}^{k-1} n_i(n - n_{i+1}) + \frac{1}{n^2} \sum_{i=1}^{k-3} n_i(n - n_{i+2}) n_{i+1}(n - n_{i+3}) \right). \tag{5.9}$$

---

*Green rightly describes this index as being similar to Loevinger's index of homogeneity which is also, as we shall see, of type S_2. However, he also seems to consider these coefficients similar to Menzel's coefficient of scalability, which is of type S_1 (Green 1956, 87), as we have seen above.

Borgatta (1959, 99), in his criticism of Menzel's coefficient, seems to define a coefficient of type S_1 when he introduces his "error ratio" as
"..simply the *ratio of errors in the scale to the maximum number of errors for a scale of the same marginal frequencies*".
However, judging from the subsequent examples he gives, his error ratio (when subtracted from one) will lead to a coefficient virtually the same as Green's Rep_t and therefore of type S_2.

The earliest example of a coefficient of type S_2 is the *coefficient of homogeneity* developed by Loevinger (1947, 1948) in her own theory of homogeneous tests, which is practically equivalent to Guttman's scale analysis*.
Reminding the reader of our convention to denote in this chapter by n_{ij} the frequency in the *error cell* for any item pair $\{i,j\}$ from our set, Loevinger's coefficient may be defined as:

$$H = 1 - \frac{\displaystyle\sum_{i=1}^{k-1}\sum_{j=i+1}^{k} n_{ij}}{\displaystyle\sum_{i=1}^{k-1}\sum_{j=i+1}^{k} \frac{1}{n} n_i(n-n_j)} \qquad (5.10)$$

where the ordering of the items, as reflected in the summation symbols, is supposed to be determined by their sample difficulties.

Both Green (1954, 357) and Torgerson attribute a possible superiority to this coefficient over other ones, the latter remarking:
"The coefficient H_t (*our H*. RJM) would seem to have a number of advantages over Rep, since it would appear that a good share of the dependency on item marginal has been eliminated. As was the case with Rep, however, its sampling characteristics are unknown. It has not been used a great deal" (Torgerson, 1958, 326).

Inspection of definition 5.10 will show us that the coefficient is based on the "error" frequencies for *all* the item pairs of the set, whereas Green's I, depending on either Rep_A or Rep_B, does so only for *adjacent* first and second order item pairs.

As H is the coefficient we have chosen to use (not wishing to add to the confusion by inventing a new one), we will return to it later (section 3.3.8).

*White and Saltz (1957, 88) state incorrectly that Jackson's Plus Percentage Ratio is essentially the same as Loevinger's H., and that the two differ only in the procedures of counting errors. They also differ, as we have seen, in the way they are formed, and belong to different types.

Other coefficients, which do not fit into one of our three types, have been suggested. For instance, Moscovici has defined two coefficients by applying certain concepts of information theory to the scaling problem (Moscovici and Durain, 1956).

2.5.4   *The problem of sampling*

In section 2.3 we saw that the sampling problem can be formulated with respect to two populations: a population of subjects from which our set of n subjects was sampled and a population, or universe of content, from which the k items were "sampled". Both problems were already mentioned, though not solved at that early time, by Guttman (1950 b).

Let us first consider the problem of sampling from a population of subjects. In most applications of scaling methods, the scalability of a set of items for a population is determined simply on the basis of a sample from that population. Our major concern is whether our co-efficient of scalability is satisfactorily high, not just for a sample, but *for the whole population*. This implies that the coefficient of scala-bility should first be defined for a population as a whole. We must then consider the problem of how to estimate that coefficient and how to test values for it on the basis of a *sample* of subjects (or items). Our sample estimator will generally be a properly chosen *sample* coefficient of scalability. We therefore need models in which on the one hand *population* coefficients of scalability can be defined and from which on the other hand *sample* coefficients of scalability may be derived to estimate and test population values.

In most studies, however, the coefficients of scalability are defined directly in terms of sample observations, without any relation to a previously defined population coefficient.

Once we have defined a coefficient of scalability for the population, the classical problems of statistical analysis have to be solved.

These classical problems of statistical analysis are:

1. Estimating the population coefficient for a sample of n subjects.
2. Establishing confidence intervals for the estimate used.
3. Testing the null hypothesis of random response behavior (*the null case*).
4. Testing coefficients for different populations (*the non null case*).

Only relatively recently have these problems been considered seriously. In accordance with classical psychometric practice, with its emphasis on sample formulations of problems without any reference to a clearly distinguished population model, the first problem was usually not stated clearly. Green (1956, 81, 85–6) mentions the possibility of calculating a variance for Rep_A or Rep_B but refers the reader to a crudely approximate and intuitive estimate originally suggested by Guttman (1950 b, 279–80). Torgerson barely mentions the problem, remarking only that the sampling characteristics are unknown (1958, 326). Matalon (1965) seems to be unaware of the problem.

Nevertheless an improvement has taken place in the situation. Sagi (1959) published a method of determining the exact distribution of Rep coefficients. This method was of very limited practical use, because for values of $n > 10$ and $k \geqslant 4$ the computational labor necessary to determine this exact distribution was so great as to prove prohibitive. Goodman (1959) gave a broader range of solutions based on the results of large sample theory in statistics. One virtue of these solutions was that they were more suitable for application in research than Sagi's. Goodman's paper in the first place gave methods for testing Rep coefficients and type S_2 coefficients against the null hypothesis of random response behavior within given item marginals. He also considered non-null distributions for some special cases to determine confidence intervals. We shall return to this later, when we derive the approximate large sample non-null distribution of H, which is not given by Goodman (See chapter 4, section 4.3.3).

The second sampling problem concerns sampling items from a broader population of possible items. It is again clear that one must then define some population model. Goodman (1959) gives a formulation in which the sample estimates can be very bad indeed. In another formulation of the model, however, the theory leads to satisfactory results and an unbiased estimation of population coefficients. The whole discussion is restricted to Rep ceofficients, which from the point of estimation are easy ones, because of their constant denominator nk (Goodman, 1959, 37–9).

In this study we will only occasionally consider such models of item populations for the purpose of gaining some general insights. We shall on the whole concentrate on the particular selection of k items.

2.6 PROCEDURES OF SCALE ANALYSIS

Many procedures of scale analysis have been suggested since the introduction of the model. The main problem that confronts the researcher is the determination of the ordering of subjects and items.

The scalogram board sketched by Suchman in *Measurement and Prediction* is well-known (Suchman, 1950 a). It was based on equipment designed to allow permutations of subjects (rows) and items (columns) in such a way as to approximate as nearly as possible the type of arrangement given in table 2.1.

Similar methods employing paper and pencil techniques have been suggested by Goodenough (1944), Guttman (1947) and Marder (1952). With the advent of sorting equipment, equivalent procedures for use on IBM and other equipment were designed by Noland (1945), Ford (1950), Kahn and Bodine (1951), Toby (1954) and Danielson (1957), among others. Most of these methods which were inspired by the Guttman-Suchman procedure had in common that items and subjects were treated similarly, through reason of the essential symmetry of the model. Subjects and items were rearranged in such a way as to make the Rep as high as possible. These methods were strongly visual and depended greatly on the judgment of the analyst. Such subjective elements were always felt to be undesirable.

We shall see (chapter 4, section 4.1.3) that the order of the items can be estimated on the basis of their marginals with more precision than the order of the subjects. Green (1956) uses this principle in his well-known procedure based on summary statistics to establish first the difficulty order of the items on the basis of their sample difficulties. Given this order, the error cell is then uniquely defined for each item pair which makes it possible to compute the coefficients and test the set of items on their scalability. The use of Rep_B had the advantage that it was sufficient for the analysis of a limited number of (2×2)-tables for adjacent item pairs, which is easily accomplished with simple sorting equipment.

Green's method was a vast improvement on the more or less artisan techniques that had been used up to them. He rightly claims that

"In a sense, the method proposed here removes scalogram analysis from the list of subjective, slightly mystical techniques available only to experienced practitioners and places it on the list of objective methods available to any statistical clerk" (Green, 1956, 80).

Mainly for these reasons, Green's method had considerable success and was widely applied.

Once the procedure of scale analysis has been established, it will be necessary to set up criteria against which the scalability of a set of items can be measured: criteria such as satisfactory values of coefficients of scalability and, if necessary, related additional criteria.

2.6.1 *Criteria of scalability*

Guttman advocates a Rep value of at least 0.90 as a necessary condition before a set of items can be considered a scale. But he adds that this criterion for scalability is not enough, and that at least four other criteria should be considered. These criteria were the following (Guttman, 1950 a, 77–80):
1. *Rep* $\geqslant$ *0.90*;
2. *An adequate range of marginal distributions.*
    Extreme distributions (0.20–0.80 or more extreme) of item marginals should be limited, and items with marginals around 0.5000 should preferably be included.
3. *The pattern of "errors"* should be random, no conspicuous frequencies of non-scale patterns should be found.
4. *The number of items*: One should not use too few items in the construction of a scale. The number of items should depend on the number of answer categories. In the case of dichotomous items he thought it
    "... probably desirable that at least ten items be used, with perhaps a lesser number being satisfactory if the marginal frequencies of several items are in the range of 30 per cent to 70 per cent. Just four or five items, with marginal frequencies outside such a range, would not give much assurance as to how scalable the universe was, no matter how scalable the sample might be" (Guttman, 1950a, 79).
5. *The number of response categories.* Especially in the case of small numbers of items, Guttman thought a large number of response categories desirable.
    In another chapter of *Measurement and Prediction* (Guttman, 1950 b, 287–8) he added the following criteria for judging items.
6. All items should have an *item-Rep* $\geqslant$ *0.85*.
7. The *criterion of improvement.* The number of errors for any item in the scale, counted over all the subjects, should be at most one half of the number of errors that would be obtained by simply predicting for every subject the answers to that item on the basis of its modal category alone, without taking into account the response pattern.
    In the case of dichotomous items, the number of scale errors per item should therefore be at most half of the frequency in its smallest category.
All these restrictions, added to the major restriction of a high Rep,

have generally led to ambivalent feelings and some uneasiness on the part of the scientists who used the method in practical applications. To quote Torgerson:

"Thus the criteria in use are mostly of a common-sense, intuitive nature. This would seem to be a necessary consequence of the deterministic approach. Until a theory of error is incorporated into the scaling model in some way or other, statistical tests of goodness of fit would not seem to be possible" (1958, 324).

We shall have to drop the deterministic model, but we shall see in this study that it will still be possible to derive from stochastic response models a type of scaling procedure that is practically equivalent to those that have been used under the heading of the Guttman scale.

From our discussion in section 2.5, it will become clear that most of the criteria listed above are necessary because Rep is just a bad coefficient.

Criteria (2), (4), (5) and (7) are necessary to protect the user of scale analysis against the effects of either of the two causes of an inflated interpretation of Rep. These effects could be done away with simply by choosing a better coefficient, preferably one of type S_2, in which both sources of inflation are eliminated. Criterion (3), a relic of the visual manual methods of scalogram analysis and the deterministic formulation of the model, may then be dropped too. Criterion (6) is a sensible one, as it seems to require good scalability characteristics of every item in the scale and guarantees a high overall coefficient. In section 5.1.8 we shall focus our definition of a scale on this criterion only, using the value of the overall coefficient to characterize the scale.

Berting (1962) suggested an additional criterion of scalability. In an analysis of the frequency of occurrence of the scale patterns in empirical scales he found that only the extreme response patterns (where all items are scored 1, or all scored 0) occurred appreciably more frequently than would be expected on the basis of chance, taking into account the total independence of the answers, and given the observed item marginals. In the majority of applications of scale analysis the unfortunate analyst, starting with typically about ten or more items, almost invariably ended up with four or five items that satisfied all the rigid criteria referred to above. Berting wondered whether this result was not due to a process of capitalizing on chance, which worked in favor of extreme item patterns. Starting with twelve dichotomized items, he randomized for given marginal frequencies the responses of 100 imaginary subjects over those items and then applied an analysis resulting in four items with Rep = 0.90.

Comparison of the frequencies observed for the response patterns with those expected by reason of the null hypothesis of random response gave the results reported in table 2.4, rearranged to follow our system of notation.

Table 2.4   A randomized 4-item scale

Pattern	P_0**	O(bs.)	E(xp.)	O–E
1111*	0.059	12	6	+6
0111*	0.116	13	12	+1
1011	0.107	11	11	0
0011*	0.207	15	21	−6
1101	0.037	1	4	−3
0101	0.071	6	7	−1
1001	0.065	7	6	+1
0001*	0.127	14	13	+1
1110	0.015	0	1	−1
0110	0.031	3	3	0
1010	0.028	2	3	−1
0010	0.054	6	5	+1
1100	0.009	1	1	0
0100	0.018	0	2	−2
1000	0.017	0	2	−2
0000*	0.033	9	3	+6

Total: $P = 1.000$ $n = 100$ $n = 100$

Rep = 0.90; I = 0.17
Source: Berting, 1962, 10

*the perfect type
**probability of pattern for random response behavior

Using Green's coefficients, Berting's analysis in the first place again confirmed the well-known fact that the Rep can be high (0.90) even in the randomized case. (The expected $Rep_t = 0.88$). It should be noted, however, that he found a low value for Green's type S_2 coefficient: $I = 0.17$. In table 2.4 we can clearly distinguish some effect of capitalization on chance in especially the extreme response patterns. They show a definite surplus over and above the frequency expected on the basis of total independence.

Berting then demonstrated a similar effect for a four-item scale which he had actually used in research. In table 2.5 these results are reformulated. This scale also has a high Rep value of 0.94 and a "chance" Rep_1 of 0.86. We should like to point out, however, that the type S_2 coefficient is also high: $I = 0.57$. In this case at least, this type of coefficient seems able to differentiate the randomized from the non-randomized case.

Table 2.5   An empirical scale

Pattern	P_0**	O(bs.)	E(xp.)	O–E
1111*	0.028	24	4	+20
0111*	0.068	11	10	+1
1011	0.052	5	7	−2
0011*	0.127	15	18	−3
1101	0.034	1	5	−4
0101	0.083	5	12	−7
1001	0.063	2	9	−7
0001*	0.155	24	22	+2
1110	0.018	3	3	0
0110	0.044	0	6	−6
1010	0.033	1	5	−4
0010	0.081	5	12	−7
1100	0.022	1	3	−2
0100	0.053	5	7	−2
1000	0.040	4	6	−2
0000*	0.099	37	14	+23

Total: $P = 1.000$ $n = 143$ $n = 143$

Rep = 0.94; I = 0.57
Source: Berting, 1962, 11

*the perfect type
**probability of pattern for random response behavior

However, in table 2.5. we see that here again, and much more strikingly, only the extreme response patterns show a high surplus over and above the frequencies expected on the basis of chance.

Berting therefore suggested an additional criterion: that not only the extreme scale patterns should show significant surpluses, but other perfect patterns as well.

Berting points out an interesting phenomenon, which we shall find occasion to treat more elaborately in section 4.2.4. There we shall see that in fact for a stochastic model of acceptable generality only and just these extreme scale patterns can be proved to occur more frequently than expected on the basis of chance, and that, in general, there is not much sense in making a sharp distinction between scale and non-scale patterns. By a counter example we shall show that the application of Berting's additional criterion may lead to the rejection of even a perfect scale. Table 2.5 gives results that are well in accordance with those to be expected for a scale. Bertings criterion, and many of the other criteria we have mentioned, therefore seem unnecessary.

For the other types of coefficients, lower critical values were invariably considered adequate for satisfactory scales. For type S_1 coefficients (*e.g.* Menzel's coefficient), values larger than 0.60 were considered adequate, for type S_2 coefficients such as Green's I and Loevinger's H, values larger than 0.50 were considered adequate for a scale. Green, however, remarks:

"To this author, it seems preferable to evaluate a scale in terms of an index of consistency that varies along a continuum rather than in terms of an arbitrary dichotomy" (Green, 1956, 87).

This will be the approach followed by us in the type of analysis given in chapter 5.

That the use of a good coefficient of type S_2 may be reasonably adequate was illustrated by Berting's data, given in tables 2.4. and 2.5. There the randomized four-item scale, in spite of all the capitalizing on chance that was involved in its construction, did not produce a better result than $I = 0.17$, whereas the empirical scale had a value of $I = 0.57$. The I-coefficient (type S_2) distinguished the two sets remarkably well in this particular case.

The criteria of scalability listed above have proved to be rigid enough in practice. Only very rarely was it possible to establish scales containing a number of items larger than, say, seven which satisfied every criterion mentioned. More typically is the process which we have referred to before, in which, starting with a good number of items, the researcher ends up with four or five items that satisfy the criteria. Stouffer *et al.* remark:

"Thus we have the somewhat paradoxical situation that increasing the number of items may strengthen our confidence in the scalability of an area under consideration and in the generality of the dimension which the scale is defining, at the same time that it creates more non-scale types and thus introduces more ambiguity in ordering respondents" (Stouffer *et al.*, 1952, 275).

Stouffer and his associates developed a technique (the H-technique) producing four or five item scales, in which a *contrived* item was constructed by means of a combination and subsequent dichotomization of a number of related items (*e.g.* three) (Stouffer *et al.*, 1952).

The scales based on four of such contrived items compared favorably with scales constructed from four single items, a result that should not surprise us too much, because, as can be deduced from the results given in chapter 4, the trace lines of contrived items will be steeper than those of single items. On the other hand, the use of at least twelve single items for a four-contrived-item scale seems a bit artificial and raises the question why we should not use scaling procedures that are directed straight at the single items, even when that implies relinquishing the apparently too stringent criteria of the classical analyses of the Guttman type.

2.6.2   The problem of scoring

Any data model used as a measurement model is focused on the allocation of numerical values to the elements that are to be measured. Once the scale has been established, it should be possible to order the subjects on the basis of their scores. Reproducibility, the property which is central to the deterministic model of the perfect scale, implies a one-one correspondence between the $k+1$ possible scores and the $k+1$ perfect patterns. An ordering in terms of scale scores would therefore coincide with an ordering of the (perfect) scale patterns. The inevitable admission of "error" destroyed this one-one correspondence and left the researcher with the question of what to do with subjects who disobligingly produced "imperfect" scale patterns. A strict adherence to the principle of reproducibility gave rise to the idea that not the simple scale score should be allocated to the subject to determine his ordinal position in the set of subjects, as would be done in the case of the perfect scale, but the score of the perfect pattern to which he "belonged". Now, in practice, quite a number of subjects usually produce non-scale patterns. Stouffer *et al.* (1952, 275) remark:

"With a four-item scale which has a reproducibility of 0.90, as many as 40 per cent of the respondents may be non-scale types. With a 10-item scale which has a reproducibility of .90, it is possible for nearly 90 per cent of the respondents to be non-scale types – that is, to have an error on at least one item".

In all these cases scale scores must be defined on the basis of the perfect scale pattern from which it is assumed that such subjects have deviated. Several procedures were devised. One of the methods was to allocate respondents to the pattern from which they deviated with the least possible number of errors (minimum error criterion), which is the same method as the one that was used in the Guttman-Suchman definition of error. But this could not always be done in a unique way. Consider our frequently used example $\{1, 1, 0, 1, 0, 0\}$, where this procedure condemns us to the unpleasant task of allocating subjects with this non-scale type to either the highest $\{1, 1, 1, 1, 1, 1\}$ or the lowest $\{0, 0, 0, 0, 0, 0\}$ class in our ordering.

Several suggestions have been made in attempts to solve the problem of uniqueness. Henry (1952) suggests a "distribution of perfect types" method, in which the modal one of the minimum-error perfect types is allocated to the respondent. Borgotta and Hays (1952) recommend choosing an average of the alternatives. Ford (1950) assigns non-scale types to the middle type or to the type closest to the middle of the scale when the number of alternative perfect types is uneven, and if they are equidistant from the middle of the scale, he assigns them to the most negative type. Many other variations may be devised if one insists on deterministic reproducibility in dealing with "error". But the question is: is it wise to do so? From the statistical point of view and from the point of view of the stochastic scaling models that incorporate the theory of error which the deterministic model lacks by definition, these procedures very much resemble tampering with the data. Response behavior which was *not* demonstrated by the respondent (a perfect type pattern) is replacing the behavior he actually did demonstrate (a non-scale type).

However, as soon as we have admitted the existence of the possibility of error, the deterministic principle of reproducibility is destroyed. We simply cannot know what perfect response pattern would be given by the respondent because of his unknown position on the attribute continuum (his θ-value) compared with that of the k items. We also saw in section 2.4.2 that even an unknown proportion of the perfect-type classes may be "in error".

We shall see elsewhere in this study that once the possibility of error is accepted and a stochastic response model is used, *every* response pattern will give information about the θ-value of the subject and must not be neglected. Even in the special models where the patterns are not important for the estimation of θ (and δ_i) because the simple scale score contains all the relevant statistical information, the perfect scale patterns do not have a particularly important role in comparison with the imperfect type patterns with the same score (see chapter 4, section 4.2.4).

Green (1956, 87) advocates for pragmatic reasons the use of the number of positive responses (the scale score) to score respondents, remarking that this score correlated highly with the scale-type-comparison score used by Suchman (1950 a) and since that time by many others. We shall see in chapter 4, section 4.2.1, that there may be other reasons too: among the simple properties of the scale score s is the fact that it correlates positively with θ, the subject value we want to measure. Practices such as those referred to above may well reduce this correlation strongly, thereby reducing the utility of scales as instruments for measurements.

2.7   THE QUASI-SCALE: A STOCHASTIC MODEL

Scalogram analysis has usually been considered to be a test of the *unidimensionality* of the item space (or population) from which the items were chosen. Low values of reproducibility were regarded as an indication against that hypothesis of unidimensionality.

It is strange that in the general application of scalogram analysis the point has virtually never been stressed that such low values may in the first place be due to the fact that a *deterministic* model is unrealistic. In this sense scalogram analysis is also a test of a hypothesis of deterministic response behavior. When a set of items does not pass the test provided by these procedures of scalogram analysis, it would be better to interpret such a result as a rather trivial contradiction of the *latter* hypothesis and not as evidence against the *former* hypothesis, which concerns a unidimensional representation of subjects and items in terms of a single continuum of behavior. This is a far less trivial conclusion.

That the procedures functioned as tests of this type fairly well in practice is proved by the fact that the majority of Guttman scales used in behavioral research consisted of four or five items sifted from a larger number of items. We might interpret this fact as ample evidence that in practice we simply cannot find reasonable approximations to deterministic models. This, of course, should not lead to a condemnation of the data as unamenable to proper measurement, but should only be seen as strong evidence that, at the present stage at least, deterministic measurement models are not of much use where problems of practical measurement are concerned. Of course, the procedures themselves did accept some "error", but, due to the lack of a theory of error, they have proved to be too rigid in practice and make it impossible to decide clearly whether scales broke down because of a lack of deterministic unidimensionality.

Guttman and his associates clearly saw the possibilities of unidimensional measurement with other than deterministic models, as witnessed by their introduction of the concept of quasi-scale.

"Some areas which are not scalable are called *quasi scales*;
... This means that although they lack the essential property of a
scale – rank order cannot reproduce persons' characteristics on the
items in the area very well – nevertheless the rank order is perfectly efficient for relating any outside variable to the area" (Guttman,
1950 a, 79);
and:
"The prediction of the external variable rests essentially on the
dominant factor that is being measured by the quasi-scale scores.
Thus a quasi scale has the full mathematical advantages of a scalable area" (Suchman, 1950 b, 162).
Guttman later explicitly said that models could be found for a
great variety of quasi-scales (Guttman, 1954a, 278–9) and has
stressed the point that for quasi-scales the notion of reproducibility
is irrelevant (Guttman, 1954 b, 414).

As a matter of fact, as soon as a set of items proves not to form a
perfect scale, we are faced with the necessity of dealing with deviations from this model. In the usual theories of error these deviations
are considered to be governed by some randomization process which,
when specified, transforms the deterministic model into a probabilistic one. We might therefore say that, strictly speaking, all the scales
that were used in practice and that were not perfect were quasi-
scales. In the orthodox practice of scalogram analysis, however,
quasi-scales are considered to be sets of items that showed too low a
coefficient of reproducibility.* The quasi-scale is, in fact, nothing but
a stochastic response model in embryonic form. We shall analyse
some of the properties of a fairly general class of models of this type
in the next two chapters.

---

*Matalon (1965, 44) even assigns the name to sets of items scaling with Reps be-
tween 0.70 and 0.90, which, given the bad qualities of the Rep, may well lead to bad
scales, which is contrary to the notion of quasi-scale.

CHAPTER 3

Probabilistic response: latent structure models

In the following two chapters we shall consider probabilistic or stochastic measurement (or scaling) models. In such models responses of the subjects to the items are not fully determined by the subject and item values in terms of the variable to be measured. Instead responses are given according to a probability distribution in which these subject and item values are important parameters. As a general outline we may sketch our approach as follows.

In the present chapter we shall give a survey of models of a specific form. In this type of model, subject and item values are introduced as separate parameters which are to be estimated in terms of the observations. This problem of the statistical estimation of parameters (*e.g.* the subject parameters) will form our measurement problem. Chapter 3 consists of two parts. In the *first* part (section 3.1) we shall attempt to demonstrate that these measurement models for dichotomous data – the chief focus of interest in this study – are simply special cases of a measurement model of a very general form to which we shall extend Lazarsfeld's term of *latent structure model*, generalizing his *latent structure analysis*.

We shall also indicate a generalization of a new approach by Rasch based on some general requirements that should be satisfied by instruments of measurement. This approach provides a guide line in choosing specific parametric forms in the class of latent structure models in any application for which these models may be used.

In the *second* part (section 3.2), we shall return to the application of what forms the chief focus of interest in our study: dichotomous data. We shall illustrate latent structure models of a specific form for these data and discuss the consequences of an application of Rasch's principles.

The next chapter, chapter 4, contains a discussion of a more general class of models for dichotomous data as quite natural formalizations of the idea of the quasi-scale. We shall derive a number of simple properties that may serve to evaluate existing scaling procedures as sketched in chapter 2, and to define and develop a procedure of scaling in chapter 5.

3.1 LATENT STRUCTURE ANALYSIS

The measurement models for dichotomous data that we are concerned with are special cases of one general model which covers a great variety, if not most, of the stochastic models that have been advocated and used in social research. This model allows for continuous or discrete, univariate or multivariate responses or (subject or item) parameters.

It can be used for the situation in which we are interested: *subjects* (objects to be measured) are related to *items* (objects instrumental to measurement) by means of an experiment resulting in *observable outcomes* of a particular data form (*e.g.* dichotomous outcomes of the "pass-fail" type).

In a model for such data, certain vectors and related spaces may be introduced:
1. A *response vector* x representing an observable outcome of this type of experiment.* We shall represent x as a p-dimensional vector, which takes on values given by a sub-set $\mathscr{X}$ of Euclidean p-space. $(E_p; x \in \mathscr{X} \subset E_p)$
2. A *subject parameter* θ representing the values which subjects can have on the variable with which we are concerned. The subject parameter θ will be represented as a q-dimensional vector which takes on values within a sub-set Θ of Euclidean q-space. $(E_q; \theta \in \Theta \subset E_q)$.
3. An *item parameter* δ representing item values in the form of an r-dimensional vector, which takes on its values in a sub-set Δ of Euclidean r-space. $(E_r; \delta \in \Delta \subset E_r)$.

Correspondingly we may distinguish a *manifest response space* of observable outcomes $(\mathscr{X})$ and two *latent spaces*: a *latent subject parameter space* (Θ) and a *latent item parameter space* (Δ). (Lazarsfeld, 1959 a, 489–90; Lord and Novick, 1968, 359, 530).

The term latent space has in general been reserved for the Θ-space only. This practice is related to the main purpose of these measure-

---

*Vectors and matrices will be given in bold print.

ment models: the measuring of subjects in terms of Θ (*i.e.* the estimation of θ-values) with the aid of the items.

Nevertheless it may be useful to stress a different role played by the items by introducing a second latent space of item parameters in general models such as these. In our model the manifest space is related to the latent space in such a way that it becomes possible for us to infer values of the latent parameters from the observations.

Lazarsfeld formulates it as follows (1959 a, 490):

"Empirical observations locate our objects in a manifest property space. But this is not what we are really interested in. We want to know their location in a latent property space. *Our problem is to infer this latent space from the manifest data*".

In probabilistic latent structure models, this is achieved by the introduction of a probability distribution of the manifest variate x over $\mathscr{X}$.

Assuming the regularity which is always our aim in attempting to design mathematical models for data, we introduce a probability density

$$p(x; \theta, \delta)$$

which governs this distribution as a function of the subject parameter θ and the item parameter δ.

We shall call this specific type of density the *response function*; it is by this function that the manifest variate x is related to the latent variables θ and δ.

Some remarks should be made concerning this response function. With respect to θ and δ, the response function $p(x; \theta, \delta)$ is a *conditional density*: it is determined for particular, fixed values of θ and δ.

In applications involving the presentation of k items to n subjects it may be necessary to consider a variability of the values of subject and item parameters across subjects and items. For instance, subjects are selected or sampled from a certain population. They respond to sets of items which too are selected from a range of possible items. Therefore different subject values θ_α ($\alpha = 1, 2, \ldots, n$) and item values δ_i ($i = 1, 2, \ldots, k$) have to be accounted for.

The way in which subjects are selected may have an effect on the estimation of the values of the item parameters δ. And even when the procedures of the selection of subjects are the same, the distribution of subjects with respect to θ may vary between the populations for which the δ-values are to be estimated.

Without loss of generality these problems concerning selection or sampling procedures and the distribution of θ-values over populations may be subsumed in just one population distribution of subject values.

If we wish to account for the effects of population distributions in our model, it may be necessary to introduce a probability measure $P^{\underline{\theta}}$ over Θ, which may formalize the selection procedure or population distribution for the subjects. We can try to devise models with certain invariance properties with respect to procedures of subject selection.

On the whole we shall assume in this chapter and the chapters that follow that *subjects are selected or sampled independently*.

Similar considerations hold good for the way in which items are selected for a test or a scale. Here the particular selection of values for the item parameters may effect the estimates (measurements) of the subject parameter θ.

If necessary, one might consider the incorporation of an item selection procedure (item sampling) in the model. This may amount to the introduction of a probability measure $P^{\underline{\delta}}$ on Δ. It may be difficult, however, to assume the independent selection of items. In practice this can be highly unrealistic, as scales and tests are frequently set up on the basis of a thorough intercomparison of the items in terms of, for instance, their difficulties. However, we may assume that the selection of subjects is performed independently of that of the items.*

Moreover, we may search for models incorporating certain invariance properties with respect to item selection. A typical situation is where a given subject responds to k items. The response function for this situation may be denoted by

$$p^{(k)}(x^{(k)}; \theta, \delta^{(k)})$$

---

*This implies that a combined probability measure on the product of Θ and Δ may be defined as:

$$P^{\underline{\theta},\underline{\delta}} = P^{\underline{\theta}} \times P^{\underline{\delta}}$$

Even when a test is composed for specific population segments, we may translate this into terms of restrictions on Θ and Δ. For instance, we may define $\Theta' \subset \Theta$ and $\Delta' \subset \Delta$ and a selection procedure $P^{\underline{\theta}} \times P^{\underline{\delta}}$ on the basis of Θ' and Δ'. As a result we may also consider $P^{\underline{\theta}}$ as a version of $P^{\underline{\theta}|\underline{\delta}}$, the conditional probability distribution given the value of δ.

where

$$\delta^{(k)} \stackrel{d}{=} \{\delta_1, \delta_2, \ldots, \delta_k\} \in \Delta^k \subset E_{r \times k};$$
$$x^{(k)} \stackrel{d}{=} \{x_1, x_2, \ldots, x_k\} \in \mathscr{X}^k \subset E_{p \times k}. \tag{1.1}$$

Once a set of k items has been selected, every subject that is selected from the population of subjects will have to respond to this same set of k items.

The simultaneous response function may be simplified considerably by the introduction of the postulate of *local* or *conditional independence*. This principle states that once the subject value θ has been determined and kept constant, all response behavior to items is purely random in the sense of statistical independence (Anderson, 1959, 11; Lord and Novick, 1968, 360–2).

Three kinds of argument may be used to defend the introduction of this requirement into any measurement based on probabilistic models.

In the *first* place there are some general substantive considerations concerning proper measurement which may give rise to this principle. What these considerations amount to is that when we have determined the value of a subject and kept it constant, all systematic variation in the outcomes of measurement of that value should disappear, leaving only purely random variation. Any residual systematic variation would point at the existence of other related dimensions and possible biases. All subjects with the same value of θ may be called homogeneous in θ and may be said to form a homogeneous class. This principle therefore implies that within a homogeneous class of subjects, responses to items are distributed independently.* For respondents with the same θ-value, any association between the items should disappear.

In the words of Lazarsfeld (1959 a, 487):

"If a class of people are alike in an underlying property, then the indicators of this property should not be statistically related in this class".

The *second* argument is based on the considerable mathematical simplicity which is achieved by the adoption of this postulate, and which leads to models of practical value.

The *third* argument concerns the possibilities of an empirical verification of the postulate of local independence. In practice some evidence has been accumulated that in a rough way the principle does work (*e.g.* Lazarsfeld, 1959a, 495–8). However, a strict empirical

---

*Lazarsfeld (1959 a, 498) reverses the situation by defining a homogeneous class as one in which this statistical independence prevails.

verification of the hypothesis presupposes that homogeneous classes of respondents can be formed through an exact determination of their θ-values which is not possible empirically.

The principle does not imply that responses to items are unrelated over the whole population or group of subjects. It only states that any such relation is due solely to a common relation of this group of subjects to the underlying θ. All observable statistical dependence between responses arises only as the result of a mixing over homogeneous classes of subjects according to the distribution of subjects over those classes (for an example see section 4.1.4).

In our model, the postulate of local or conditional independence of responses to items entails that for a fixed subject value θ, the responses to *different** items are statistically independent. The simultaneous response function is thereby reduced to a product of response functions in the following way:

$$p^{(k)}(x^{(k)}; \theta, \delta^{(k)}) = \prod_{i=1}^{k} p_i(x_i; \theta, \delta_i);\qquad(1.2)$$

where the functional form of the density $p_i(x_i;\theta,\delta_i)$ is completely determined by the i-th item.

A general review along lines similar to ours was given by Anderson (1959). A less complete treatment of this type of model in terms of Stieltjes integrable densities was given by McDonald (1962)**. Anderson labeled the class of models for dichotomous data "latent structure analysis" (1959, 22).

This term was introduced by Lazarsfeld in his general formulation of these models, a formulation which was subsequently developed by him and his associates in a number of studies (Lazarsfeld, 1950; 1959a; Lazarsfeld and Henry, 1968). This formulation covers virtually all the dichotomous models of attitude scaling and mental and achievement testing as special cases of latent structure analysis.

Nevertheless, as McDonald (1962, 205) emphasizes, Lazarsfeld did not in principle restrict his model to dichotomous data only. It therefore seems to us that extending the term *latent structure analysis* to cover the yet more general meaning given in this section is well in agreement with his attempt to give a measurement model in general form.

---

*Due to learning and memory effects the hypothesis of local independence (Assumption (1.2)) seems to be untenable for replications with the *same* items.

**McDonald's formulation contains an occasional incorrect use of the concepts "distribution function" and "density function" (1962, 203).

3.1.1   *Response functions*

We may now define our general latent structure model as follows.
Let the *response vector* be denoted by

$$x \in \mathscr{X} \subset E_p;$$

the *subject parameter* by

$$\theta \in \Theta \subset E_q;$$

and the *item parameter* by

$$\delta \in \Delta \subset E_r.$$

Let $\mathscr{A}$ denote a σ algebra defined on $\mathscr{X}$ and let us consider the event $x \in A, A \in \mathscr{A}$. We may denote the probability of that event by

$$P(A) = P\{\underline{x} \in A; A \in \mathscr{A}\}.$$

Then we may introduce a family of probability measures $P(A; \theta, \delta)$ on $(\mathscr{X}, \mathscr{A})$ which depend on the parameters θ, δ and govern the probability distribution of $\underline{x}$ as a variate over $(\mathscr{X}, \mathscr{A})$ for fixed θ and δ.

Assuming the existence* of a σ-finite measure μ on $(\mathscr{X}, \mathscr{A})$ dominating the family $\bar{P}(A; \theta, \delta)$ for all θ and δ, we may introduce a probability density with respect to μ:

$$dP(x; \theta, \delta) = p(x; \theta, \delta)d\mu(x). \tag{1.3}$$

The density $p(x; \theta, \delta)$ may be called the *response function* of our latent structure model.

In many latent structure models the expectation of $\underline{x}$ for fixed θ and δ is important:

$$\mathscr{E}(\underline{x}; \theta, \delta) = \int_{\mathscr{X}} xp(x; \theta, \delta) \, d\mu(x). \tag{1.4}$$

---

*Although for the sake of generality we follow a measure theoretic formulation in this chapter, we shall presuppose the neat and regular situations which we require in models for empirical applications. Therefore we shall assume Euclidean spaces; for instance, let $\mathscr{A}$ stand for Borel-σ-algebras and let us take Lebesgue or counting measure for μ. We shall assume the existence of families $P(A; \theta, \delta)$ which are absolutely continuous with respect to μ for all θ, δ. If necessary we shall implicitly assume the existence of the appropriate product measures. These assumptions of regularity will also guarantee the existence of the conditional expectations and probabilities involved. Variates (*e.g.* $\underline{x}$) are underlined in this study.

This function gives the regression of $\underline{x}$ with respect to $\boldsymbol{\theta}$ (and $\boldsymbol{\delta}$). In its present general form we propose to call it the *trace function* of the model.* For dichotomous x and scalar θ this function as a function of θ was called a *trace line* by Lazarsfeld (1950, 364). The trace function therefore generalizes the concept of trace line.

When one subject with value $\boldsymbol{\theta}$ ($\boldsymbol{\theta}$ fixed) responds to k items, we have a probability density

$$dP^{(k)}(x^{(k)}; \boldsymbol{\theta}, \boldsymbol{\delta}^{(k)}) = p^{(k)}(x^{(k)}; \boldsymbol{\theta}, \boldsymbol{\delta}^{(k)}) \, d\mu^{(k)}(x^{(k)}) \tag{1.5}$$

where

$$d\mu^{(k)}(x^{(k)}) = \prod_{i=1}^{k} d\mu(x_i)$$

and $x^{(k)}$, $\boldsymbol{\delta}^{(k)}$ were defined in (1.1).

Taking into account our requirement of local or conditional independence (see 1.2) we may write (1.5) as

$$dP^{(k)}(x^{(k)}; \boldsymbol{\theta}, \boldsymbol{\delta}^{(k)}) = \prod_{i=1}^{k} dP_i(x_i; \boldsymbol{\theta}, \boldsymbol{\delta}_i)$$

$$= \prod_{i=1}^{k} p_i(x_i; \boldsymbol{\theta}, \boldsymbol{\delta}_i) \, d\mu(x_i). \tag{1.6}$$

For a sample of n subjects, and with an independent selection of subjects, we get

$$dP^{(nk)}(x^{(nk)}; \boldsymbol{\theta}^{(n)}, \boldsymbol{\delta}^{(k)}) = \prod_{\alpha=1}^{n} \prod_{i=1}^{k} dP_i(x_{\alpha i}; \boldsymbol{\theta}_\alpha, \boldsymbol{\delta}_i)$$

$$= \prod_{\alpha=1}^{n} \prod_{i=1}^{k} p_i(x_{\alpha i}; \boldsymbol{\theta}_\alpha, \boldsymbol{\delta}_i) \, d\mu(x_{\alpha i}); \tag{1.7}$$

where $\boldsymbol{\theta}^{(n)}$ is defined analogously to (1.1) and

$$x^{(nk)} = \{x_1^{(k)}, x_2^{(k)}, \ldots, x_\alpha^{(k)}, \ldots, x_n^{(k)}\} \in \mathcal{X}^{nk} \subset E_{n \times p \times k}. \tag{1.8}$$

(1.7) can also be seen as the likelihood function of a sample of n subjects.

In its present general form, the latent structure model covers a great variety of data models as special cases, each corresponding to a

---

*Another term used is *item characteristic function* (Lord and Novick, 1968, 360). This terminology seems rather unfortunate, as characteristic functions have a very specific meaning in probabilistic contexts.

specific assumption concerning the structure and nature of the manifest response space $\mathscr{X}$ and the underlying latent spaces Θ and Δ.

For instance, when Θ is *discrete*, $\boldsymbol{\theta}$ taking on a finite number of values, and $\mathscr{X}$ is also *discrete*, we have a generalized *latent class* model (Lazarsfeld and Henry, 1968). For $\underline{x}$ *continuously* distributed on $\mathscr{X}$ this model generalizes the *latent profile* model proposed by Gibson (1959).

For discrete $\mathscr{X}$ the models that are most prolific are those that are restricted to dichotomous $\mathscr{X}$, the type which will be the chief focus of interest in this study. For other cases, models have been used with a discrete response space $\mathscr{X}$, which can also be considered special cases of our general latent structure model. For instance, the Danish statistician Rasch, taking $\mathscr{X}$ to be one-dimensional, positive and denumerable, and taking Θ and Δ to be both one-dimensional and continuous, developed a model for mistakes in oral reading of texts by applying a special type of Poisson law (Rasch, 1960, 13–33). This approach was based on an interesting theory of measurement which we shall investigate in section 3.1.2, and in the example just given led to considerable success in the construction of a test of reading ability.

For discrete and finite $\mathscr{X}$ (polychotomous items in tests) few models seem to have been developed. Only Rasch has recently (1961, 1967a and 1967b) made some suggestions as a generalization of his approach to dichotomous data.

The model of *factor analysis* may also be formulated as a special case of latent structure analysis. Here $\underline{x}_i$ is continuously distributed on $\mathscr{X} \subset E_1$ for $i = 1, 2, \ldots, k$ ($p = 1$) and dim $\Theta = q \leqslant k$.

Starting from the assumption of conditional independence, (1.2), we may define the model of factor analysis for k items (or tests) as follows:

$$p^{(k)}(\boldsymbol{x}^{(k)}; \boldsymbol{\theta}, \boldsymbol{\delta}^{(k)}) = \prod_{i=1}^{k} p_i(x_i - \boldsymbol{\lambda}_i^T \boldsymbol{\theta} - \mu_i) \qquad (1.9)$$

or

$$\underline{x}^{(k)} = \Lambda_{(k)}^T \boldsymbol{\theta} + \boldsymbol{\mu}^{(k)} + \underline{z}^{(k)} \qquad (1.10)$$

where:
$\boldsymbol{\lambda}_i$ is a column vector of q real constants; $i = 1, 2, \ldots, k$;

$$\Lambda_{(k)}^T = \{\boldsymbol{\lambda}_1, \boldsymbol{\lambda}_2, \ldots, \boldsymbol{\lambda}_i, \ldots, \boldsymbol{\lambda}_k\}^T$$

is a matrix of order $k \times q$;

$\underline{x}^{(k)}$ as defined in (1.1), is a stochastic column vector with components $\underline{x}_i; i = 1, 2, \ldots, k;$

$\mu^{(k)}$ is a column vector of constants $\mu_i; i = 1, 2, \ldots, k;$ and where $\underline{z}^{(k)}$ is a column vector with stochastic elements $\underline{z}_i; i = 1, 2, \ldots, k,$ which are mutually independently distributed, each with mean zero and variance σ_i^2 depending on the i-th item.

In terms of our model, the item parameter δ_i, and correspondingly $\delta^{(k)}$, can be written as the column vector

$$\delta_i = (\lambda_{i1}, \lambda_{i2}, \ldots, \lambda_{iq}, \mu_i, \sigma_i^2)^T \tag{1.11}$$

so that in this case $r = q + 2$.

On the basis of (1.4) and (1.10) it can be shown that the trace function of $\underline{x}_i$ for given θ and δ_i is

$$\mathscr{E}(\underline{x}_i; \theta, \delta_i) = \lambda_i^T \theta + \mu_i \tag{1.12}$$

and therefore

$$\mathscr{E}(\underline{x}^{(k)}; \theta, \delta^{(k)}) = \Lambda_{(k)}^T \theta + \mu^{(k)}; \tag{1.13}$$

so that the trace function shows a linear regression of $\underline{x}_i$ and $\underline{x}^{(k)}$ on θ (see also Anderson, 1959, 17–22).

In some models of factor analysis, distributional assumptions concerning the θ values are introduced, such as a continuous distribution of $\underline{\theta}$ on Θ according to a probability distribution $P^{\underline{\theta}}$. A well-known assumption is

$$\theta \doteq N_q(0, I)$$

that is, the $\underline{\theta}$ have a q-variate normal distribution, with mean vector zero and covariance matrix equal to the unity matrix. Hence the components of $\underline{\theta}$ are postulated to be uncorrelated.

Specification of the latent structure model. In order to select from the class of latent structure models given in (1.3)–(1.7) a specific form which may serve as a model for a given set of data, the researcher has to make a number of interrelated decisions which will determine his choice out of the alternatives open to him. This set of decisions will be suggested by the data definition and the theoretical considerations which he may be using as a guide. We may summarize the major elements of this set of decisions as follows.

*1. Dimension (p) of the response vector **x**.* This entails the choice of p as the dimension of the manifest (observable) response vector, representing the response of a subject to an item. Generally, the right decision will be to some extent suggested by the data, as will the related decision of choosing $\underline{x}$ as a *discrete* or *continuous* variate.

*2. Dimension (q) of the subject parameter **θ**.* The choice of the proper value of $q = \dim \Theta$, as well as the representation of θ as a *discrete* or *continuous* variable will partly depend on theoretical considerations concerning the nature of the latent subject space Θ. For instance, the restriction that θ may assume only a finite, preferably small, number of values, will mean that we will have to use a *latent class* model.

The choice of q may also be partly determined by the type of response function that we choose for our model. We shall see in section 3.1.2 that such a restriction on the possible values of q may be very strong when certain requirements of a strong theory of measurement are involved, as in the approach of Rasch, which will be described in that section.

In other models, such as that of factor analysis, the particular choice of q may be decided empirically from the data just as, for instance, the number of common factors is determined in factor analysis.

*3. Dimension (r) of the item parameter **δ**.* Here principles similar to those mentioned in connection with the subject parameters may guide us in choosing an adequate representation.

4. The choice of the response function. The particular response function $p_i(\mathbf{x}_i; \boldsymbol{\theta}, \boldsymbol{\delta}_i)$ in (1.6) and (1.7) will be chosen on the basis of both empirical and theoretical considerations.

Generally it will not be necessary to search for models which allow the highest levels of mathematical generality. It may be more rewarding to look for much simpler models, in which a parsimonious description of the data is adequate. One simplification, for instance, may be to choose, instead of separate functions p_i for responses $\mathbf{x}_i$ to item i, just one function $p(\mathbf{x}_i; \boldsymbol{\theta}, \boldsymbol{\delta}_i)$, which depends on this item only through the argument $\boldsymbol{\delta}_i$.

The possible form of the response function will, of course, also be determined by the dimensions of $\mathscr{X}$, Θ, and Δ as established in 1, 2 and 3. It is clear that the choice made should allow for at least a partial empirical verification by means of the data.

5. The choice of the subject distribution $(P^{\underline{\theta}})$. We have seen that the model may sometimes also imply certain assumptions concerning a distribution $P^{\underline{\theta}}$ of the subject variate $\underline{\theta}$ on Θ as a kind of *a priori* distribution of subjects. In practical applications it will be necessary either to determine or to postulate a family of probability distributions to which $P^{\underline{\theta}}$ should belong. Once this matter has been settled, a particular member of this family of distributions must be selected with the right choice of a particular value ξ_0 of the selection parameter vector ξ which uniquely determines a member of that family. *I.e.*, let a member of the family be denoted by its density

$$dP^{\underline{\theta}} = dP^{\underline{\theta}}(\theta; \xi);$$

then a particular distribution of subject values $\underline{\theta}$ will be selected from that family with the choice $\xi = \xi_0$ and will be given by

$$dP^{\theta}_0 = dP^{\theta}(\theta; \xi_0).$$

For instance, in the model of factor analysis we may postulate that the distribution of $\underline{\theta}$ belongs to the family of the q-variate normal distributions $N_q(\mu, \Sigma)$. Here ξ is denoted by the set $\{\mu, \Sigma\}$.

We may determine a member of this family by means of the postulate that

$$P^{\underline{\theta}}_0 = N_q(0, I),$$

so that

$$\xi_0 = \{0, I\}.$$

Sometimes such a specification of a population distribution may be used to eliminate the dependence of the response function on θ by the following transformation of (1.6)

$$dP^{(k)}(x^{(k)}; \cdot, \delta^{(k)}, \xi_0) = \left[\int_\Theta \prod_{i=1}^{k} p_i(x_i; \theta, \delta_i) \, dP^{\theta}(\theta; \xi_0) \right] \prod_{i=1}^{k} d\mu(x_i); \tag{1.14}$$

$$= p^{(k)}(x^{(k)}; \cdot, \delta^{(k)}, \xi_0) \prod_{i=1}^{k} d\mu(x_i); \tag{1.15}$$

where $p^{(k)}(x^{(k)}; \cdot, \delta^{(k)}, \xi_0)$ is a density of a (marginal) probability distribution over $\mathscr{X}^k$, obtained by an integration over Θ with respect to $P^{\underline{\theta}}_0$.

This marginal density will depend on the family of distributions chosen for $P^{\underline{\theta}}$ and on the parameter value ξ_0.

Sometimes this method may be used to determine the item parameters δ_i from the density $p^{(k)}(x^{(k)}; \cdot, \delta^{(k)}, \xi_0)$ and a sample of subjects. As an example of this method for dichotomous data and one-dimensional θ, Lazarsfeld used a uniform distribution of θ on the interval [0, 1] in his *latent distance* model (Torgerson, 1958, 374–85).

In other cases a Bayesian analysis may be performed, by means of which an *a posteriori* distribution of $\underline{\theta}$ for given value $\underline{x}_i = x_i$; ($i = 1, 2, \ldots, k$) may be derived from P_0^θ and (1.6) (Anderson, 1959, 10). Andersen (1968) introduces such an *a posteriori* distribution for given values of statistics sufficient for θ to solve some estimation problems.

6. *The choice of the item distribution* (P^δ). Sometimes the introduction of a sampling model concerning the selection of items may be warranted. In those cases a family of probability distributions P^δ may be postulated and methods as mentioned *sub* 5 applied.

Problems of inference. A decision as regards the six points listed above will lead to a specification of the general forms (1.6) and (1.7), which will then represent a specific measurement model. In such a model a number of problems of inference may arise, problems which have been mentioned by Anderson (1959, 17). In summarizing these we shall first mention three general problems concerning the existence, uniqueness and solvability of the model.

I. The existence of the model. Once the model is specified in a form such as that given in (1.6) or (1.7), the existence of the model depends on the mutual consistency of the choices that have been made as regards the six points listed above and the value of n to be realized. For instance, the numbers of parameters involved in a particular model may have to satisfy a number of restrictions related to p, k and even n, as the dimensions of the manifest (observable) phenomena.

II. The identification of the parameters. This problem concerns the uniqueness of a given parametric representation within the model. Given the dimensions p, q and r of, respectively, x, θ and δ, are the values of θ and δ uniquely determined by the model, or do other values satisfy the model as well?

III. The solution of the structure. When I and II have been settled satisfactorily, so that the existence of the model may be taken for granted and its parameters have been identified, we can look for methods to determine the class of solutions of θ and δ from (1.7).

In addition to these three classes of problems we may mention a number of statistical problems which determine the utility of our data model as a measurement model.

IV. The determination of the dimensions of the latent parameters θ *and* δ. We have stated before that a latent structure model may permit different and various values for the dimensions q and r of respectively θ and δ. If this is the case, we may try to determine a "best" value for these dimensions from the data.

In factor analysis the estimation of the number of common factors belongs to this class of problems. In a somewhat different form the problem of the determination of the number of latent classes in the latent class model can be classified under this heading.

V. The estimation of the parameters θ *and* δ. Our measurement problem, which concerns a set (test or scale) of k items as an instrument of measurement, consists of the estimation of the value of θ_α for subject α, if we regard the measurement of subjects as our main aim. To fulfil this aim we shall have to estimate the item parameters δ_i as well, because a latent structure model is defined for a particular selection of values δ_i. Here these given values δ_i take on the role of nuisance parameters* which have to be estimated as well unless, as in particular models (see section 3.1.2), the θ_α values may be estimated independently of the particular values chosen for δ_i.

VI. Testing the fit of the model. When the estimation problems mentioned *sub* IV and V have been solved, we can look for statistical criteria by means of which we can judge whether the data are in good correspondence with the observable outcomes that we may expect from our model. Generally, such expected observable outcomes may be computed from the model, using the estimated values for θ_α, δ_i and, if necessary, the dimensions q and r. These expected values should be compared with the observed data with the aid of adequate criteria in order to decide whether the data fit the model more or less satisfactorily. The model must come through such a test of the goodness-of-fit successfully to warrant its practical use for measurement purposes.

VII. Testing other hypotheses. Within the context of our data model other hypotheses may be of interest. *E.g.* we may test a hypothesis of the equality of item difficulties between items ($\mathcal{H}_0$: $\delta_i = \delta_j$, where δ_i and δ_j are difficulty parameters of items i and j (see section 3.2.1). Or we may test the equality of the difficulty of a given item i across h populations ($\mathcal{H}_0$: $\delta_i^{(1)} = \delta_i^{(2)} = \ldots = \delta_i^{(h)}$; populations $1, 2, \ldots, h$).

---

*In other situations the measurement of δ_i may be of interest on its own account *e.g.* as a difficulty level of a test, or a readability parameter for texts.

3.1.2   An exponential model

In the last section we gave the latent structure model in its full generality. As such its scope exceeds by far what is required for the dichotomous data which are the chief focus of interest in this study. Before we specialize the latent structure model in section 3.2 for these purposes, we shall first try to give a general theory concerning a special choice of response function $p(x; \theta, \delta)$, which will enable us to introduce a new approach in probabilistic measurement theory as advocated by Rasch.

In section 3.1.1 we mentioned the fact that our estimates of particular parameters will generally depend on the selected values of other (nuisance) parameters. More precisely: if we want to estimate the values of the δ_i, our estimates will depend on the θ_α values selected in (1.7). By symmetry, estimates (measurements) of the subject value θ_α will depend on the particular selection of item parameters δ_i.

Since the 1950's Rasch (1960, 1961, 1966, 1966 [with Leunbach], 1967a, 1967b) has been developing an approach leading to "population-free" estimates of the parameters (1960, 172), as a consequence of a separability property in subject and item parameter(s) which he originally introduced in models for oral reading and intelligence tests. In a later publication he subsequently tried to generalize this property (1961, 326).

We shall not follow Rasch's method of derivation. We prefer to use a different formulation, which will enable us to relate his theory to some well-known results concerning sufficient statistics.

Rasch's approach simply results in a particular choice of response function which belongs to a sub-family of the well-known exponential family of probability densities.

Generalizing his models, we may write the response function (1.3) as:

$$dP(x, \theta, \delta) = C(\theta, \delta) \exp\left\{ \sum_{j=1}^{q} \theta_j t_j(x) + \sum_{s=1}^{r} \delta_s d_s(x) \right\} d\mu(x),$$

where $C(\theta, \delta)$ is a constant depending on θ and δ; θ_j and δ_s denote components of vectors θ and δ; $t_j(x)$ and $d_s(x)$ are statistics defined on $\mathscr{X}$; and where a factor depending solely on x may have to be absorbed in $\mu(x)$ in order to obtain form (1.16).

Using vector notation and defining the column vectors

$$t(x) = (t_1(x), t_2(x), \ldots, t_q(x))^T;$$

$$d(x) = (d_1(x), d_2(x), \ldots, d_2(x))^T;$$

we may write (1.16) as

$$dP(x; \boldsymbol{\theta}, \boldsymbol{\delta}) = C(\boldsymbol{\theta}, \boldsymbol{\delta}) \exp\{\boldsymbol{\theta}^T t(x) + \boldsymbol{\delta}^T d(x)\} \, d\mu(x). \tag{1.17}$$

For a sample of n subjects with values $\boldsymbol{\theta}_\alpha$; $(\alpha = 1, 2, \ldots, n)$, responding to k items $\boldsymbol{\delta}_i$ $(i = 1, 2, \ldots, k)$, we may use (1.17) to write (1.7) as:

$$dP^{(nk)}(x^{(nk)}; \boldsymbol{\theta}^{(n)}, \boldsymbol{\delta}^{(k)}) = \prod_{\alpha=1}^{n} \prod_{i=1}^{k} dP(x_{\alpha i}; \boldsymbol{\theta}_\alpha, \boldsymbol{\delta}_i) \tag{1.18}$$

$$= C^*(\boldsymbol{\theta}^{(n)}, \boldsymbol{\delta}^{(k)}) \exp\left\{\sum_{\alpha=1}^{n} \boldsymbol{\theta}_\alpha^T t^*(x_\alpha^{(k)}) + \sum_{i=1}^{k} \boldsymbol{\delta}_i^T d^*(x_i^{(n)})\right\}$$

$$\times \prod_{\alpha=1}^{n} \prod_{i=1}^{k} d\mu(x_{\alpha i});$$

where

$$C^*(\boldsymbol{\theta}^{(n)}, \boldsymbol{\delta}^{(k)}) = \prod_{\alpha=1}^{n} \prod_{i=1}^{k} C(\boldsymbol{\theta}_\alpha, \boldsymbol{\delta}_i);$$

$$t^*(x_\alpha^{(k)}) = \sum_{i=1}^{k} t(x_{\alpha i});$$

$$d^*(x_i^{(n)}) = \sum_{i=1}^{n} d(x_{\alpha i});$$

and where $x^{(nk)}$, $x_\alpha^{(k)}$, $x_i^{(n)}$, $\boldsymbol{\theta}^{(n)}$ and $\boldsymbol{\delta}^{(k)}$ are defined as in (1.1) and (1.8).

Some remarks should be made concerning the forms (1.18) and (1.17).

In the *first* place it will be clear that (1.18) is of the same type as (1.17). We shall therefore begin by analyzing the properties of form (1.17).

Secondly, (1.17) is clearly a member of the *exponential family*, which is important in mathematical statistics because of its nice properties (see Lehmann, 1959, 50).

These properties make it possible to use the corresponding analytic means concerning the estimation of parameters and the testing of hypotheses of modern statistical theory (see *e.g.* Lehmann, 1959). It seems that the field of social measurement has seen a consistent and more elaborate application of these methods of analysis to parametric measurement models only very recently (Birnbaum, 1965; 1968).

In the *third* place, in forms (1.16), (1.17) and (1.18), the functions

$t_j(x)$ and $d_s(x)$, $t(x)$ and $d(x)$, and $t^*(x_\alpha^{(k)})$ and $d^*(x_i^{(n)})$ are the sufficient statistics that are characteristic for the exponential family. They are sufficient for, respectively, the parameter components θ_j and δ_s in (1.16) or the parameter vectors $\boldsymbol{\theta}$ and $\boldsymbol{\delta}$ in (1.17) or $\boldsymbol{\theta}_\alpha$ and δ_i in (1.18); *i.e.* they carry all the probabilistic information concerning the parameter values that is conveyed by the manifest probability space.

For the purpose of making inferences about these parameters, a considerable simplification of the observational basis is possible under these circumstances: not the values of the original observations $x_{\alpha i}$ but those of the sufficient statistics are adequate for the estimation of $\boldsymbol{\theta}_\alpha$ and δ_i.

In the *fourth* place we may add some remarks concerning the level of mathematical generality with which we are concerned when we choose a particular form of type (1.16; 1.17). Especially the possible forms and properties of the functions $t_j(x)$ and $d_s(x)$ and the parameterization of the components θ_j and δ_s may vary considerably and take on rather unpleasant forms in the more "pathological" cases. Fortunately, the empirical scientist can choose the simplest functions that will suit his theoretical purposes and provide adequate descriptions of his data that are subject to empirical verification. Therefore we need only consider the neater forms of (1.16).

A particular virtue of this model is that it permits a certain form of "population-free" estimation as given in the following theorem, which can be seen as a straightforward reformulation of a lemma by Lehmann (1959, 52, Lemma 8).

Theorem 1.2.1   Let the common response function $p(x; \boldsymbol{\theta}, \boldsymbol{\delta})$ be chosen in such a way that x is distributed as in (1.16). Then there exist probability measures $v_{\underline{t}}$ and $v_{\underline{d}}$ over r and q dimensional Euclidean space respectively such that
1. *the conditional distribution of $\underline{t}$, given $d(\underline{x}) = d$, is an exponential family of the form*

$$dP(t; \boldsymbol{\theta}|\underline{d} = d) = C_d(\boldsymbol{\theta}) \exp\left\{\sum_{j=1}^{q} \theta_j t_j\right\} dv_{\underline{d}}(t) \tag{1.19}$$

and

2. *the conditional distribution of $\underline{d}$, given $t(\underline{x}) = t$, is an exponential family of the form*

$$dP(d; \boldsymbol{\delta}|t = t) = C_t(d) \exp\left\{\sum_{s=1}^{r} \delta_s d_s\right\} dv_{\underline{t}}(d) \tag{1.20}$$

where $C_d(\boldsymbol{\theta})$ and $C_t(\boldsymbol{\delta})$ denote appropriate constants.

For a proof of this theorem we refer to Lehmann (1959, 52). For a good understanding of some of the points to be made elsewhere in this chapter we must add a remark concerning the non-trivial validity of theorem 1.2.1. To ensure this validity it is necessary that no functional relationship should exist between the components of the statistic t and those of the statistic d, for this may lead to degenerate conditional distributions, (1.19) or (1.20).

For instance, let $t = g(d)$. Then if $\underline{d} = d$ the value of $\underline{t}$ will also be fixed, so that the conditional distribution of $\underline{t}$ given by (1.19) will be the degenerate distribution.

The importance of theorem (1.2.1) lies in the fact that for any inference concerning θ we may choose the conditional distribution (1.19), *which does not depend on δ.*

In this sense any estimation procedure for θ based on (1.19) is independent of the particular choice of items, *item-selection free.*

Similarly (1.20) is independent of θ, and any estimation procedure for δ based on the conditional distribution (1.20) may be called *subject-selection free* or *population-free*, to borrow Rasch's term.

Moreover, according to statistical theory, inferences such as these, proceeding from these conditional distributions, may often have optimal properties such as minimum variance estimates (Fraser, 1957; Lehmann, 1959).

Rasch advocated a more restricted model than that given in (1.16) by adding further requirements based on certain heuristic considerations concerning the objective measurement or rather the objective comparison of items and subjects in a certain sense* (Rasch, 1967a, b).

Although a strict mathematical formulation of his ideas is still lacking, his line of thought may be sketched as follows.

The response function formalizes the intercomparison of subject value and item value in terms of the observable or manifest variate $\underline{x}$. The intercomparison of these values may be summarized by a vector-valued function $\xi(\theta, \delta)$ of θ, δ which represents the interrelation of θ and δ in the response function. We assume that dim $\xi = m$. In the stochastic models under consideration, $\xi(\theta, \delta)$ plays the role of a (m component) parameter which determines the response function and therefore the distribution of $\underline{x}$ on the manifest probability space.

In terms of the comparison vector ξ we may write:

$$p(x; \theta, \delta) = q(x; \xi(\theta, \delta)) \tag{1.21}$$

*The requirement of "specific objectivity" according to Rasch's terminology.

We may then follow a line of reasoning which amounts to a special way of ensuring identification (see section 3.1.1, sub II) if appropriate regularity conditions are assumed. We shall require the comparison function ξ in the measurement model to be such that for all δ any given value $\xi(\theta, \delta) = \xi$ will determine a unique value θ. This requirement is equivalent to a condition of unambiguous measurement, in the sense that for given δ a value θ is uniquely determined by any outcome ξ of the comparison function $\xi(\theta, \delta)$. It establishes a 1-1 correspondence between values ξ and θ for given δ. Therefore, solving for θ, we may write

$$\theta = \lambda(\delta, \xi) \tag{1.22}$$

Consequently, if $\dim \theta < \dim \xi$, some functional dependencies will exist among components of ξ which may be eliminated by a proper reparameterization of ξ.

Again, if $\dim \theta > \dim \xi$, functional dependencies will exist among the components of the subject parameter which will needlessly complicate our measurement model and which can be eliminated by a reparameterization of Θ.

Excluding therefore such dependencies by assumption, we can choose the parametric form of our measurement model in such a way that

$$q = \dim \theta = \dim \xi = m \tag{1.23}$$

However, the same reasoning may be applied to the measurement of the item parameter δ. For all θ, any value $\xi(\theta, \delta) = \xi$ should correspond uniquely with a value δ.

Hence we may solve for δ

$$\delta = \eta(\theta, \xi); \tag{1.24}$$

establishing a 1-1 correspondence between δ and ξ for all θ.

An application of the same reasoning given above will lead to the requirement of a parametric form where

$$r = \dim \delta = \dim \xi = m \tag{1.25}$$

As a result we can derive from (1.23) and (1.25) that

$$\dim \theta = \dim \delta = \dim \xi = m \tag{1.26}$$

The strong measurement theory proposed in this form by Rasch therefore requires that subject parameters and item parameters should have the same dimension.

In the specific models from which Rasch developed his theory, the response function may be written as a density belonging to the exponential family with parameter $\boldsymbol{\xi}$,

$$dQ(x; \boldsymbol{\xi}) = q(x; \boldsymbol{\xi}) \, d\mu(x) = C^{(\varphi)}(\boldsymbol{\xi}) \exp\left\{\sum_{h=1}^{m} \xi_h g_h(x)\right\} d\mu(x)$$

(1.27)

where $C^{(\varphi)}(\boldsymbol{\xi})$ is a constant in $\boldsymbol{\xi}$.

In order to ensure "selection-free" estimation of subject and item parameters it is also necessary for the response function to belong to type (1.16) in terms of $\boldsymbol{\theta}$ and $\boldsymbol{\delta}$.

Applying Rasch's strong measurement theory ("specific objectivity"), we furthermore require the equality of dimensions (1.26) to hold good.

We then get (see 1.21)

$$q(x; \boldsymbol{\xi}(\boldsymbol{\theta}, \boldsymbol{\delta})) = C^{(\varphi)}(\boldsymbol{\xi}(\boldsymbol{\theta}, \boldsymbol{\delta})) \exp\left\{\sum_{h=1}^{m} \xi_h(\boldsymbol{\theta}, \boldsymbol{\delta}) g_h(x)\right\}$$

$$\equiv C(\boldsymbol{\theta}, \boldsymbol{\delta}) \exp\left\{\sum_{j=1}^{m} \theta_j t_j(x) + \sum_{s=1}^{m} \delta_s d_s(x)\right\} = p(x; \boldsymbol{\theta}, \boldsymbol{\delta});$$

(1.28)

where $C(\boldsymbol{\theta}, \boldsymbol{\delta})$ is the corresponding constant.

According to an argument of Dynkin's (1951; see also Fraser, 1966), the set of functions $\{g_1(x), g_2(x), \ldots, g_m(x)\}$ are linearly independent. They therefore form a basis for the linear space of rank m generated in the exponent of the left-hand member of (1.28).

In terms of this basis the right-hand member of (1.28) may be defined as

$$C(\boldsymbol{\theta}, \boldsymbol{\delta}) \exp\left\{\sum_{h=1}^{m} a_h(\boldsymbol{\theta}) g_h(x) + \sum_{h=1}^{m} b_h(\boldsymbol{\delta}) g_h(x)\right\}$$

(1.29)

As we are free to choose our parameters in any way we like, and as the functions $a_h(\boldsymbol{\theta})$ as well as the functions $b_h(\boldsymbol{\delta})$ are independent, we may well use these functions for the parametric values of subjects and items. After reparameterization, (1.28) reduces to

$$C^{(\varphi)}(\boldsymbol{\xi}(\boldsymbol{\theta}, \boldsymbol{\delta})) \exp\left\{\sum_{h=1}^{m} \xi_h(\boldsymbol{\theta}, \boldsymbol{\delta}) g_h(x)\right\}$$

$$\equiv C(\boldsymbol{\theta}, \boldsymbol{\delta}) \exp\left\{\sum_{h=1}^{m} (\theta_h + \delta_h) g_h(x)\right\};$$

(1.30)

which implies that

$$\xi = \theta + \delta \tag{1.31}$$

As a result, the "comparison function", the vector ξ, is additive in the vectors θ and δ. However, although (1.30) is of the form of (1.16), theorem 1.2.1 applies only in a degenerate way, as the statistics are sufficient only for $\xi_h = \theta_h + \delta_h$. The parameters θ_h and δ_h are not separable, for $g_h(x)$ applies to both of them.

Yet for n subjects and k items this problem does not exist. We may write (1.30) in the form of (1.17)

$$C(\theta, \delta) \exp \{\theta^T g(x) + \delta^T g(x)\}; \tag{1.32}$$

where

$$g(x) = (g_1(x), g_2(x), \dots, g_m(x))^T.$$

For n subjects (θ_α) and k items (δ_i) we get, analogous to the form of (1.18)

$$dP^{(nk)}(x^{(nk)}; \theta^{(n)}, \delta^{(k)})$$

$$= C^*(\theta^{(n)}, \delta^{(k)}) \exp \left\{ \sum_{\alpha=1}^{n} \theta_\alpha^T T(x_\alpha^{(k)}) + \sum_{i=1}^{k} \delta_i^T D(x_i^{(n)}) \right\}; \tag{1.33}$$

where

$$T(x_\alpha^{(k)}) = \sum_{i=1}^{k} g(x_{\alpha i}); \quad D(x_i^{(n)}) = \sum_{\alpha=1}^{n} g(x_{\alpha i}).$$

As the statistics $T(x_\alpha^{(k)})$ and $D(x_i^{(n)})$ are functionally independent, theorem 1.2.1 applies non-degenerately, and the ensuing separability in the sets of parameters $\{\theta_\alpha\}$ and $\{\delta_i\}$ permits "selection-free" estimation in the sense of this theorem if the conditional distributions corresponding to (1.19) and (1.20) are used.

This is the model put forward by Rasch. It is clear that his approach, insofar as it is based on his requirements concerning procedures of comparing subjects and items for purposes of measurement, implies very strong assumptions, as they virtually determine unique response functions for any type of measurement model. However, strong assumptions of this type are not uncommon in modern measurement theory. How restrictive the requirements are can be seen in discrete data models, where $\mathscr{X}$ is finite, consisting of, say, $m+1$ points x_ν $(\nu = 1, \ldots, m+1)$.

In this case $\boldsymbol{\xi}$ will determine a probability distribution over $\mathscr{X}$:

$$P(\underline{x} = x_\nu; \boldsymbol{\xi}) = P(x_\nu; \boldsymbol{\xi});$$ (1.34)

and therefore

$$\sum_{\nu=1}^{m+1} P(x_\nu; \boldsymbol{\xi}) = 1.$$ (1.35)

The requirement of the functional independence of the components of $\boldsymbol{\xi}$ therefore implies that

$$\dim \boldsymbol{\xi} \leqslant m$$ (1.36)

In the case under consideration in this study, $\mathscr{X}$ is dichotomous and consists of two points, therefore ξ, θ and δ have to be one-dimensional and (1.31) leads to the scalar requirement

$$\xi = \theta + \delta$$ (1.37)

Within the framework of the approach of Rasch, therefore, the use of dichotomous data models for measurement models is only adequate for, or presupposes, one-dimensional item parameters.

3.2 LATENT STRUCTURE MODELS FOR DICHOTOMOUS DATA

We shall now specialize our general latent structure model for the dichotomous data and the one-dimensional subject values with which we are concerned in this study. First we shall investigate the concept of the trace line as a special form of the trace function.*After a brief analysis of some of the specific parametric forms that have been used in actual practice, we shall formulate a general two-parameter model as one generalization of the Guttman model, some of the properties of which will be analyzed in the next chapter.

---

*Throughout this chapter we shall adhere to the customary term *trace line*. In the next chapter we shall restrict the use of this term and introduce the term *trace function* for cases in which variation in item parameters are also involved (see section 4.1).

3.2.1   Trace lines

In the case of dichotomous data, the concept of the quasi-scale implies the notion of error. We have argued that the possibility of error should be taken into account in the model used to describe response behavior for measurement purposes. One way of achieving this is by assuming that the scale response will be given with a certain probability which will depend on the subject's position on the variable that we want to measure in the first place, and on the particular item to which he is responding in the second place. Let us consider a subject with value θ responding to a particular item. Let us denote a response to item i by x_i, x_i having the value 1 for the scale response alternative ("positive" response) and 0 for the other alternative.
   If

$$P(\underline{x}_i = 1; \theta) = \pi_i(\theta); \tag{2.1}$$

the response function may then in this case by formulated as

$$p(x_i; \theta, \delta_i) = \pi_i(\theta)^{x_i}(1 - \pi_i(\theta))^{1-x_i} \tag{2.2}$$

where δ_i will not be specified for the moment. The response function will therefore be determined by the probability $\pi_i(\theta)$.
   Considered as a function of θ, this probability has been called "trace line" by Lazarsfeld in his first exposition of latent structure analysis (Lazarsfeld, 1950, 363). It will easily be seen that (1.4) will give

$$\mathscr{E}(x; \theta, \delta_i) = \pi_i(\theta); \tag{2.3}$$

so that the trace line is a special case of a trace function. As such $\pi_i(\theta)$ may also be regarded as a measure of the *local difficulty* of item i, *i.e.* the difficulty at the point θ. We may also distinguish *local discrimination* at an item in a point θ as the degree to which $\pi_i(\theta)$ varies over different θ values in a neighbourhood of θ. Confining our attention to items for which $\pi_i(\theta)$ is a monotone non-decreasing function of θ, we may consider some of the possibilities given in figure 3.1.
   Item 1 is a Guttman item: $\pi_1(\theta) = 0$ for $\theta \leq \delta_1$ and 1 for values $\theta \geq \delta_1$. Defining the function $\iota(x)$ as follows:

$$\iota(x) = 0; \quad x < 0;$$
$$\iota(x) = 1; \quad x \geq 0;$$

we may formulate for any Guttman item as for item 1:

$$\pi_1(\theta) = \iota(\theta - \delta_1);$$
(2.4)

where the value δ_1 is clearly an item difficulty parameter.

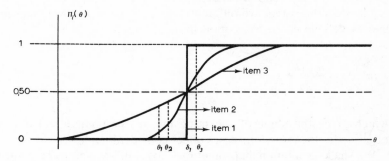

Figure 3.1   Three trace lines.

It will furthermore be seen that item 1 discriminates locally only in θ neighborhoods containing the point δ_1. There the discrimination is very sharp: for $\theta_1 < \delta_1$, and $\theta_3 > \delta_1$ we have $\pi_1(\theta_1) = 0$ and $\pi_1(\theta_3) = 1$. But in other neighborhoods (intervals) along the θ axis not containing δ_1, item 1 does not discriminate θ values at all. For instance, subjects with different values θ_1 and θ_2 in figure 3.1 will respond identically to item 1 thus:

$$\pi_1(\theta_1) = \pi_1(\theta_2) = 0.$$

The trace lines of items 2 and 3 in figure 3.1 present a different picture. For these trace lines, local discrimination is for no point θ as sharp as for the point $\theta = \delta_1$ in the case of the Guttman item (G-item) 1. On the other hand, local discrimination in neighborhoods not containing δ_1 is better for items 2 and 3 than for item 1. For different values of θ in, say, the interval $[\theta_1, \theta_2]$, the expected value of a positive response varies, increasing from θ_1 to θ_2 for both item 2 and item 3:

$$\pi_2(\theta_1) < \pi_2(\theta_2)$$

and

$$\pi_3(\theta_1) < \pi_3(\theta_2).$$

We will also see from figure 3.1 that over the interval $[\theta_1, \theta_2]$, $\pi_2(\theta)$, (item 2), increases more steeply in terms of its slope than $\pi_3(\theta)$ (item 3). We may therefore regard item 2 as discriminating locally more sharply than item 3 over the interval $[\theta_1, \theta_2]$. But other points may easily be found along the θ axis where the relatively "flat" item 3 discriminates more sharply than item 2.

For trace lines that are differentiable in θ, the *local discrimination* may be defined on the basis of the first derivative

$$\pi_i'(\theta) = \frac{d\pi_i(\theta)}{d\theta} \tag{2.5}$$

which gives the slope of the trace line in the point θ and is non-negative for the monotone cases under consideration here.*

We shall see later on that sometimes "overall" parameters are introduced which do not depend on θ and which bear some relation to the difficulty level or to the discriminating ability of an item. For instance, we may define for any item i an *item difficulty* parameter δ as that value δ, for which we have (for $\theta = \delta$)

$$\pi_i(\delta) = 0.50.**$$

In figure 3.1, items 1, 2 and 3 have equal difficulty δ_1.

*A not too serious objection that may be raised against the use of $\pi_i'(\theta)$ as a direct definition of local discrimination in θ is that it depends on the scale of measurement used for θ. It is easy to point out ways in which such difficulties may be evaded. For instance, when we are comparing discriminating power across items or points, the unit of measurement is cancelled out if we use ratios. Consequently, if we compare local discrimination as a function of θ for two items (2 and 3), we may use the ratio

$$R_{23}(\theta) = \frac{\pi_2'(\theta)}{\pi_3'(\theta)}$$

The sets θ for which $R_{23}(\theta) > 1$, $R_{23}(\theta) = 1$ and $R_{23}(\theta) < 1$ define the sets θ where item 2 has a higher, equal or lower local discrimination respectively than item 3.

**If for the weakly monotone case we are considering there are more values for θ for which $\pi_i(\theta) = 0.50$ (*e.g.* if $\pi_i(\theta) = 0.50$ and is constant over an interval), we may take for δ the smallest value of θ in that range. In the case of discontinuity points, we may if necessary take the point $\delta = \theta_0$ in which $\pi_i(\theta)$ jumps from a value smaller than 0.50 to a value larger than 0.50.

3.2.2 Specific forms of trace lines

In his original development of latent structure analysis, Lazarsfeld suggested the use of a *polynomial* model (Lazarsfeld, 1950, 371):*

$$\pi(\theta, \delta_i) = \delta_{0i} + \delta_{1i}\theta + \delta_{2i}\theta^2 + \cdots + \delta_{ri}\theta^r. \tag{2.6}$$

In this model θ is one-dimensional**, whereas dim $\delta = r + 1$. Lazarsfeld reasoned that even complicated functions can be expanded in polynomial form. Moreover, the integration of (2.6) by means of the population distribution $P^{\underline{\theta}}$ for combinations of items leads to expressions in terms of observable moments of θ which he termed "accounting equations" (1950, 369), and which could be used for the estimation of the δ_i. The use of these accounting equations for the estimation of item parameters, as a variant of the *method of moments*, is characteristic for latent structure analysis.

As a special case of (2.6) we may mention the *linear* model where

$$\pi(\theta, \delta_i) = \delta_{0i} + \delta_{1i}\theta. \tag{2.7}$$

In this model there are two item parameters. Other possibilities have been advocated by Lazarsfeld and his associates.

The *latent distance* model (Lazarsfeld, 1950, 410; Torgerson, 1958, 374) may be defined as:

$$\pi(\theta, \delta_i) = \delta_{0i} - \delta_{2i}[1 - 2\iota(\theta - \delta_{1i})], \tag{2.8}$$

which contains three item parameters. $\iota(x)$ is defined as in (2.3).

In the general *latent content* model the trace lines have the following form:

$$\pi(\theta, \delta_i) = \delta_{0i} + \delta_{2i}(\theta - \delta_{1i})^{\delta_{3i}}; \tag{2.9}$$

---

*For the purposes of this chapter we shall not consider the case of a finite set Θ containing, say, m points θ. This *latent class* model, although it is the most developed part of latent structure analysis, does not fit in with the measurement models which we regard as being characterized by continuous θ. (Lazarsfeld and Henry, 1968).

**Of course in forms (2.6)–(2.10) we should see to it that $0 \leq \pi(\theta, \delta_i) \leq 1$. Therefore $\pi(\theta, \delta_i)$ is defined as being equal to zero or one for the θ values that would lead to values for $\pi(\theta, \delta_i)$ which are, respectively, smaller than zero or larger than one. An equivalent approach is perhaps to limit the population distribution (and hence the θ scale) to the θ values for which $0 \leq \pi(\theta, \delta_i) \leq 1$.

which involves four item parameters (Lazarsfeld, 1959a, 529). A special case is of the form

$$\pi(\theta, \boldsymbol{\delta}_i) = \delta_{0i} + \delta_{2i} \exp\{\delta_{1i}\,\theta\};\tag{2.10}$$

where $\underline{\theta}$ is assumed to be distributed uniformly over (0, 1) (see Anderson, 1959; Lazarsfeld, 1959a). Most of the cases of continuous trace lines dealt with by Lazarsfeld and his associates were characterized by a relative abundance of item parameters or by rather strong assumptions concerning the distribution $P\underline{\theta}$.

We shall now consider parametric models with a somewhat simpler structure. Although they were developed in the field of mental and achievement testing, they fit into the general latent structure model and may well prove to be more versatile than the models described above.

3.2.3   Normal ogive and logistic models

The application of the model of the normal distribution function has its roots in the psychophysical origins of psychometric scaling which reach back as far as Thurstone's introduction of "discriminal processes" and their application in scaling problems. (Thurstone, 1927; Torgerson, 1958, 156). Several heuristic approaches underlie the formulation of models which rely on this *normal ogive* function. The simplest way to illustrate this is, perhaps, by means of a discriminal process of the type shown in figure 3.2.

A subject α, characterized by his value θ_α, perceives the "value" δ_{1i} on the continuum as the location of item i. He does this, however, with some error, resulting in a deviation z_i from the "true" item value δ_{1i}. These errors may be regarded as being governed by a probability distribution which is determined entirely by parameters that are characteristic for the item. Hence this error distribution is considered

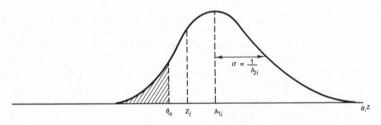

Figure 3.2   The discriminal process of item perception.

to be the same for all the subjects. The response of the subject is determined entirely by the Guttman assumption: subject α will give a positive answer only if $\theta_\alpha \geq z_i$, the perceived value of the item.

In figure 3.2 the probability of a positive response is therefore represented by the shaded area. Assuming the error distribution to be a normal distribution with mean δ_{1i} and variance δ_{2i}^{-2}, we get

$$\pi(\theta, \boldsymbol{\delta}_i) = \mathcal{N}(\delta_{2i}(\theta - \delta_{1i})); \quad \delta_{2i} > 0 \tag{2.11}$$

where

$$\mathcal{N}(u) = \frac{1}{\sqrt{2\pi}} \int_{-\infty}^{u} e^{-1/2x^2} dx, \quad -\infty < u < \infty;$$

which leads to a trace line with two item parameters. This example at the same time clearly demonstrates how a theory of error, added to the model of Guttman response, leads to a stochastic model.

The item parameter δ_{2i} is the inverse of the standard deviation which determines the dispersion of the normal distribution in figure 3.2. It also bears some relation to the general steepness of the trace line and has been called the discriminating power of the item probably for this reason (Lord and Novick, 1968, 367). As a matter of fact it can be seen that for the discrimination parameter δ_2, $\lim_{\delta_2 \to \infty} \mathcal{N}(\delta_2(\theta - \delta_1))$ is equivalent to the trace line of a (perfect) G-item, as the variance of the distribution for $\delta_2 \to \infty$ approaches zero.

That is for

$$\theta > \delta_1, \lim_{\delta_2 \to \infty} \mathcal{N}(\delta_2(\theta - \delta_1)) = \mathcal{N}(\infty) = 1;$$

for

$$\theta < \delta_1, \lim_{\delta_2 \to \infty} \mathcal{N}(\delta_2(\theta - \delta_1)) = \mathcal{N}(-\infty) = 0.$$

Defining

$$\lim_{\delta_2 \to \infty} \mathcal{N}(\delta_2(\theta - \delta_1)) = 1 \quad \text{for } \theta = \delta_1,$$

we have

$$\lim_{\delta_2 \to \infty} \mathcal{N}(\delta_2(\theta - \delta_1)) = \iota(\theta - \delta_1),$$

which is the form of the Guttman trace line (2.3).*

*The only exception is in the point $\theta = \delta_{1i}$ where the limit is equal to 0.50.

The difficulty parameter in (2.11) is δ_{1i}, because when $\theta = \delta_{1i}$,

$$\pi(\theta, \boldsymbol{\delta}_i) = \mathcal{N}(0) = 0.50.$$

Hence δ_{1i} is a general indicator of the difficulty level of item i (Lord and Novick, 1968, 368). This model has been dealt with extensively by Torgerson (1958, 385). Maximum likelihood estimates were indicated by Lord (1953); Tucker (1952) gave approximate solutions in the least-squares sense.

A special case is the model in which the variances of (2.11) are equal for all the items, or, what amounts to the same thing, where all the items have the same discrimination parameter δ_2, which is therefore independent of the items. We can then write:

$$\pi(\theta, \boldsymbol{\delta}_i) = \mathcal{N}(\delta_2(\theta - \delta_{1i})). \tag{2.12}$$

We may as well absorb the common value δ_2 in the parameters θ and δ_{1i}; this amounts to a re-scaling of these parameters.

Hence the form for the model with equal discrimination parameters may be written as:

$$\pi(\theta, \delta_i) = \mathcal{N}(\theta - \delta_{1i}); \tag{2.13}$$

which gives us a one-parameter trace line. In this model, items differ only in their difficulty parameters.

As from 1957, Birnbaum (1965; 1968) has advocated a class of models, the basis of which is the *logistic distribution function* given by

$$\mathcal{L}(u) = \frac{1}{1 + e^{-u}}; \quad -\infty < u < \infty; \tag{2.14}$$

Birnbaum developed a *logistic model* with two item parameters which according to our notation results in a trace line of the following form:

$$\pi(\theta, \boldsymbol{\delta}_i) = \mathcal{L}(\delta_{2i}(\theta - \delta_{1i})) = \frac{1}{1 + \exp\{-\delta_{2i}(\theta - \delta_{1i})\}};$$
$$\delta_{2i} > 0; \quad -\infty < \theta, \delta_{1i} < \infty. \tag{2.15}$$

Note that (2.15) may be written as

$$\pi(\theta, \boldsymbol{\delta}_i) = \frac{1}{1 + \left(\dfrac{e^{\theta}}{e^{\delta_{1i}}}\right)^{-\delta_{2i}}}. \tag{2.16}$$

Introducing the transformation:

$$t^* = \exp(t); \quad 0 < t^* < \infty; \tag{2.17}$$

we may write the right-hand member of (2.16) as

$$\frac{\theta^{*\delta_{2i}}}{\theta^{*\delta_{2i}} + \delta_{1i}^{*\delta_{2i}}}$$

We can therefore state that

model (2.15) is isomorphic to the model

$$\pi(\theta, \delta_i) = \frac{\theta^{\delta_{2i}}}{\theta^{\delta_{2i}} + \delta_{1i}^{\delta_{2i}}} = \frac{1}{1 + \left(\dfrac{\theta}{\delta_{1i}}\right)^{-\delta_{2i}}} \tag{2.18}$$

with

$$0 < \theta, \delta_{1i}, \delta_{2i} < \infty.$$

What was said with respect to the normal ogive model concerning the form of trace lines also holds good for the logistic model. As a matter of fact we shall see in section 3.2.5 that the logistic and normal ogive models are empirically equivalent.

Again, we can see that

$$\lim_{\delta_{2i} \to \infty} \mathscr{L}(\delta_{2i}(\theta - \delta_{1i})) = \iota(\theta - \delta_{1i}),$$

so that there too the trace line for $\delta_{2i} \to \infty$ approaches the trace line for a Guttman item.

It will easily be seen that $\mathscr{L}(0) = 0.50$, so that for the logistic model too δ_{1i} may be regarded as an item difficulty parameter.

The statistical theory of the logistic model has been treated extensively and rigorously by Birnbaum (1968), who carried out a straightforward application of relatively recent developments in the theory of statistical tests and decisions. The logistic model proved to be mathematically considerably more tractable than the normal ogive model. A recent application of the model with empirical data in the field of mental testing underlines this versatility (Ross, 1966).

The relative simplicity of the logistic model arises from the fact that the distribution of responses belongs to the exponential family.

It should be noted that (2.2) can be written as

$$p(x_{\alpha i}; \theta_\alpha, \boldsymbol{\delta}_i) = (1 - \pi(\theta_\alpha, \boldsymbol{\delta}_i)) \left(\frac{\pi(\theta_\alpha, \boldsymbol{\delta}_i)}{1 - \pi(\theta_\alpha, \boldsymbol{\delta}_i)} \right)^{x_{\alpha i}}$$

$$= (1 - \pi(\theta_\alpha, \boldsymbol{\delta}_i)) \exp \{ x_{\alpha i} [\log \pi(\theta_\alpha, \boldsymbol{\delta}_i) - \log (1 - \pi(\theta_\alpha, \boldsymbol{\delta}_i))] \};$$

(2.19)

where subject α and item i have specified parameters.

For k items and subsequently n subjects we get the following versions of the likelihood functions (1.6) and (1.7):

$$\prod_{i=1}^{k} p(x_i; \theta, \boldsymbol{\delta}_i) = \prod_{i=1}^{k} (1 - \pi(\theta, \boldsymbol{\delta}_i)) \exp \left\{ \sum_{i=1}^{k} x_i [\log \pi(\theta, \boldsymbol{\delta}_i) \right.$$

$$\left. - \log (1 - \pi(\theta, \boldsymbol{\delta}_i))] \right\};$$

(2.20)

$$\prod_{\alpha=1}^{n} \prod_{i=1}^{k} p(x_{\alpha i}; \theta_\alpha, \boldsymbol{\delta}_i)$$

$$= \prod_{\alpha=1}^{n} \prod_{i=1}^{k} (1 - \pi(\theta_\alpha, \boldsymbol{\delta}_i)) \exp \left\{ \sum_{\alpha=1}^{n} \sum_{i=1}^{k} x_{\alpha i} [\log \pi(\theta_\alpha, \boldsymbol{\delta}_i) \right.$$

$$\left. - \log (1 - \pi(\theta_\alpha, \boldsymbol{\delta}_i))] \right\}.$$

(2.21)

For a logistic model with two item parameters in the form of (2.16) we get

$$\prod_{i=1}^{k} p(x_i; \theta, \boldsymbol{\delta}_i) = C_k(\theta, \boldsymbol{\delta}^{(k)}) \exp \left\{ \theta \sum_{i=1}^{k} \delta_{2i} x_i - \sum_{i=1}^{k} \delta_{1i} \delta_{2i} x_i \right\};$$

(2.22)

where

$$C_k(\theta, \boldsymbol{\delta}^{(k)}) = \prod_{i=1}^{k} \frac{1}{1 + \exp \{ \delta_{2i} (\theta - \delta_{1i}) \}};$$

and

$$\prod_{\alpha=1}^{n} \prod_{i=1}^{k} p(x_{\alpha i}; \theta_\alpha, \boldsymbol{\delta}_i)$$

$$= C_{n,k}(\boldsymbol{\theta}^{(n)}, \boldsymbol{\delta}^{(k)}) \exp \left\{ \sum_{\alpha=1}^{n} \theta_\alpha \sum_{i=1}^{k} \delta_{2i} x_{\alpha i} - \sum_{i=1}^{k} \delta_{1i} \delta_{2i} \sum_{\alpha=1}^{n} x_{\alpha i} \right\},$$

(2.23)

where

$$C_{n,k}(\boldsymbol{\theta}^{(n)}, \boldsymbol{\delta}^{(k)}) = \prod_{\alpha=1}^{n} C_k(\theta_\alpha, \boldsymbol{\delta}^{(k)}).$$

In connection with these forms, some remarks must be made which are more or less analogous to the remarks made in connection with forms (1.30) and (1.33). In the first place, we must note that (2.22) and (2.23) identify distributions that belong to the exponential family. In the second place, we can nevertheless easily see that there is no complete separability of subject parameters and item parameters in (2.23).

From the properties of the exponential family it follows at once that

$$t(x_\alpha^{(k)}) \stackrel{d}{=} \sum_{i=1}^{k} \delta_{2i} x_{\alpha i} \tag{2.24}$$

is a sufficient statistic for θ and that

$$d(x_i^{(n)}) \stackrel{d}{=} \sum_{\alpha=1}^{n} x_{\alpha i} \tag{2.25}$$

is a sufficient statistic for $\delta_{1i}\delta_{2i}$.

We know from theorem 1.2.1 that the conditional distribution of $t(x_\alpha^{(k)})$ for $d(x_i^{(n)}) = d_i$, $(i = 1, \ldots, k)$, will not depend on $\delta_{1i}\delta_{2i}$. Therefore, the use of this distribution makes it possible for us to estimate θ independently of, in particular, δ_{1i}, the difficulty parameter of the model. Here the separability of the subject parameter θ and the item difficulty parameter holds good. However, in this conditional distribution, the statistic $t(x_\alpha^{(k)})$ which is sufficient for θ still depends on the second item parameter δ_{2i}. In fact, this statistic can only be used if δ_{2i} is known.

And even then it is clear that the statistic t does not reduce the sample space of the original observations. In general, for known values δ_{2i}, the statistic $t(x_\alpha^{(k)})$ of (2.24) will be a 1-1 mapping of the response pattern

$$(\underline{x}_{\alpha 1}, \underline{x}_{\alpha 2}, \ldots, \underline{x}_{\alpha k})^T$$

and may therefore be considered as an index of that response pattern. Consequently, $t(\underline{x}_\alpha^{(k)})$ will be exactly equivalent to the *trivial sufficient statistic*: the vector of original responses $x_{\alpha i}$, $(i = 1, 2, \ldots, k)$ (Dynkin, 1951). We could therefore base our estimation procedures on the original response patterns as well, because they are *minimal sufficient statistics* in this model (see also Birnbaum, 1968, 425–35).

This also has some consequences for the "population free" estimation of the difficulty parameters δ_{1i}, if we want to apply theorem 1.2.1 to find the conditional distribution of the statistic $d(\underline{x}_i^{(n)})$ of (2.25) for the given values

$$t(\underline{x}_\alpha^{(k)}) = t_\alpha, \quad (\alpha = 1, 2, \ldots, n).$$

In general, the 1-1 mapping (for known δ_{2i})

$$t(\underline{x}_\alpha^{(k)}) = t_\alpha$$

will imply that the response vectors

$$(\underline{x}_{\alpha 1}, \underline{x}_{\alpha 2}, \ldots, \underline{x}_{\alpha k})^T, \quad \alpha = 1, 2, \ldots, n,$$

are also kept constant.

Consequently, the statistic $d(\underline{x}_i^{(n)})$ too will be constant, so that the conditional distribution of $d(\underline{x}_i^{(n)})$, given $t(\underline{x}_\alpha^{(k)}) = t_\alpha$, will be the degenerate distribution. We must therefore conclude that in terms of δ_{2i} the statistics d_i of (2.25) are functionally related to the t_α of (2.24) and that for this reason a population free estimation of the δ_{1i} is not possible.

As such the statistic $t(\underline{x}_\alpha^{(k)})$ of (2.24) is simply a weighted score taken over the item scores $x_{\alpha i}$. The weighting coefficients are the discrimination parameters δ_{2i}. They are, however, unknown and their estimation is connected with that of θ. Birnbaum (1965; 1968, 436–49) studied the problem of the determination of such weights, a_i, $i = 1, \ldots, k$, in linear score formulas of the type

$$\sum_{i=1}^{k} a_i x_i \tag{2.26}$$

taken over the responses to items which are the best with respect to the discrimination of two parameter points θ_1 and θ_2. By means of a straightforward application of the theory of statistical tests, he demonstrated that for $\theta_2 \to \theta_1$ (in neighborhoods of θ_1) these *locally best weights* $a_i(\theta_1)$ would generally depend on θ_1. The optimal linear score for discrimination in a neighborhood of θ would therefore be of the type

$$\sum_{i=1}^{k} a_i(\theta) x_i \tag{2.27}$$

Birnbaum also demonstrates that the weights of (2.27) do not depend on θ if and only if the trace lines are logistic curves. Therefore only in that case (2.26) is *uniformly* best.

We may consider models with an equal discrimination parameter δ_2 for all the items in the same way as the normal ogive models:

$$\pi(\theta, \delta_i) = \mathcal{L}(\delta_2(\theta - \delta_{1i})). \tag{2.28}$$

By a rescaling of θ and δ_1, we may absorb the value of δ_2 into the parameter values and formulate the model as:

$$\pi(\theta, \delta_i) = \mathcal{L}(\theta - \delta_{1i}) = \frac{1}{1 + \exp\{-(\theta - \delta_{1i})\}} \tag{2.29}$$

with

$$-\infty < \theta, \delta_{1i} < \infty,$$

which again is a model with one item parameter. This type of model (2.27) is the one advocated by Rasch (1960) and mentioned by Birnbaum (1968, 402) as a special case of his logistic model.

3.2.4 *The approach of Rasch: the two-parameter logistic model.*

The heuristics underlying the construction of response models for scales and tests had their origin mainly in "discriminal dispersion" theory, which was based on a theory of subject stimulus perception underlying responses to stimuli. Torgerson's monograph (1958) clearly indicates this origin and the role played by L. L. Thurstone in the development of the many different versions, all of which led to some normal ogive formulation. The logistic model introduced by Birnbaum (1965) was not based on any heuristic considerations except for the fact (dealt with in section 3.2.5) that the logistic distribution function could be used as a good approximation of the normal distribution function.

During the 1950's Rasch developed a number of models on the basis of certain considerations which amounted to an appreciably different approach, although it led to similar models. Judging from the absence in his published work of extensive references to the vast literature on scaling and test theory, he apparently developed his models mainly independently of other approaches.*

As his formulation implies certain heuristics for the logistic model, we shall briefly reproduce his argument here (Rasch, 1960, 117).

1. Let the probability of a positive response to any item be determined for each subject and for each item by a subject parameter θ and an item difficulty parameter δ; $0 \leqslant \theta, \delta$.

2. Let this probability be denoted by a function $\pi(\theta, \delta)$, depending on subjects and items only through θ and δ;

$$0 \leqslant \pi(\theta, \delta) \leqslant 1.$$

Such a function should preferably fulfil the following conditions.

A subject with a θ value (ability, attitude or other attribute) higher than that of another subject should have a higher probability of giving a positive response to a given item than the other subject. Again, an item with a δ value (item difficulty) higher than that of another item should have a lower probability of eliciting a positive response from a given subject than the other item.

These desirable properties would result in two additional conditions.

3. $\pi(\theta, \delta)$ should be *monotone increasing* in θ.

4. $\pi(\theta, \delta)$ should be *monotone decreasing* in δ.

Trace lines $\pi(\theta, \delta)$ satisfying conditions (3) and (4) were called *holomorph* by Rasch (1960, 169).

Another crucial assumption in Rasch's model is that of *conformity* (Rasch, 1960, 114–115), according to which the probability of a positive response is determined by the quotient of subject and item parameter.

This property may be defined as follows. Suppose a given subject α_1 with value θ_1 responds to an item i_1 with difficulty δ_1. Consider next a second subject α_2 with twice the value of α_1 ($\theta_2 = 2\theta_1$), responding to another item i_2 with twice the difficulty of item i_1 ($\delta_2 = 2\delta_1$). It seems reasonable to require that in this situation the two subjects should

---

*Although Rasch's work is referred to in several American works, including Birnbaum's, Rasch seems to have been unaware at this time of the work by Birnbaum, to which his own models are closely related.

respond positively to their respective items with equal probability. We may define the condition of *conformity* more generally by requiring that for $k > 0$,

$$\pi(\theta, \delta) = \pi(k\theta, k\delta); \tag{2.31}$$

hence $\pi(\theta, \delta)$ should be linearly homogeneous of order zero and

$$5. \ \pi(\theta, \delta) = \pi\left(\frac{\theta}{\delta}, 1\right) = \pi\left(\frac{\theta}{\delta}\right) = \pi(\xi); \tag{2.32}$$

π being a function of the ratio $\xi = \theta/\delta$ only*, the scaling of θ and δ being such that $0 < \theta$, $\delta < \infty$. (Rasch later denoted the measure of easiness by $\epsilon = 1/\delta$, and the condition of conformity by $\pi(\theta\epsilon)$.)

Other requirements may be added to ensure that for low or high values of ξ (in the limit) positive responses will be impossible (probability zero) or will be given with certainty (probability one).

$$6. \ \pi(\theta, 0) = 1, \quad \text{for} \quad \theta > 0$$

$$\tag{2.33}$$

$$7. \ \pi(0, \delta) = 1, \quad \text{for} \quad \delta > 0**$$

8. The addition of the requirements mentioned in section 3.2.1, such as that of "specific objectivity" or selection-free measurement and estimation will lead to a virtually unique determination of the form of π, as we shall now demonstrate.

Using (2.19) we may write the response function as follows

$$p(x; \pi) = (1 - \pi) \left(\frac{\pi}{1 - \pi}\right)^x$$

$$= (1 - \pi) \exp\left\{x \log\left(\frac{\pi}{1 - \pi}\right)\right\} \tag{2.34}$$

$$= C(\xi^*) \exp(x\xi)^*,$$

**I.e.* it is assumed that θ and δ are measured in the *same* ratio scale and that the probability of a positive response is invariant for changes in the unit of measurement used for that scale.

**The reader may note that $\pi(\theta, \delta)$ is undetermined for $\theta = 0$ and $\delta = 0$ and is discontinuous in that point.

where

$$\xi^* = \log\left(\frac{\pi}{1-\pi}\right)$$

and $C(\xi^*)$ is derived by the substitution of ξ^* in $1-\pi$. The form (2.34) is clearly of the exponential type of (1.27) described in section 3.1.2. If we are looking for a parametric form which will satisfy the requirements of "specific objectivity", (8), we can therefore use the results of that section. In particular (requiring equal dimensions of ξ^*, θ^* and δ^*, our θ being one-dimensional by assumption) result (1.31) of section 3.1.2 can be used:

$$\xi^* = \theta^* + \delta^* = \log\left(\frac{\pi}{1-\pi}\right);$$

or

$$\exp(\xi^*) = \exp(\theta^*)\exp(\delta^*) = \frac{\pi}{1-\pi}.$$

Substitution of

$$\theta = \exp(\theta^*); \epsilon = \exp(\delta^*); \theta, \epsilon > 0$$

gives

$$\theta\epsilon = \frac{\pi}{1-\pi}$$

and therefore

$$\pi = \frac{\theta\epsilon}{1+\theta\epsilon} \tag{2.35}$$

Multiplication of the numerator and denominator of (2.35) with $\delta = 1/\epsilon$ gives

$$\pi(\theta,\delta) = \frac{\theta}{\theta+\delta} = \frac{1}{1+\xi^{-1}}; \tag{2.36}$$

which makes the trace line the type (2.30) given by Rasch. The reader can easily verify that this trace function satisfies requirements 1–8 given above.

We have seen that an equivalent form is (2.29)

$$\pi(\theta, \delta) = \mathscr{L}(\theta - \delta) = \frac{1}{1 + \exp\{-(\theta - \delta)\}}. \tag{2.37}$$

The only difference in this logistic model concerns the values assigned to parameters θ and δ: $-\infty < \theta, \delta < \infty$.

Following the developments that led to (2.22) and (2.23), for the likelihood function for k items, n subjects, we obtain:

$$\prod_{i=1}^{k} p(x_i; \theta, \delta_i) = C_k(\theta, \boldsymbol{\delta}^{(k)}) \exp\left\{\theta \sum_{i=1}^{k} x_i - \sum_{i=1}^{k} x_i \delta_i\right\}; \tag{2.38}$$

and

$$\prod_{\alpha=1}^{n} \prod_{i=1}^{k} p(x_{\alpha i}; \theta_\alpha, \delta_i) = C_{n,k}(\boldsymbol{\theta}^{(n)}, \boldsymbol{\delta}^{(k)}) \exp\left\{\sum_{\alpha=1}^{n} \theta_\alpha \sum_{i=1}^{k} x_{\alpha i} - \sum_{i=1}^{k} \delta_i \sum_{\alpha=1}^{n} x_{\alpha i}\right\};$$
$$\tag{2.39}$$

where

$$C_k(\theta, \boldsymbol{\delta}^{(k)}) = \prod_{i=1}^{k} \frac{1}{1 + \exp(\theta - \delta)}$$

and

$$C_{n,k}(\boldsymbol{\theta}^{(n)}, \boldsymbol{\delta}^{(k)})$$

is as defined in (2.23).

Formulating (2.38) and (2.39) as respectively:

$$\prod_{i=1}^{k} p(x_i; \theta, \delta_i) = C_k(\theta, \boldsymbol{\delta}^{(k)}) \exp\left\{\theta s - \sum_{i=1}^{k} x_i \delta_i\right\} \tag{2.40}$$

and

$$\prod_{\alpha=1}^{n} \prod_{i=1}^{k} p(x_{i\alpha}; \theta_\alpha, \delta_i) = C_{n,k}(\boldsymbol{\theta}^{(n)}, \boldsymbol{\delta}^{(k)}) \exp\left\{\sum_{\alpha=1}^{n} \theta_\alpha s_\alpha - \sum_{i=1}^{k} \delta_i n_i\right\}; \tag{2.41}$$

where

$$s_\alpha = \sum_{i=1}^{k} x_{\alpha i} \quad \text{is the } simple\ score \text{ over the items for subject } \alpha \text{ and}$$

$$n_i = \sum_{\alpha=1}^{n} x_{\alpha i} \quad \text{is the number of respondents giving the positive answer to item } i;$$

we see that (2.40) and (2.41) are of form (1.18) of section 3.1.2. Hence the conditions of theorem 1.2.1 have been satisfied, which means that it is now possible to estimate θ_α *independently* of the values of the δ_i on the basis of its sufficient statistic $\underline{s}_\alpha$, whereas in (2.41) the estimation of δ_i may be carried out on the basis of its sufficient statistic $\underline{n}_i$ independently of the values of the θ_α.

In our discussion of the logistic model with two-item parameters ("Birnbaum" items) we pointed out that the full application of theorem 1.2.1 was impeded by the fact that for this model the statistic $\underline{d}_i$ of (2.25) was functionally related to $\underline{t}_\alpha$ of (2.24). For this reason population-free estimation of the item difficulties δ_{1i} was not possible. In the case of the logistic model with one parameter we can easily see that the statistics $\underline{n}_i$ are functionally independent of the $\underline{s}_\alpha$, so that a "population-free" estimation of the difficulty parameters δ_i may be carried out by means of the conditional distributions, given $\underline{s}_\alpha = s_\alpha$, which can be derived by theorem 1.2.1 and which are independent of the θ_α.

We may therefore conclude that in this model, due to the separability of subject and item parameters, *subjects θ may be estimated "item-selection free," i.e. independently of the items sampled or selected for their measurement, and item δ's may be determined "population free," i.e. independently of the particular subjects sampled or selected for the measurement.*

The problem of statistical estimation for these "Rasch" models has been solved by Andersen (1967, 1968, 1969) by means of a thorough application of mathematical statistical theory. Andersen demonstrated that an application of the maximum likelihood method to the likelihood function (2.40) would lead to bad estimates which would not even be consistent. A (conditional) application of the maximum likelihood method to the conditional distributions of the statistics $\underline{n}_i$ (and $\underline{s}_\alpha$) warranted by theorem 1.2.1 would, however, lead to estimates with desirable properties.

In section 2.2.3 we saw that for a perfect Guttman scale, all information concerning the response patterns as indicators of the location of respondents along the θ continuum was contained in the simple scale scores, for the exact response pattern could be reproduced from this score s. In the logistic model with one-item parameter we see that the simple scale score s, taken over the response pattern as a sufficient statistic for θ, carries all the probabilistic information concerning θ and is therefore the best thing to use for the estimation (measurement) of θ. This emergence of $\underline{s}$ as an important statistic for purposes of measurement of θ gives the model special significance as a probabilistic analogue of the deterministic Guttman scale. It should be noted that only requirement (8) leads to a virtually unique determination of the form of the trace lines. Requirements 1–7 leave the way open for a wide range of possibilities. In terms of the difficulty parameter it will easily be seen that, for instance, the normal ogive models and Birnbaum's logistic model fulfil all these requirements, with the possible exception of condition 4 (see section 4.1.3).

3.2.5 *The empirical equivalence of normal ogive and logistic models*

For practical purposes the normal ogive and logistic models in the form 2.15 may be regarded as being the same, because the logistic distribution function is a remarkably good approximation of the normal distribution function. Birnbaum (1965, 11) mentions one of the results of Haley (1952, 7) which was that

$$|\mathcal{N}(u) - \mathcal{L}(1.7u)| < 0.01 \quad \text{for all } u. \tag{2.42}$$

$\mathcal{L}(1.7u)$ approximates $\mathcal{N}(u)$ more closely than 0.01 *uniformly* in u. $\mathcal{N}(u)$ and $\mathcal{L}(1.7u)$ may therefore be considered empirically equivalent. Hence (2.11), (2.13), (2.15) and (2.29) may be related as follows:

$$\mathcal{N}(\delta_{2i}(\theta - \delta_{1i})) \approx \mathcal{L}(1.7\delta_{2i}(\theta - \delta_{1i})); \tag{2.43}$$

$$\mathcal{N}(\theta - \delta_{1i}) \approx \mathcal{L}(1.7(\theta - \delta_{1i})). \tag{2.44}$$

Therefore, even if for theoretical or other reasons the normal ogive model is preferred, the logistic model, with its greater mathematical simplicity may be used as a good approximation. For practical purposes many of its properties (*e.g.* those derived from the exponential family) may be seen as holding good for the normal ogive model too. The models used here are also well-known in biometric research, where, in the field of bioassay, Finney introduced a quantal response model, based on the normal ogive function, under the name of *probit analysis* (Finney, 1952). Berkson (1953) suggested that the logistic function be used for this type of analysis.

3.2.6 *A digression: some paired-comparison models*

The measurement models mentioned above bear a striking resemblance to those that have been developed in the type of data models with which we are not concerned in this study: stimulus comparison data or, in Coombs's terminology, quadrant IIIa data.

In the great variety of experimental situations that may be classified under this heading, the common defining feature is that objects (items, stimuli) are compared by subjects by means of a process giving rise to a probability distribution which describes the outcomes of the comparisons, and which does not contain any subject parameters and is therefore independent of the subjects performing the comparisons. One of the procedures which produces this type of data is the well-known *method of paired comparison*. In this model, pairs of items (objects) from a set of k items are compared. For each pair (i, j) of items one has to decide which item dominates the other one with respect to the attribute to be scaled. Let $\pi(i, j)$ be the probability that i will be judged "greater" than j, and $\pi(j, i)$ the probability that j will be judged "greater" than i, and let the experimental situation be such that

$$\pi(i, j) + \pi(j, i) = 1 \tag{2.45}$$

Again, Thurstone (1927) has defined a class of models which determine the functions $\pi(i, j)$, naming it the "Law of comparative judgment". Without attempting to give a full account of the various approaches that lead to the models within this class (see Torgerson, 1958), we will sketch the general characteristics as follows. Again the outcome of the comparison of two objects is determined by a "discriminal process" as illustrated in figure 3.3. Only when z_i, the

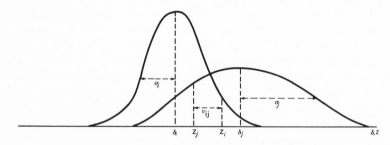

Fig. 3.3   The discriminal process for the comparison of two items.

perceived value for item i, is larger than z_j, the perceived value of item j, that is when

$$v_{ij} = z_i - z_j > 0 \tag{2.46}$$

will item i be judged "greater" than (or be preferred to) item j. These perceived values, z_i and z_j, are assumed to be stochastic variables from whose distribution can be derived the distribution of v_{ij}.

Assuming a bivariate normal distribution for z_i and z_j with means δ_i and δ_j and assuming certain values for variances and covariance, it is not difficult to show that

$$P(v_{ij} > 0) = \pi(i,j) = \mathcal{N}\left(\frac{\delta_i - \delta_j}{\sigma_{ij}}\right) \tag{2.47}$$

where σ_{ij} is the variance of the distribution of v_{ij}. To achieve identifiability, the most general case we can use is Thurstone's case III of the law of comparative judgment:

$$\pi(i,j) = \mathcal{N}\left(\frac{\delta_i - \delta_j}{(\sigma_i^2 + \sigma_j^2)^{1/2}}\right); \tag{2.48}$$

where, as in figure 3.3, σ_i^2 and σ_j^2 are the variances of the distributions of z_i and z_j. In Thurstone's case V, $\sigma_{ij}^2 = \sigma^2$ for all item pairs. Absorbing the common value of σ into the parameters, this model becomes, by a transformation of the δ scale

$$\pi(i,j) = \mathcal{N}(\delta_i - \delta_j) \tag{2.49}$$

Bradley and Terry (1952) advocated another model for the analysis of paired comparison data, for which the former later published elaborate statistical techniques (for a reference see David, 1963). Luce (1959), starting from an axiomatic theory substantially different from that of the Thurstone approach, also advocated the model of Bradley and Terry.

This Bradley-Terry-Luce model is:

$$\pi(i,j) = \frac{\delta_i}{\delta_i + \delta_j}; \quad 0 < \delta_i, \delta_j < \infty. \tag{2.50}$$

Following a similar reasoning as for the Rasch model (2.27) by an appropriate application of transformation (2.17), we see that (2.45) is equivalent (in the sense of isomorphism) to

$$\pi(i,j) = \mathcal{L}(\delta_i - \delta_j) = \frac{1}{1 + \exp\{-(\delta_i - \delta_j)\}}; \quad -\infty < \delta_i, \delta_j < \infty; \tag{2.51}$$

which gives us a logistic distribution with two parameters, as in the Rasch model. Several authors have noted the fact that the logistic distribution function seems to form a good approximation to the normal cumulative distribution (Gulliksen, 1960, 3; Torgerson, 1958, 202). Luce (1959, 55–6) gives a numerical illustration. After the discussions of the previous section this will be quite understandable.

An application of the remarks made in section 3.2.4 on the basis of Haley's result (2.42) underlines the empirical equivalence of Thurstone's case V and the Bradley-Terry-Luce model:

$$\pi(i,j) = \mathcal{N}(\delta_i - \delta_j) \approx \mathcal{L}(1.7(\delta_i - \delta_j)). \tag{2.52}$$

We may even suggest an empirically equivalent formulation for Thurstone's case III (2.48):

$$\pi(i,j) = \mathcal{N}\left(\frac{\delta_i - \delta_j}{(\sigma_i^2 + \sigma_j^2)^{1/2}}\right) \approx \mathcal{L}\left(1.7\frac{\delta_i - \delta_j}{(\sigma_i^2 + \sigma_j^2)^{1/2}}\right); \tag{2.53}$$

which, as a four-parameter model, is considerably more complicated than (2.15).

CHAPTER 4

Homogeneity and holomorphism in scaling models: some simple properties

In chapter 3 we considered scaling models with trace lines of a specific parametric form. Their application necessitates the search for and development of methods of, preferably, efficient estimation, by means of which the values of the parameters may be approximately determined for samples of subjects and items. For the full utilization of such models, techniques and methods, a good deal of prior knowledge concerning items and population of subjects seems to be required.

In the first place we must have some evidence at our disposal about the functional form of the trace lines used for our measurement. In practice this seems to be possible only when we have acquired considerable experience and insight into the ways and means of constructing items which satisfy the requirements of specific parametric models. At this stage the scientist will have at his disposal a fund or pool of items from which he may select in such a way that an efficient choice of specific measurement models may be made. Through such an optimal selection and the subsequent application of good techniques of estimation of the parameters in the model, relatively precise measurements of subjects can be obtained. For instance, in the case of Birnbaum models we first have to define by means of research the class of items which satisfies the requirements of the trace lines mentioned in section 3.2.4. Then the item parameters (δ_i) will have to be estimated as precisely as possible before the sets of items can be used as instruments for the measurement of subjects: the estimation of θ values. In general, such a fund of knowledge concerning the construction of tests by selecting the appropriate items can only be the product of an accumulation of results of a continuous research program of scale or test construction involving large sets of items and large numbers of subjects.

This situation may be typical for most of the field of mental, ability and, perhaps, achievement tests. In other fields of social research a different situation seems to prevail. For various reasons, no variables seem to have been isolated in these fields which may be worth the effort of an elaborate and continuous program of this type, directed at the improved measurement of these variables. For instance, in some fields many variables have been introduced only rather recently, so that the level of the knowledge concerning items that may be used for the measurement of these variables will be rather low. Moreover, many variables are defined within the context of a particular research project because of their specific importance for the object of investigation. Again, knowledge about the items used for their measurement may be very scanty.

In many cases it may be impossible to investigate in one single research project large sets of items for different variables for the purpose of constructing instruments involving specific parametric models. One reason may be that the use of many variables in one research program will limit the number of items that can be used per variable. Such limits may be forced on the researcher because of respondent fatigue, or questionnaire length. In other cases the scientist may not yet possess enough knowledge about a variable to select and construct a sufficient number of items.

Under all these circumstances, which seem to be fairly typical of, for instance, the present stage of research in much of sociology and political science, the prospects for the full application of specific parametric models of the type of chapter 3 seem rather unpromising. In these fields of research we therefore need measurement techniques derived from models formulated on the basis of less specific postulates, which are more closely in correspondence with the low level of the knowledge concerning items and variables possessed by the researcher.

At the same time, however, we shall want these more general and simple models to bear a clear relation to the sophisticated models with specific trace lines. Then it may be possible to construct and analyze sets of items in the earlier stages of research with the help of the simpler techniques based on the more general models with few assumptions and at the same time to prepare the ground for the application of specific parametric models in future research at more advanced stages.

One solution is to investigate the general properties of the class of models with trace lines of the type mentioned in chapter 3, the specific functional form of which is left unspecified apart from some relatively mild restrictions. We may then attempt to derive from such general properties measurement procedures that can be used in research. The application of such procedures may help the researcher in detecting the items with trace lines which belong to the general class underlying the model. As items with specific trace lines are special cases of the model, it may then be possible to isolate them from the general class by means of the application of models for items with these specific response functions.

Using this method, we shall in this chapter derive some simple properties of a general two-parameter model, containing one subject and one item parameter; we shall confine ourselves to dichotomous items. These properties are in a certain sense distribution-free: they are based on the manifest ("observable") marginal distribution obtained by an integration over the population (subject) distribution P^θ. Hence these properties are valid irrespective of the population distribution of the subjects. The properties may form the rationale of the scaling procedures of the Guttman type which are used in actual practice. As a matter of fact our two-parameter model is a simple example of a quasi-scale in a general form. Our results enable us to define a scale and devise the procedures for item selection and scale construction which will be described in chapter 5.

4.1   HOLOMORPHIC TWO-PARAMETER MODELS

As stated above, we shall consider only dichotomous items. We shall again assume that the trace function* is the function $\pi(\theta,\delta)$ of a one-dimensional subject parameter θ and a one dimensional item difficulty parameter δ.

Sets of items with trace lines depending on the same argument are called *homogeneous* (Meredith, 1965, 430–2). However, this definition is far too general to be of much practical use: it will easily be seen that on this level of generality any set of items may be considered to be homogeneous for any population. In order to obtain empirically useful models, we shall therefore have to make further assumptions concerning the functional form of the trace lines, assumptions which will lead to closer interrelations between the response probabilities for items and subjects which may be verified from observations. One assumption will usually be that the trace lines have the same functional form. In what follows we shall assume, unless specified otherwise,

---

*We may use the term *trace line* when we consider the probability of a positive response as a function of θ only, while the term *trace function* should be used to stress the point that variations in δ are also considered.

that *the trace lines of all items have the same functional form and depend on the items only through the values of the common argument* δ *in this form.*

In this case we shall denote the trace function by $\pi(\theta, \delta)$. If the trace function depends on item i through other sources than its difficulty δ we shall write it as $\pi_i(\theta, \delta)$*. In this study, moreover, we shall only consider items with trace lines that are monotone non-decreasing or strictly monotone increasing in θ. Trace lines that satisfy these conditions, which are similar to conditions (1), (2) and (3) of section 3.2.4, will be called *monotonely homogeneous* trace lines.

We saw in section 3.2.4 that by means of condition (4), one further plausible requirement may be made: the trace function should be monotone decreasing (or monotone non-increasing) in the item difficulty δ for all θ. Following the terminology of Rasch (1960, 169), we may call such trace functions *holomorph*. Holomorphism is introduced here as a property of a single trace function. We shall see in this chapter that holomorphism is more important as a property of a *set of items:* sets of items with trace lines of the same functional form and satisfying conditions (3) and (4) of section 3.2.4 will be called *holomorphic sets of items.* For a holomorphic set of items, therefore, the trace lines will be monotone increasing in θ (for all δ) and monotone decreasing in δ (for all θ)**. Consequently, the trace lines of these items will never intersect; this will prove to be of some importance later on.

In fact we shall see that it is possible to generalize the concept of holomorphism to include sets of items with trace functions of a different functional form $\pi_i(\theta, \delta_i)$.

For a set of k items, if for i = 1, 2, . . ., k we have

  1. $\pi_i(\theta, \delta_i)$ *is monotonely homogeneous;*

  2. $\delta_i < \delta_j \Rightarrow \pi_i(\theta, \delta_i) > \pi_j(\theta, \delta_j)$;

then we shall call that set of items doubly monotone.†

*For instance, the logistic trace functions with two item parameters in the models proposed by Birnbaum (see section 3.2.3) do not depend solely on their difficulties δ_{1i} but also on their discrimination parameters δ_{2i}. The trace functions for constant δ_{2i} are equivalent to the logistic model with one item parameter proposed by Rasch (see section 3.2.4), depend solely on the difficulty parameter, and have the same functional form in the terminology used here.

**In what follows we shall generally use the term "monotony" to mean strict monotony without further specification. But the reader may regard the term as including weak monotony, as most of the results are valid for cases of weak monotony too.

†We may also call the corresponding sets of trace lines doubly monotone or holomorphic.

The reader should note, for instance, that a set of "Rasch" items (logistic with one item difficulty parameter) as described in section 3.2.4 is a holomorphic set of items. A set of "Birnbaum" items (logistic with two item parameters) with different discrimination parameters (δ_{2i}), however, is not even doubly monotone, although for each item the trace function is holomorph. It should be stressed once more that in spite of these restrictions we still have a great deal of freedom in choosing the mathematical specification of the model, as may be seen from the following example.

Let $\pi(\theta,\delta)$ be a particular model. Let $(\theta^*,\delta^*) = (t(\theta),d(\delta))$ be an appropriately chosen one-to-one transformation of (θ,δ) and let

$$(\theta,\delta) = (t^{-1}(\theta^*), d^{-1}(\delta^*))$$

be the corresponding inverse transformation; then

$$\pi^*(\theta^*,\delta^*) = \pi(t^{-1}(\theta^*), d^{-1}(\delta^*)) = \pi(\theta,\delta);\qquad(1.1)$$

is an equivalent model in the sense of isomorphism. Examples are the equivalent forms (2.26) and (2.27) in section 3.2.3.

Without further specification of our model, we shall now derive some results that are generally valid for models of this class. Some are analogous to the results obtained by Meredith (1965) for a non-homogeneous model, others appear to be characteristic for the class of two-parameter models defined here.

4.1.1 *Some lemmas*

In what follows we shall occasionally use some lemmas which we shall state here. First we shall prove a lemma derived in a special form from Hardy, Littlewood and Polya (1934, 168).* Let $(\mathcal{X}, \mathcal{B}, \mu)$ be a σ-finite measurable space with $\mathcal{X} \subset E_i$. Let $f(x)$ and $g(x)$ be $\mathcal{B}$-measurable and μ-integrable functions.**

Definition 1.1.1

a. $f(x)$ and $g(x)$ are *"similarly ordered"* (s.o.) on $\mathcal{X}$ if for all x_1, $x_2 \in \mathcal{X}$

$$(f(x_1) - f(x_2))(g(x_1) - g(x_2)) \geq 0\qquad(1.2)$$

---

*The one-variable form presented here is taken from Tchebychef.

**f (and g) are μ-integrable if the integrals with respect to μ over their positive and negative parts are both finite.

b. $f(x)$ and $g(x)$ are *oppositely ordered*, (*o. o.*), if $f(x)$ and $-g(x)$ are *s.o.*

We are now able to state*

Lemma 1.1.1   If $f(x)$ and $g(x)$ are s.o. on $\mathscr{X}$, then, for all $B \in \mathscr{B}$

$$\mu(B) \int_B f(x)g(x)d\mu(x) \geq \int_B f(x)d\mu(x) \int_B g(x)d\mu(x) \qquad (1.3)$$

with equality iff $\mu(B) = 0$ or $f(x)$ or $g(x)$ are constant on B μ–a.e. When $f(x)$ and $g(x)$ are o.o. the inequality sign in (1.3) is reversed.

Proof: Consider

$$\mu(B) \int_B f(x)g(x)d\mu(x) - \int_B f(x)d\mu(x) \int_B g(x)d\mu(x)$$

$$= \tfrac{1}{2}\Big[\int_B d\mu(x_2) \int_B f(x_1)g(x_1)d\mu(x_1)$$

$$+ \int_B d\mu(x_1) \int_B f(x_2)g(x_2)d\mu(x_2)$$

$$- \int_B f(x_2)d\mu(x_2) \int_B g(x_1)d\mu(x_1) - \int_B f(x_1)d\mu(x_1) \int_B g(x_2)d\mu(x_2)\Big]$$

$$= \tfrac{1}{2}\int_B \Big\{ \int_B \Big[f(x_1)g(x_1) + f(x_2)g(x_2) - f(x_2)g(x_1) - f(x_1)g(x_2) \Big] d\mu(x_1)\Big\}$$

$$\times d\mu(x_2)$$

$$= \tfrac{1}{2}\int_B \Big\{ \int_B (f(x_1) - f(x_2))(g(x_1) - g(x_2))d\mu(x_1)\Big\} d\mu(x_2) \geq 0$$

as the integrand is non-negative by (1.2).**□

When we have a probability space ($\mathscr{X}$, $\mathscr{B}$, P) we have as a corollary, noting that $P(\mathscr{X}) = 1$:

Corollary 1.1.1   If $f(x)$ and $g(x)$ are s.o. on $\mathscr{X}$ then

$$\int_{\mathscr{X}} f(x)g(x)dP(x) \geq \int_{\mathscr{X}} f(x)dP(x) \int_{\mathscr{X}} g(x)dP(x) \qquad (1.4)$$

with equality iff $f(x)$ or $g(x)$ are constant on $\mathscr{X}$ P–a.e. When $f(x)$ and $g(x)$ are o.o. the inequality sign in (1.4) is reversed.

---

*Of course the lemma remains true when (1.2) is true on $\mathscr{X}$ except on sets $B_N \in \mathscr{B}$ of μ-measure zero, that is when $f(x)$ and $g(x)$ are s.o. μ–a.e. "Iff" denotes "if and only if"

**The proof of the necessity of the condition $f(x)$ or $g(x)$ constant on $B\mu$-a.e. (if $\mu(B) > 0$) is somewhat complicated and will not be given here for reasons of space.

The next lemma is a matrix generalization of a certain expression for the unconditional variance of a stochastic vector $\underline{u}$ in its simultaneous distribution with another stochastic vector $\underline{v}$ (Hemelrijk, 1965). Assuming the existence of all the moments concerned, we have the well-known relation:

$$\mathscr{E}\,\underline{u} = \mathscr{E}_{\underline{v}}\,\mathscr{E}_{\underline{u}}\,(\underline{u}|\underline{v}) \tag{1.5}$$

where the stochastic subscripts on the expectation symbols indicate the variate with respect to which the expectation is taken.

Let $\Sigma(\underline{u})$ denote the unconditional covariance-matrix of $\underline{u}$; let $\Sigma_{\underline{u}}(\underline{u}|v)$ denote the conditional covariance matrix of $\underline{u}$, given $\underline{v} = v$, and let $\Sigma_{\underline{v}}(f(\underline{v}))$ be the covariance matrix with respect to $\underline{v}$ of a (vector-valued) function f. We can now state:

Lemma 1.1.2

$$\Sigma(\underline{u}) = \mathscr{E}_{\underline{v}}\,\Sigma_{\underline{u}}(\underline{u}|\underline{v}) + \Sigma_{\underline{v}}(\mathscr{E}_{\underline{u}}(\underline{u}|\underline{v})) \tag{1.6}$$

Proof:

$$\mathscr{E}\,\{(\underline{u}-\mathscr{E}\underline{u})\,(\underline{u}-\mathscr{E}\underline{u})^{T}\} = \mathscr{E}_{\underline{v}}\,[\,\mathscr{E}_{\underline{u}}\{(\underline{u}-\mathscr{E}\underline{u})(\underline{u}-\mathscr{E}\underline{u})^{T}|\underline{v}\}\,]$$

Note that

$$\mathscr{E}_{\underline{u}}\,\{(\underline{u}-\mathscr{E}\underline{u})(\underline{u}-\mathscr{E}\underline{u})^{T}|v\}$$
$$= \mathscr{E}_{\underline{u}}\,\{\,[\underline{u}\underline{u}^{T} - \mathscr{E}_{\underline{u}}\,(\underline{u}|v)\,\mathscr{E}_{\underline{u}}\,(\underline{u}^{T}|v) + \mathscr{E}_{\underline{u}}\,(\underline{u}|v)\,\mathscr{E}_{\underline{u}}\,(\underline{u}^{T}|v) - \underline{u}\mathscr{E}\,\underline{u}^{T}$$
$$- (\underline{u}\mathscr{E}\,\underline{u}^{T})^{T} + \mathscr{E}\underline{u}\mathscr{E}\underline{u}^{T}\,]|v\}$$
$$= \Sigma_{\underline{u}}(\underline{u}|v) + \mathscr{E}_{\underline{u}}\,(\underline{u}|v)\mathscr{E}_{\underline{u}}\,(\underline{u}^{T}|v) - \mathscr{E}_{\underline{u}}\,(\underline{u}|v)\mathscr{E}\underline{u}^{T} - \mathscr{E}\underline{u}\mathscr{E}_{\underline{u}}\,(\underline{u}^{T}|v) + \mathscr{E}\underline{u}\mathscr{E}\underline{u}^{T}.$$

Taking expecta: ons with respect to $\underline{v}$ we get

$$\Sigma(\underline{u}) = \mathscr{E}\,\{(\underline{u}-\mathscr{E}\underline{u})\,(\underline{u}-\mathscr{E}\underline{u})\}$$
$$= \mathscr{E}_{\underline{v}}\,\Sigma_{\underline{u}}(\underline{u}|\underline{v}) + \mathscr{E}_{\underline{v}}\,\{\mathscr{E}_{\underline{u}}\,(\underline{u}|\underline{v})\mathscr{E}_{\underline{u}}\,(\underline{u}^{T}|\underline{v}) - \mathscr{E}\underline{u}\mathscr{E}\underline{u}^{T}\}$$
$$= \mathscr{E}_{\underline{v}}\,\Sigma_{\underline{u}}(\underline{u}|\underline{v}) + \Sigma_{\underline{v}}(\mathscr{E}_{\underline{u}}(\underline{u}|\underline{v})) \quad \square$$

As a corollary we get for scalar $\underline{u}, \underline{v}$:

Corollary 1.1.2

$$\sigma^{2}(\underline{u}) = \mathscr{E}_{\underline{v}}\sigma_{\underline{u}}^{2}(\underline{u}|\underline{v}) + \sigma_{\underline{v}}^{2}(\mathscr{E}_{\underline{u}}(\underline{u}|\underline{v})). \tag{1.7}$$

4.1.2 *Some marginal relations*

In this chapter and in accordance with the conventions of this section we have for the response $\underline{x}_i$ of a subject (θ_α) to item δ_i:

$$P\{\underline{x}_i = 1 | \theta_\alpha, \delta_i\} = \pi(\theta_\alpha, \delta_i);$$

$$(1.8)$$

$$P\{\underline{x}_i = 0 | \theta_\alpha, \delta_i\} = 1 - \pi(\theta_\alpha, \delta_i).$$

Let us consider the unconditional probability that $\underline{x}_i$ takes on the values 1 or 0 irrespective of the θ-value of the subjects drawn by our sampling process defined by $P^{\underline{\theta}}$. Clearly

$$\pi_i \overset{d}{=} P\{\underline{x}_i = 1 | \delta_i\} = \mathscr{E}_{\underline{\theta}}\mathscr{E}_{\underline{x}_i}(\underline{x}_i | \underline{\theta}) = \mathscr{E}_{\underline{\theta}}\pi(\underline{\theta}, \delta_i) = \int_\Theta \pi(\theta, \delta_i) \, dP^{\underline{\theta}}(\theta);$$

$$(1.9)$$

and

$$1 - \pi_i = P\{\underline{x}_i = 0 | \delta_i\}.$$

In the research situations covered by our model, π_i is the probability that a subject, drawn randomly by the selection process governed by $P^{\underline{\theta}}$, will give the positive answer to item i*.

Let $\underline{n}_i$ be the number of subjects of a sample of n subjects giving the "positive" answer.
Then

$$\hat{\pi}_i = \frac{\underline{n}_i}{n}$$

$$(1.10)$$

will be the maximum likelihood estimate of π_i. These results may be generalized to the response pattern of subjects responding to k items.

Let $\underline{\mathbf{x}} = (\underline{x}_1, \underline{x}_2, \ldots, \underline{x}_i, \ldots, \underline{x}_k)^T$ $\qquad (1.11)$

denote a stochastic (column) vector of responses to k items.

Let $\mathbf{x}_\nu = (x_{1\nu}, x_{2\nu}, \ldots, x_{i\nu}, \ldots, x_{k\nu})^T;$ $\qquad (1.12)$

$$x_{i\nu} = 1, 0; i = 1, 2, \ldots, k;$$

---

*In cases where it can be done without leading to ambiguity, the argument δ_i will be dropped for the sake of simplicity. Items will then be indicated by their indices i.

be one of the 2^k possible values $\underline{x}$ can assume. Then, keeping in mind our assumption (1.2) of local independence (see section 3.1):

$$P\{\underline{x} = \mathbf{x}_\nu | \theta, \delta_1, \delta_2, \ldots, \delta_k\} = \prod_{i=1}^{k} \pi(\theta, \delta_i)^{x_{i\nu}} (1 - \pi(\theta, \delta_i))^{1-x_{i\nu}}. \quad (1.13)$$

Therefore

$$\pi^{(\nu)} = \pi(\mathbf{x}_\nu) \stackrel{d}{=} P\{\underline{x} = \mathbf{x}_\nu | \delta_1, \ldots, \delta_k\} = \int_\Theta \prod_{i=1}^{k} \pi(\theta, \delta_i)^{x_{i\nu}}$$

$$\times (1 - \pi(\theta, \delta_i)^{1-x_{i\nu}} dP^{\underline{\theta}}(\theta); \quad (1.14)$$

with

$$\sum_{\nu=1}^{2^k} \pi^{(\nu)} = 1. \quad (1.15)$$

Let

$$\underline{n}^{(\nu)} = \underline{n}(\mathbf{x}_\nu) \quad (1.16)$$

be the number of subjects producing the response pattern $\mathbf{x}_\nu$; then the set

$$\{\underline{n}^{(\nu)}\}; \quad \nu = 1, 2, \ldots, 2^k$$

is multinomially distributed with the set of parameters $\{\pi^{(\nu)}\}$; $\quad$ (1.17)

Maximum likelihood estimates of the $\pi^{(\nu)}$ are given by

$$\hat{\underline{\pi}}^{(\nu)} = \frac{\underline{n}^{(\nu)}}{n}; \quad \nu = 1, 2, \ldots, 2^k. \quad (1.18)$$

The parameter $\pi^{(\nu)} = \pi(\mathbf{x}_\nu)$ gives the probability that a subject drawn randomly from the population according to the P^θ distribution will respond to the set of k items with pattern $\mathbf{x}_\nu$. The parameters $\pi^{(\nu)}$ from (1.14) and π_i from (1.9) are called the *manifest* parameters and determine the marginal (or "observable") distribution of the responses of subjects to items*.

*This terminology is usual in latent structure analysis. Actually, these "manifest" parameters do depend on the item parameters and are therefore, strictly speaking, conditional with respect to the given item selection.

Note that

$$\pi_i = \sum_{\nu=1}^{2^k} x_{i\nu} \pi(\mathbf{x}_\nu);$$

and (see (1.15))

$$1 - \pi_i = \sum_{\nu=1}^{2^k} (1 - x_{i\nu}) \pi(\mathbf{x}_\nu); \tag{1.19}$$

where $x_{i\nu}$ is the i-th component of $\mathbf{x}_\nu$.

4.1.3 *Ordering items and subjects*

For *holomorphic sets of items* we may formulate:

Theorem 1.3.1   If $\delta_i > \delta_j$ then $\pi_j \geqslant \pi_i$, with equality iff

$$\pi(\theta, \delta_i) = \pi(\theta, \delta_j) \ P^\theta\text{-}a.e.^*$$

Proof:

$$\pi_j - \pi_i = \int_\Theta [\pi(\theta, \delta_j) - \pi(\theta, \delta_i)] \, dP^{\underline{\theta}}(\theta) \geqslant 0$$

by condition (4) of section 3.2.4. $\square$

Remarks
1. Under condition (4) of section 3.2.4, the equality sign will hold good only if $\pi(\theta, \delta)$ is monotone non-decreasing in δ for all θ and when $\pi(\theta, \delta_i)$ and $\pi(\theta, \delta_j)$ are equal over the population of subjects ($P^{\underline{\theta}}$-a.e.). We will usually assume that in condition (4) a strict monotony of $\pi(\theta, \delta)$ in δ holds good for all θ. For practical purposes we may therefore assume that the strict inequality holds good in theorem 1.3.1. Consequently the π_i values (the *population difficulties*) reflect (inversely) the order of the item difficulties δ_i, a result which is well in

---

*In some theorems it seems desirable to consider sets with $P^{\underline{\theta}}$-measure zero and therefore functions on Θ that are equal on Θ except on sets with $P^{\underline{\theta}}$-measure zero (equal $P^{\underline{\theta}}$-a.e.), if only to emphasize the importance of the population distribution $P^{\underline{\theta}}$. Besides the term "$P^{\underline{\theta}}$-a.e." we shall also use, more loosely, the formulation "over the population" which restricts propositions to sets of subjects with positive probability of selection.

agreement with intuition and with the common practice of describing the estimates

$$\hat{\pi}_i = \frac{n_i}{n}$$

as "difficulties" or "popularities".

2. This common practice, however, needs some qualification when seen from the point of view of our scaling theory. Theorem 1.3.1 is valid for holomorphic sets of items, *i.e.* items possessing the same trace function and different values δ_i. It is not valid for a set of items in which each item has a holomorphic but different trace function. This is illustrated in figure 4.1, where two population distributions are represented by their bell-shaped density functions

$$\left(\frac{dP^{\theta}(\theta)}{d\theta}\right).$$

The monotone trace lines of the two items i and j are also given. Taking these trace lines to represent two logistic trace lines with two item parameters, we see that item i has difficulty $\delta_{1i} > \delta_{1j}$, which is the difficulty of item j. For the items, different functions are used, because $\delta_{2i} \neq \delta_{2j}$. Each trace function is holomorphic: monotone increasing in θ, monotone decreasing in δ_1.

A glance at figure 4.1 will show that for population I, although each

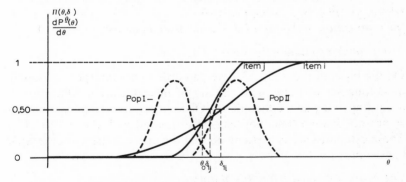

Figure 4.1 Two trace lines for two populations.

of these logistic trace functions is holomorphic (for variable δ), we have $\delta_{1i} > \delta_{1j}$ but $\pi_{1i} > \pi_{1j}$ (counter to theorem 1.3.1), because population distribution I covers mainly that part of the θ axis for which

$\pi(\theta, \delta_i) > \pi(\theta, \delta_j)$. For population II the situation is reversed: there $\pi_{\mathrm{II}i} < \pi_{\mathrm{II}j}$. Consequently, although for both populations the trace lines are the same, a consideration of the π_i values, the *population difficulties*, may lead to different conclusions concerning the δ_i values, the item difficulties. *Therefore the common practice of ordering items in terms of their sample difficulties without making further assumptions will not reveal much about their trace lines.*

In such cases, the comparison of population difficulties π_i *between* populations or sub-populations involves risks because the item difficulties may be "twisted" by the particular population distributions.

3. The difficulty discussed in (2) arises from the fact that the trace lines of items i and j intersect. In consequence, in figure 4.1, item i is "easier" than item j for all $\theta < \theta_0$, $(\pi(\theta, \delta_i) > \pi(\theta, \delta_j))$ whereas for $\theta > \theta_0$, $(\pi(\theta, \delta_i) < \pi(\theta, \delta_j))$ item i is the most difficult of the two. The θ continuum is divided into two segments, in one of which the comparative (local) difficulty (see section 3.2), of the items is the reverse of the other. Consequently, items can only be ordered by their trace lines in terms of difficulty parameters when these trace lines do not intersect, *i.e.* when a set is *doubly monotone*. For intersecting trace lines in the order of π_i the effects of the population distribution are blended with the effects of the characteristics of the particular trace lines.

Theorem 1.3.1 is therefore more generally valid for the much wider class of doubly monotone sets of items.

For a doubly monotone set of k items with trace functions $\pi_i(\bar{\theta}, \delta_i)$, where, for all θ, $\delta_i > \delta_j$ implies $\pi_i(\theta, \delta_i) < \pi_j(\theta, \delta_j)$, $i, j = 1, 2, \ldots, k$, the proposition of theorem 1.3.1, with strict inequality, is true.

Proof: similar to that of theorem 1.3.1.   □

On the basis of theorem 1.3.1 we can order a holomorphic or doubly monotone set of items with the aid of the population difficulties π_i according to the item difficulties δ_i. Of course, the manifest parameters π_i are not known, but they can be estimated with the $\hat{\pi}_i$ of (1.10). These estimates are consistent, so that the order of the π_i is estimated consistently by that of the $\hat{\pi}_i$.

The $\hat{\pi}_i$ are unbiased estimates of the π_i.

Proof:

$$\mathcal{E}\,\underline{\hat{\pi}}_i = \mathcal{E}\,\frac{\underline{n}_i}{n} = \frac{1}{n}\mathcal{E}_{\underline{\theta}_\alpha}\mathcal{E}_{\underline{x}_{\alpha i}}\left\{\sum_{\alpha=1}^{n} \underline{x}_{\alpha i}\big|\underline{\theta}_\alpha\right\} = \frac{1}{n}\mathcal{E}_{\underline{\theta}_\alpha}\sum_{\alpha=1}^{n}\mathcal{E}_{\underline{x}_{\alpha i}}(\underline{x}_{\alpha i}|\underline{\theta}_\alpha);\qquad (1.20)$$

where use has been made of (1.5), the δ_i have not been specified and

$$\underline{n}_i = \sum_{\alpha=1}^{n} \underline{x}_{\alpha i}. \qquad (1.21)$$

Noting that the $\underline{\theta}_\alpha$ are identically distributed and that for the Bernoulli variate $\underline{x}_{\alpha i}$:

$$\mathscr{E}_{\underline{x}_{\alpha i}}(\underline{x}_{\alpha i}|\theta_\alpha) = \pi_i(\theta_\alpha),$$

we have (see 1.9):

$$\mathscr{E}\underline{\hat{\pi}}_i = \frac{1}{n} \sum_{\alpha=1}^{n} \pi_i = \pi_i \quad \square$$

The $\underline{\hat{\pi}}_i$ are, of course, mutually dependent.
For large n (the number of subjects) they are relatively precise, as can be seen from their variances. As the subjects are sampled independently, we see that

$$\sigma^2(\underline{\hat{\pi}}_i) = \sigma^2\left(\frac{\underline{n}_i}{n}\right) = \frac{1}{n^2}\sigma^2(\underline{n}_i) = \frac{1}{n^2}\sigma^2\left(\sum_{\alpha=1}^{n} \underline{x}_{\alpha i}\right) = \frac{1}{n^2} \sum_{\alpha=1}^{n} \sigma^2(\underline{x}_{\alpha i}). \qquad (1.22)$$

Application of corollary 1.1.2 gives

$$\sigma^2(\underline{x}_{\alpha i}) = \mathscr{E}_{\underline{\theta}_\alpha}\sigma^2_{\underline{x}_{\alpha i}}(\underline{x}_{\alpha i}|\theta_\alpha) + \sigma^2_{\underline{\theta}_\alpha}[\mathscr{E}_{\underline{x}_{\alpha i}}(\underline{x}_{\alpha i}|\theta_\alpha)] \qquad (1.23)$$

$$= \mathscr{E}_{\underline{\theta}_\alpha}\sigma^2_{\underline{x}_{\alpha i}}(\underline{x}_{\alpha i}|\theta_\alpha) + \underline{\sigma}^2_{\underline{\theta}_\alpha}[\pi_i(\theta_\alpha)]. \qquad (1.24)$$

Because for the Bernoulli variate $\underline{x}_{\alpha i}$

$$\sigma^2_{\underline{x}_{\alpha i}}(\underline{x}_{\alpha i}|\theta_\alpha) = \pi_i(\theta_\alpha)(1 - \pi_i(\theta_\alpha));$$

we get

$$\mathscr{E}_{\underline{\theta}_\alpha}\sigma^2_{\underline{x}_{\alpha i}}(x_{\alpha i}|\underline{\theta}_\alpha) = \pi_i - \pi_{ii} \qquad (1.25)$$

where

$$\pi_{ii} \overset{d}{=} \mathscr{E}_\theta[\pi_i(\underline{\theta})]^2 = \int \pi^2(\theta, \delta_i)\,dP^{\underline{\theta}}(\theta);$$

and

$$\sigma^2_{\underline{\theta}_\alpha}(\pi_i(\underline{\theta}_\alpha)) = \mathscr{E}_{\underline{\theta}_\alpha}[\pi_i(\underline{\theta}_\alpha) - \pi_i]^2 = \pi_{ii} - \pi_i^2. \qquad (1.26)$$

Substitution of (1.25) and (1.26) in (1.24) gives

$$\sigma^2(\underline{x}_{\alpha i}) = \pi_i(1 - \pi_i) \tag{1.27}$$

a result which is not surprising, because the $\underline{x}_{\alpha i}$ are still unconditionally Bernoulli variates, with probabilities π_i. Substitution of (1.27) in (1.22) finally gives

$$\sigma^2(\hat{\underline{\pi}}_i) = \frac{1}{n}\pi_i(1 - \pi_i) \leq \frac{1}{4n}. \tag{1.28}$$

This result and the (rather trivial) upper bound for $\sigma_2(\hat{\underline{\pi}}_i)$, is similar to Rasch's treatment of the problem of the ordering of subjects and respondents (Rasch, 1960, 169).* As the $\hat{\underline{\pi}}_i$ have standard deviations smaller than or equal to $1/2\sqrt{n}$ we may, for large n, estimate the population difficulties fairly accurately. Although the values of the π_i depend on the population distribution, their order is determined by the δ_i and this order is therefore "population free".

These considerations can be extended to the ordering of subjects. Assuming that the particular procedures of item selection may be formalized in some item sampling model governed by an item distribution $P^{\underline{\delta}}$, as we saw in section 2.3.2 we get that

$$\omega_\alpha \stackrel{d}{=} \int_\Delta \pi(\theta_\alpha, \delta)dP^{\underline{\delta}}(\delta) = \mathscr{E}_{\underline{\delta}}\pi(\theta_\alpha, \delta) \tag{1.29}$$

defines the unconditional or marginal probability that a certain subject α (with value θ_α) will answer positively to (or "pass") an item presented to him according to the particular probabilistic selection procedure dominated by $P^{\underline{\delta}}$.

For *monotonely homogeneous models* we may formulate, similarly to theorem 13.1:

Theorem 1.3.2   If $\theta_\alpha \geq \theta_\beta$ then $\omega_\alpha \geq \omega_\beta$ with equality iff $\pi(\theta_\alpha, \delta) = \pi(\theta_\beta, \delta)$, $P^{\underline{\delta}}$-a.e.

with qualifications similar to those which follow theorem 1.3.1. Here it is the monotony in θ that essentially establishes theorem 1.3.2.

---

*Rasch's derivation, though leading to the same upper bound, seems to be erroneous because in his expressions (2.4) he appears to equate

$$\sigma^2(\hat{\underline{\pi}}_i) \quad \text{with} \quad \frac{1}{n^2}\sum_{\alpha=1}^{n} \mathscr{E}_{\underline{\theta}_\alpha}\sigma^2_{\underline{x}_{\alpha i}}(\underline{x}_{\alpha i}|\theta_\alpha) = \frac{1}{n}(\pi_i - \pi_{ii}).$$

In a similar way

$$\hat{\underline{\omega}}_\alpha = \frac{\underline{s}_\alpha}{k}$$

may be considered an unbiased estimate of ω_α where k is the number of items presented, and

$$\underline{s}_\alpha = \sum_{i=1}^{k} \underline{x}_{\alpha i}$$

is the number of positive responses given to these items (the simple score). We see from theorem 1.3.2 that the ω_α reflect the ordering of the subjects independently of the $P^{\underline{0}}$ distribution. This ordering can *be estimated by that of the estimates $\underline{s}_\alpha/k$.*

In practice, we are not entitled to expect the $\underline{s}_\alpha$ to reproduce the ordering of the values θ_α without an assumption such as that of monotonely homogeneous trace lines.

The precision of the estimates is indicated by the variances of the estimates for which, similarly to (1.28), we may state

$$\sigma^2(\hat{\omega}_\alpha) = \sigma^2\left(\frac{\underline{s}_\alpha}{k}\right) = \frac{1}{k}\omega_\alpha(1-\omega_\alpha) \leqslant \frac{1}{4k}. \qquad (1.30)$$

In most practical applications, however, the number of items, k, used for the measurement of subjects is relatively small and the precision of the estimates, as indicated by a standard deviation with upper bound $1/2\sqrt{k}$ will not be high. *We may therefore expect our scores, $\underline{s}_\alpha$, to reflect the order of subjects only roughly in practice.* On the one hand, this result diminishes our hopes of achieving a precise measurement of subjects where we have small numbers of items. On the other hand, (1.30) clearly demonstrates the well-known insight, that the precision of these estimates may be increased by increasing k, the number of items used for measurement.

4.1.4 *Marginal moments of item pairs*

We shall now investigate some properties of mixed second moments and related parameters for pairs of items, which belong to a holomorphic set of k items. The discussion will not be exhaustive, as many similar properties may be derived for higher moments. We shall restrict ourselves to a number of properties that seem to present some opportunities for the evaluation of the pragmatic scaling methods that will be developed later in this study.

We must first extend our notations and definitions. Where the order of the items matters we shall follow the convention mentioned in section 2.2.3, that of the numbering of the items according to decreasing item difficulty:

$$i < j \Longleftrightarrow \delta_i > \delta_j \Longleftrightarrow \pi_i < \pi_j; \, i,j = 1, 2, \ldots, k. \tag{1.31}$$

applying theorem 1.3.1 and excluding the equality sign. Considering the set $\{\underline{x}_i, \underline{x}_j\}$ as the responses to item i and j, and denoting

$$\pi_{ij}(x_i, x_j) = P\{\underline{x}_i = x_i, x_j = x_j\}; \, x_i, x_j = 1, 0; \, i,j = 1, 2, \ldots, k; \tag{1.32}$$

we may present the marginal bivariate distribution of $(\underline{x}_i, \underline{x}_j)$ in table 4.1.

Table 4.1

item j: x_j

		1	0	
	1	$\pi_{ij}(1,1)$	$\pi_{ij}(1,0)$	π_i
item i: x_i				
	0	$\pi_{ij}(0,1)$	$\pi_{ij}(0,0)$	$1-\pi_i$
		π_j	$1-\pi_j$	1

The parameters of table 4.1 are defined as follows:

$$\pi_{ij}(x_i, x_j) = \int_{\Theta} \pi_i(\theta)^{x_i}(1 - \pi_i(\theta))^{1-x_i}\pi_j(\theta)^{x_j}(1 - \pi_j(\theta))^{1-x_j}dP^{\underline{\theta}}(\theta); \tag{1.33}$$

$$\pi_{ij} \overset{d}{=} \pi_{ij}(1, 1) = \int_{\Theta} \pi_i(\theta) \, \pi_j(\theta) \, dP^{\underline{\theta}}(\theta); \tag{1.34}$$

and

$$\pi_{ij}(1, 0) = \pi_i - \pi_{ij}; \; \pi_{ij}(0, 1) = \pi_j - \pi_{ij}; \; \pi_{ij}(0, 0) = 1 - \pi_i - \pi_j + \pi_{ij},$$

These parameters are again manifest parameters.

We may now state:

Theorem 1.4.1   For monotonely homogeneous sets of k items,

$$\pi_{ij} \geq \pi_i \pi_j \text{ for all } i,j; \ i,j = 1, 2, \ldots ,k; \tag{1.35}$$

with equality iff $\pi_i(\theta)$ *or* $\pi_j(\theta)$ *is constant* P^θ-*a.e.*

Proof: Because of the monotony in θ required by condition (3) of section 3.2.4, $\pi_i(\theta)$ and $\pi_j(\theta)$ are s.o. Hence the result follows by a straightforward application of lemma 1.1.1. $\square$

Remarks

1. Only if $\pi_i(\theta)$ or $\pi_j(\theta)$ is constant over the population will π_{ij}, under the conditions of the model, be equal to $\pi_i\pi_j$, the value expected for π_{ij} under the hypothesis of the marginal independence of $\underline{x}_i$ and $\underline{x}_j$. Therefore, in the case of item sets with trace lines that are monotone non-decreasing and non-constant over the population, all item pairs will be positively correlated. The degree of correlation will be determined by the population distribution. We shall use this argument in chapter 8, section 8.2, figure 8.1.

2. Of course, as a corollary, the "error cell" in the theory of traditional Guttman scaling, which is $\pi_{ij}(1, 0)$ for $i < j$, will be "small", that is:

$$\text{for all } i < j: \pi_{ij}(1, 0) < \pi_i(1 - \pi_j) \tag{1.36}$$

Hence $\pi_{ij}(1, 0)$, the marginal probability of an "error" response to item pair i, j will be smaller than it would be under the hypothesis of marginal independence.

3. The relation of positive correlation given in theorem 1.4.1 is valid not only for monotonely homogeneous sets of items but also for sets with similarly ordered trace lines. However, it can be argued (as we shall do elsewhere) that from the point of view of measurement theory, these two cases, monotone homogeneity and similarly orderedness, may well be considered equivalent.

4. In the case of perfect Guttman items or G-items with trace lines as defined in (2.3), section 3.2.1, it can easily be seen that

$$\text{for } i < j: \pi_{ij} = \pi_i \text{ and } \pi_{ij}(1, 0) = 0. \tag{1.37}$$

But it can also be shown that these relations, (1.37) can be fulfilled by items with other forms of trace lines as well. Consider, for instance, the "error" probability $\pi_{ij}(1, 0)$, $(i < j; \delta_i > \delta_j)$. From (1.34) we have

$$\pi_{ij}(1, 0) = \int_{\Theta} \pi(\theta, \delta_i)(1 - \pi(\theta, \delta_j)) \, dP^{\underline{\theta}}(\theta) = 0 \text{ iff} \qquad (1.38)$$

$$\pi(\theta, \delta_i)(1 - \pi(\theta, \delta_j)) = 0, P^{\underline{\theta}}\text{-}a.e.$$

as the integrand is non-negative.

Now, if we allow non-decreasing monotony in θ, (1.38) will be valid when $\pi(\theta, \delta_j)$ reaches the value one before $\pi(\theta, \delta_i)$ leaves the value zero. Sets of items with trace lines that satisfy this condition for all consecutive pairs of items along the δ ordering (see figure 2.7, chapter 2) will satisfy (1.38) and will prove to be perfect Guttman scales. For theoretical and mathematical purposes it therefore seems desirable to distinguish between *latent* G-items, with trace lines of type (2.3) (section 3.2.1), and a *set of manifest G-items* as a set of items in which all item pairs satisfy (1.37).

It will easily be seen that the following proposition is true.

A set of items forms a perfect Guttman scale iff it is a set of manifest G-items. (1.39)

Proof:
1. Necessity trivial.
2. Sufficiency: the assumption of the occurrence of a non-perfect response pattern with positive probability implies that in this pattern a pair of items i, j, exists, $i < j$ and $x_i = 1$, $x_j = 0$. This again implies

$$\pi_{ij}(1, 0) > 0,$$

which is counter to (1.37), the defining property of a set of manifest G-items. $\square$

In practical applications, sets of manifest G-items have been met rarely, if at all.

Using the property of holomorphism of a set of items, we may demonstrate another property of the manifest parameters $\pi_{ij}(x_i, x_j)$ of (1.34) and table 4.1.

Theorem 1.4.2   For a holomorphic set of k items, for all triads of items $i, j_1, j_2; i, j_1, j_2 = 1, 2, \ldots, k;$ and $\delta_{j_1} > \delta_{j_2}, (j_1 < j_2)$:

1. $\pi_{ij_1} = \pi_{ij_1}(1, 1) \leqslant \pi_{ij_2}(1, 1) = \pi_{ij_2}$
2. $\pi_{ij_1}(1, 0) \geqslant \pi_{ij_2}(1, 0)$
3. $\pi_{ij_1}(0, 1) \leqslant \pi_{ij_2}(0, 1)$ (1.40)
4. $\pi_{ij_1}(0, 0) \geqslant \pi_{ij_2}(0, 0)$.

Proof:

1. $\pi_{ij_1} - \pi_{ij_2} = \pi_{ij_1}(1, 1) - \pi_{ij_2}(1, 1) = \int_\Theta \pi(\theta, \delta_i)[\pi(\theta, \delta_{j_1})$

$$- \pi(\theta, \delta_{j_2})] dP^\theta(\theta) \leq 0;$$

as, due to the monotony in δ, the integrand is non-positive. The proofs of (2), (3) and (4) may be completed along similar lines. $\square$

Remarks

1. *For practical purposes, assuming neat conditions (e.g. strict monotony in δ), strict inequality may be seen as holding good in (1), (2), (3) and (4) of (1.40), unless $\delta_{j_1} = \delta_{j_2}$.*
As in the former theorems stating inequalities, full mathematical generality will impose equality on system (1.40) (apart from the case $\delta_{j_1} = \delta_{j_2}$) in a number of cases involving particular trace lines and P^θ null sets, but we need not describe this in detail here. The perfect Guttman scale (a set of manifest G-items) is one of these cases. For instance, for $i < j_1 < j_2$, $\pi_{ij_1} = \pi_{ij_2} = \pi_i$, though strict inequality holds good in all other cases. The "error" probabilities involved in (1.40), (2) and (3) are then all zero.

2. Following the line of reasoning given under remark (3) of theorem 1.3.1, we will see that *the propositions of theorem 1.4.2 are also valid for the more general class of doubly monotone sets of items.*

3. Theorem 1.4.2 formulates a number of conditions which the manifest parameters must fulfil if the items are to form a holomorphic set. The conditions may be checked by an inspection of all the (2×2)-tables like that given in table 4.1 for all the pairs of items of the set. Do we have to check all four inequalities for any set of items? The answer is no.
It will easily be seen that given the ordering of the items for any triad, i, j_1 and j_2, $(j_1 < j_2)$

(1) inequality (1) of (1.40) iff inequality (2);   (1.41)
(2) inequality (3) of (1.40) iff inequality (4).

Therefore to verify the inequalities (1), (2), (3) and (4) of theorem 1.4.2 for any set of k items it is sufficient to verify only the inequalities (1) and (4).

4. Let us define the following conditional probabilities (see table 4.1):

$$\pi_{j|i} = \frac{\pi_{ij}(1,1)}{\pi_i};$$

$$\pi_{j|\bar{i}} = \frac{\pi_{ij}(0,1)}{1-\pi_i};$$

it will then easily be seen that for the given difficulty ordering, conditions (1)–(4) of theorem 1.4.2 are equivalent to the statement that $\pi_{j|i}$ and $\pi_{j|\bar{i}}$ are monotone increasing in j or monotone decreasing in δ_j. Therefore the (conditional) difficulty ordering of the items j, given the response to item i, is the same as the unconditional ordering under conditions (1)–(4).

5. Let $\mathbf{\Pi} = \|\pi_{ij}\|$ of order $k \times k$ be the symmetric matrix of manifest parameters $\pi_{ij}; i,j = 1, 2, \ldots, k$ (1.42)

Inequality (1) of theorem 1.4.2 states that for holomorphic (or doubly monotone) sets of items, the row elements will increase monotonely in j. By symmetry, the column elements will increase monotonely in i. The diagonal elements π_{ii} of $\mathbf{\Pi}$ are defined by (1.26) and are included in the propositions of (1.40) of theorem 1.4.2; that is, we may choose δ_{j_1} or δ_{j_2} equal to δ_i.

In section 4.2.2 we shall use this last property for an approximation of the reliability coefficients. But it may be pointed out here that the π_{ii} should not be considered *manifest* parameters, because, as we shall argue in section 4.2.2, they cannot really be regarded as referring to an observable experiment unless *independent* replications over subjects of the same set of items (test-retest) are possible. Therefore, it is not necessary to specify the π_{ii} elements here.

6. Similarly, let

$$\mathbf{\Pi}^{(0)} = \|\pi_{ij}(0,0)\| \text{ of order } k \times k \qquad (1.43)$$

be the symmetric matrix, with unspecified diagonal elements, the off-diagonal elements being equal to the probabilities of a 0-0 response for the corresponding pair of items. Then, according to inequality (4) of theorem 1.4.2, the row elements in $\mathbf{\Pi}^{(0)}$ will decrease monotonically in the column index j and, by symmetry, column elements of $\mathbf{\Pi}^{(0)}$ will decrease in i.

The verification of (1) and (4) of theorem 1.4.2 by means of an inspection of the matrices $\mathbf{\Pi}$ and $\mathbf{\Pi}^{(0)}$ is sufficient for a complete verification of the system (1.40). The reader may note that for arbitrary (2×2)-tables and for given i, all elements $\pi_{ij} \leq \min(\pi_i, \pi_j)$. Consequently, for given i and $j_1 < j_2$ the possible variation of π_{ij_1} may be more restricted than that of π_{ij_2} (consider, for instance, $\pi_{j_1} < \pi_{j_2} < \pi_i$). Therefore, the restriction due to the difficulty ordering of the items may tend to impose the trends predicted by theorem 1.4.2 even on randomly answered items. But we shall see in chapter 8, section 8.4, in which our results are used as checks of the double monotony of scales, that it may be possible to detect deviations from double monotony.

We shall now derive the item variance-covariance matrix $\Sigma(\underline{x})$ where $\underline{x}$ again denotes the stochastic vector of responses

$$\underline{x} = (\underline{x}_1, \underline{x}_2, \ldots, \underline{x}_k)^T; \quad x_i = 0, 1; \quad i = 1, 2, \ldots, k.$$

An application of lemma 1.1.2 gives:

$$\Sigma | (\underline{x}) = \mathscr{E}_{\underline{\theta}} \Sigma_{\underline{x}}(\underline{x}|\underline{\theta}) + \Sigma_{\underline{\theta}}(\mathscr{E}_{\underline{x}}(\underline{x}|\underline{\theta})) \tag{1.44}$$

Analyzing the two components:

A. $\Sigma_{\underline{x}}(\underline{x}|\theta)$

is a diagonal matrix by the assumption (1.2) (section 3.1) of local independence. Its only non-zero elements are the item variances in the diagonal, which (according to (1.25)) are

$$\sigma_{\underline{x}_i}^2(\underline{x}_i|\theta) = \pi_i(\theta)(1 - \pi_i(\theta)) \tag{1.45}$$

Hence we may define

$$\mathbf{D}(\underline{x}) = \mathscr{E}_{\underline{\theta}} \Sigma_{\underline{x}}(\underline{x}|\underline{\theta}) \tag{1.46}$$

as a diagonal matrix with diagonal elements

$$d_{ii} = \mathscr{E}_{\underline{\theta}} \sigma_{\underline{x}_i}^2(\underline{x}_i|\underline{\theta}) = \pi_i - \pi_{ii}; \tag{1.47}$$

where, as in (1.26)

$$\pi_{ii} = \mathscr{E}_{\underline{\theta}}\{\pi_i(\underline{\theta})\}^2 = \int_{\Theta} \pi^2(\theta, \delta_i) \, dP^{\underline{\theta}}(\theta); \tag{1.48}$$

B. $\mathscr{E}_{\underline{x}}(\underline{x}|\theta) = \pi(\theta)$

where

$$\boldsymbol{\pi}(\theta) = (\pi_1(\theta), \pi_2(\theta), \ldots, \pi_i(\theta), \ldots, \pi_k(\theta))^T. \tag{1.49}$$

Therefore, noting that (see (1.9)), $\mathscr{E}_{\underline{\theta}}(\pi_i(\underline{\theta})) = \pi_i$ and denoting

$$\boldsymbol{\pi} = (\pi_1, \pi_2, \ldots, \pi_i, \ldots, \pi_k)^T; \tag{1.50}$$

$$\mathbf{M}(\underline{\mathbf{x}}) = \boldsymbol{\Sigma}_{\underline{\theta}}(\mathscr{E}_{\underline{\mathbf{x}}}(\underline{\mathbf{x}}|\underline{\theta})) = \mathscr{E}_{\underline{\theta}}\{(\boldsymbol{\pi}(\underline{\theta}) - \boldsymbol{\pi})(\boldsymbol{\pi}(\underline{\theta}) - \boldsymbol{\pi})^T\}$$

$$= \mathscr{E}_{\underline{\theta}} \boldsymbol{\pi}(\underline{\theta}) \boldsymbol{\pi}(\underline{\theta})^T - \boldsymbol{\pi}\boldsymbol{\pi}^T$$

$$= \boldsymbol{\Pi} - \boldsymbol{\pi}\boldsymbol{\pi}^T \tag{1.51}$$

where $\boldsymbol{\Pi}$ is the matrix defined in (1.42), (see also 1.34), so that

$$m_{ij} = \pi_{ij} - \pi_i\pi_j; \quad i \neq j$$

$$m_{ii} = \sigma_{\underline{\theta}}^2(\mathscr{E}_{\underline{x}_i}(\underline{x}_i|\underline{\theta})) = \pi_{ii} - \pi_i^2 \tag{1.52}$$

Hence

$$\boldsymbol{\Sigma}(\underline{\mathbf{x}}) = \|\sigma_{ij}\| = \mathbf{D}(\underline{\mathbf{x}}) + \mathbf{M}(\underline{\mathbf{x}})$$

and

$$\sigma_{ii} = d_{ii} + m_{ii} = \pi_i(1 - \pi_i) \tag{1.53}$$

which, of course, reproduces (1.27) and

$$\sigma_{ij} = m_{ij} = \pi_{ij} - \pi_i\pi_j; \quad i \neq j;$$

which gives us the familiar marginal (manifest) variances and co-variances for the case under consideration. From theorem 1.4.1 we know that for monotonely homogeneous sets of items $\pi_{ij} > \pi_i\pi_j$. Consequently the items are all positively correlated for such models.

For sets of manifest G-items, forming a perfect Guttman scale, $\boldsymbol{\Sigma}(\underline{\mathbf{x}})$ is of the form:

$$\sigma_{ij} = \pi_i - \pi_i\pi_j = \pi_i(1 - \pi_j); \quad i < j;$$

$$\sigma_{ii} = \pi_i(1 - \pi_i). \tag{1.54}$$

The correlation matrix $\boldsymbol{R} = \|\rho_{ij}\|$ satisfying

$$\rho_{ij} = \frac{a_i}{a_j} \leqslant 1, \quad i \leqslant j; \quad i, j = 1, 2, \dots, k. \tag{1.55}$$

where a_i and a_j are positive constants characteristic for respectively the i-th row and the j-th column, has been called by Guttman a *perfect simplex*. This concept plays an important role in the alternative single-factor model which we developed in the context of his radex theory. (Guttman, 1954a, 269–75).

Consequently we have

$$\rho_{ij_1} > \rho_{ij_2}, \quad \text{for} \quad i < j_1 < j_2;$$

$$\tag{1.56}$$

$$\rho_{ij_1} < \rho_{ij_2}, \quad \text{for} \quad j_1 < j_2 < i.$$

It can easily be verified that for a set of manifest G-items the correlation matrix is of the form (1.55), given the appropriate difficulty ordering of the items, so that the inequalities (1.56) are satisfied.

From (1.54) it can be seen that the covariance matrix of a set of manifest G-items also satisfies (1.55) and (1.56). Covariance or correlation matrices not satisfying (1.55) but showing the ordering implied by the inequalities (1.56) have been called a *quasi-simplex* (Guttman, 1954a, 278). Because the simplex theory applies to sets of items forming a perfect scale, Gibson (1967) suggested that the method of single-factor analysis proper to quasi-simplex correlation structures be used as a method of Guttman scaling. We might therefore ask whether in general our holomorphic model does imply a quasi-simplex structure, *i.e.* whether (1.54) or (1.56) are valid in this general case. This does not seem to be true for covariances (1.54), as can be seen from what follows.

For $i < j_1 < j_2 : \delta_i > \delta_{j_1} > \delta_{j_2}; \pi_i < \pi_{j_1} < \pi_{j_2}; i, j_1, j_2 : 1, 2, \dots, k$

the validity of (1.56) implies

$$\sigma_{ij_1} > \sigma_{ij_2} \quad \text{or} \quad \pi_{ij_1} - \pi_i \pi_{j_1} - (\pi_{ij_2} - \pi_i \pi_{j_2}) > 0$$

or

$$(\pi_{ij_1} - \pi_{ij_2}) - \pi_i (\pi_{j_1} - \pi_{j_2}) > 0. \tag{1.57}$$

Denoting

$$\Delta_{j_1 j_2}(\theta) = \pi_{j_1}(\theta) - \pi_{j_2}(\theta) < \theta$$

assuming strict monotony in δ) we may use the method of proof of lemma 1.1.1 to write the left-hand member of (1.57) as a repeated integral

$$\tfrac{1}{2} \int_\Theta \int_\Theta \left(\pi_i(\theta_1) - \pi_i(\theta_2) \right) \left(\Delta_{j_1 j_2}(\theta_1) - \Delta_{j_1 j_2}(\theta_2) \right) dP^{\underline{\theta}}(\theta_1) \, dP^{\underline{\theta}}(\theta_2);$$

$$(1.58)$$

which may well be negative or positive for (θ_1, θ_2) values because $\Delta_{j_1 j_2}(\theta)$ and $\pi_i(\theta)$ are not necessarily ordered in the "s.o." or "o.o." sense. Therefore whether (1.58) will produce the inequality demanded by (1.57) or the reverse inequality will depend on the functional form of $\pi(\theta, \delta)$ and the weight that $P^{\underline{\theta}}$ gives to the negative and positive parts of the integrand. For the same reasons it seems unlikely that (1.56) will generally hold good for correlation matrices in the case of double monotony or holomorphism.

This negative result again demonstrates the fact that the properties (*i.e.* simplex structure) illustrated by the *deterministic* perfect scale model are lost when a more realistic *probabilistic* model is considered. Gibson's essentially deterministic procedure based on this simplex theory therefore does not seem to present many possibilities for less than perfect scales.

4.2   SCALE STATISTICS: SCORE, RELIABILITY, SCALABILITY AND PATTERNS

In this section we shall discuss certain other parameters and statistics which are characteristic for a set of items as a scale. We shall consider successively the simple score, item and scale reliability, a coefficient of scalability and the significance of response patterns.

4.2.1   *Properties of the simple score $\underline{s}$*

We shall first investigate certain properties of the simple score $\underline{s}$, taken over the vector of item responses

$$\mathbf{\underline{x}} = (\underline{x}_1, \underline{x}_2, \ldots, \underline{x}_i, \ldots, \underline{x}_k)^T; \quad x = 0, 1$$

$$\underline{s} = s(\mathbf{\underline{x}}) \overset{d}{=} \sum_{i=1}^{k} \underline{x}_i.$$

$$(2.1)$$

It follows immediately that

$$\mathscr{E}_{\underline{s}}(\underline{s}|\theta) = \mathscr{E}_{\underline{x}}(s(\underline{x})|\theta) = \sum_{i=1}^{k} \pi_i(\theta). \tag{2.2}$$

$\mathscr{E}_{\underline{s}}(\underline{s}|\theta)$ gives the (curvilinear) regression of $\underline{s}$ on θ. As such it may be regarded as a trace line for the set of k items. Its local discrimination for all θ is not worse and is often better than that of the trace lines of each of the k items in the set, as can be seen from the inequality

$$\frac{\partial}{\partial\theta}\mathscr{E}_{\underline{s}}(\underline{s}|\theta) = \sum_{i=1}^{k} \frac{\partial}{\partial\theta}\pi_i(\theta) \geqslant \frac{\partial}{\partial\theta}\pi_i(\theta) \geqslant 0; \quad i = 1, 2, \ldots, k; \tag{2.3}$$

if we assume differentiability of the item trace lines in θ over Θ.

Assuming strict monotony in θ of all the trace lines in (2.3), the strict inequalities will hold good. From (2.3) it also follows that $\mathscr{E}_{\underline{s}}(\underline{s}|\theta)$ as a trace line is monotone increasing in θ. Even then there may be θ regions where the local discrimination of the test score will not be much better than that of one particular item.

One example, the case of widely spaced items, is given in figure 4.2. For values $\theta < \theta_0$, local discrimination of the test score $\underline{s}$ is the same as that for item 1. Evidently

$$\mathscr{E}(\underline{s}) = \mathscr{E}_\theta\mathscr{E}_{\underline{s}}(\underline{s}(\theta)) = \sum_{i=1}^{k} \pi_i. \tag{2.4}$$

The variance of $\underline{s}$ can easily be derived by regarding the variance of linear combinations of the $\underline{x}_i$

$$a(\underline{x}) = \mathbf{a}^T\underline{x}, \quad \text{where} \quad \mathbf{a} = (a_1, a_2, \ldots, a_k)^T$$

is a vector of constants a_i.

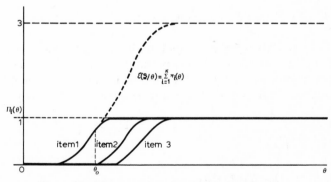

Figure 4.2   The regression of test scores for three items.

Using (1.46), (1.47), (1.51), (1.52) and (1.53) and corollary 1.1.2,

$$\sigma^2(a(\underline{x}) = \mathscr{E}_\theta \sigma_{\underline{x}}^2(a(\underline{x})|\underline{\theta}) + \sigma_\theta^2(\mathscr{E}_{\underline{x}}(a(\underline{x})|\underline{\theta})) = \mathbf{a}^T \mathbf{\Sigma}(\underline{x})\mathbf{a}; \qquad (2.5)$$

where

$$\mathscr{E}_\theta \sigma_{\underline{x}}^2(a(\underline{x})|\underline{\theta}) = \mathbf{a}^T \mathbf{D}(\underline{x})\mathbf{a} \qquad (2.6)$$

and

$$\sigma_\theta^2(\mathscr{E}_{\underline{x}}(a(\underline{x})|\underline{\theta})) = \mathbf{a}^T \mathbf{M}(\underline{x})\mathbf{a} \qquad (2.7)$$

Taking $a_i = 1$; $i = 1, 2, \ldots, k$, and simplifying the notation somewhat we get

$$\sigma^2(\underline{s}) = \mathscr{E}_\theta \sigma_{\underline{s}}^2(\underline{s}|\underline{\theta}) + \sigma_\theta^2(\mathscr{E}_{\underline{s}}(\underline{s}|\underline{\theta})); \qquad (2.8)$$

where

$$\mathscr{E}_\theta \sigma_{\underline{s}}^2(\underline{s}|\underline{\theta}) = \sum_{i=1}^k \mathscr{E}_\theta \sigma_{\underline{x}_i}^2(x_i|\underline{\theta}) = \sum_{i=1}^k [\pi_i - \pi_{ii}] \qquad (2.9)$$

and

$$\sigma_\theta^2|\mathscr{E}_{\underline{s}}(\underline{s}|\underline{\theta})) = \sum_{i=1}^k [\pi_{ii} - \pi_i^2] + 2 \sum_{i=1}^{k-1} \sum_{j=i+1}^k [\pi_{ij} - \pi_i \pi_j]. \qquad (2.10)$$

Hence

$$\sigma^2(\underline{s}) = \sum_{i=1}^k \pi_i(1 - \pi_i) + 2 \sum_{i=1}^{k-1} \sum_{j=i+1}^k [\pi_{ij} - \pi_i \pi_j], \qquad (2.11)$$

which, of course, could have been obtained immediately from (2.5).

We shall next consider the correlation of $\underline{s}$ with the latent variate $\underline{\theta}$. Meredith (1965) has studied the correlation of linear scores and linear combinations of the $\pi_i(\theta)$. In the case of monotonely homogeneous sets of items, we may consider the correlation between $\underline{s}$ and $\underline{\theta}$ itself.
  Defining:

$$\mu = \int_\Theta \theta \, dP^\theta(\theta)$$

$$\sigma^2(\underline{\theta}) = \int_\Theta (\theta - \mu)^2 \, dP^{\underline{\theta}}(\theta)$$

it can easily be shown that for single items $i = 1, 2, \ldots, k$;

$$\text{cov}\,(\underline{x}_i, \underline{\theta}) = \mathscr{E}\underline{x}_i\underline{\theta} - \mu\pi_i = \mathscr{E}_{\underline{\theta}}\mathscr{E}_{\underline{x}_i}\underline{x}_i\underline{\theta} - \mu\pi_i$$

$$= \mathscr{E}_{\underline{\theta}}\underline{\theta}\pi_i(\underline{\theta}) - \mu\pi_i > 0 \tag{2.12}$$

where the inequality follows from the fact that θ and $\pi_i(\theta)$ are s.o. and from an application of lemma 1.1.1.

Similarly

$$\text{cov}\,(\underline{s}, \underline{\theta}) = \sum_{i=1}^{k} [\mathscr{E}_{\underline{\theta}}\underline{\theta}\pi_i(\underline{\theta}) - \mu\pi_i] > 0; \tag{2.13}$$

so that $\underline{s}$ and $\underline{\theta}$ are *positively* correlated over the population with correlation coefficient

$$\rho(s, \theta) = \frac{\text{cov}\,(\underline{s}, \underline{\theta})}{\sigma(\underline{s})\sigma(\underline{\theta})} > 0. \tag{2.14}$$

Finally we may again mention the results of section 4.1.3, in which the simple score was related to the ordering of subjects. The properties mentioned here seem to support the common practice of using the simple score as a reasonable method for the measurement of subjects. But this use of the simple score is not necessarily an *optimal* procedure. To achieve optimality of some kind one might, for instance, consider other linear combinations of the item response alternatives x_i. In that case one is liable to run into a number of difficulties depending on the manner in which and the methods according to which optimality is defined. There is, for instance, no reason to expect linear combinations that are optimal *uniformly in* θ. In general, one might expect at most some *local optimality*, *i.e.* the coefficients $a_i(\theta)$ determining the optimal linear score $\sum_{i=1}^{k} a_i(\theta)x_i$ will depend on θ.

In this context we should recall an important result of Birnbaum's (see section 3.2.3.): only the logistic model has uniformly optimal linear scores, *i.e.* scores with coefficients independent of θ. We have seen that only in the model of Rasch, a special case of the logistic model, was the simple score $\underline{s}$ that uniformly best score. Therefore only in the logistic model with one item parameter is $\underline{s}$ optimal in the general sense in which Birnbaum uses the term.

Investigating other types of optimality, Meredith (1965) concluded that the optimal linear score would depend on $P^{\underline{\theta}}$, the (unknown) population distribution. In concluding this section, we must remark that only in specific parametric models does investigating a problem such as that of finding optimal linear scores seem to make sense. In applications where such specific information about the model is not available, and the researcher has to resort to the general model considered in this chapter, he might as well fall back on the simple score s in the absence of criteria that are clearly better.

4.2.2   Reliability

One of the reasons for giving the somewhat laborious derivations of variance and covariance formulas in the former sections was that these formulas enable us to define reliability adequately. First we shall consider *item reliability*.

We saw that (see (1.47) and (1.52)):

$$
\sigma^2(\underline{x}_i) = \mathscr{E}_\theta \sigma^2_{\underline{x}_i}(\underline{x}_i|\theta) + \sigma^2_\theta(\mathscr{E}_{\underline{x}_i}(\underline{x}_i|\theta))
$$
$$
= \mathscr{E}_\theta \sigma^2_{\underline{x}_i}(\underline{x}_i|\theta) + \sigma^2_\theta(\pi_i(\underline{\theta}))
$$
(2.15)

where

$$
\mathscr{E}_\theta \sigma^2_{\underline{x}_i}(\underline{x}_i|\theta) = \pi_i - \pi_{ii}
$$
(2.16)

and

$$
\sigma^2_{\underline{\theta}}(\pi_i(\theta)) = \pi_{ii} - \pi_i^2
$$
(2.17)

On the basis of (2.16) we may remark that

$$
\pi_i - \pi_{ii} = \int_\Theta [\pi_i(\theta) - \pi_i^2(\theta)] \, dP^{\underline{\theta}}(\theta) \geq 0
$$
(2.18)

with equality iff the set $\{\theta; 0 < \pi_i(\theta) < 1\}$ has $P^{\underline{\theta}}$–measure (probability) zero.

Allowing non-strict monotony in θ for $\pi_i(\theta)$, we may call items with trace lines $\pi_i(\theta)$ that satisfy the condition for equality in (2.18) $P^{\underline{\theta}}$–G(uttman)-items*. Note that sets of $P^{\underline{\theta}}$–G-items form a sub-class of the class of manifest G-items, defined in remark (4) of theorem 1.4.1. The distinction is somewhat artificial but is necessary in order

---

*Latent G-items, with trace lines of type (2.3), section 3.2.1, are of course included in this class of $P^{\underline{\theta}}$–G-items.

to indicate the different theoretical boundaries for the coefficient of reliability and the coefficient of scalability of section (4.2.3)

We may therefore state that

$$\mathscr{E}_{\underline{\theta}}\sigma^2_{\underline{x}_i}(\underline{x}_i|\underline{\theta}) = 0 \quad \text{iff item } i \text{ is a } P^{\underline{\theta}}\text{-}G\text{-item} \tag{2.19}$$

We may now consider (2.17).
From theorem 1.4.1 we know that

$$\pi_{ii} - \pi_i^2 \geq 0 \text{ with equality iff } \pi_i(\theta) \text{ is constant over the population}$$
$$(P^{\underline{\theta}}\text{-}a.e.). \tag{2.20}$$

$$Hence \; \sigma^2_{\underline{\theta}}(\pi_i(\underline{\theta})) = 0 \; iff \; \pi_i(\theta) \; is \; P^{\underline{\theta}}\text{-}a.e. \; constant. \tag{2.21}$$

Combining statements (2.15), (2.16), (2.17) and (2.21), we will see that:

$$0 \leq \sigma^2_{\underline{\theta}}(\pi_i(\underline{\theta})) \leq \sigma^2(\underline{x}_i) = \pi_i(1 - \pi_i). \tag{2.22}$$

Regarding $\sigma^2(x_i)$ as a total variance, $\sigma^2_{\underline{\theta}}(\pi_i(\underline{\theta}))$ as a variance between means over θ, and $\mathscr{E}_{\underline{\theta}}\sigma^2_{\underline{x}_i}(\underline{x}_i|\underline{\theta})$ as an error variance, we will see that $\sigma^2_{\underline{\theta}}(\pi_i(\underline{\theta}))$ is a measure of the *overall* discriminating power of an item over the population with distribution $P^{\underline{\theta}}$. (Meredith, 1965, 431). In view of (2.22) we may therefore define the variance ratio as a measure of overall discriminating power

$$0 \leq \rho(\underline{x}_i) = \frac{\sigma^2_{\underline{\theta}}(\pi_i(\theta))}{\sigma^2(\underline{x}_i)} = 1 - \frac{\mathscr{E}_{\underline{\theta}}\sigma^2_{\underline{x}_i}(\underline{x}_i|\underline{\theta})}{\sigma^2(\underline{x}_i)} \tag{2.23}$$

or

$$\rho(\underline{x}_i) = \frac{\pi_{ii} - \pi_i^2}{\pi_i(1 - \pi_i)}; \tag{2.24}$$

which proves to be also an adequate definition of the *coefficient of item reliability*.

Meredith (1965,423) derives this coefficient in a related way and demonstrates its equivalence to the definition of $\rho(\underline{x}_i)$ usual in psychometric practice.

One way of defining an item reliability coefficient is as the correlation between two replications with the same item (stability or test-retest), *i.e.* the model in which subjects respond twice to the same item through different replications. This type of experiment, however, gives rise to difficulties because memory and learning effects, for instance, may invalidate a hypothesis of independent responses *between* replications *within* subjects.

This hypothesis is not supported by our basic assumption (1.2) (see section 3.1, chapter 3) of local independence of responses within subjects: this assumption only states that a subject responds independently to *different* items, it does not claim such independence for the replication of responses to *identical* items. For the test-retest model we therefore need additional assumptions about the distribution of replications, assumptions which will lead to a definition of reliability that will differ from the usual one.

Another way of defining reliability is as the correlation between responses to pairs of parallel or equivalent items: pairs of *different* items i, j, with the same δ values $\delta_i = \delta_j = \delta$.* In this case, independence of responses is warranted by our assumption (1.2) of local independence. But now another difficulty arises: that of the *existence* of equivalent items. For a finite (or denumerable) population of items this existence requires an additional assumption. Apart from the problem of the existence of equivalent pairs of items, there is the problem of finding them: in the case of a continuous population distribution of items (P^{δ}), the probability that two equivalent items will be selected will be zero.

Similarly we may define two (or more) equivalent or parallel sets of items (parallel tests or scales) as two sets of k items of such a kind that $\delta_i^{(1)} = \delta_i^{(2)}; i = 1, 2, \ldots, k$.

We will now demonstrate the equivalence of the definitions of reliability for the reliability of the simple score. From (2.8) we have

$$\sigma^2(\underline{s}) = \mathscr{E}_{\underline{\theta}}\sigma_{\underline{s}}^2(\underline{s}|\theta) + \sigma_{\theta}^2(\mathscr{E}_{\underline{s}}(\underline{s}|\theta));$$

so that we can define the variance ratio

$$\rho(\underline{s}) = \frac{\sigma_{\theta}^2(\mathscr{E}_{\underline{s}}(\underline{s}|\theta))}{\sigma^2(\underline{s})} = \frac{\sum\limits_{i=1}^{k}[\pi_{ii}-\pi_i^2] + 2\sum\limits_{i=1}^{k-1}\sum\limits_{j=i+1}^{k}[\pi_{ij}-\pi_i\pi_j]}{\sum\limits_{i=1}^{k}\pi_i(1-\pi_i) + 2\sum\limits_{i=1}^{k-1}\sum\limits_{j=i+1}^{k}[\pi_{ij}-\pi_i\pi_j]} \quad (2.25)$$

From (2.18)–(2.22) we can state that:

$$0 \leq \rho(\underline{s}) \leq 1 \quad (2.26)$$

*More generally, we should require that $\pi_i(\theta, \delta_i) = \pi_j(\theta, \delta_j)$ for *all* θ.

with equality to zero iff the $\pi_i(\theta)$ are P^{θ}-a.e. constant for all i (i = 1, 2, ..., k) and with equality to one iff all items i are P^{θ}-G-items.

Apart from being a measure of the overall discriminating power of $\mathcal{E}(\underline{s}|\theta)$ as a trace line over the population, $\rho(\underline{s})$ is also the *coefficient of reliability* of the simple score. Let us consider two parallel sets of items and their simple scores $\underline{s}_1$ and $\underline{s}_2$.

Note that $\underline{s}_1$ and $\underline{s}_2$ are identically distributed as, say, $\underline{s}$, and that $\underline{x}_{i1}$ and $\underline{x}_{i2}$ are identically distributed as $\underline{x}_i$. Then the coefficient of correlation between $\underline{s}_1$ and $\underline{s}_2$ is given by

$$\text{cor}\ (\underline{s}_1, \underline{s}_2) = \frac{\text{cov}\ (\underline{s}_1, \underline{s}_2)}{\sigma(\underline{s}_1)\sigma(\underline{s}_2)} = \frac{\text{cov}\ (\underline{s}_1, \underline{s}_2)}{\sigma^2(\underline{s})}; \tag{2.27}$$

$$\text{cov}\ (s_1, s_2) = \mathcal{E}\underline{s}_1\underline{s}_2 - \mathcal{E}\underline{s}_1\mathcal{E}\underline{s}_2 = \mathcal{E}\underline{s}_1\underline{s}_2 - \left(\sum_{i=1}^{k} \pi_i\right)^2$$

$$= \mathcal{E}\sum_{i=1}^{k}\sum_{j=1}^{k} \underline{x}_{i1}\underline{x}_{j2} - \left(\sum_{i=1}^{k} \pi_i\right)^2 = \sum_{i=1}^{k}\sum_{j=1}^{k} \mathcal{E}\underline{x}_{i1}\underline{x}_{j2} - \sum_{i=1}^{k}\sum_{j=1}^{k} \pi_i\pi_j$$

$$= \sum_{i=1}^{k} [\pi_{ii} - \pi_i^2] + 2 \sum_{i=1}^{k-1}\sum_{j=i+1}^{k} [\pi_{ij} - \pi_i\pi_j]. \tag{2.28}$$

Substitution of (2.28) in (2.27) establishes the identity of cor $(\underline{s}_1, \underline{s}_2)$ with $\rho(\underline{s})$ of (2.25).

We may stress here the well-known fact that $\rho(\underline{x}_i)$ and hence also $\rho(\underline{s})$ are not manifest parameters; they are functions of π_{ii} which is not a manifest parameter and cannot be estimated from the data in the same way as the π_i and π_{ij} (for $i \neq j$). We must know the form of $\pi(\theta, \delta)$, the value of δ_i, and the form and parameters of the population distribution P^{θ} before we can determine π_{ii}. As the value of δ_i is unknown, the method of parallel test reliability, which leads to the same formula, does not contribute to the estimability of the π_{ii}. The methods of test-retest reliability used to determine stability coefficients presuppose additional conditions, which do not result in the same definition of reliability.

Therefore we may state:

The $\rho(\underline{s})$ -coefficient of reliability is not estimable.

In practical applications crude methods have been devised in which the problem is avoided. Various lower and upper bounds have been suggested and have sometimes been used. The *split-half* method is often used as a practical way of estimating parallel test reliability (equivalence). In this method a set of items is split into two (or more) parts, each part containing items which are approximately matched to the items of the other part according to their sample difficulties. This method is based on the rather strong assumption that a set of 2 k items (test or scale) consists of two parallel sets of k items each. Apart from the fact that the δ_i are unknown, which makes it impossible to realize such an assumption in practice, the estimated reliability coefficient based on the correlation of two tests of half the length of the original one has to be corrected for length with the well-known Spearman-Brown formula (Gulliksen, 1950, 78; Lord and Novick; 1968, 112).

For holomorphic or doubly monotone models another, though admittedly equally crude, method of determining an approximate reliability is suggested by theorem 1.4.2. Noting first that, given the difficulty ordering of the items,

$$\pi_i^2 < \pi_{ii} < \pi_i \tag{2.29}$$

and

$$\pi_{ii} < \pi_{jj}; \quad i < j;$$

this theorem suggests two other bounds:

$$\pi_{i,i-1} < \pi_{ii} < \pi_{i,i+1}; \tag{2.30}$$

resulting from the monotony proved in the theorem.

In terms of manifest parameters, we may approximate π_{ii} by a manifest value $\tilde{\pi}_{ii}$ obtained by an interpolation procedure based on $\pi_{i,i-1}$ or $\pi_{i,i+1}$ or both, hoping that $\pi_{ii} \approx \tilde{\pi}_{ii}$ for all i, and define an approximate coefficient of reliability

$$\tilde{\rho}(s) = \frac{\sum\limits_{i=1}^{k} [\tilde{\pi}_{ii} - \pi_i^2] + 2 \sum\limits_{i=1}^{k-1} \sum\limits_{j=i+1}^{k} [\pi_{ij} - \pi_i \pi_j]}{\sum\limits_{i=1}^{k} \pi_i (1 - \pi_i) + 2 \sum\limits_{i=1}^{k-1} \sum\limits_{j=i+1}^{k} [\pi_{ij} - \pi_i \pi_j]}; \tag{2.31}$$

which is a manifest parameter and directly estimable in terms of the manifest parameters $\pi_{ij} (i \neq j)$.

The advantage of this method is mainly that the reliability coefficient can be estimated for the scale or test *at its own length,* without necessitating additional assumptions with regard to the composition of the set. With holomorphic sets of items, neatly spaced according to difficulty without any wide gaps, the appropriately defined $\tilde{\pi}_{ii}$ may well be very reasonable approximations to the π_{ii}.

Two procedures of defining π_{ii} suggest themselves. For both procedures we assume the item indices to be determined by their difficulty ordering according to the convention followed in this book: $i < j$, $\pi_i < \pi_j; (\delta_i > \delta_j)$.

Procedure 1. Choose for each π_{ii} that value $\pi_{i,i-1}$ or $\pi_{i,i+1}$ for which

$$|\pi_i - \pi_j|, j = i-1, i+1 \tag{2.32}$$

is smallest. Let that be $\pi_{i,i+1}$.

Assume

$$\frac{\pi_{ii}}{\pi_{i,i+1}} \approx \frac{\pi_i^2}{\pi_i \pi_{i+1}} = \frac{\pi_i}{\pi_{i+1}} \quad \text{or}$$

$$\pi_{ii} \approx \frac{\pi_i \pi_{i,i+1}}{\pi_{i+1}} = \tilde{\pi}_{ii}^{(1)}. \tag{2.33}$$

This procedure treats π_{11} and π_{kk} in the same way as the other values π_{ii} $(i = 2, \ldots, k-1)$.

Procedure 2. Choose for π_{11} and π_{kk} the approximations $\tilde{\pi}_{11}^{(1)}$ and $\tilde{\pi}_{kk}^{(1)}$ of (2.33). Assume that for $i = 2, 3, \ldots, k-1$

$$\pi_{i,i-1} : \pi_{ii} : \pi_{i,i+1} \approx \pi_i \pi_{i-1} : \pi_i^2 : \pi_i \pi_{i+1} = \pi_{i-1} : \pi_i : \pi_{i+1}; \tag{2.34}$$

so that (interpolating linearly)

$$\pi_{ii} \approx \tilde{\pi}_{ii}^{(2)} = \pi_{i,i-1} + \frac{\pi_i - \pi_{i-1}}{\pi_{i+1} - \pi_{i-1}} (\pi_{i,i+1} - \pi_{i,i-1}). \tag{2.35}$$

Finally, we may estimate the values of $\tilde{\pi}_{ii}$ from sample data by inserting the appropriate estimates $\hat{\pi}_{ij}$ in the formula for $\tilde{\pi}_{ii}$.

It is true that this method is very simple and crude, but there is no *a priori* reason to think that the estimated reliability coefficients obtained by means of this method will be less accurate than those provided by the usual equally fortuitous methods. The method itself is of course restricted to scales consisting of holomorphic or doubly monotone sets of items. For the results of some applications we refer the reader to section 8.5 of chapter 8.

4.2.3 *A coefficient of scalability: H*

Loevinger (1947, 1948) was the first to develop an explicit theory of homogeneous tests on the basis of "cumulative" or monotone items. As such, her method proved to be equivalent to the approach of Guttman *et al.* Hence the models discussed in this chapter and especially the general class of monotonely homogeneous (and holomorphic) models, which are meant to be a more general formulation of Guttman's concept of the quasi-scale, are in a way also a further mathematical elaboration of her work.

We saw in section 2.5.3 that Loevinger devised a criterion of scalability, or homogeneity in her (and our) sense, that was of type S_2 (see section 2.5.2) and therefore possessed all the desirable properties of coefficients of that class. This coefficient of homogeneity (H) can be derived in several ways. In section 2.5.3, H was defined in terms of observed frequencies. As we are considering a probabilistic model, we shall now define H in terms of the manifest parameters and the "error" probabilities $\pi_{ij}(1,0)$, $(i < j)$ (see table 4.1).

In doing so, we must realize that H will be defined as a function of the parameters $\pi(\mathbf{x}_\nu)$ of the manifest multinomial distribution (1.14)–(1.19).

In the first place, we can define H as a coefficient of scalability of the type S_2. Reminding the reader that, *given the ordering of the items according to their values* δ_i, we may denote the "error" probabilities as:

$$\pi_{ij}^{(e)} = \pi_{ij}(1,0) \quad \text{if} \quad i < j;$$

$$\pi_{ij}^{(e)} = \pi_{ij}(0,1) \quad \text{if} \quad i > j; \tag{2.36}$$

and, similarly, their expectations under the hypothesis of marginal independence, as:

$$\pi_{ij}^{(0)} = \pi_i(1 - \pi_j) \quad \text{if} \quad i < j;$$

$$\pi_{ij}^{(0)} = (1 - \pi_i)\pi_j \quad \text{if} \quad i > j. \tag{2.37}$$

We define

$$E \overset{d}{=} \sum_{i=1}^{k-1} \sum_{j=i+1}^{k} \pi_{ij}^{(e)}; \tag{2.38}$$

$$E_0 \overset{d}{=} \sum_{i=1}^{k-1} \sum_{j=i+1}^{k} \pi_{ij}^{(0)}. \tag{2.39}$$

The *coefficient of scalability* can now be defined as

$$H \overset{d}{=} 1 - \frac{E}{E_0} = \frac{\displaystyle\sum_{i=1}^{k-1} \sum_{j=i+1}^{k} [\pi_{ij} - \pi_i \pi_j]}{\displaystyle\sum_{i=1}^{k-1} \sum_{j=i+1}^{k} \pi_i (1 - \pi_j)}. \tag{2.40}$$

Loevinger's own derivation starts from an analysis of "homogeneous"* item pairs as given in table 4.1. Given $\delta_i > \delta_j$; $i < j$ the conditional probability

$$\pi_{j|i} = \frac{\pi_{ij}}{\pi_i} \tag{2.41}$$

should be equal to one in the case of "perfect homogeneity" (*i.e.* when i and j form a set of manifest G-items).

We may add that in the definition of the coefficient of scalability the *order* of the population difficulties π_i is essential. Therefore the property of monotone homogeneity may not be sufficient if we relax our deterministic requirements and admit a probabilistic model. We may then need holomorphic or doubly monotone sets of items as in these items the order of the π_i always corresponds with that of the δ_i (see theorem 1.3.1, remarks (2) and (3)).

Noting that the requirement $\pi_{j|i} > \pi_{i|j}$ is merely equivalent to the already established order $\pi_i < \pi_j$ and that $\pi_{j|i}$ as an indicator of homogeneity is subject to the bounds (see theorem 1.4.1):

$$\pi_j \leqslant \pi_{j|i} \leqslant 1 \tag{2.42}$$

a proper normalization gives

$$0 \leqslant H_{ij} \overset{d}{=} \frac{\pi_{j|i} - \pi_j}{1 - \pi_j} = \frac{\pi_{ij} - \pi_i \pi_j}{\pi_i (1 - \pi_j)} \leqslant 1. \tag{2.43}$$

For monotonely homogeneous models, H_{ij}, the coefficient of homogeneity of item pair i,j, ($i < j$) will be equal to zero iff $\pi_i(\theta)$ or

---

*Loevinger's definition of "perfect homogeneity" is equivalent to Guttman's concept of the perfect scalability of items (Loevinger, 1947, 28).

$\pi_j(\theta)$ *is constant over the population* ($P^{\underline{\theta}}$ - *a.e. constant), and will be equal to one iff i, j forms a set of manifest G-items.*

For monotonely homogeneous models H_{ij} is non-negative. In general however, in arbitrary (2×2)-tables such as table 4.1, the coefficient H_{ij} may be negative. Hence negative values of H_{ij} are a sure sign of the non-homogeneity of the pairs of items under consideration.

Following Loevinger (1947, 29–32), we may define H, the coefficient of homogeneity of a set of k items, as a normalized weighted sum over the H_{ij} for all item pairs:

$$H \stackrel{d}{=} \frac{\sum\limits_{i=1}^{k-1} \sum\limits_{j=i+1}^{k} \pi_i(1-\pi_j) H_{ij}}{\sum\limits_{i=1}^{k-1} \sum\limits_{j=i+1}^{k} \pi_i(1-\pi_j)} = \frac{\sum\limits_{i=1}^{k-1} \sum\limits_{j=i+1}^{k} [\pi_{ij}-\pi_i\pi_j]}{\sum\limits_{i=1}^{k-1} \sum\limits_{j=i+1}^{k} \pi_i(1-\pi_j)}. \tag{2.44}$$

On the basis of theorem 1.4.1 we may state that:

For monotonely homogeneous models of sets of k items, H as defined by (2.44) will be non-negative

$0 \leqslant H \leqslant 1$

with equality to zero iff at least k − 1 items have trace lines that are constant over the population ($P^{\underline{\theta}}$ - *a.e. constant) and equality to one iff the items form a set of manifest G-items.*

We may note here that although H is in some ways related to ρ ($\underline{s}$) of (2.25)–(2.26), there are some essential differences too.

In the first place, H is a manifest parameter and can be estimated, while ρ ($\underline{s}$) is not manifest due to its term $\sum\limits_{i=1}^{k} [\pi_{ii}-\pi_i^2]$. Theoretically, moreover, even for monotonely homogeneous models they attain their bounds under different conditions: $H = 1$ for any set of manifest G-items, whereas $\rho(\underline{s})$ may still be smaller than one, attaining that value only for sets of $P^{\underline{\theta}}$–G-items. H will be zero, as soon as $k-1$ items are constant over the population, whereas then:

$\rho(\underline{s}) > 0$;   (one term $\pi_{ii}-\pi_i^2 > 0$);

$\rho(\underline{s})$ attaining the value zero only if *all* the items are constant over the population.

Finally, we may derive H as a sort of normalized variance ratio by considering $\sigma^2(\underline{s})$, the variance of the simple score. Defining

$$\sigma_0^2(\underline{s}) \overset{d}{=} \sum_{i=1}^{k} \pi_i(1-\pi_i); \tag{2.45}$$

$$\sigma_{\max}^2(\underline{s}) \overset{d}{=} \sigma_0^2(\underline{s}) + 2 \sum_{i=1}^{k-1} \sum_{j=i+1}^{k} \pi_i(1-\pi_j); \tag{2.46}$$

and noting that $\pi_{ij} \leq \pi i$; $(i < j)$, inspection of (2.11) will show that for monotonely homogeneous models

$$\sigma_0^2(\underline{s}) \leq \sigma^2(\underline{s}) \leq \sigma_{\max}^2(\underline{s}). \tag{2.47}$$

This suggests the definition of

$$H \overset{d}{=} \frac{\sigma^2(\underline{s}) - \sigma_0^2(\underline{s})}{\sigma_{\max}^2(\underline{s}) - \sigma_0^2(\underline{s})} = \frac{\sum\limits_{i=1}^{k-1} \sum\limits_{j=i+1}^{k} [\pi_{ij} - \pi_i\pi_j]}{\sum\limits_{i=1}^{k-1} \sum\limits_{j=i+1}^{k} \pi_i(1-\pi_j)}; \tag{2.48}$$

according to which H bears a clear relation to the variance of the test score. (2.48) corroborates a similar proposition by Loevinger (1947, 31).

We may also define a coefficient of scalability as a measure of the homogeneity of an item with respect to a set of items in a way similar to (2.40);

let $E_i \overset{d}{=} \sum\limits_{\substack{j=1 \\ j \neq i}}^{k} \pi_{ij}^{(e)}$ \hfill (2.49)

and

$$E_{0i} \overset{d}{=} \sum_{\substack{j=1 \\ j \neq i}}^{k} \pi_{ij}^{(0)} \tag{2.50}$$

where $\pi_{ij}^{(e)}$ and $\pi_{ij}^{(0)}$ are defined by (2.36) and (2.37).

Then we may define the *item coefficient of scalability* of item i as:

$$H_i \overset{d}{=} 1 - \frac{E_i}{E_{0i}} = \frac{\sum\limits_{\substack{j=1 \\ j \neq i}}^{k} [\pi_{ij} - \pi_i\pi_j]}{\sum\limits_{j=1}^{i-1} \pi_j(1-\pi_i) + \sum\limits_{j=i+1}^{k} \pi_i(1-\pi_j)}. \tag{2.51}$$

Loevinger defined an item coefficient of homogeneity which is different from ours and cannot be related to H_{ij} and $H.$* The item coefficient which we defined in (2.51) seems to be new. However, it fits very well into the scaling theory which we shall develop. It will, for instance, enable us to evaluate for any item belonging to a certain scale its homogeneity with respect to any other scale. In procedures of multiple scaling (see chapter 5, section 5.2.3), items allocated to one scale may be related to other scales by means of our item coefficients. (For an application see chapter 9, section 9.3).

Our coefficient of scalability, H, can be written as a weighted and normalized sum over the H_i for all items, in a way similar to (2.44). For our item coefficient we have

$$H_i = \frac{\displaystyle\sum_{\substack{j=1 \\ j\neq i}}^{k} [\pi_{ij} - \pi_i \pi_j]}{\displaystyle\sum_{\substack{j=1 \\ j\neq i}}^{k} \pi_{ij}^{(0)}} \tag{2.52}$$

and from (2.37 and 2.40) H can be written as

$$H = \frac{\displaystyle\sum_{i=1}^{k}\sum_{\substack{j=1 \\ j\neq i}}^{k} [\pi_{ij} - \pi_i \pi_j]}{\displaystyle\sum_{i=1}^{k}\sum_{\substack{j=1 \\ j\neq i}}^{k} \pi_{ij}^{(0)}} = \frac{\displaystyle\sum_{i=1}^{k}\sum_{\substack{j=1 \\ j\neq i}}^{k} \pi_{ij}^{(0)} H_i}{\displaystyle\sum_{i=1}^{k}\sum_{\substack{j=1 \\ j\neq i}}^{k} \pi_{ij}^{(0)}}. \tag{2.53}$$

From theorem 1.4.1 we can now state that:

For monotonely homogeneous models of sets of k items, for any i, i = 1, 2, . . . , k, H_i as defined by (2.51) will be non-negative

$$0 \leqslant H_i \leqslant 1$$

with equality to zero iff either $\pi_i(\theta)$ is constant over the population (constant P^θ - a.e.) or the other $k-1$ items have trace lines that are constant over the population.

We may note that for H_i to reach unity it is not necessary that the set of items be a set of manifest G-items.

---

*In fact, her coefficient is related to the Wilcoxon statistic or Mann-Whitney U-test for two samples which became well-known as non-parametric tests in later years. Her procedure of item analysis was equivalent to the substitution of this test for the usual ones based on the point-biserial correlation-coefficient (Loevinger, 1947, 35).

From (2.53) we have

$$H_i \geqslant c > 0 \text{ for } i = 1, 2, \ldots, k \text{ implies: } H \geqslant c; 0 \leqslant c \leqslant 1; \qquad (2.54)$$

i.e. H is always at least as great as the smallest item coefficient of homogeneity contained in the set.

4.2.4 Response patterns

In section 2.6.1 we saw that in applications of Guttman scaling much attention is often paid to the adequate occurrence of the "perfect" response patterns in comparison with that of the "imperfect" ones. We mentioned (see table 2.4 and 2.5 of chapter 2) some investigations that stressed the point that these perfect response patterns should occur with a frequency higher than the one which can be expected under the *null hypothesis of total marginal independence,* which states, in the notation of (1.11)–(1.19),

$$\pi_0(\mathbf{x}_\nu) = \prod_{i=1}^{k} \pi_i^{x_{i\nu}}(1-\pi_i)^{1-x_{i\nu}}; \quad \nu = 1, 2, \ldots, 2^k. \qquad (2.55)$$

This view is, of course, inspired by the particular role assigned to these perfect patterns in the deterministic Guttman model. As these features are carried over to practical applications in which perfect Guttman scales do not occur, it might be as well to investigate whether, in the stochastic models under consideration, there is any reason to treat these perfect patterns with special attention.

Considering a holomorphic model, we get for a particular response vector $\mathbf{x} = (x_1, x_2, \ldots, x_i, \ldots, x_k)^T$:

$$P\{\underline{\mathbf{x}} = \mathbf{x} | \theta, \delta_i; i = 1, \ldots, k\} = \prod_{i=1}^{k} \pi(\theta, \delta_i)^{x_i}(1 - \pi(\theta, \delta_i))^{1-x_i}$$

$$= C(\theta, \delta_1, \ldots, \delta_k) \prod_{i=1}^{k} \left\{ \frac{\pi(\theta, \delta_i)}{1 - \pi(\theta, \delta_i)} \right\}^{x_i} \qquad (2.56)$$

where

$$C(\theta, \delta_1, \ldots, \delta_k) = \prod_{i=1}^{k} (1 - \pi(\theta, \delta_i)).$$

Noting that for $\pi \in (0, 1)$ the function

$$\frac{\pi}{1 - \pi}$$

is monotonically increasing in π, and that, given the item ordering $\delta_1 > \delta_2 > \cdots > \delta_k$, our holomorphic model implies $\pi(\theta, \delta_1) < \pi(\theta, \delta_2) < \cdots < \pi(\theta, \delta_k)$ uniformly in θ (supposing strict monotony in δ), we may consider the probability, given θ, of (2.56) for every pattern with $s(\mathbf{x}) = s = \overset{k}{\underset{i=1}{\Sigma}} x_i$. It will be clear that for these patterns the probability will be highest for the pattern, in which $x_i = 1$ for $i = k - s + 1, k - s + 2, \ldots, k$ and $x_i = 0$ for the other $k - s$ items. This pattern is the "perfect" pattern with score s. As this property is true uniformly in θ for every value of the simple score s, we have in fact proved the same proposition for the marginal (manifest) probabilities in holomorphic sets of items:

Let $\mathbf{x}_\nu^{(s)}$ be a response pattern with simple score s; then for every s ($s = 0, 1, \ldots, k$) $\pi(\mathbf{x}^{(s)})$ attains its highest value for the "perfect" response pattern with score s, as consistent with the ordering of the items.

In other words, for *holomorphic* sets of items the "perfect" response patterns have greater probability than other patterns with equal score.

However, this property does not seem to be a strong one at all. *It also applies to the patterns expected under the null hypothesis of total marginal independence of (2.55), as can be seen from*

$$\pi_0(\mathbf{x}) = \prod_{i=1}^{k} (1 - \pi_i) \prod_{i=1}^{k} \left(\frac{\pi_i}{1 - \pi_i}\right)^{x_i}; \tag{2.57}$$

and an application of the same reasoning. We might therefore try to find out whether in monotonely homogeneous or even holomorphic models the perfect response patterns perhaps occur with manifest probabilities higher than those expected for these patterns under the null hypothesis of total marginal independence.

For extreme response patterns only, this can be proved always to be the case. Let $\pi(1, 1, \ldots, 1)_k$ denote the probability of the response pattern with positive responses to all k items:

$$\pi(1, 1, \ldots, 1)_k = \int_\Theta \prod_{i=1}^{k} \pi_i(\theta) dP^g(\theta); \tag{2.58}$$

let

$$\pi_0(1, 1, \ldots, 1)_k = \prod_{i=1}^{k} \pi_i; \tag{2.59}$$

let, similarly, $\pi(0, 0, \ldots, 0)_k$ be the probability of the response pattern with zero response to all k items and

$$\pi(0, 0, \ldots, 0)_k = \int_\Theta \prod_{i=1}^{k} (1 - \pi_i(\theta)) \, dP^{\underline{\theta}}(\theta) \qquad (2.60)$$

and let

$$\pi_0(0, 0, \ldots, 0)_k = \prod_{i=1}^{k} (1 - \pi_i) \qquad (2.61)$$

then we have:

Theorem 2.4.1   For monotonely homogeneous sets of k items:

$$\pi(1, 1, \ldots, 1)_k \geqslant \prod_{i=1}^{k} \pi_i = \pi_0(1, 1, \ldots, 1)_k \qquad (2.62)$$

and

$$\pi(0, 0, \ldots, 0)_k \geqslant \prod_{i=1}^{k} (1 - \pi_i) = \pi_0(0, 0, \ldots, 0)_k. \qquad (2.63)$$

Proof: By induction. We may note that for $k = 2$, propositions (2.62) and (2.63) are valid by theorem 1.4.1. Let (2.62) and (2.63) be valid for $k - 1$ items forming a monotonely homogeneous set and let us consider the monotonely homogeneous set of k items that results from adding a k-th item with a properly monotone trace line $\pi_k(\theta)$. (For reasons of generality we shall introduce different forms of trace lines $\pi_i(\theta)$).

As $\prod_{i=1}^{k} \pi_i(\theta)$ and $\pi_k(\theta)$ are s.o., we have from corollary 1.1.1 and the induction hypothesis (2.62) for $k - 1$ iterns:

$$\pi(1, 1, \ldots, 1)_k \geqslant \int_\Theta \prod_{i=1}^{k-1} \pi_i(\theta) \, dP^{\underline{\theta}}(\theta) \int_\Theta \pi_k(\theta) \, dP^{\underline{\theta}}(\theta) \geqslant \prod_{i=1}^{k} \pi_i, \qquad (2.64)$$

which proves (2.62) for all $k \geqslant 2$. As $\prod_{i=1}^{k} (1 - \pi_i(\theta))$ and $(1 - \pi_k(\theta))$ are s.o., (2.63) can be proved for all k in the same way. $\square$

Remarks

1. The equality signs will only hold good if any item is constant over the population ($P^{\underline{\theta}} - a.e.$). We may assume in practice that the strict inequalities will apply in (2.62) and (2.63).

2. Theorem 2.4.1 states that *for monotonely homogeneous scaling models only the extreme response patterns will always occur with manifest probabilities higher than expected on the basis of chance (total marginal independence). Even when we assume holomorphism or double monotony, adding monotony in δ, (the item difficulties), it will not be possible in general to prove similar inequalities for the other "perfect" response patterns independently of the particular population as the s.o. relation used in the proof does not hold good for them.*

3. As a matter of fact, the criterion of comparing the (relative) frequency of response patterns with their expectation under the null hypothesis of marginal total independence seems irrelevant, since even for perfect scales the probability of the intermediate perfect patterns can well be smaller than expected on the basis of this null hypothesis.

A simple counter example may suffice. Let three items i, j, k form a perfect scale.
Let $\pi_i = 0.10,$ $\pi_j = 0.30$ and $\pi_k = 0.60$

Then

$$\pi(0, 0, 1) = \pi_k - \pi_j = 0.60 - 0.30 = 0.30;$$
$$\pi_0(0, 0, 1) = \pi_k(1 - \pi_j)(1 - \pi_i) = 0.38,$$

so that the probability of the perfect pattern (0, 0, 1) is appreciably lower than that expected on the basis of independence.

4. As we saw in section 2.6.2, the deterministic starting point has in many cases led to such an exaggerated emphasis on the "perfect" pattern that many procedures of Guttman scaling included devices to "correct" "imperfect" patterns by allocating them to a nearest perfect pattern before the simple score s was computed. In this and the previous chapter we have accumulated abundant evidence that, in comparison with the more realistic starting point of a stochastic model, the deterministic starting point can lead to bad practices.

We saw especially that in all models except one (Rasch's model) for a given simple score s, each pattern, "perfect" or "imperfect", carries its own information, necessary for the estimation of θ, *i.e.* for the measurement of subjects. (The patterns are minimal sufficient statistics). Only in the model of Rasch is the scale score $\underset{\sim}{s}$ a minimal sufficient statistic, so that all patterns with the same score s carry the same information for the measurement (estimation) of subject parameters, but in this case it is senseless to substitute a perfect pattern for the imperfect ones. In all other cases, the practices referred to may lead to distortions resulting from the allocation of other scale scores than the actual value of s which corresponds to the imperfect pattern. By doing this, properties of $\underline{s}$ (see section 4.2.1) such as the positive correlation with the underlying attribute may be destroyed. To us it seems that such practices lack all reasonable foundation.

4.3 APPROXIMATE SAMPLING DISTRIBUTIONS

In the preceding paragraphs we have investigated a number of properties in terms of the manifest parameters of two classes of general two-parameter latent structure models, which we called monotonely homogeneous and holomorphic. In this section we shall consider the relatively simple problem of estimation and the problem of the sampling distribution of our main criterion of scalability, the coefficient of homogeneity $\underline{\hat{H}}$.

4.3.1 *Some remarks on estimation*

In contrast to the practice common to many traditional texts, we have not defined our fractions and coefficients in terms of our observations (frequencies), but have chosen to derive them as manifest parameters or functions of these parameters. As such they can all be related to the multinomial distribution governing the frequencies $\underline{n}(\mathbf{x}_\nu)$ that we derived in section 4.1.2, (1.14)–(1.16).

The problem of efficient estimation is solved for this distribution, the estimates $\hat{\underline{\pi}}^{(\nu)}$ of (1.18) being the maximum likelihood estimates of the parameters $\pi^{(\nu)}$ of that distribution. All the other manifest parameters in this chapter are mainly appropriate summations over the $\pi^{(\nu)}$ and may be estimated efficiently and unbiasedly by means of their maximum likelihood estimates, obtained by taking the corresponding sums over the $\underline{\pi}^{(\nu)}$.

However, several properties, such as the monotony in the π_{ij} for the holomorphic models of theorem 1.4.2, and some of the functions of the parameters, such as the coefficient of scalability H, depend on the (unknown) order of the item difficulties δ_i, which by theorem 1.3.1 is the same as that of the π_i.

In most practical applications this order must first be estimated from the data before it can be used for the derivation of other entities. This order itself can be estimated consistently from the $\hat{\pi}_i$ (see section 4.1.3) (Goodman and Kruskal, 1963). When the ordering of the items should be established, as in the definition of H as a parametric function in the π_{ij} and π_i, an estimation of this type will probably lead to good approximations.*

In the sections that follow we shall assume that the ordering of the items has been established, and that the numbering of the items has been determined according to the conventions followed throughout this chapter:

$$\pi_1 < \pi_2 < \cdots < \pi_k. \tag{3.1}$$

For all practical purposes we may also assume that a strict ordering as given in (3.1) holds good.

Following the definitions and notations of (1.14)–(1.18) we should note that (analogous to (1.19)) E as defined in (2.38) and E_0 from (2.39) can be written as

$$E = \sum_{\nu=1}^{2^k} \pi(\mathbf{x}_\nu) \sum_{i=1}^{k-1} \sum_{j=i+1}^{k} x_{i\nu}(1 - x_{j\nu}); \tag{3.2}$$

and

$$E_0 = \sum_{i=1}^{k-1} \sum_{j=i+1}^{k} \left[\sum_{\nu=1}^{2^k} x_{i\nu}\pi(\mathbf{x}_\nu) \sum_{\mu=1}^{2^k} (1 - x_{j\mu})\pi(\mathbf{x}_\mu) \right]. \tag{3.3}$$

By definition (2.40) we have

$$H = 1 - \frac{E}{E_0},$$

so that H is a parameter defined in terms of the parameters of the multinomial distribution (1.14–1.16).

Again we may see from (2.49) and (2.50) that

---

*If the order of the items is given prior to the estimation procedure, we may want our estimates to satisfy this order. This leads to restricted maximum likelihood estimates which are highly unmanageable. The assumption of a strict order $\delta_1 > \delta_2 > \cdots > \delta_k$ or $\pi_1 < \pi_2 < \cdots < \pi_k$ implies the asymptotic equivalence of restricted and unrestricted ML-estimates. The asymptotic distribution theory will therefore be the same.

$$E_i = \sum_{\nu=1}^{2^k} \pi(\mathbf{x}_\nu) \left[\sum_{j=1}^{i-1} (1-x_{i\nu})x_{j\nu} + \sum_{j=i+1}^{k} x_{i\nu}(1-x_{j\nu}) \right]; \tag{3.4}$$

and that

$$E_{0i} = \sum_{j=1}^{i-1} \left\{ \sum_{\nu=1}^{2^k} (1-x_{i\nu})\pi(\mathbf{x}_\nu) \sum_{\mu=1}^{2^k} x_{j\mu}\pi(\mathbf{x}_\mu) \right\}$$

$$+ \sum_{j=i+1}^{k} \left\{ \sum_{\nu=1}^{2^k} x_{i\nu}\pi(\mathbf{x}_\nu) \sum_{\mu=1}^{2^k} (1-x_{j\mu})\pi(\mathbf{x}_\mu) \right\}. \tag{3.5}$$

Hence the item coefficients H_i are also functions of the parameters $\pi^{(\nu)}$ of (1.14–1.16).

We may estimate the parameters H and H_i by means of the method of maximum likelihood, using a substitution in (3.2), (3.3), (3.4) and (3.5) of the maximum likelihood estimates of the $\pi^{(\nu)}$ given by (1.18): $\hat{\pi}^{(\nu)} = \underline{n}^{(\nu)}/n$; $\nu = 1, 2, \ldots, 2^k$ (Zehna, 1966). We may then define, equivalently to (2.36) and (2.37):

$$\hat{\underline{\pi}}_{ij}^{(e)} = \frac{n_{ij}^{(e)}}{n} = \hat{\underline{\pi}}_{ij}(1,0) = \sum_{\nu=1}^{2^k} x_{i\nu}(1-x_{j\nu})\hat{\underline{\pi}}(\mathbf{x}_\nu) \quad \text{if} \quad i < j; \tag{3.6}$$

$$= \hat{\underline{\pi}}(0,1) = \sum_{\nu=1}^{2^k} (1-x_{i\nu})x_{j\nu}\hat{\underline{\pi}}(\mathbf{x}_\nu) \quad \text{if} \quad i > j;$$

and

$$\underline{\pi}_{ij}^{(0)} = \frac{n_{ij}^{(0)}}{n} = \hat{\underline{\pi}}_i(1-\hat{\underline{\pi}}_j) \quad \text{if} \quad i < j; \tag{3.7}$$

$$= (1-\hat{\underline{\pi}}_i)\hat{\underline{\pi}}_j \quad \text{if} \quad i > j;$$

where, from (1.19),

$$\hat{\underline{\pi}}_i \overset{d}{=} \sum_{\nu=1}^{2^k} x_{i\nu}\hat{\underline{\pi}}(\mathbf{x}_\nu). \tag{3.8}$$

We may remark that $\underline{n}_{ij}^{(e)}$ and $\underline{n}_{ij}^{(0)}$ in (3.6) and (3.7) correspond to somewhat differently denoted quantities in section 2.5.3, $\underline{n}_{ij}^{(e)}$ being the uniquely defined "error" frequency and $\underline{n}_{ij}^{(0)}$ being its expectation under the hypothesis of random response, given the marginal frequencies n_i and n_j in table 2.2 which is related to table 4.1 of this chapter.

Therefore, substitution of (3.6) and (3.7) in (2.40) will give us an ML-estimate $\hat{H}$ for H which is identical to the coefficient H defined in terms of observed frequencies in section 2.5.3.

4.3.2   *The approximate sampling distribution of $\hat{H}$: the null-case*

None of the standard texts on methods of scaling known to the author at the time of writing contains a treatment of the sampling distribution of coefficients of scalability and methods of statistical inference based on the availability of such a distribution. Insofar as the problem is mentioned at all, the authors simply point out the lack of any distribution theory. This is especially true for the sample coefficient treated in this study, $\hat{H}$. In a recent survey of scaling methods, Sixtl again mentions the absence of any statistical theory for the coefficient $\hat{H}$:

> "Dieser Homogenitätsindex lässt sich zur Zeit nur zu deskriptiven Zwecken verwenden, da seine Stichprobenverteilung unbekannt ist" (Sixtl, 1967, 406).

Only the specialized paper by Goodman (1959) contained some results on the sampling distribution of a number of coefficients, including the null distribution of $\hat{H}$.

We have defined the coefficients H and H_i as *population* coefficients, *i.e.* as coefficients for a given population of subjects and a given set of k items.

Two types of problems are involved in the derivation of a distribution theory for $\hat{H}$ and $\underline{H}_i$, the *sample* coefficients in terms of which we may test hypotheses concerning these population coefficients.

In the *first* place, we have seen that for monotonely homogeneous models, H (and all H_i) were equal to zero, if and only if for all i, j, $(i, j: 1, 2, \ldots, k)\ i \neq j$,

$$\pi_{ij} = \pi_i \pi_j \tag{3.9a}$$

which represents the *null hypothesis of marginal independence* for all item pairs. (*The null case.*) A similar hypothesis may be formulated with respect to a particular item coefficient H_i which will be equal to zero if and only if for $j = 1, 2, \ldots, k; j \neq i$,

$$\pi_{ij} = \pi_i \pi_j \tag{3.9b}$$

in order to be able to test the scalability of a particular item with respect to a set of $k - 1$ items. Assuming the null hypotheses (3.9a) or

(3.9b), we may establish the distribution of the sample statistics $\underline{\hat{H}}$ and $\hat{H}_i$ and use it to test these null hypotheses so as to investigate the scalability of the set of items and particular items for given populations.

Secondly, we may want to derive the distribution of these sample coefficients in the more general cases in which their population values are greater than zero. (*The non-null case.*) We may then use these statistics to test for a set of k items the hypothesis of equal population (H) values for *different* populations, as an indication of the equal scalability of a set of items. Moreover, we may not be satisfied by knowing that a high sample scalability ($\underline{\hat{H}}$) could not be a chance result in a sample of n subjects sampled from a population with H value zero (the null case), but may want to calculate a confidence interval for the actual value of the population coefficient H.

In this section we shall consider *the null case*. In general, due to the relatively complicated nature of the sample statistics $\hat{H}$ and $\hat{H}_i$, the derivation of their exact distribution for small (finite) sample sizes is virtually impossible. Sagi (1959) derived this distribution for relatively simple coefficients of the Rep type (with denominator nk) and stated that for $\hat{H}$ the computational labor would be exceedingly great for samples of $n > 10$ and number of items $k > 4$, even in the simple null case. Goodman (1959), however, published some simple asymptotic results concerning the large sample distributions of a number of coefficients, including $\hat{H}$, for the case in which responses to different items are independent with given marginal frequencies of positive response n_i (*conditional marginal independence*).

From the results of section 4.3.1 it follows that $\underline{H}$ can be written as

$$\underline{\hat{H}} = \frac{\sum_{i=1}^{k-1} \sum_{j=i+1}^{k} [\hat{\pi}_{ij} - \pi_i \hat{\pi}_j]}{\sum_{i=1}^{k-1} \sum_{j=i+1}^{k} \hat{\pi}_i (1 - \hat{\pi}_j)} = \frac{\sum_{i=1}^{k-1} \sum_{j=i+1}^{k} \Delta_{ij}}{\hat{E}^{(0)}} \tag{3.10}$$

As the denominator of (3.10) is constant for given marginal frequencies, it will be sufficient to consider the statistic

$$\underline{\Delta} = \sum_{i=1}^{k-1} \sum_{j=i+1}^{k} \Delta_{ij} \tag{3.11}$$

for any inference concerning H.

Under the null hypothesis of marginal independence we have particularly

$$\mathscr{E}\hat{\underline{H}} = \mathscr{E}\underline{\Delta} = 0.$$

It can be proved (see Anderson and Goodman, 1957) that the statistics $\underline{\Delta}_{ij}$ are *asymptotically independent* under the conditions which hold good here.

Van Eeden and Runnenburg (1960), demonstrated that

$$\text{for } n \rightarrow \infty: (n-1)^{1/2}\underline{\Delta}_{ij} \xrightarrow{\mathscr{L}} N(0, \sigma^2_{ij}) ; \tag{3.12}$$

where the convergence is in distribution, $N(0, \sigma^2_{ij})$ indicates the normal distribution with mean zero and variance σ^2_{ij} and where

$$\sigma^2_{ij} = \hat{\pi}_i(1-\hat{\pi}_i)\hat{\pi}_j(1-\hat{\pi}_j). \tag{3.13}$$

Combining the asymptotic normality and independence of the $\underline{\Delta}_{ij}$ we obviously get:

$$\text{for } n \rightarrow \infty: (n-1)^{1/2}\underline{\Delta} = (n-1)^{1/2} \sum_{i=1}^{k-1} \sum_{j=i+1}^{k} \underline{\Delta}_{ij} \xrightarrow{\mathscr{L}} N(0, \sigma^2_{(k)}); \tag{3.14}$$

where

$$\sigma^2_{(k)} = \sum_{i=1}^{k-1} \sum_{j=i+1}^{k} \sigma^2_{ij}. \tag{3.15)}$$

(3.14) is equivalent to the statement that

$$\underline{\Delta}^* = \frac{(n-1)^{1/2}\underline{\Delta}}{\sigma_{(k)}} \xrightarrow{\mathscr{L}} N(0,1) \quad \text{for} \quad n \rightarrow \infty \tag{3.16}$$

i.e that, for large n, $\underline{\Delta}^*$ has approximately a standard normal distribution.

An application of the methods given by Anderson and Goodman (1957) shows that this test is asymptotically adequate as a test of the unconditional hypotheses (3.9a) and (3.9b). We may also test the scalability of an item with the statistic:

$$\underline{\Delta}_i^* = \frac{(n-1)^{1/2}\underline{\Delta}_i}{\sigma_{i,k-1}} \xrightarrow{\mathscr{L}} N(0,1) \quad \text{for} \quad n \rightarrow \infty \tag{3.17}$$

where

$$\underline{\Delta}_i = \sum_{\substack{j=1 \\ j \neq i}}^{k} \underline{\Delta}_{ij};$$ (3.18)

$$\sigma_{i,k-1}^2 = \sum_{\substack{j=1 \\ j \neq i}}^{k} \sigma_{ij}^2;$$ (3.19)

and where according to (3.17) $\underline{\Delta}_i^*$ has for large n approximately a standard normal distribution. For possible improvements and corrections for small n we may refer to Goodman (1959).

To test the hypothesis of scalability we may simply apply standard statistical theory. First we may point out that from theorem 1.4.1, the population coefficients H and H_i should be positive in the case of monotone homogeneity.

Therefore we may apply a one-sided test:

$$\mathcal{H}_0 : H = 0$$
$$\mathcal{H}_1 : H > 0$$ (3.20)

Choosing our confidence level, α_r, (*e.g.*: $\alpha_r = 0.05$) we may determine

$$u_{\alpha_r} = \Phi^{-1}(1 - \alpha_r)$$

defined by:

$$1 - \alpha_r = \frac{1}{\sqrt{2\pi}} \int_{-\infty}^{u_{\alpha_r}} e^{-(1/2)x^2} dx$$ (3.21)

(u_{α_r} being the standard normal deviate with right-tail probability α_r). Defining a critical value

$$\Delta_r = u_{\alpha_r} (n-1)^{-1/2} \sigma_{(k)}$$ (3.22)

and a critical region consisting of values

$$\Delta \geq \Delta_r;$$ (3.23)

there is no reason to reject $\mathcal{H}_0$ when the observed value

$$\underline{\Delta} < \Delta_r$$ (3.24)

and we reject $\mathcal{H}_0$ in favor of $\mathcal{H}_1$ when

$$\underline{\Delta} \geq \Delta_r. \tag{3.25}$$

The test for hypotheses concerning H_i can be constructed in exactly the same way.

It can be seen from (3.10) and (3.13) that the only data necessary for the computation of these tests are the $\hat{\pi}_{ij}$ which can be obtained from the cross-tabulation of the items (table 2.2) and the sample difficulties $\hat{\pi}_i$.

The computation of the approximate distribution in the non-null case demands the calculation of more complicated statistics.

4.3.3   *The approximate sampling distribution of $\hat{\underline{H}}$: the non-null case*

Goodman (1959) also considers the non-null distribution for a limited class of coefficients, all of the Rep type (denominator nk; see section 2.5.1). He does not give approximate non-null sampling distributions for the class of coefficients of type S_2 (see section 2.5.2) to which $\hat{H}$ belongs. As the asymptotic distribution of $\hat{H}$ in the non-null case seems to be unknown, we shall derive it in this section.

We shall again use the notation and definitions of (1.14)–(1.19) concerning the multinomial distribution of $\underline{n}(\mathbf{x}_\nu)$, with parameters $\pi(\mathbf{x}_\nu) = \pi^{(\nu)}$ associated with the 2^k possible response patterns $\mathbf{x}_\nu$. We shall also assume that the difficulty order of the k items has been determined and that the items are numbered according to the convention followed throughout these chapters: $\hat{\pi}_i \leq \hat{\pi}_j$; $i < j$.

Therefore

$$\mathbf{x}_p = (x_{1\nu}, x_{2\nu}, \ldots, x_{i\nu}, \ldots, x_{k\nu})^T; \ x_{i\nu} = 1, 0;$$

$$\nu = 1, 2, \ldots, 2^k; \tag{3.26}$$

may represent one of the 2^k possible outcomes for a response vector in which the elements $x_{i\nu}$ are numbered in i according to that convention.

First let us list a number of definitions. We saw from (3.2) and (3.6) that:

$$E = \sum_{\nu=1}^{2^k} \pi(\mathbf{x}_\nu) \sum_{i=1}^{k-1} \sum_{j=i+1}^{k} x_{i\nu}(1-x_{j\nu}) = \sum_{i=1}^{k-1} \sum_{j=i+1}^{k} \pi_{ij}^{(e)}; \tag{3.27}$$

and from (3.3), (3.7) and (3.8) that:

$$E_0 = \sum_{i=1}^{k-1} \sum_{j=i+1}^{k} \left[\sum_{\nu=1}^{2^k} x_{i\nu} \pi(\mathbf{x}_\nu) \sum_{\mu=1}^{2^8} (1 - x_{j\mu}) \pi(\mathbf{x}_\mu) \right]$$

$$= \sum_{i=1}^{k-1} \sum_{j=i+1}^{k} \pi_i(1 - \pi_j) = \sum_{i=1}^{k-1} \sum_{j=i+1}^{k} \pi_{ij}^{(0)};$$

(3.28)

then we know from (2.40) that

$$H = 1 - \frac{E}{E_0}.$$

(3.29)

Partial differentiation shows that for

$$\alpha = 1, 2, \ldots, 2^k,$$

$$\dot{E}_\alpha \triangleq \frac{d}{\partial \pi^{(\alpha)}} = \sum_{i=1}^{k-1} \sum_{j=i+1}^{k} x_{i\alpha}(1 - x_{j\alpha})$$

(3.30)

and

$$\dot{E}_{0\alpha} \triangleq \frac{d}{\partial \pi^{(\alpha)}} = \sum_{i=1}^{k-1} \sum_{j=i+1}^{k} \left[x_{i\alpha} \sum_{\nu=1}^{2^k} (1 - x_{j\nu}) \pi(\mathbf{x}_\nu) \right.$$

$$\left. + (1 - x_{j\alpha}) \sum_{\nu=1}^{2^k} x_{i\nu} \pi(\mathbf{x}_\nu) \right]$$

$$= \sum_{i=1}^{k-1} \sum_{j=i+1}^{k} [x_{i\alpha}(1 - \pi_j) + (1 - x_{j\alpha}) \pi_i].$$

(3.31)

From (3.30) and (3.31) we have

$$\dot{H}_\alpha \triangleq \frac{d}{\partial \pi^{(\alpha)}} = \frac{\dot{E}_{0\alpha} E - \dot{E}_\alpha E_0}{E_0^2}$$

(3.32)

Let

$$\dot{H} = (\dot{H}_1, \dot{H}_2, \ldots, \dot{H}_\alpha, \ldots, \dot{H}_{2^k})^T$$

(3.33)

be a column vector with elements $\dot{H}_\alpha$.

Let the covariance matrix of the multinomial distribution of the $\underline{n}(\mathbf{x}_\nu)$ be denoted by

$$\mathbf{\Sigma} = \|\sigma_{\alpha\beta}\|; \alpha, \beta = 1, 2, \ldots, 2^k$$

$$\sigma_{\alpha\beta} = \pi^{(\alpha)}\delta_{\alpha\beta} - \pi^{(\alpha)}\pi^{(\beta)}, \tag{3.34}$$

where

$$\pi^{(\alpha)} = \pi(\mathbf{x}_\alpha)$$

and

$\delta_{\alpha\beta}$ is Kronecker's *delta* defined as:

$\delta_{\alpha\beta} = 1 \qquad$ if $\alpha = \beta$;

$\delta_{\alpha\beta} = 0 \qquad$ if $\alpha \neq \beta$.

Correspondingly, from a random sample of n subjects, let:
$\hat{E}_n$ be derived from (3.27) by a substitution of the estimates $\hat{\pi}_{ij}^{(\varrho)}$ for $\pi_{ij}^{(\varrho)}$; $\hat{E}_{0n}$ be derived from (3.28) by a substitution of the estimates $\hat{\pi}_{ij}^{(0)}$ based on $\hat{\pi}_i$ and $\hat{\pi}_j$ for $\pi_{ij}^{(0)}$; $\hat{H}_n$ be defined as

$$\hat{H}_n = 1 - \frac{\hat{E}_n}{\hat{E}_{0n}};$$

$\dot{E}_{0\alpha,n}$ be derived from (3.31) by a substitution of the estimates $\hat{\pi}_i$ and $\hat{\pi}_j$ for π_i and π_j;

$$\hat{H}_{\alpha n} = \frac{\dot{\hat{E}}_{0\alpha,n}\hat{E}_n - \dot{E}_\alpha\hat{E}_{0n}}{\hat{E}_{0n}^2};$$

$$\hat{H}_n = (\hat{H}_{1n}, \hat{H}_{2n}, \ldots, \hat{H}_{\alpha n}, \ldots, \hat{H}_{2^k n})^T$$

be a column vector; $\hat{\mathbf{\Sigma}}_n$ be derived from (3.34) by a substitution of $\hat{\pi}^{(\alpha)}$ for $\pi^{(\alpha)}$; then we may state the following theorem.

Theorem 3.3.1

$$For\ n \to \infty: \frac{\hat{H}_n - H}{S(\hat{\underline{H}}_n)} \xrightarrow{\mathscr{L}} N(0, 1),$$

where $\quad S^2(\hat{\underline{H}}_n) = \frac{1}{n}\hat{\underline{H}}_n^T \hat{\underline{\Sigma}}_n \hat{\underline{H}}_n;$ $\qquad\qquad\qquad$ (3.35)

and where $N(0, 1)$ *denotes the standard normal distribution, and the convergence is in distribution.*

Proof: the theorem is an immediate corollary* of a theorem given by Rao (1965, (ii), 321). □

Remarks

1. Theorem 3.3.1 gives the asymptotic distribution of $\hat{H}_n$. As in most asymptotic theories, this distribution "for large n" is only an approximate distribution where the degree of approximation as a function of n is generally not known. In this special case we may expect k, the number of items in the scale, to play a role, as it determines exponentially the dimension, 2^k, of the multinomial vector, the estimated covariance matrix of which, $\hat{\underline{\Sigma}}_n$, determines the variance of $\hat{H}_n$.
For values of k between 4 and 10, the values that occur predominantly in practice, the approximation may not be too inaccurate; for larger values of k one might expect very large samples to be needed. The effect of large values of k on the asymptotic approximation for large n is still, however, a matter of investigation.

2. The computation of $S^2(\hat{H}_n)$ from (3.35) is a very complicated matter, because it involves a quadratic form, the elements of which are related to each of the possible form, the elements of which are related to each of the possible response patterns. In this computation one therefore starts from the complete frequency distribution $n^{(\nu)} = n(\mathbf{x}_\nu)$ of the sample of n subjects over the possible response patterns $\mathbf{x}_\nu$. This is feasible only with a computer. In our case the whole procedure was programmed on the Electrologica X8 computer of the Mathematical Centre at Amsterdam.
Once the observed values of $\hat{H}$ and $S^2(\hat{H})$ have been computed,

---

*In our differentiation with respect to the parameters we have not taken into account the restriction,

$$\sum_{\nu=1}^{2^k} \pi_\nu = 1.$$

It can easily be proved that unrestricted differentiation does not affect the asymptotic results we derived.

we may apply standard statistical theory to derive a confidence interval for H at confidence level 2α (*e.g.* $2\alpha = 0.05$).

Let (see (3.21))

$$u_\alpha = \Phi^{-1}(1-\alpha) \tag{3.36}$$

(u_α being the standard normal deviate with right-tail probability α). Then, dropping the suffix n to simplify notation,

$$\hat{\underline{H}} - u_\alpha S(\hat{\underline{H}}) \leqslant H \leqslant \hat{\underline{H}} + u_\alpha S(\hat{\underline{H}}) \tag{3.37}$$

is for large n an approximate confidence interval for the population coefficient H at confidence level 2α.

Another application of the theory developed here involves testing the equality of the coefficient of scalability of a given set of k items for different populations.

Let us assume that random samples of subjects have been drawn from p different populations and that the same set of k items has been presented to each of the p samples.

Let n_h; $h = 1, 2, \ldots, p$ denote the size of the sample drawn from the h-th population.

Let $\hat{\underline{H}}_h$ and $S^2(\hat{H}_h)$ be the sample coefficient and its estimated asymptotic variance (3.35) computed for the sample from the h-th population.

$$\bar{H} \overset{d}{=} \frac{\sum\limits_{h=1}^{p} [S^2(\hat{H}_h)]^{-1}\hat{H}_h}{\sum\limits_{h=1}^{p} [S^2(\hat{H}_h)]^{-1}} \tag{3.38}$$

and let us define the statistic T as:

$$T \overset{d}{=} \sum\limits_{h=1}^{p} [S^2(\hat{H}_h)]^{-1}(\hat{H}_h - \bar{H})^2$$

$$= \sum\limits_{h=1}^{p} [S^2(\hat{H}_h)]^{-1}\hat{H}_h^2 - \frac{\left(\sum\limits_{h=1}^{p} [S^2(\hat{H}_h)]^{-1}\hat{H}_h\right)^2}{\sum\limits_{h=1}^{p} [S^2(\hat{H}_h)]^{-1}}. \tag{3.39}$$

Let

$$N = \sum\limits_{h=1}^{p} n_h \quad \text{and} \quad p_h = \frac{n_h}{N}; \quad h = 1, 2, \ldots, p.$$

Then the application of a theorem by Rao (1965, (v), 323) will prove:

Theorem 3.3.2 *If the p_h are constant for $N \to \infty$, then under the null hypothesis*

$$\mathscr{H}_0 : H_1 = H_2 = \ldots = H_h = \ldots = H_p = H; \tag{3.40}$$

for $N \to \infty$: $\underline{T} \overset{\mathscr{L}}{\to} \chi^2_{p-1}$.

Hence under the null hypothesis (3.40) of equal H for the p populations, the statistic $\underline{T}$ of (3.39) will for large $N = \sum\limits_{h=1}^{p} n_h$ be approximately distributed as χ^2 with $(p-1)$ degrees of freedom. Consequently $\underline{T}$ can be used to test this assumption: for large values of $\underline{T}$ the null hypothesis of equal H values will be rejected.

In the case of small values of $\underline{T}$ and non-rejection of $\mathscr{H}_0$, we may use $\bar{H}$ defined by (3.38) as a pooled estimate of the common H value for the p populations. The estimated asymptotic variance of $\bar{H}$ will in that case be given by

$$S^2(\underline{\bar{H}}) = \left(\sum_{h=1}^{p} [S^2(\hat{\underline{H}}_h)]^{-1} \right)^{-1} \tag{3.41}$$

so that an approximate confidence interval can be computed along the lines of (3.37).

In a similar way we may compute approximate sampling distributions for each of the item coefficients $\hat{H}_i$, construct confidence intervals, and test common H_i values across populations. It is also possible to derive the asymptotic k-dimensional normal joint distribution of all the item coefficients $\hat{\underline{H}}_i$ ($i = 1, 2, \ldots, k$).

For applications and examples we refer the reader to section 8.2, chapter 8.

CHAPTER 5

A class of scaling procedures

We may now review the general results of the last two chapters and see what use may be made of them in developing instruments of measurement in social research. This review will serve two purposes. In the first place we may trace the general line of thought for the non-mathematically inclined reader. This will be done fairly briefly in section 5.1.1 for the parametric approach dealt with in chapter 3 and in more detail for the non-parametric models of chapter 4 in the subsequent sub-sections of section 5.1.

The second purpose, which is the most important in the section dealing with the non-parametric models, aims at the realignment of these results for the purpose of assessing their utility for the development of a class of simple scaling procedures.

In section 5.2 we shall then go on to sketch the procedures on which the research reported in this book is based.

5.1 SUMMARY AND EVALUATION OF THE FINDINGS

In our summary evaluation of the findings of chapters 3 and 4 we will first briefly consider our review of specific parametric models and will concentrate mainly on the findings which concern the general class of models of chapter 4 that seem more relevant for the type of scale analysis reported in this study. From the latter findings we hope to derive some relevant criteria for judging the scalability of sets of items and for defining a scale in terms of these criteria which can be supplied for purposes of measurement.

5.1.1 *Parametric models*

In section 3.1 we first formulated a stochastic measurement model of a very general form. In this model the response data may be discrete (*e.g.* dichotomous) or continuous (*e.g.* numerical scores) and unidimensional or multidimensional. It was supposed that these observed responses are generated by some probability process determined by a latent subject parameter (θ) and a latent item parameter (δ). These parameters too may be discrete or continuous, and unidimensional or multidimensional. It was shown that the model includes as special cases the factor analytic models as well as the full spectrum of the specific latent structure models that have been advocated in the literature.

For this reason we proposed that the term *latent structure analysis* should be extended to the class of measurement models defined by this general model. One purpose of this general formulation was to point out that its parametric structure makes it amenable to the standard analytical methods of inference and estimation of mathematical statistics.

In section 3.1.2 we discussed a specific class included in the model which was characterized by some desirable properties. This model, which belongs to the exponential family, well-known in mathematical statistics, is characterized by a separability in the subject and item parameters which is due to the existence of "sufficient statistics". The existence of these sufficient statistics enables us to estimate or, in terms of our measurement model, to measure the parameters, not only efficiently, but also independently of the particular population distributions involved in the selection of the values of these parameters. Thus item parameters may be measured (estimated) "*population free*", that is, independently of the particular choice of subjects, or the form of the population distribution, as defined by the particular procedure of subject selection.

Again, subject values (parameters) may be measured (estimated) "*item selection free*", that is, independently of the particular selection of items used for the measurement, or more precisely, independently of the population distribution (model of item sampling) that formalizes the procedure of item selection used in the construction of the scale. Parametric measurement models possessing these properties seem to have a number of advantages, so that it may be worthwhile to construct instruments of measurement based on such models and showing a reasonable empirical fit to these models.

For instance, in cross-cultural and cross-national comparative research (see chapters 6 and 7), where the problem of the comparison of measurements over very different populations is of great significance, it may be worthwhile to aim at the construction of measurement instruments on the basis of such parametric models.

In section 3.2, in which we specialized the general model of section 3.1 for the dichotomous data which are the chief focus of interest in this study, we saw that the logistic trace line with two item parameters (Birnbaum) embodies these features only for the difficulty parameter and not for the discrimination parameter of the items, the latter not being separable from the subject parameter. Rasch's model, a special case of the general logistic model of Birnbaum in which the trace line is the logistic distribution function with only one item parameter (the item difficulty), belongs wholly to the class of models of section 3.1.2.

In section 3.2.5. we saw that comparable normal ogive models and logistic models are equivalent for all practical purposes, so that the assumptions underlying the normal ogive model may be projected onto the logistic model. Given in addition the relative mathematical tractability of logistic models, it seems that their use should be preferred in actual practice. Their application seems, however, to be of relatively recent date: only those of Ross (1966) and Rasch (1960) in the field of mental testing are known to the author. Rasch (1967 a) mentions an application (dating from 1966) with questionnaire data in social psychology. In cases where it seems justifiable to apply parametric models in the field of survey research or other fields of the study of political behavior, it may be worthwhile to investigate the possibilities of the application of logistic scaling models in view of the desirable properties referred to above.

In the introduction of chapter 4, however, we argued that in vast areas of social research the application of parametric models may often be too far fetched. Their application presupposes a relatively deep insight into the structure of the variable to be measured and the properties of the items by which it can be measured. Such insight must be based upon sound data on the trace lines, difficulties etc. of a pool of items, and this can usually be achieved only in the more advanced stages of research through more or less continuous studies of scale evaluation and construction. This situation may be more characteristic of the field of mental and ability testing than of other fields such as sociological research and the study of political behavior. There the researcher is engaged in more intermediate or exploratory phases of research in which the level of knowledge concerning variables and items is still relatively low or undeveloped. The explorative context in which his measurement problems must be formulated implies a low level of insight concerning the structure and properties of the items which can be used for measurement.

Moreover, in these fields of research we seldom see a dominating emphasis on the measurement of one variable implemented by a continuous program of research. Instead the main emphasis seems to lie on the more or less *ad hoc* measurement and analysis of a relatively large number of variables. Therefore usually only a small number of items, typically four to ten, are available for the measurement of a variable.

For these reasons it seems legitimate to try to find starting points for scaling models which do not rely too heavily upon specific parametric assumptions, as these lead to procedures of inference and estimation that are too pretentious and intricate for the level of information and the precision that can be claimed for the data used in actual measurement. At the same time we may want these models and procedures to bear a clear relationship to the parametric models, although the former are less specific in their assumptions and more in harmony with our limited knowledge concerning the data. If we use these simpler but related models primarily for investigating the scalability of sets of items, their relation to more sophisticated parametric models may enable us to specialize them to a specific parametric model in the more advanced stages of the research.

In chapter 4 we therefore investigated models of a fairly general type which seemed to us natural generalizations of the cumulative quasi-scale, but without any assumption of a special parametric form such as determined, for instance, the logistic or normal ogive models.

The scaling procedures which we shall derive from these models in this chapter may well be used in the intermediate stages of empirical research in which the sole use of more or less arbitrarily defined indices or unreliable techniques of "single item measurement" is considered unsatisfactory. At the same time, many parametric models are special cases of the models given in chapter 4. Therefore, once sets of items have been found which form scales in terms of these general models, one may subsequently investigate whether certain parametric models can be used. For instance, we might first investigate which items for which variables form holomorphic sets or scales, and then proceed to find out whether we can discover or construct sub-sets which fit the parametric model of Rasch.

5.1.2   *Non-parametric models: homogeneity and holomorphism*

In chapter 4 we undertook what might be regarded as a reappraisal and possibly as a revindication of the scaling techniques inspired by the Guttman model. Our approach was to formulate a stochastic scaling model for dichotomous data of the general form considered in chapter 3 and to investigate what general properties would be preserved in the manifest data irrespective of the specific parametric form of the latent structure (the functional form of the trace line) and the resulting distribution of subjects (population distribution). In doing this we considered sets of items with trace lines belonging to a fairly general class characterized by the property of *monotone homogeneity, i.e.* trace lines which give the probability of a positive response $(\pi(\theta, \delta))$ as a function that *increases* with *increasing* subject values θ. A number of the properties found in chapter 4 were the result of this monotone homogeneity.

For other properties we had to examine a sub-class of these models which is characterized by the additional property of *double monotony* or *holomorphism** as a property of a set of items. The trace lines of this class give the probability of a positive response as a function which *decreases* with *increasing* values of the item difficulty δ_i.

In *monotonely homogeneous* models we only have monotony in θ: the higher the θ value of a subject, the higher the probability of a positive response. *Holomorphic* models (holomorphic sets of items) are marked by a *double monotony*: in addition to a monotony in θ (subject values), we have a monotony in δ (item difficulties). The higher the item difficulty δ of an item, the smaller the probability that any given subject will give a positive response.

This is illustrated in figure 5.1, where the graphs of four trace lines are given as functions along a θ-axis. If, for their difficulty values δ, we use the value on the θ-axis for which $\pi_i(\theta, \delta) = 0.50$, we can

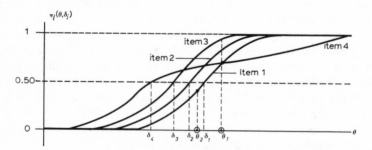

Figure 5.1   An illustration of monotone homogeneity and holomorphism.

*In section 4.1 we distinguished between the theoretically important concepts of double monotony and holomorphism of sets. As this distinction will not be emphasized in this part of our study, the general reader may regard the terms as synonymous.

indicate their item difficulties δ_i along the θ-axis. In figure 5.1 we have, following our convention of numbering the items according to their difficulty order, $\delta_1 > \delta_2 > \delta_3 > \delta_4$.

In the case of figure 5.1, all trace lines are monotonely homogeneous: for any two values θ_1 and θ_2 such that $\theta_1 > \theta_2$, we have $\pi_i(\theta_1, \delta_i) > \pi_i(\theta_2, \delta_i)$, as is illustrated by the two points θ_1 and θ_2 and their values $\pi_1(\theta_1, \delta_1) > \pi_1(\theta_2, \delta_1)$ for item 1 in figure 5.1. The items 1, 2 and 3 form a holomorph or doubly monotone set of items, as for any given value θ_1 we have from $\delta_1 > \delta_2 > \delta_3$:

$$\pi_1(\theta_1, \delta_1) < \pi_2(\theta_1, \delta_2) < \pi_3(\theta_1, \delta_3)*$$

as illustrated in figure 5.1.

We see that for holomorphic sets of trace lines the order of the probabilities of a scale (positive) response is the same uniformly in θ. I.e., the trace lines can be ordered according to their degrees of difficulty. In figure 5.1 item 4 disturbs the property of holomorphism, as can be seen from its point of intersection at θ_1 with the trace line of item 1.

For values $\theta > \theta_1$ we have

$$\pi_4(\theta, \delta_4) < \pi_1(\theta, \delta_1),$$

whereas for $\theta < \theta_1$ we have

$$\pi_4(\theta, \delta_4) > \pi_1(\theta, \delta_1).$$

We see that in a holomorphic model the trace lines of the items in a set are monotonely related through a dependence on their difficulties δ, a functional dependence that is not essential in the more general case of monotone homogeneity.

The property of monotone homogeneity underlies and defines the "monotone" or "cumulative" items described in section 2.2.2. But the doubly monotone or holomorph model incorporating "cumulative" trends in the subject parameter θ as well as in the item difficulty parameter δ may correspond even better with one's intuitive idea of the cumulative quasi-scale. By integrating it over the unknown population distribution we transformed the latent structure to the manifest parameters which resulted in some properties that were valid irrespective of the population distribution. This, however, did not mean that the structure was entirely independent of the population distribution.

*More generally, many properties can be derived assuming weak monotony, such as, for all $\theta_1 > \theta_2$: $\pi(\theta_1, \delta) \geq \pi(\theta_2, \delta)$ and for all θ: $\delta_i > \delta_j$: $\pi_i(\theta, \delta_i) \leq \pi_j(\theta, \delta_j)$.

For instance, we saw in section 4.1.3 that the manifest probabilities π_i, *i.e.* the population difficulties, reflected the order of the (latent) item difficulties, given the form of the trace line for any population. This *order* is therefore preserved for every population. But the *particular values* of all the manifest probabilities and parameters, such as the π_i are determined by the population distribution.

By these methods, assuming monotone homogeneity or holomorphism of the trace lines, certain simple properties and relations concerning these manifest probabilities were derived which hold good for every population for sets of items belonging to these classes. We shall summarize these properties in section 5.1.4 and following sub-sections.

Scaling procedures of the type we are looking for may be based on such general assumptions as monotone homogeneity and holomorphism and the manifest (observable) properties which result from these assumptions only. This has the following three advantages.

In the first place we need not specify the functional form of the trace line and the population distribution beyond these general and rather mild assumptions.

Secondly, these properties may enable us to verify the fit of the model to empirical data with simple methods based on the estimation of the manifest parameters and with relatively simple procedures. These may also give us methods of measurement of a more simple kind than those based on intricate solutions of latent structural parameters.

Thirdly, the properties of homogeneous and holomorphic scaling models as a class of quasi-scales will supply sounder support for the use of scaling techniques of the Guttman type than arguments based on the untenable deterministic model discussed in chapter 2.

In the following sub-sections we shall therefore re-examine the findings of chapter 4 with regard to their pragmatic value in this respect.

5.1.3   *Summary of the notation*

We will now give a summary and rearrangement of our notation.

A *response pattern* is denoted by the response row vector:

$$\mathbf{x}_\nu = (x_{1\nu}, x_{2\nu}, \ldots, x_{i\nu}, \ldots, x_{k\nu})^T \quad x_{i\nu} = 1, 0;$$
$$i = 1, 2, \ldots, k$$
$$\nu = 1, 2, \ldots, 2^k.$$

The *manifest probability* of observing response vector $\mathbf{x}_\nu$ is denoted by

$$\pi^{(\nu)} = \pi(\mathbf{x}_\nu), \ \sum_{\nu=1}^{2^k} \pi^{(\nu)} = 1. \tag{1.1}$$

The *population difficulty of item i* is denoted by

$$\pi_i = \sum_{\nu=1}^{2^k} x_{i\nu} \pi^{(\nu)}. \tag{1.2}$$

In keeping with the convention which we use throughout this study, we assume the *difficulty ordering of the items* to be such that

$$\delta_i > \delta_j : i < j \Longleftrightarrow \pi_i < \pi_j$$

The *score of a response pattern* $\mathbf{x}_\nu$ is denoted by

$$s^{(\nu)} = \sum_{i=1}^{k} x_{i\nu}; \tag{1.3}$$

or sometimes by s or s_α as the score of subject α.

The *manifest probability of observing two positive responses* for the pair of items i, j is denoted by

$$\pi_{ij} = \pi_{ij}(1, 1) = \sum_{\nu=1}^{2^k} x_{i\nu} x_{j\nu} \pi^{(\nu)} \tag{1.4}$$

(See also table 4.1 and chapter 4 (1.34)).

Analogously, we denote the manifest "error" probabilities (see chapter 4, (1.44)) by

$$\pi_{ij}^{(e)} = \pi_{ij}(1, 0) = \pi_i - \pi_{ij} \quad \text{if} \quad i < j;$$

$$\pi_{ij}^{(e)} = \pi_{ij}(0, 1) = \pi_j - \pi_{ij} \quad \text{if} \quad i > j. \tag{1.5}$$

Under the null hypothesis of marginal independence (random response to items) we denote (as in chapter 4 (2.37))

$$\pi_{ij}^{(0)} = \pi_i(1 - \pi_j) \quad \text{if} \quad i < j;$$

$$\pi_{ij}^{(0)} = (1 - \pi_i)\pi_j \quad \text{if} \quad i > j. \tag{1.6}$$

as the value of $\pi_{ij}^{(e)}$ in the case of marginal independence.

For the observed frequencies a similar notation will be used. The observed frequency of positive response to item i from a sample of n subjects is denoted by n_i; $n^{(\nu)} = n(\mathbf{x}_\nu)$ denotes the frequency of response pattern $\mathbf{x}_\nu$, and n_{ij}, $n_{ij}^{(e)}$ denote the observed frequencies of two positive responses and the "error" response to the item pair i, j respectively.

The functions (see (1.10), section 4.12)

$$\hat{\pi}^{(\nu)} = \frac{n^{(\nu)}}{n};$$

$$\hat{\pi}_i = \frac{n_i}{n};$$

$$\hat{\pi}_{ij} = \frac{n_{ij}}{n}; \tag{1.7}$$

$$\hat{\pi}_{ij}^{(e)} = \frac{n_{ij}^{(e)}}{n};$$

are unbiased and efficient (maximum likelihood) estimates of respectively $\pi^{(\nu)}$, π_i, π_{ij} and $\pi_{ij}^{(e)}$.

We may further define and denote (see also chapter 4 (3.7)) the estimated "error" probabilities under the null hypothesis of independence (random response for given marginals π_i) by:

$$\hat{\pi}_{ij}^{(0)} = \hat{\pi}_i(1 - \hat{\pi}_j) \quad \text{if} \quad i < j;$$

$$\hat{\pi}_{ij}^{(0)} = (1 - \hat{\pi}_i)\hat{\pi}_j \quad \text{if} \quad i > j. \tag{1.8}$$

5.1.4   *The ordering of items and subjects*

In chapter 2, section 2.2.3, we saw that for the perfect Guttman scale the order of items and subjects could be determined from the sample difficulties $\hat{\pi}_i$ and the scale scores s_α; $(\alpha = 1, 2, \ldots, n)$. We also saw that for large samples (large n) of subjects the order of the items could be determined much better than the order of the subjects in the typical case of a small number (k) of items. In fact, the sample can reproduce perfectly the system of ordered classes determined by the item difficulties (δ_i).

Ordering of items. From theorem 1.3.1 of chapter 4, we concluded that for holomorphic sets of items the population difficulties, π_i, reflected inversely the order of the item difficulties ($\delta_i > \delta_j \Rightarrow \pi_i < \pi_j$). We also concluded that this property is not generally valid in the case of non-holomorphic (intersecting) trace liges. Strictly speaking the common practice of ordering items on the basis of their sample difficulties seems to be warranted *only in the case of holomorphism of the set of items* in question. Theoretically, monotone homogeneity by itself is not enough!

The population difficulties can be estimated consistently with reasonable precision, by the sample difficulties $\hat{\pi}_i$ for large n. Therefore the order of the π_i (and hence that of the δ_i) can also be estimated consistently and with good precision. For sample data we shall therefore usually base our numbering and ordering of the items on the estimated order of their population difficulties.

$$\hat{\pi}_i \leqslant \hat{\pi}_j \Rightarrow i < j \tag{1.9}$$

The ordering of subjects. Similarly, the relative score as a fraction s_α/k of the total number of items (k) may in an item sampling model be regarded as an estimate of the probability (ω_α) that a subject with fixed value θ_α will respond positively to an item which is drawn at random from a population of items according to some distribution, due to the monotone homogeneity in θ. Irrespective of the form of this distribution, the order of the subjects according to their θ_α-values can be reproduced exactly by their ω_α-values.

$$\theta_\alpha < \theta_\beta \Rightarrow \omega_\alpha < \omega_\beta \tag{1.10}$$

Hence this ordering of the subjects may be estimated efficiently with s_α/k. Due to relatively small values of k (small numbers of items) the precision of this estimate will usually be small for any subject. (See theorem 1.3.2 of chapter 4).

Ordering properties of the scale score s can also be derived from a consideration of its trace line, giving its regression $\mathscr{E}(s|\theta)$ on θ. For monotonely homogeneous models this trace line is also monotone increasing in θ. (See section 4.2.1) This implies that respondents may be ordered stochastically on the basis of their scores.

5.1.5 *Positive correlation: small "error" probabilities*

In chapter 2 we saw that most procedures of Guttman scaling defined scales in ways which involved the requirement that in the (2×2)-

tables giving the response frequencies for item pairs, (see table 2.2), the frequency in the "error" cell, or "error" frequency, should be small.

These "error" frequencies play a central role in defining coefficients of scalability as the main criteria of scalability. Theorem 1.4.1 of chapter 4 supports this approach not so much because of the use of a concept of error as because of the fact that in the case of monotone homogeneity, responses to item pairs are positively correlated. This implies a "small" "error" probability in the (2×2)-table for every pair of items from a set of monotonely homogeneous items:

$$\pi_{ij} > \pi_i \pi_j \iff \pi_{ij}^{(e)} < \pi_{ij}^{(0)} \tag{1.11}$$

5.1.6 *Checks for holomorphism*

Theorem 1.4.2 of chapter 4, section 4.1.4, suggested some interesting means of investigating the holomorphism of a set of items which, as we saw in section 5.1.2, is a stronger property than just monotone homogeneity. When in such a set we consider for any item i its (2×2)-tables with any other two items j_1 and j_2 in the set, we see that theorem 1.4.2 demonstrates some strikingly simple relations between these tables (see theorem 1.4.2, (1.40), (1), (2), (3) and (4)). We also stated in remark (3) following theorem 1.4.2 that it is sufficient to verify only the inequalities (1) and (4) of (1.40).

Let us define as in remarks (5) and (6) to theorem 1.4.2 the following symmetric matrices of manifest probabilities:

$$\mathbf{\Pi} = \|\pi_{ij}(1, 1)\| \text{ of order } k \times k;$$

$$\mathbf{\Pi}^{(0)} = \|\pi_{ij}(0, 0)\| \text{ of order } k \times k; \tag{1.12}$$

where $\pi_{ij}(0, 0)$ is the probability of a $\{0, 0\}$ response to items i and j (the response to both items being not positive) and where the diagonal elements $(\pi_{ii}(1, 1)$ and $\pi_{ii}(0, 0))$ are not specified.

Let us assume that the rows (and columns) are numbered according to our item ordering, *i.e.* $i < j, \pi_i < \pi_j, \delta_i > \delta_j$.

Then, given the ordering of items, inequality (1) of theorem 1.4.2 implies that the elements of row i of $\mathbf{\Pi}$ will *increase* monotonely with column index j.

Similarly, according to inequality (4), the elements of row i of $\mathbf{\Pi}^{(0)}$ will *decrease* monotonically with increasing column index j.

Of course, because of the symmetry of Π and $\Pi^{(0)}$ the same statements will hold good for their columns.

An illustration is given in the fictitious example of table 5.1. It gives the Π- and $\Pi^{(0)}$-matrices for a set of five items in their conventional difficulty order. These matrices are symmetric by definition.

Consider rows 2 and 4 of the Π-matrix. The elements of these rows show clearly the trend expected from theorem 1.4.2. for a holomorphic or doubly monotone set of items: they *increase monotonically* from left to right. For the $\Pi^{(0)}$-matrix the rows 2 and 4 also show the right trend, the elements *decreasing monotonically* from left to right.

Table 5.1   A fictitious case of double monotony

Π-matrix

Items	1	2	3	4	5
1	–	0.12	**0.18**	0.16	0.18
2	0.12	–	0.20	0.22	0.25
3	**0.18**	0.20	–	0.26	0.38
4	0.16	0.22	0.26	–	0.42
5	0.18	0.25	0.38	0.42	–
Population difficulties (π_i):	0.20	0.30	0.40	0.50	0.60

$\Pi^{(0)}$-matrix

Items	1	2	3	4	5
1	–	0.62	0.58	0.46	0.38
2	0.62	–	0.50	0.42	0.35
3	0.58	0.50	–	0.36	**0.38**
4	0.46	0.42	0.36	–	0.32
5	0.38	0.35	**0.38**	0.32	–
Population difficulties (π_i):	0.20	0.30	0.40	0.50	0.60

However, when we consider row 1 of the Π-matrix, we see that the trend is disturbed by the element π_{13} (1, 1), which has too high a value (0.18). Yet, in the $\Pi^{(0)}$-matrix the first row does not deviate from the pattern to be expected for a doubly monotone set of items: its elements decrease monotonically.

The reverse holds good for row 5 of the $\Pi^{(0)}$-matrix, where the element $\pi_{5,3}$ (0, 0) is too high (0.38). The trend for that row in Π, however, is what it should be when double monotony exists for the set of items: the elements increase neatly from left to right.

We may conclude that a necessary condition for holomorphism of a set of items is that both the Π- *and the* $\Pi^{(0)}$-*matrices must show the monotone trends predicted from theorem 1.4.2.**

The set of items in table 5.1 cannot therefore be regarded as a holomorphic set. With large samples, the properties of holomorphism may be checked by inspecting the observed sample estimates for a sample of size n:

$$\hat{\Pi} = \|\hat{\pi}_{ij}(1, 1)\|, \text{ order } k \times k;$$

$$\hat{\Pi}^{(0)} = \|\hat{\pi}_{ij}(0, 0)\|, \text{ order } k \times k;$$

(1.13)

where

$$\hat{\pi}_{ij}(1, 1) = \frac{n_{ij}(1, 1)}{n}, \hat{\pi}_{ij}(0, 0) = \frac{n_{ij}(0, 0)}{n};$$

$n_{ij}(0, 0)$ is the observed frequency of non-positive response to both i and j, $i \neq j$ and where the diagonal is not specified.

Empirical examples will be reported in section 8.4 of chapter 8.

Finally, we saw in section 4.2.2 that (1) of theorem 1.4.2 enabled us to suggest two procedures for estimating approximations of the non-manifest probabilities π_{ii}, the diagonals of Π. As a consequence, the covariance terms of the form $\pi_{ij} - \pi_i^2$ can be estimated. The method was used in section 4.2.2 to suggest estimates for reliability coefficients.

An empirical illustration will be given in section 8.5 of chapter 8.

5.1.7   *A criterion of scalability:* H

The findings of chapter 4 also provide a means of defining a criterion of scalability. In section 5.1.5 we saw that the old notion of "small" "error" probabilities was supported as a corollary of monotone homogeneity. Most coefficients of scalability incorporate this notion and therefore seem promising as measures of *scalability* as far as monotone homogeneity is concerned.

From the discussion in chapter 2 it will be clear that we prefer a coefficient of type S_2 (see section 2.5.2, chapter 2). We prefer to use the coefficient of homogeneity, H, as a criterion of scalability in the sense of monotone homogeneity, for a number of reasons.

---

*The reader may note that the trends tend to be caused by the population difficulties π_i. For a further argument we may refer the reader to remark 6 of theorem 1.4.2 in chapter 4.

The choice of H seems particularly appropriate in this respect because it is based on the "error" probabilities $(\pi_{ij}^{(e)})$ for *all* item pairs (see (2.40), chapter 4) and can be written as a weighted function of H_{ij}-coefficients for all item pairs (see 2.44), chapter 4) and also as a weighted function of the item coefficients H_i (see (2.53), chapter 4).

Another advantage is the fact that H, as a measure of homogeneity, can also be derived as a normalized variance ratio for the scale score* $\underline{s}$, so that H bears a clear relation to $\underline{s}$.

Furthermore, H seems to answer the four criteria of White and Saltz mentioned in section 2.5.2, as well as the fifth criterion added by us in that section:

1. Its theoretical maximum is 1 and hence invariant over scales.

2. Its theoretical minimum is 0 assuming monotone homogeneity (see section 4.2.3) and hence invariant over scales.

Of course, its sample estimate $\hat{\underline{H}}$ may assume values smaller than zero even when $0 \leqslant H \leqslant 1$ is true for the population coefficient. However as a test of the value of H, the permissible range of $\hat{\underline{H}}$ will be between zero and one, *i.e.* only one-sided tests of the null hypothesis $H = 0$ will be in order.

3. With H or its sample estimate $\hat{\underline{H}}$, it is possible to evaluate scales as a whole as well as the scalability of individual items on the basis of our item coefficients H_i and their sample estimates $\hat{\underline{H}}_i$. This will be possible on the basis of points 1 and 2 and of points 4 and 5 below. As a matter of fact, we can base our definition of a scale and our characterization of scales solely on this evaluation.

4. It is possible to test the sample values $\hat{\underline{H}}$ and $\hat{\underline{H}}_i$ against the null hypothesis mentioned *sub* 2 by an application of the asymptomatic null distribution derived in section 4.3.2.

5. It is possible to estimate population values for a scale and to determine approximate confidence intervals for these estimates. We can also set up approximate tests of the equality of the H-values of a set of items for different populations. This can be done by an application of theorems 3.3.1, and 3.3.2, in which we derived the approximate large-sample distributions for the non-null case.

These considerations suggest that H (and its components H_i and

*$\underline{s}$: stochastic variables are underlined in this report.

H_{ij}) seems to be as good a coefficient of scalability as we could desire. We therefore propose to use it as our criterion of scalability for any scaling procedure to be designed hereafter. Our definition of the item coefficient H_i as a component of H is new.

5.1.8   *Definition of a scale*

Our coefficient of scalability as such will be our sole criterion of scalability. This enables us to discard the many additional and cumbersome criteria of scalability (see chapter 2, section 2.6.1) accompanying the more orthodox methods of Guttman scaling.

We saw in section 2.6.1 that in traditional methods of Guttman scaling, high values of the coefficients of scalability were required for a set of items to be considered a scale. For coefficients of type S_2 such as H, this value had to be higher than 0.50, which in practice proved to be a strong requirement for sets of more than five or six items. Sometimes lower values were used for sets of items which were then called quasi-scales. However, we have seen that the admission of "error" in a deterministic model immediately reduces our set of items to a quasi-scale, a stochastic model. Therefore any scale used in actual practice should be considered a quasi-scale, even when its H-value by far exceeds 0.50. For these reasons we shall avoid a terminological redundancy by using the term "scale" only.

We define a scale in simple terms:
a scale is a set of items which are all positively correlated and with the property that every item coefficient of scalability (H_i) is larger than or equal to a given positive constant (c).
From (2.53), section 4.2.3, we have:

$$\text{if } H_i \geqslant c > 0 \text{ for } i = 1, 2, \ldots, k, \text{ then } H \geqslant c. \tag{1.14}$$

From our foregoing analysis it is not clear why a requirement as strong as an H-value $\geqslant 0.50$ should be imposed on the data. We therefore propose to relax our requirements regarding the values of our coefficients.

On the other hand, we shall want a reasonable homogeneity for every item in our scale as measured by the item coefficient H_i. Of course, we could have imposed a still stronger requirement in terms of high H_{ij} values for every pair of items of the set. H_i as a measure of the overall homogeneity of item i with respect to the other $k-1$ items, however, seems to be a perfectly reasonable, if not an obvious choice. We shall choose $c = 0.30$ so that $\hat{H}_i \geqslant c; i = 1, 2, \ldots, k.$

We may nevertheless distinguish some degrees of scalability in terms of the overall coefficient H. Although an empirical basis for this distinction is still lacking, we can suggest the following classification of scales.

a. $0.50 \leq H$: a strong scale;
b. $0.40 \leq H < 0.50$: a medium scale; $\qquad$ (1.15)
c. $0.30 \leq H < 0.40$: a weak scale.

The concept of a strong scale corresponds to the original strong requirements for a Guttman-scale. The medium scale may well prove very useful in research. In fact even our weak scales may possess enough structure to be used in research with profit for the measurement of an underlying dimension.

It may also be important to investigate the holomorphism of a scale by checking the points mentioned in section 5.1.6.

5.1.9 *The significance of response patterns*

In perfect scales only perfect response patterns can occur. This main property of reproducibility led to a strong emphasis on the "perfect" response patterns in the case of "error" too. We saw in section 2.6.1 that even an additional criterion was suggested: the observed frequency of these "perfect" patterns had to be higher than expected under the hypothesis of independent response to items. Another example is that of Verba *et al* (1967), who reported a special analysis of these response patterns, using the procedures advocated by Stouffer *et al* (1952), which we consider needlessly complicated and cumbersome.

Again, in section 2.6.2 we saw how this exaggerated emphasis on "perfect" response patterns led to a number of procedures of classifying "imperfect" response patterns as "perfect" ones in order to determine the "proper" scores. We demonstrated in chapter 4 that these practices, which were the result of a too rigid adherence to the deterministic model, lacked all foundation. And in section 4.2.4, it was proved that only the extreme patterns (all responses positive or no responses positive) always occurred with probability (or frequency) higher than could be expected on the basis of random response (theorem 2.4.1). But no such property could be proved to exist for the other "perfect" patterns, as was demonstrated with a counter example. Even with a perfect scale, these intermediate perfect patterns can occur with a probability smaller than that expected under the null hypothesis of random response (total marginal independence).

In fact it was shown for holomorphic models that among the patterns characterized by the same score, the "perfect" pattern has the highest probability of occurrence, but this proved to be a weak property, as it is valid for total marginal independence too.

From these results we concluded that the example of table 2.5 of section 2.6.1 corresponded well to what could be expected for a scale. In fact we know from the statistical considerations referred to in chapter 3, that in the general case every response pattern contains specific probabilistic information concerning the subject values and item parameters. Only in the case of Rasch's model is this information conveyed wholly by a cruder statistic, the pattern score $s^{(\nu)}$. The interesting point is, however, that in this particular case too the "perfect" patterns are equivalent to the "imperfect" ones for purposes of measurement.

5.1.10   *The simple score*

When a set of items forms a satisfactory scale as described in section 5.1.8, we have to decide how to obtain measurements with it.

The classical procedure of using the simple score s as a means of obtaining ordinal measurements seems a reasonable one, if we do not use specific parametric measurement models of the types discussed in chapter 3. In section 5.1.4 we saw that the score s is a good estimate of the order of subjects, and in section 4.2.1 we showed that the simple score is positively correlated with the latent variate θ (see (2.13) and (2.14)) and that it may have better local discrimination than single items (see (2.3)). In this section we also pointed out that s will not usually be an optimal estimate even among linear combinations of the item responses.

Of course, the response patterns themselves (as minimal sufficient statistics) will in general be necessary for the measurement of subject values. Hence weighted linear combinations of the item responses bearing a 1–1 relation to the response patterns may have a higher correlation with θ. In the general case, however, such linear combinations, when optimal, will depend on the *unknown* value of θ or its equally *unknown* population distribution. Only in the logistic model of Birnbaum (see section 3.2.3) are such optimal scores obtained independently of the value of θ (optimal *uniformly* in θ). Again, only in the special case of the model of Rasch do these optimal scores coincide with the simple score s.

5.1.11 *Conclusion*

We must stress the fact that all the relations and properties described in the last chapter as being consequences of respectively monotone homogeneity and holomorphism are necessary but not sufficient conditions for homogeneity and holomorphism. This means that even when the parameters reproduce all the relations and properties mentioned, we are, strictly speaking, not entitled to conclude that homogeneous and holomorphic models are actually involved. This situation is not peculiar to our findings, for it is characteristic for virtually all the models in use. In practice we can seldom find a set of conditions that uniquely determine a model. Usually other models exist which will lead to the same set of conditions. The most we can usually do is to see whether our observations do not contradict the necessary conditions implied by the model.

It they do not contradict these conditions, we may assume the model to be valid for practical purposes.

It should moreover be noted that we did not prove all the possible relations and properties in chapter 3. Many more properties could have been obtained. For instance, in the investigation of moments in section 4.1, we kept to the time-honored tradition of analyzing first and second moments only. Many more results of the type of theorem 1.4.2 might have been obtained.

Our aim, however, was to find a number of related and simple properties which might serve as starting points for scaling procedures which are simple but capable of sorting the data in a reasonable way.

5.2 DESCRIPTION OF SCALING PROCEDURES

We are now ready to apply our findings in constructing a class of scaling procedures. These procedures will be based on the definition of a scale given in section 5.1.8 by substituting the estimates for the parameters. In spite of the essentially very simple structure of the procedures, practical applications would entail a vast amount of tedious calculation.

For this reason we designed the whole system in a form appropriate to computer processing.* In this form it was subsequently pro-

---

*Hofstetter, Boyd and Van Houweling (1967) recently pointed out the striking scarcity of programs for scaling procedures of this type:

"Despite the widespread use of the technique in attitudinal research, few computer programs are available that rapidly perform scalogram analyses for large numbers of cases, items and scales".

grammed for use on the Dutch Electrologica X-8 computer at the Mathematical Centre at Amsterdam.*

In our procedure we shall assume from the beginning that the data are dichotomous. We shall not discuss what in section 2.2.1 we called "one-sided dichotomization". This does not mean that this is un-important. Especially the "no opinion" and "no answer" categories, which harass every scholar who has to glean his data from observa-tions based on survey questions may still hold some unsolved problems very relevant to the way in which we transform our observa-tions into dichotomous data.

As one solution to the problem of dichotomization, we might have incorporated into our procedure a consideration of all possible dichotomizations, choosing those leading to an "optimal" scale.

Apart from the not too serious drawback that this approach would complicate and lengthen the procedure, we feel that relegating the problem of dichotomization to a more or less mechanical com-puter technique would result in a change process which could en-danger our interpretation of the scale. Hence we shall consign the responsibility for choosing dichotomies where it belongs: to the researcher who decides on the basis of item content. After construct-ing a scale, he may analyze the possible influence of "no-opinion" or "no-answer" responses as part of the validation of the scale.

The scalability of a set of items may be investigated from many angles and at different levels of analysis which may require different approaches and correspondingly different procedures. Most of these possibilities have been incorporated into our system of programs as options.

The most important alternatives are the following:

- *the evaluation of a set of items as one scale*; this will be the subject of section 5.2.1;
- *the construction of a scale from a given pool of items* (section 5.2.2);
- *multiple scaling*; the construction of a number of scales from a given pool of items (section 5.2.3);
- *the extension of an existing scale* by means of a larger pool of items (section 5.2.4);

*We owe many thanks to programmer Douwe de Jong of the Mathematical Centre for his programming of the system throughout its subsequent development. Copies of the Algol-60 program and the input and output descriptions can be obtained from the author.

— the investigation of the double monotony or holomorphism of a set of items (section 5.2.6);
— the computation of reliability coefficients; (section 5.2.7).

We shall sketch these procedures in the following sections.

5.2.1 *The evaluation of a set of items as one scale*

In most cases where the traditional techniques of Guttman scaling were applied, the researcher was supposed to have selected before-hand a set of k items which could be considered homogeneous with respect to some variable. With the aid of these techniques the *whole* set of items was then evaluated as just *one* scale. In the end some defective items were eliminated as a result.

This procedure offers no special difficulties within the framework of our theory. In terms of our definition of a scale of section 5.1.8, such an evaluation will be relatively simple: it will be based on the estimates of the item coefficients H_i and the scale coefficient H and a considera-tion of the intercorrelation of all item pairs.

Such an evaluation can take place at two levels of statistical analysis.

I. Testing against the criterion of random response (marginal independence)
First we compute the values of the estimates:

$$\hat{H} = \frac{\sum_{i=1}^{k-1} \sum_{j=i+1}^{k} [\hat{\pi}_{ij} - \hat{\pi}_i \hat{\pi}_j]}{\sum_{i=1}^{k-1} \sum_{j=i+1}^{k} [\hat{\pi}_i (1 - \hat{\pi}_j)]} \tag{2.1}$$

$$\hat{H}_i = \frac{\sum_{j=1; j \neq i}^{k} [\hat{\pi}_{ij} - \hat{\pi}_i \hat{\pi}_j]}{\sum_{j=1; j \neq i}^{k} \hat{\pi}_{ij}^{(0)}}; \text{(see (1.8))}. \tag{2.2}$$

A test of these observed values against the null hypothesis of indepen-dence may be effected by performing separately the one-sided test based on the statistics $\underline{\Delta}^*$ and $\underline{\Delta}_i$ treated in section 4.3.2 (see (3.16) and (3.17)). We may reject the items with $\hat{H}_i$-values which are negative or not significantly different from zero by these one-sided tests or smaller than the scale-defining constant c (0.30 in what follows). An inspection of the intercorrelation of all item pairs should show that no pair of items is negatively correlated.

Finally, the hypothesis of scalability may be rejected for the whole set of items when its H-value proves to be not significantly higher than zero according to the test. An example of this analysis will be given in chapter 7, sections 7.1.2 and following.

II. Estimating population values for a population
The specific problem is to give confidence intervals for the *population* coefficients H and H_i as estimated with our *sample* coefficients $\hat{H}$ and $\underline{\hat{H}}_i$ at a given level of confidence $(1 - \alpha)$. The theory and methods are given in section 4.3.3 and need not be reiterated here.

Once the scale has been applied, it may still be corrected by eliminating items whose *population* coefficients are likely to be lower than the scale-defining constant c (say 0.30), *i.e.* coefficients whose confidence intervals contain values lower than c.

This last practice, however, which implies that the confidence interval for any population item coefficient H_i should contain only values larger than c, requires all *sample* coefficients H_i to be correspondingly larger than c. In our system of programs the statistical procedures of this second type have been incorporated into a separate program. The reader will find some applications in chapter 8, sections 8.1 and 8.2.

5.2.2   *Constructing a scale from a pool of items*

In section 5.2.1 the scaling problem was to evaluate directly a set of items as one scale. It will be clear that this approach presupposes a good deal of confidence in the scalability of the set of items concerned, based on prior experience and knowledge concerning the interrelation and meaning of the items and the variable we want to measure. Without such prior knowledge and insight it would not make much sense to use this approach on a set of items. In that case we may be primarily interested in the exploration of the homogeneity of a pool of items which on the basis of their content alone are thought to be more or less homogeneous. From this pool we must select a set of items, as large as possible, which satisfies our scale criteria and which may be used for the ultimate measurement of our variable.

Apart from the statistical criteria used, the general structure of this problem is a familiar one in statistical methods aiming at the optimal selection of k variables from a larger pool. In theory this problem is very simple for given k: we inspect all possible k-tuples from the pool and select the best one. In practice this problem cannot be dealt with by even a computer, because astronomically large numbers of k-tuples are often involved. We therefore have to settle for a method which, though not necessarily optimal, at least guarantees a reasonable scale.

Several authors have proposed exploratory methods of item analysis in some form of cluster analysis. Toby and Toby (1954) reported an idea attributed to Stouffer, which was based on an analysis of the cross-tabulation of all item pairs. Loevinger (1945, 520) suggested a cluster analysis based on the H_{ij} for all item pairs, an idea reiterated by Matalon (1965, 58). Several procedures of item analysis have been advocated, *e.g.* an analysis on the lines of Likert-procedures which started with equal-appearing interval techniques based on judgments and ended with a scalogram analysis. (The scale discrimination technique (Edwards and Kilpatrick, 1948; Edwards, 1957, 201–19)).

The method developed here aims at a rather straightforward maximization of $\hat{H}$ in terms of the definition of a scale given in section 5.1.8. It consists of a step-wise technique of constructing a scale from a given set of items. A value for the defining constant c is chosen (*e.g.* 0.30 in most applications). The analysis then proceeds from the cross-tabulations (2×2)-tables) for all item pairs.

The procedure begins with the choice of a "best" item *pair*: the pair of items which satisfies the following criteria:

1. Its coefficient $\hat{H}_{ij}$ differs significantly from zero at a selected level of confidence, according to the one-sided test ($H_{ij} > 0$) based on the statistic $\underline{\Delta}^*$ from (3.16) in section 4.3.2.

2. Its coefficient $\hat{H}_{ij}$ is the highest of all item pairs which satisfy condition 1.

To ensure unicity and the closure of the algorithm required by the computer, for the case in which item pairs are equally eligible we choose the item pair containing the smallest item number (in the order of sample difficulties: $i < j \Rightarrow n_i \leqslant n_j$). If a unique pair can still not be determined, the item pair which is smallest in the other item index is chosen.

After the choice of an "optimal" item pair in the *first* step, *single* items are added to the scale in the steps that follow. *I.e.* in the *second* step another item is selected from the remaining set of items and added to the chosen pair of items, if it satisfies conditions (3)–(8) listed below. In the *third* step a fourth item is added to the chosen triplet and so on.

In general we may describe the recursive process of adding an item to a scale as follows.

Let a set of r-1 items be selected for our scale in r-2 steps. Then we may from the remaining set of items add an r-th item (i_r) to our scale if it satisfies the following conditions ($r \geqslant 3$).

3. The r-th item (i_r) should correlate positively ($\hat{\pi}_{i_r j} > \hat{\pi}_{i_r}\hat{\pi}_j$; "error" frequency smaller than expected under marginal independence) with each item j of the r-1 selected items. As a consequence an item that correlates negatively with any of the r-1 items already selected will be left out of further consideration in the consecutive steps for the construction of the scale at hand. This requirement follows from the condition of positive correlation of all item pairs stated in section 5.1.8.

4. Its coefficient $\hat{H}_{i_r}$ with respect to the selected r-1 items should be significant at a selected level of confidence according to the one-sided test based on the statistic $\underline{\Delta}_i^*$ from (3.17) in section 4.3.2.

5. Its coefficient $\hat{H}_{i_r}$ with respect to the selected r-1 items should be larger or equal to the scale-defining constant c (*e.g.* 0.30). Conditions 3, 4 and 5 determine the set of items that are admissible in terms of our definition of a scale. The following conditions ensure the choice of the best item from this set and the unicity of this choice.

6. The scale consisting of the r-1 selected items and item i_r should have the highest value $\hat{H}$ among scales consisting of these r-1 items and one item that also satisfies conditions (3), (4) and (5).

7. If no unique choice is possible, because several items fulfilling conditions (3), (4) and (5), have equal maximal $\hat{H}$-values, then the item i_r is chosen which has the highest H_{i_r}-value with respect to the r-1 selected items.

8. If more than one item can still be chosen which satisfies conditions (4), (5), (6) and (7), then the item with the lowest item number (in the order of sample difficulties: $i < j \Rightarrow n_i \leqslant n_j$) is chosen; this guarantees a unique choice.

The procedure continues to add items to the scale as long as there are items in the remaining pool of items which satisfy conditions (3), (4) and (5).

Hence this search procedure stops:

a. when there are no more items in the remaining pool satisfying conditions (3), (4) and (5) or

b. when there are no more items available or when there are no more items eligible in terms of condition (3).

At the end of the procedure, we may evaluate the resulting scale by means of one of the methods mentioned in section 5.2.1 and by inspecting the items with regard to their content. In the programmed system, the final scale is submitted to the test of method I, by testing the overall H and the item coefficient H_i against the null hypothesis of marginal independence. Examples are given in chapter 6, section 6.6, and chapter 8, sections 8.1.2 and 8.3.

A few qualifications should be made.

In the first place the selection of the items takes place mainly in terms of conditions (3), (4) and (5), *i.e.* the items are selected with coefficients $\hat{H}_i$ of at least 0.30. The procedure as it is programmed does not recheck the coefficients $\hat{H}_i$ of the items already selected in the scale in previous steps. Because of the closure of the algorithm, the program always ends. However, in the final scale some of the items selected in the scale in previous steps may have item coefficients $\hat{H}_i$ somewhat smaller than c. In order to evade loops in the program (two items continually being adopted in the scale and rejecting each other again) we did not try to eliminate this relatively rare phenomenon. It can be corrected by inspecting the scale and rejecting the items, whose coefficients $\hat{H}_i$ are smaller than c. In theory it is even possible for so many item $\hat{H}_i$ coefficients to drop below c that the final scale value $\hat{H}$ appears to be smaller than c. In actual practice, however, the possibility seems so small as to be negligible. To the knowledge of the author at the time of writing this never occurred during the many runs which the program was put through. In the many cases where scales were produced, the method resulted in scales in the sense of our definition of section 5.1.8.

As a second remark we repeat the statement made at the beginning of this section: as is always the case in step-wise "maximization" procedures in multivariate analysis, our procedure does not necessarily produce an *optimal* scale, even in terms of our defining criteria. It will, however, produce reasonable or even good scales, which after all is something of value.

Finally, we want to stress the point that our definition of a scale (section 5.1.8) is simply a mathematical one. It does not guarantee any operational relation to an underlying variable, or, in other words, it does not guarantee validity. In the same way, our procedure of scale construction, being based on this definition, is nothing but an algorithmic device for the constructing of scales in conformance with this definition. Hence it cannot be a substitute for a theoretically meaningful analysis of the value of the instruments for social research. It does not eliminate the need for a final intuitive, theoretical and common sense evaluation of the scale and its items on the basis of their content. The final value of the scale stems not from its internal consistency, but from its construct validity: from the theoretical significance of the way in which the scale relates the variable it is supposed to measure to other variables in a broader operational context.

5.2.3   *Multiple scaling*

In the last section we dealt with a situation in which one could construct a pool of items which were all considered to be homogeneous with respect to a certain dimension. From this pool all the items suitable for a scale were selected for the measurement of this dimension. However, we may not be sure that only one dimension is involved in the area of content which we are trying to cover. We may be prepared to make allowances for the existence of more than one dimension or variable and hence for the existence of one or more corresponding scales.

We may then use the procedure described in section 5.2.2 repeatedly as follows. The procedure starts with the selection of items for the first scale. After the selection of this scale, the *remaining* pool of items, including the items that were rejected on condition (3) are subjected to the same procedure once more for the purpose of selecting a second scale; this process is repeated until no more scales can be found.

This procedure of *multiple scaling* merely entails the repeated application of the procedure of section 5.2.2 to the diminishing residual set of items which remains when the items allocated to the first, second and following scales have been removed. Consequently, items that are assigned to a certain scale at some stage of the procedure will not be considered for the construction of scales to be formed at later stages. Yet some of the items allotted to earlier scales may fit other scales constructed at later stages just as well. If, therefore, the scales had been formed in a different order than that defined by the algorithm, the resulting scales would perhaps have contained different items.

The item coefficient $\hat{H}_i$ defined in this study (see 2.2), gives us the opportunity of building some controls into our set of procedures. These controls allow us to evaluate each item with respect to each of the scales produced, by means of the item coefficient belonging to this scale. When a given scale has been produced, the procedure gives, for the remaining items *and* for the items allotted to the earlier scales the item coefficients with respect to this scale. In this way a comparison of item coefficients *between* scales is also possible in terms of our coefficient H_i. In chapter 9, sections 9.3 and 9.4, we shall give examples of how the results of our multiple scaling procedure can be evaluated with the help of these item coefficients. Procedures of multiple scaling, by means of which "unidimensional" scales are produced one after the other by a repeated application of a scaling procedure to a diminishing set of residual items may be contrasted with methods of multidimensional scaling of a metric (*e.g.* factor analysis; see Torgerson, 1958, 247–97) or non-metric nature (Guttman, 1968; Kruskal, 1964 a and b; Shepard, 1962 a and b). In methods of the latter type, items (stimuli) are evaluated simultaneously on all the dimensions defined in terms of a special model.

Methods of multiple scaling or cluster analysis have been criticized because of the fact that in multiple scaling an item is allotted to one and only one scale (or cluster), whereas in multidimensional techniques an item can be evaluated against all the dimensions (or clusters). For instance, Alker and Russett (1965, 28–30) seem to use arguments of this type against multiple scaling in their defense of the use of factor analysis in the field of roll call analysis. It is clear that this is not a valid argument, because in our version of multiple scaling an item can be related to all the scales by means of our item coefficient.

5.2.4 *Extending an existing scale*

Once a scale has been found and has demonstrated its usefulness in research, it may be worthwhile to develop and extend it further in subsequent research. In the explorative phases referred to in the last two sections, a final scale often consists of only a few, say four to six, items. Our insight into the scale and its theoretical and empirical referents may enable us to invent or collect new items for other investigations. We may then try to extend and improve the old scale by adding these new items, with the purpose of varying difficulty levels for better discrimination.

We may then use a modification of the procedure of section 5.2.2. Instead of beginning with the selection of the initial best pair of items, we may at once select the old validated or accepted set of items for a scale and add new items on the lines given in section 5.2.2. In this way the original scale is enlarged by the addition of those items from the pool of new items which satisfy conditions (3)–(8) of this section. An example will be given in chapter 8, section 8.1.1.

5.2.5   *Selecting a level of confidence*

In the procedure sketched above, a number of statistical tests are performed at each step, on the outcome of which the ultimate selection of an item in this step will depend. In doing so, we are continually committing the mortal sin called by statisticians "capitalizing on chance". This sin consists in the rearranging of results that are purely the product of chance, until something statistically significant is produced; its penalty is that results will be obtained which have a very low probability of being repeated in other trials.

There are several ways of guarding against the risks of "capitalizing on chance". One of them is to replicate the analysis in a new experiment to see whether the same results are found.

This replication may be achieved by splitting the sample of subjects randomly into two halves, constructing the scales on the one half and testing them on the other half. This procedure was used in an application of an earlier version of the author's scaling procedure (Smolenaars, 1968). It does, however, have its drawbacks. Due to the reduction of the size of the sample, the power of the tests is reduced and the estimates are consequently less accurate.

In the present procedure the author has therefore tried to moderate the effects of possible chance results by a continual reduction of the level of confidence in consecutive steps. Although this procedure was inspired by a method used in the construction of slippage tests (Doornbos, 1966, 1966, 11–9; 54–5), it should be stressed that our procedure of fixing the level of confidence (α) in each step at a lower level is a probably reasonable but more or less arbitrary way of reducing α by decreasing it constantly throughout the consecutive steps.

The procedure is as follows:
1. One general level of confidence α (typically 0.05 or 0.01) is chosen.
2. Let there be an initial pool of r items. Then the test for the selection of the first "outlying" pair of items is performed at the level of confidence:

$$\frac{\alpha}{\frac{1}{2}r(r-1)} \tag{2.3}$$

the denominator indicating the number of co nparisons involved.
3. After the elimination of items on the basis of condition (3), let the remaining pool of items consist of k_2 items.
Then the tests necessary for the selection of the third item are performed at level of confidence:

$$\frac{\alpha}{\frac{1}{2}r(r-1)+k_2} \tag{2.4}$$

4. In general, let l items be selected for the scale, k_1 items being retained in the remaining pool (after elimination by condition (3)). The tests necessary for the selection of the $(l+1)$-th item are then computed at confidence level:

$$\frac{\alpha}{\frac{1}{2}r(r-1)+\sum_{j=2}^{l} k_j} \tag{2.5}$$

5. In the construction of more than one scale, as described in section 5.2.3, we proceed as follows. Let l_1 items altogether be selected in the first scale, so that $r-l_1$ items remain in the pool for the construction of other scales.

The procedure for the second scale entails the selecting of confidence levels in exactly the same way, starting with the new value $r-l_1$ for r in (2.3).

For further scales the confidence levels are determined in a strictly analogous way.

It is hoped that these probably strong requirements concerning the confidence levels will mitigate the effects of manipulating chance results. In our applications, these requirements have not prevented the construction of scales for even relatively small samples.

A further safeguard consists in testing the scale according to one of the methods described in section 5.2.1 in any new application of a scale.

5.2.6   *Investigating double monotony*

As was stated in section 5.1.6, the investigation of holomorphism or double monotony can be performed with the help of the $\hat{\Pi}$ and $\hat{\Pi}^{(0)}$ matrix for the set of items. In the programmed system these matrices are always given for a scale when it is completed. Examples are given in chapter 8, section 8.4.

5.2.7   *Reliability coefficients*

The reliability coefficient for any scale may be computed by means of the two methods given in section 4.2.2. For the $\hat{\Pi}$ matrix, the diagonal elements are estimated with each of the two methods and the reliability coefficient is computed directly on the scale itself at its full length. The application of these methods presupposes some confidence in the holomorphism (double monotony) of the set of items concerned. We shall give examples in chapter 8, section 8.5.

5.2.8   *The effects of the order of selection*

We saw in the preceding sections that in the process of scale construction, items are selected for the purpose of forming a scale in consecutive steps. The order in which they are selected is determined by the step-wise algorithmic procedure sketched above. Consequently this order in itself is part of the definition of the final scale(s) produced by the procedure and may sometimes determine the outcome in a very specific way. For instance, starting the procedure in a different way (*e.g.* with another set of items instead of the "best" pair, as in section 5.2.4) may sometimes lead to a different order of selection and possibly to an entirely different final scale.

Such effects are not peculiar to our scaling procedure. They are to be expected in other processes of step-wise selection of pseudo-optimal sets of variables such as tree analysis and step-wise regression, where the order of selection is a defining element.

For these reasons we should also analyze critically the outcomes produced by such procedures. For instance, the first "best" pair of items selected for starting the procedure may dominate the resulting scale, as it is the pair with the highest association. Sometimes such a pair is highly untypical from some theoretical point of view, and may seriously bias the final results. For this reason it may occasionally be necessary to guard against a particular pair of items playing such a dominant role. In applications of our procedure we have occasionally been forced to start with other pairs of items, using the procedure of section 5.2.4, in order to prevent an atypical pair from biasing the determination of the resulting scale. An example is given in chapter 9, section 9.2.

The order in which items are added to a scale may occasionally give us other information as well. For instance, items that are added last to the scale may not be the best ones. They may be less "robust" (see section 8.4 of chapter 8) or may disturb the double monotony of the scale (see section 8.4).

The order of selection also determines the final scales produced by our procedure of multiple scaling. In section 5.2.3 we already mentioned the fact that items, once they are allocated to a certain scale, do not play a role in the construction of later scales, although they might have fitted one of these later scales just as well. Consequently, if we had followed another order of scale construction, starting, for instance, with one of the later scales (see section 5.2.4), this scale might have collected other items and the final results might have been quite different. The method of comparison of item coefficients between scales referred to in section 5.2.3 may serve as an analytic tool for investigating and evaluating the outcomes of our multiple scaling program from this point of view as well. The reader will find some examples in sections 9.3 and 9.4 of chapter 9.

PART II

Applications in political research

CHAPTER 6

Cross-cultural comparison: the discovery of dimensional identity

In the following chapters we shall illustrate the scaling theory developed in the first part of this study with a number of examples taken from the research of the author. The first two chapters of part II will consist mainly of the results of some comparative analyses of a cross-national nature. Our purpose is to suggest the utility of cross-cultural comparative analyses of the scalability of sets of items in searching for common dimensions.

Methods such as factor analysis and scale analysis are particularly suitable for discovering such dimensions. Establishing certain dimensions for any given nation, community or culture is, however, not enough for purposes of comparative analysis. Duijker and Frijda, stating that the comparison of objects amounts to an ordering along a common dimension, conclude that *dimensional identity* is a necessary condition for comparability across cultures (1960, 138). In this and the next chapter we shall report some attempts to establish such dimensional identity for some cross-national data.

6.1 ON CROSS-CULTURAL COMPARISON

Cross-cultural analysis as a means of collecting evidence of a very general nature in the social sciences is almost as old as the sciences themselves. Ethnographers and cultural anthropologists, because of the nature of their discipline, were the pioneers in this field, as is demonstrated by one of the older references (Whiting, 1954). Their early efforts dominated methodological investigations to such a degree that Whiting could still write of *the* cross-cultural method. In a recent review, Berrien (1967, 34), acknowledging their pioneering role in the field, points out that psychologists are relative newcomers in this province of comparative analysis. The same statement may be made with reference to the advent of cross-cultural research in other fields of social research such as mass communications research and political research. The increasing influx of methods from other disciplines into the area of cross-national research since the fifties has greatly enlarged both the scope and the variety of methodological investigations compared to those encompassed by *"the"* cross-cultural method discussed by Whiting.

An early discussion of the outlook for cross-national research distinguished three principal types of comparative cross-national analysis: *field and laboratory* studies, *documentary* studies, and *current statistics* studies, and predicted the significant rise of especially the first type of study (Duijker and Rokkan, 1954, 11); the cross-national field studies of the last decade in particular have more than fulfilled this prophecy.

It is not our purpose to give a general review of cross-cultural methodology (see *e.g.* Duijker, 1955; Duijker and Frijda, 1960 (Chapter VIII); Almond and Verba, 1963 (Chapter II); Frijda and Jahoda, 1966). Our purpose will mainly be to indicate where the research reported here might fit in the methodological arsenal of cross-cultural analysis.

In cross-national research two approaches may be distinguished.

The *first* we may call the *direct* approach. Researchers search for answers to their substantial problems by means of a direct comparison of the answers to the questions, or to the scores on indices and other variables which they have collected in different national or cultural contexts.

This fairly straightforward method is often chosen quite consciously, in spite of the many linguistic, semantic and other risks inherent in the comparison of what are sometimes widely different cultural systems.

The problem of translation clearly brings out these risks in disciplines which depend on culturally-loaded terms to convey observational information, because of their reliance on verbal techniques of observation. Even in the case of cross-national comparison across cultural sub-systems, the researcher may encounter pitfalls of this type.

This direct approach has led to a general emphasis on the importance of standardization in most reviews of cross-cultural methodology. This emphasis is, for instance, implicit in an early definition of cross-national research as

"..... *research undertaken for comparative purposes on the same categories of data across several different national populations or equivalent sections of different national populations"* (Duijker and Rokkan, 1954, 9).

In other contexts the terms "cross-national" and "cross-cultural" have been used more loosely, "cross-national" usually denoting a comparison of western nations and "cross-cultural" denoting a comparison of non-western populations. Because the methodological problems involved in "cross-national" and "cross-cultural" or even "intra-cultural" comparative research are not fundamentally different as Frijda and Jahoda (1966, 110) note, we may follow them in using the general term "cross-cultural" as we think fit.

The necessity of standardization with its accompanying problems and the experiences with the early cross-national surveys led to a special stress on equivalence in methods of data collection, *e.g.* equivalent sampling designs, equivalent arrangements of interview situations, and linguistic or semantic equivalence in question wording and interview design.

Especially the last problem, that of linguistic equivalence, was greatly emphasized and led to the invention and application of ingenious practices such as using bilingual individuals and translating verbal material back into the original language as a criterion of semantic equivalence (Ervin and Bower, 1952; Jacobson, 1954; Jacobson, Kumata and Gullahorn, 1960).

More recently it was realized that this direct approach, with its stress on the linguistic equivalence of verbal material and its elaborate standardization of methods of data collection, could be supplemented by a *second*, more *indirect* approach. In this approach a basis for comparative analysis could be sought in a cross-cultural comparison of specific interrelationships of sets of variables. Almond and Verba remark in the introduction to their five-nation study:

"The fact that a particular indicator has to be interpreted to some extent in terms of its context has led those interested in cross-national comparisons to stress, not direct comparisons of variables cross-nationally, but cross-national comparisons of the *pattern* of relations among variables" (Almond and Verba, 1963, 70).

This indirect approach may provide opportunities for using more sophisticated techniques of measurement and analysis to ensure some cross-cultural equivalence and validity. Procedures such as the use of bilingual individuals and the translating of verbal material back into the original language could at best guarantee some content validity. The application of methods based on the indirect approach might establish some construct validity cross-culturally as well.

At the same time this approach might occasionally allow a slackening of the very strong requirements imposed on cross-cultural analysis by rigid standardization.

In this and the next chapter we shall consider some examples of this indirect approach: the cross-cultural comparison of applied data models and their empirical outcomes.

We have seen that such data models may be used as measurement models to detect, define and measure uni- or multidimensional variables. Factor analysis and scaling methods are examples of models and techniques of measurement of this type, by which specific data structures and configurations are used as manifestations of "underlying" variables.

Their application in cross-cultural research, however, requires a positive answer to the basic question of the general existence of these structures in the set of cultures compared. Duijker and Frijda stress the point that the dimensions involved in comparative analysis cannot be imposed by *fiat*:

"Empirically speaking, it is unwarranted to posit *a priori* the existence of specific cross-cultural dimensional identities. They have to be discovered and validated" (1960, 151).

Thus far only factor analysis has been much used to discover such cross-cultural dimensional identities.

An early and well-known example of this type of comparison is the work of Osgood and his associates on the pan-cultural generality of his factor-analytically defined semantic space (Osgood, Suci and Tannenbaum, 1957; Osgood, 1964; Jakobovits, 1966). The research reported in this chapter is of a far more modest scope. We shall mention some results of a comparative analysis of the interest structure of newspaper readership in two American communities and a Dutch city based on the outcomes of three factor analyses performed in the studies involved.

We introduce these results mainly to illustrate the point that in different communities or nations, with very different methods and even strongly different theoretical starting points, essentially the same dimensions and data configurations may nevertheless be detected as a sign of dimensional identity. From this point of view our discussions will prepare the ground for a similar cross-national comparative analysis of the *scalability* of sets of items, a method far less common in cross-cultural methodology than factor analysis. This analysis will be the subject of chapter 7.

The results of the present chapter may serve a second purpose. Once certain dimensions have been detected by means of, for instance, factor analysis, we may want to design instruments to measure one or more of the newly found variables in intended research. This may be done, of course, by means of a factor analysis model which measures the variables in terms of factor scores. Another possibility is to design items that appear to be appropriate indicators for a particular dimension and to try to analyze them with some one-dimensional technique such as scale analysis. An illustration of this possibility will be the subject of section 6.6.

Although dimensional identity may exist in a cross-national context, the dimensions involved may be interpreted in a very different manner by different researchers. In his component analysis of ratings of readership interest in types of newspaper contents, the author found for a Dutch city a factor structure strongly akin to those reported independently by two researchers in different American communities. Each of the authors, as we shall see, labeled these structures in entirely different terms. In the following sections we shall recapitulate successively the results reported for Madison, Wisconsin, by Anast (1961), for Minneapolis, Minnesota, by Carter Jr. and Clarke (1963), and the related findings of our own research.

6.2 THE STUDY BY ANAST (MADISON, WISC.)

The study reported by Anast was intended to evaluate the public attitude towards the press in relation to specific types of news interest. Anast wanted to test the hypothesis that newspaper readers primarily interested in current issues of a controversial nature would be more critical of their newspaper than readers mainly interested in non-controversial news. We shall not go into the adequacy and interpretation of this hypothesis, which he subsequently verified. What is of importance here is that Anast performed a factor analysis on his readership interest ratings to see if the controversial and non-controversial dimensions of readership interest could be found. As Anast thus indulged in the often rather dangerous practice of applying factor analysis as an inductive technique which is particularly suitable for purposes of detection, with some firmly preconceived theoretical factors in mind, we need not be very surprised that he found these factors. We shall see in what follows that his interpretation of the factor structure may have been biased by this theoretical starting point.

6.2.1   *Method*

We shall report here only those details that may be relevant to our purpose. The data were collected by means of a questionnaire distributed to 241 residents of Madison, Wisconsin, chosen on a non-probability basis "with certain features of area sampling" (Anast, 1961, 377). The questionnaires were filled in by the respondents and collected a couple of days later. The survey was conducted in December 1958 and January 1959.

News interest was determined by means of a list of 130 statements which resembled newspaper headlines, except that they were longer, and which represented various types of news. The *controversial news* category comprised: foreign affairs, politics, economics – industry, columns – editorials, and education – social welfare. The *non-controversial news* category comprised: crime, society, comics, the world of entertainment, sports, religious, human interest, mishaps, natural disasters, science and health.

Each of the 130 items was rated by the respondent on a seven-point interest scale. For each of the news categories listed above a mean score was computed for each respondent. These scores were subsequently factor analyzed over the respondents.

6.2.2   *Results*

The results are given in table 6.1. In the report by Anast some rather essential data are missing. It seems natural to assume that in conformance with more or less universal practice the correlation matrix was factored according to the method of principal components followed by an orthogonal rotation to simple structure as defined by the normal-varimax criterion. It is less clear how many principal components were extracted or how many principal components were involved in the rotation. Because the ultimate factor structure is also determined by the dimension of the component-space involved in the rotation, this item of information is not unimportant. Also lacking is an indication of the percentage of variance "explained" by the space spanned by the four factors presented. Apart from these technicalities which are certainly not trivial, the factor structure presented in table 6.1 is quite interesting.

Anast (p.378) sees support for the existence of the controversial – non-controversial dichotomy in news interest in this factor structure, because factor II plainly contains most of his controversial items,

Table 6.1 Varimax-factor loadings of the Madison study*

Items	Varimax-factors			
	I	II	III	IV
Mishaps	**0.900**	0.023	0.072	0.116
Crime	**0.874**	0.009	0.044	−0.034
Natural disasters	**0.781**	0.179	0.077	0.183
Human interest	**0.775**	−0.050	*0.320*	0.062
Foreign	−0.079	**0.742**	0.122	0.164
Political	0.064	**0.828**	0.032	0.080
Economic	0.027	**0.853**	−0.066	0.009
Welfare – education	0.185	**0.510**	0.229	*0.305*
Scientific	0.211	*0.440*	−0.040	*0.471*
Society	*0.472*	−0.129	**0.592**	−0.079
Entertainment	0.243	0.145	**0.648**	0.190
Religious	*0.363*	*0.302*	*0.368*	0.029
Sports	*0.394*	0.111	−0.103	−0.250
Health	*0.309*	*0.373*	0.081	**0.582**
Columns	−0.049	*0.403*	*0.398*	−0.026
Comics	0.205	−0.212	*0.317*	0.043

*Source: Anast, 1961, 378.

factor I contains the bulk of the non-controversial items, and the rest of the items are distributed mainly over the other two factors. Quite apart from our view of Anast's theoretical input, we did not share his conclusions. The interpretation of factor structures is, of course, a highly subjective activity, often depending on the values of the loadings for a few critical items. In this case we think that the values of the loadings for "scientific" news items ("non-controversial") and for "columns" ("controversial") should have put Anast on his guard. The "non-controversial" category "scientific" has a higher loading on factor II (meant to be "controversial") than the "controversial" item "columns".

Inspection of the factor loadings of table 6.1 suggests another interpretation of the highly salient factors I and II.

Factor I, associated as it is with mishaps, crime, natural disasters, and human interest, suggests a dimension of interest in sensational news and reports which we may dub *human interest*.

Factor II is definitely associated with an interest in "serious" information about public affairs. We may therefore dub this factor *political interest*.

The other two factors are not clear-cut enough to hazard an opinion.

6.3 THE STUDY BY CARTER JR. AND CLARKE (MINNEAPOLIS, MINN.)

A similar approach was followed by Carter Jr. and Clarke (1963) in the Minneapolis area, although they started from an appreciably different theoretical point of view. Starting from research concerning the role of the community press as a local communication system reported by Janowitz (1952), and using content analyses of weekly newspapers and a subsequent investigation of, among other things, the relationships between news contents and readership interest, Carter and Clarke sought to analyse somewhat further the functions of urban weekly newspapers. They specifically tried to identify patterns of interest in *local news*, to assess preferences for different sources of local news and to interrelate these to certain other variables. Again we shall not go into their general findings, and report only the findings relevant to our purposes.

Carter and Clarke hypothesized in their study that interest in *local news*, the main focus of their study, may be structured into two independent factors: a *disruptive* and an *integrative* factor. "Disruptive" was meant to denote news describing events that indicate a temporary failure of social institutions or norms, whereas "integrative" news emphasized common community values and conveyed information about social organizations in which people cooperate in order to achieve objectives (Carter and Clarke, 1963, 549). In the same way as Anast, Carter and Clarke carried out a factor analysis armed with a firmly preconceived picture of the structure of readership interest, and not surprisingly saw their ideas confirmed.

6.3.1 *Method*

A probability sample of 237 respondents stratified according to residence in city or suburb was interviewed in a survey held in December 1961 in the form of a readership survey concerning the weekly local issue of an evening paper. Only interviewees who reported having read the previous evening's paper qualified as respondents.

The general focus was local news, defined as "news about this part of town or this suburb". The respondents were not handed copies of or statements concerning specific news items, but were given a description of the type of contents. Three types of *disruptive* news were mentioned: stories about crime and police activities, stories about accidents, and "stories about disputes or controversies involving your part of town (suburb)" (p. 549). In a similar way five types of *integrative* news were mentioned: meetings of clubs and organizations, street and highway improvements, local school affairs, accomplishments of people in the neighbourhood and high school sports. In addition a statement was made about local advertisements.

The respondents indicated their degree of interest on a three-point rating scale for each of the nine types of content. On these ratings a factor analysis was performed over the respondents.

6.3.2 Results

The results are given in table 6.2. Judging by the references, the whole factor analysis was done by hand: a centroid analysis was followed by an orthogonal rotation by hand to simple structure. No

Table 6.2 Factor loadings of the
Minneapolis study*

Items	Factors		
	I	II**	III
Crime	0.10	**0.75**	−0.15
Accidents	0.19	**0.77**	0.09
Clubs	**0.72**	0.02	0.02
Streets	**0.59**	0.18	0.09
Disputes	**0.66**	0.04	−0.27
Schools	**0.66**	−0.21	0.06
Accomplishments	**0.60**	0.15	0.01
Advertisements	**0.51**	0.21	*0.42*
Sports	**0.52**	−0.04	−0.26

*Source: Carter Jr. and Clarke, 1963, 550.
**Sign of loadings reversed.

further details are given. Again the factor structure is striking. Carter and Clarke regard their hypothesis concerning the existence of the two factors as confirmed. They note the deviant results for the "disputes" items, which were meant to be "disruptive" items but obtained high loading on their "integrative" factor I.

The interpretation of Carter and Clarke is not very convincing: they state that the "disputes" items must have been interpreted as an integrative type of news by the respondents.

"The phrase 'disputes and controversies' may have carried over-tones of civic betterment for people, suggesting to them such issues as larger schools, industrial promotion, and similar activities" (Carter and Clarke, 1963, 550).

We feel that the behavior of the "disputes" item is rather critical and rather detrimental to their theory of the structure of readership interest. If factor I corresponds to an interest dimension of general local sub-jects and problems, we may expect news items of a clearly disruptive nature such as disputes and conflicts to load high on this dimension.

We shall therefore give another interpretation. Despite the strongly different research context and especially the emphasis on local prob-lems, we believe that the two factors of readership suggested in the Anast study can nevertheless be detected in the Carter and Clarke study. Factor I is that of *political interest*, on which we should have predicted the high loading for "disputes" actually given by the data. Factor II seems to be the dimension of interest in sensational news which we dubbed *human interest*.

6.4   A DUTCH STUDY (AMSTERDAM, 1964)*

In the two studies summarized in the last two sections, we detected a striking common dimensional structure in the readership interest in the contents of newspapers. The discovery of this dimensional iden-tity, important for the analysis of news media, suggested a similar exploratory comparative analysis for the Netherlands for the purpose of investigating the possibility that this identity may be found to exist in a broader cross-cultural context.

*The research reported in this section is the result of a survey conducted during the university year 1963–1964 by students of political science as part of their course in mass communications at the Institute of Mass Communications ("Instituut voor Pers-wetenschap") of the University of Amsterdam. The research was directed and super-vised by Drs. F. Bergsma and the author.

On the basis of the data of the American studies, we though that it might also be possible to describe the interest structure of newspaper readership in terms of similar underlying, uncorrelated factors. We decided, however, to ban as much as possible any biasing considerations derived either from our own interpretation of this factor structure or from possibilities of further analysis suggested by our experiment, and to direct our full attention to an exploration of the interest structure of news categories which are representative as far as possible for the general composition of daily newspaper contents.

With an eye to subsequent analysis, it was decided to facilitate a possible validation of the factors by incorporating into the survey some variables which were likely to be relevant.

6.4.1 *Method*

We decided to confront respondents in the interview situation with copies of new items as realistic as possible within the context of a survey and taking into account the costs involved. First several hundred newspaper clippings were obtained from a sample taken from the national and regional press over the past year. These clippings were sorted out (the participating students acting as judges) into thirty news categories thought to be representative of general newspaper contents, and defined by explicit instructions followed by an introductory training of the students. To preclude an ambiguity that might lead to unreliable responses and interpretations in the analysis stage, only relatively clear-cut examples of these news categories were included. Because of the population to be studied, residents of Amsterdam, the selected items were confined to more general types of news, which were not clearly irrelevant to the interviewees (as local news about other parts of the country would have been).

We were forced by the requirements of the survey to limit the final design to 24 categories of news, where a few categories formed more or less obvious combinations. The 24 categories are given in table 6.3. The whole procedure, questionnaire and scales, were pre-tested in November 1963. The final field work, though starting in December of that year, took place mainly in January 1964, and resulted in 199 completed interviews from an original two-stage probability sample of 283 addresses drawn from the electoral register of Amsterdam.*

*For further details concerning the method of selection and presentation of the items and the sampling design we refer the reader to the appendix.

6.4.2   Results*

The summated ratings for the twenty-four categories of newspaper content were correlated. The resulting matrix of correlations was subsequently factor analyzed by means of the familiar procedure of principal components and a subsequent normal-varimax rotation of the selected number of first principal components.** The familiar stopping rule prescibing the extraction of all the principal components with eigenvalues of at least unity resulted in six principal components "explaining" about 66% of the total variance. A subsequent normal-varimax rotation of these six principal components resulted in the factor structure reported in table 6.3.

The results of table 6.3 seem rather satisfactory. The first two factors will be familiar to the reader by now. In factor I we recognize the factor "general political interest". The fact that "local news" loads high on this factor supports this interpretation, while the high loadings on this factor for the two informative "popular education" items "technology and science" and "humanities" do not seem to contradict it, as such items may well indicate or be associated with such a general type of interest.

Factor II also cannot be mistaken: it seems to measure the dimension we called "human interest". The four categories "crime", "disasters", "calamities" and "human interest" all have high loadings and hence are highly correlated with the "underlying" factor we constructed.

We found more evidence of a cross-culturally identical dimensional structure of readership interest in newspaper contents in at least two interest dimensions: a factor "general political interest" and a factor "human interest". We may therefore conclude that in spite of entirely different theoretical premises, and highly different designs, techniques of data collection and even methods of analysis, the results discussed here for two American cities and one Dutch city show clear evidence of at least two prominent, cross-culturally common, and uncorrelated factors defining part of the structure of readership interest. The interesting point is of course that, clear as the cross-cultural existence of these two factors may be, the theoretical interpretation of these factors in three different studies are highly divergent! Our opinion, as

*In this study we shall only report the findings of the factor analysis. Our results regarding the subsequent validation of these factors by means of a transformation to factor scores will be published elsewhere.

**The whole analysis was performed on the Dutch Electrologika X-1 computer of the Mathematical Centre at Amsterdam.

Table 6.3   Factor loadings of the Amsterdam study (1964)

Items	Varimax Factors					
	I	II*	III	IV*	V	VI*
Crime, trials	−0.05	**0.88**	0.04	0.09	−0.13	−0.01
Disasters, calamities	0.18	**0.77**	0.10	0.09	−0.05	0.08
Accidents	−0.05	**0.82**	−0.01	0.10	−0.04	0.08
Human interest	−0.09	**0.69**	−0.03	*0.44*	−0.05	−0.08
International politics	**0.83**	0.09	0.06	−0.03	0.03	−0.11
International trade & economics	**0.78**	−0.06	0.21	−0.18	0.10	0.12
National politics	**0.80**	0.06	0.08	−0.09	0.13	0.03
National trade & economics	**0.77**	0.08	0.13	−0.24	−0.02	0.24
Technology & science	**0.72**	−0.11	−0.01	0.21	−0.20	0.01
Humanities	**0.66**	−0.26	0.28	0.15	0.01	−0.04
Local news	**0.60**	0.24	0.11	0.20	0.05	0.09
Entertainment (shows, musicals)	0.13	*0.46*	**0.59**	0.07	−0.27	0.09
Theatre, literary reviews	*0.37*	−0.18	**0.73**	0.05	0.21	0.15
Concerts	*0.36*	−0.13	**0.58**	−0.03	*0.40*	0.03
Cinema	0.14	0.16	**0.69**	*0.36*	−0.07	0.00
Royalty	−0.19	0.22	0.19	**0.67**	0.17	0.21
Film stars (entertainment)	0.04	*0.39*	*0.30*	**0.68**	−0.14	−0.05
Other public personalities	**0.63**	−0.09	0.19	*0.42*	0.04	−0.08
Religion	*0.33*	−0.01	0.13	−0.01	**0.75**	−0.00
Sports	*0.38*	0.29	0.11	−0.19	**−0.60**	0.14
Strips, comics, serials	0.02	−0.02	0.12	0.09	−0.10	**0.77**
Advertisements	−0.09	**0.50**	−0.07	0.09	0.24	*0.46*
Home and household matters	*0.34*	0.17	−0.03	**0.57**	0.09	*0.39*
Health, medical news	*0.36*	*0.42*	0.08	0.11	0.01	*0.41*
Communalities	5.14	3.72	2.08	2.03	1.41	1.34

Explained variance: 15, 72; 66%.

*Sign of loadings reversed.

given above, is that these two cross-cultural common dimensions of interest can perhaps best be interpreted as "general political interest" and "human interest".

Apart from these two factors, the Amsterdam data give evidence of the existence of at least two additional dimensions of readership interest which could not be distinguished clearly in the American data. We have dubbed one of these additional factors "cultural interest" (factor III) because it seems to be related to entertainment in general. The fourth factor, which is related to interest in glamorous public personalities, we may dub "status interest" or "society interest".

Factors V and VI, though suggestive of some dimension, seem to be less clear cut.* In subsequent analyses we focussed part of our research on the first four factors and tried to obtain a battery of copies of news items which were purer for these four separate factors so that a still clearer description of the four-factor space might be made possible.

6.5   A SECOND DUTCH STUDY (AMSTERDAM, 1965)**

In our first study, mentioned in section 6.4, to which we shall refer as "the '64-study", further analyses focused our interest on the first four factors given in table 6.3. Measurements on these factors, which concerned professed interest for certain newspaper clippings, had proved to be useful in other research contexts which involved mass media such as television and radio.

We decided to improve our description and measurement of the readership interest structure in a subsequent research study.

6.5.1   *Method*

The method of presentation of the items was exactly the same as that for the '64-study: respondents were shown copies of newspaper clippings and were asked to indicate their interest in general for this type of newspaper contents on the same rating scale as was used in the first study. Twenty-four items were chosen altogether, six items for each of the first four factors constructed in the '64-study. We tried to obtain a still clearer factor structure by a selection of "purer" items on each factor. All in all twelve items from the '64-study were used.

---

*A more elaborate analysis of these results will be published elsewhere.

**The research reported in this section is part of a survey conducted during the university year 1964–1965 by students of political science as part of their course in mass communications at the Institute of Mass Communications ("Instituut voor Pers-wetenschap") of the University of Amsterdam. This research was directed and supervised by Drs. F. Bergsma and the author.

Four new items were used for our factor "general political interest", three new items for the factor "society interest" and five new items for the factor "cultural interest", so that all in all half the number of items used was new. The whole procedure was pre-tested in November 1964. Field work, starting in December, took place mainly in January 1965. In the end 234 completed interviews were obtained from an initial total of 288 addresses. The higher response percentage (81%) may partly be due to a call-back procedure considerably more intensive than two times after an initially successful visit.

The population definition and sampling procedure were exactly the same as in the '64-study. Amsterdam residents of 23 years of age or older, registered in the electoral register, were our subjects.

6.5.2 *Results*

Again the correlation matrix of the interest ratings for the twenty-four newspaper items was first factored into its principal components. The procedure, suggested by similar findings in the '64-study, was to postulate a four-factor model choosing an appropriate rotation within the space spanned by the first four principal components and not to follow the more or less conventional procedure of extracting all the principal components with eigenvalues exceeding or equal to one, and rotating these components within the space spanned by the set of these eigenvectors.

We thought it legitimate to give preference to the former procedure, because on both occasions it resulted in a clearly better factor structure.*

*Some remarks may be necessary to justify our choice. In the first place it is well known that factor loadings and hence the whole factor structure are dependent on the dimension of the space (the number of first principal components) within which rotation to simple structure takes place. This procedure (which involves the initial determination of all eigenvectors with eigenvalues larger than or equal to one) is based on a tradition going back to Thurstone, according to which the full dimension of the common factor space should be determined first. Only within that full space of common factors may an adequately chosen rotation reveal simple structure. Therefore in most applications the problem of simple structure is mainly a problem of rotation, the problem of the dimension of the common factor space (the problem of minimum rank) being quite a separate problem.

Without denying the utility of this common practice in many cases, one might, however, wonder whether one could not just as well re-define the problem of simple

The results are given in table 6.4, in which item content is also indicated. In this table we clearly recognize our four factors. Our efforts
to obtain a better description and measurement of that part of readership interest which was generated by these four factors were fairly
successful.

From the point of view of simple structure, our factor structure is
probably as good as we could wish, the items generally being pure in
one factor on which they load high, and showing low loadings on the
other three factors. A possible exception may be the "Audrey
Hepburn" item, which shows a relatively high loading (0.38) on the
factor "cultural interest".

Although the ordering of the factors (according to their communalities) is different from that of table 6.3, the general meaning of the
dimensions seems clearly the same. The four factors together explain
59% of the total variance. In view of the probably high unreliability
of the ratings, this is not too bad. We may therefore conclude that
readership interest may be described in part by four uncorrelated
(orthogonal factors:
- "general political interest"   (factor II);
- "human interest"   (factor I);
- "society interest"   (factor III);
- "cultural interest"   (factor IV).

6.6   A SCALE OF POLITICAL INTEREST

In the preceding sections we investigated a number of dimensions of
readership interest, one of which interested us particularly in further
research: the dimension of political interest. Having discovered this
dimension with the help of factor-analytic methods, we may consider
how we can devise an instrument consisting of items that are homogeneous on this dimension. We may then also pose the question what

---

structure in such a way as to *include* simultaneously the determination of the dimension
of the common factor space.

One could then choose the combination of a particular dimension (number of first
principal components) and particular analytic rotation which produces the most satisfactory factor structure from the point of view of the essentially intuitive idea of simple
structure.

At any rate, besides the fact that we started with a four-factor problem, a normal
varimax rotation of the first four principal components resulted in a clearer factor structure than rotations performed in spaces spanned by higher numbers of principal components. Therefore, we chose that solution.

Table 6.4 Factor loadings of the Amsterdam study (1965)

Items	Varimax factors			
	I*	II*	III*	IV
Traffic accident	**0.81**	−0.02	0.19	0.14
Murder case	**0.76**	−0.05	0.28	−0.05
Roadside accident	**0.82**	−0.08	0.18	0.10
Trial for fraud	**0.82**	−0.01	0.14	−0.00
Railroad disaster	**0.80**	0.05	0.07	−0.07
Hurricane with high death toll	**0.71**	0.21	0.08	0.12
Role of France in Nato (n)**	−0.02	**0.80**	−0.06	0.22
Culture of the Aztecs	−0.12	**0.63**	0.04	0.20
Modern technology	−0.03	**0.67**	0.11	−0.01
Wage negotiations with the government (n)	0.18	**0.65**	−0.13	0.01
Marathon session of the EEC council (n)	0.07	**0.76**	0.07	0.17
Red summit in Moscow (n)	0.07	**0.84**	−0.01	0.04
Audrey Hepburn (n)	0.10	0.01	**0.65**	*0.38*
Ponti-Loren wedding	0.18	0.03	**0.66**	0.19
Princess Irene and Don Carlos (n)	0.15	0.02	**0.76**	−0.02
Lord Snowdon	0.12	0.11	**0.64**	0.26
Farah Diba and Fabiola	0.11	−0.14	**0.81**	0.20
Lyndon Johnson (n)	0.17	0.01	**0.76**	0.05
Yehudi Menuhin recital	−0.14	0.11	0.18	**0.70**
Italian opera performance (n)	0.07	0.07	0.01	**0.67**
Musical "My Fair Lady" (n)	0.19	0.02	*0.32*	**0.68**
Visconti motion picture (n)	0.10	0.22	0.14	**0.64**
Theatre: Look Back in Anger (n)	−0.04	0.18	0.12	**0.81**
Dutch cabaret (n)	0.22	0.04	0.17	**0.58**
Communalities	4.04	3.38	3.51	3.26

Explained variance: 14.19; 59%.

*Sign of loadings reversed.
**New items are indicated by (n).

measurement model can be used. Of course, we could again use our factor analysis model to measure the general variable we have in mind.*

On the other hand we might consider whether our scaling model could be used. At this juncture we may add a few remarks concerning the relation between factor analysis and scale analysis. Guttman (1950 c, 191–205) showed that there is no immediate and clear mathematical relation between the model of factor analysis and that of scale analysis which ensures the scalability of a set of items which load high on a given factor.

For the dichotomous data for which our scaling model applies, a factor analysis of the inter-item correlation matrix will usually give more than one factor even when there is just one underlying variable.** In these cases, a well-known and frequent empirical finding is that such factors often correspond with different difficulty levels of the items.†

One reason for this discrepancy between the two models is that factor analysis presupposes the use of *quantitative* data, whereas scale analysis is designed for *qualitative* data, and in this study is even used for dichotomous data. Loevinger, who developed a theory of cumulative scales too, also indicated that factor analysis and scales (homogeneous tests) were quite different things, remarking:

"There is no reason to suppose that the factor analysis of tests helps directly in the composition of 'pure' tests" (1948, 523).

The factor analyses reported in the preceding section were, however, performed under different circumstances. Responses to items were of a pseudo-numerical nature, as they were based on seven-point rating scales. Apart from the difficult problem of the *mathematical* interrelation of the two models, we may investigate the *empirical* question whether dimensions found by such an application

---

*In this case, if we have good "pure" items that are homogeneous on the variable concerned, we may define the first principal component of the matrix of inter-item correlations (the diagonal containing estimated communalities) as measuring that variable. This amounts to a general factor model.

**These results also depend on the type of correlation coefficients used. But even when, as is usually the case, tetrachoric correlation coefficients are used, postulating normal distributions which are dichotomized by the items, a factor analysis will reveal just one common factor only under very special conditions and assumptions (Lord and Novick, 1968, 382).

†A comparison of one scale analysis made with our procedure and the results of a factor analysis of this type led to the identification of two such "difficulty" factors, referring to two levels of difficulty in the set of items used.

of factor analysis to pseudo-numerical response values may subsequently be scaled using well selected and properly dichotomized items.

For a study of opinion leadership in mass communications with respect to the diffusion of political information, we decided to design a scale of interest in general political information based on the dimension discovered in the preceding sections, using news items in the form of newspaper clippings.* Respondents were shown eleven clippings and asked to indicate on a rating scale how often they read news of that type. After a proper dichotomization ("always or nearly always" or "often" forming the scale alternative), a scale analysis was performed using the procedure proposed in section 5.2.2, the results of which may be seen in table 6.5, where the items are given in the conventional order of their difficulties.

For reasons of space we shall not give the literal texts of the

Table 6.5   Scale of political interest (10 items) (Sample of male Amsterdam voters) n = 269

News Item	Sample difficulty	Item coefficient $(\hat{H}_i)$
1. Nkrumah referendum Ghana	0·16	0·47
2. Amsterdam City Council on harbour (1)*	0·16	0·39
3. Local miscellanea (1)**	0·25	0·25
4. France and the Atlantic alliance	0·26	0·50
5. Soviet offer at disarmament conference	0·31	0·48
6. American-Russian "Berlin" talks	0·32	0·46
7. Amsterdam City Council on traffic policy (1)	0·33	0·38
8. Cabinet minister on wages and prices	0·38	0·36
9. Amsterdam building program (Bijlmermeer) (1)	0.40	0·36
10. Vietnam: U.S. offer to cease bombings	0.43	0.43
11. Fall of Marijnen cabinet	0.49	0.48

Coefficient of scalability: $\hat{H} = 0.43$.
*Local items indicated by (1).
**Non-scale item.

*The research reported in this section is part of a survey conducted during the university year 1965–1966 by students of political science as part of their course in mass communications at the Institute of Mass Communications ("Instituut voor Per-wetenschap") of the University of Amsterdam. It was directed and supervised by Drs. F. Bergsma and the author.

For further details concerning design and sample we refer the reader to section 9.1.2.

clippings, but shall confine ourselves to an indication of the nature of their contents. The set of items referred to news of different types, as may be judged from table 6.5. Nevertheless, except for one (local) item the set proved to form a medium scale ($\hat{H} = 0.43$).

From our factor analysis we found that items concerning local news loaded high on the factor "general political interest" (see table 6.3). The set of items in table 6.5 contained four items concerning local Amsterdam news.

Judging from table 6.5, most of the local items fitted the scale. For instance, the item concerning the building program in the Bijlmermeer polder (item 9), belonged to a type of local news which 40% of the (male) respondents said they read "often" or "always or nearly always" (sample difficulty 0.40) and which had an item coefficient $\hat{H}_9 = 0.36$, well above the lower bound defining the scale ($c = 0.30$).

One local item, 3, "local miscellanea", was excluded from the scale, as its item coefficient $\hat{H}_3 = 0.25$ did not reach the value of the lower bound (0.30). This may be due to the fact that this news item, which was type set in italics, formed part of a daily column usually devoted to topics of human interest.

In general the other ten items seem to scale reasonably.* In this case, therefore, we had some success in detecting with the aid of factor analysis, a dimension which could subsequently be isolated by scale analysis.

6.7   CONCLUSIONS

In the preceding sections we compared cross-culturally at a very low level of standardization ratings of readership interest.

The three studies involved differed greatly in design and data collection. The populations and sampling techniques were very different. The presentation of editorial categories was also very different. Translation problems were not dealt with. And, last but not least, the theoretical purposes underlying the studies were very different. Nevertheless, a comparison of the results of the three factor analyses showed clearly the cross-culturally common existence of at least two common factors: political interest and human interest. Even at this methodologically low and unstandardized level of cross-cultural analysis, the detection of common, theoretically meaningful under-

---

*An inspection of the holomorphism of the set led to some doubt concerning item 7, whereas the association of items 5 and 6 was higher than was expected from the trend. For an investigation of holomorphism see section 8.4.

lying variables occasionally seems possible. In the case of the Dutch studies, the description of readership interest was extended to include two other factors: "society interest" and "cultural interest", which, with adequate research designs, may be discovered in other countries as well.*

In the following chapter we shall see that such a comparative investigation of the cross-cultural existence of a certain dimension may also be performed in terms of our scaling model.

*Some remarks should be added about the methodological status of our procedure of comparing the results of the factor analyses considered in this study. In spite of the fact that in two cases (Anast's study and ours) the methods of factor analysis were highly similar (component analysis and normal varimax rotation) and that in the third case (Carter Jr. and Clarke) a related method was used (centroid and hand rotation), this status is rather low. In fact we did no more than inspect the outcomes. This method is far removed in sophistication from techniques of investigating factorial invariance in several populations that may be regarded as sub-populations selected from a larger population (see Ahmavaraa, 1954; Meredith, 1964a, 1964b). These techniques may be used to investigate the cross-cultural identity of a factor structure of the same set of items and therefore require a level of standardization which will seldom be achieved in even the strictest and best-planned research undertaken in the cross-cultural field. Even then milder methods of comparing factor structures in terms of milder criteria may be necessary, even in the case of sets of items that are cross-culturally fixed (see Pinneau and Newhouse, 1964). Still milder criteria may be necessary when, as may easily be the case, even the most thorough and strenuous efforts of standardization do not result in sets of items which may be regarded as identical or fixed cross-culturally. Therefore we shall reject the rigid principle of invariance as the sole criterion of comparability and propose the milder criterion of cross-cultural "robustness" in the following chapter.

CHAPTER 7

The cross-cultural robustness of scales: political efficacy

In the last chapter we saw that even at a very elementary unstandardized level of research, it is possible to obtain substantive results with a cross-cultural comparison by means of a factor analysis model. The same approach may be used with variables that are defined in terms of unidimensional scaling models. For our scaling model this approach entails investigating whether variables which are studied across several cultures correspond to similar scales for each of the cultures analyzed. This may very well *not* be the case. A set of items may form a good scale for one culture, and a set of similar items may fail to do so for another culture. In this case a cross-cultural comparison in terms of the variable measured by the set of items in question may be very precarious indeed.

Guttman already remarked, in discussing the relativity of attitudes:
"If a universe is scalable for one population but not for another population, we cannot compare the two populations in degree and say that one is higher or lower on the average than another with respect to the universe .... A similar consideration holds for comparisons in time" (Guttman, 1950a, 83).

Yet in other cases we may be more successful in establishing cross-culturally valid scales.

Almond and Verba refer in their study to a Guttman-type scale of "subjective political competence" as being valid across the nations involved, although one item apparently failed in Mexico due to language difficulties (Almond and Verba, 1963, 231–6). This is another argument in favour of using a cross-cultural comparison for our measurements.

Our general problem is, therefore, the same as that of chapter 6. Will the application of certain measurement models (factor analysis, scale analysis, etc.) to given sets of data lead to similar results for

224

different cultures? Do such data structures, in terms of which variables are defined, have the property of being alike in different cultural or national settings?

We may characterize this property by means of some appropriate term. "Invariance" does not seem the best term for describing the special type of cross-cultural equivalence which we are considering. It carries the implication of a (mathematical) strictness that no researcher will be prepared to use in his evaluation of this type of equivalence of the factor-analytic or scale structures that he is comparing in such different settings. Every researcher will be satisfied if they are approximately alike. We shall for that reason use the less strict term of the "robustness" of a scale: a scale (or a factor structure) is *robust* for a set of cultures or nations, when its structure is approximately the same for the cultures or nations concerned.

Wherein lies the utility of investigating the cross-cultural robustness of a scale? We may mention at least two ways in which such efforts may prove fruitful.

a. The establishing of the cross-national robustness of scales and other constructs may be regarded as evidence of a more general *validity* of these constructs. The variables involved therefore are more "fundamental" and provide a more reasonable basis for comparison within the framework of their robustness.

b. The property of robustness need not be defined in a cross-national context only; it may also be important in an intra-cultural context.

In 1962 a survey was held concerning the relation between religiosity and personality characteristics in the population of two new communities that were created by the land-reclaiming program in the Netherlands. The study showed that, according to an earlier scaling procedure which we had devised, a scale of conformity in religious behavior could be found for two religious groupings. In a third group, the orthodox Protestants, however, no such clear pattern could be found (Smolenaars, 1968).

As Frijda and Jahoda point out in their survey of cross-cultural research strategy:

"Cross-cultural comparisons may have to be supplemented by intra-cultural comparisons, in order to ascertain the intra-cultural variability due to variables which could not be controlled cross-culturally" (Frijda and Jahoda, 1966, 123).

Therefore, when a scale has proved to be cross-culturally robust within a nation, it may prove to be robust in a broader cross-national context as well. From the point of view of international comparison this may add some *instrumental* value to *intra-national* analyses of the robustness of data structures.

In this chapter we hope to illuminate these points with some research findings concerning a well-known scale, which is related to the Almond-Verba scale mentioned above. It measures the "sense of political efficacy".

7.1   DUTCH-AMERICAN COMPARISONS OF THE "SENSE OF POLITICAL EFFICACY"*

7.1.1   *Political efficacy: concept and scale*

The concept of the "sense of political efficacy" was introduced in 1954 by a research team from the Survey Research Center of the University of Michigan in a study reporting on a nation-wide survey covering voting behavior in the 1952 presidential election (Campbell, Gurin and Miller, 1954, 187–94). It was designed as a measure of the subjective sense of integration in the political system or, rather, the sense of being able to exercise a personal influence on the processes of this system. It was derived from the responses to five statements (items) with dichotomous response categories. The items were the following:

1. "Voting is the only way that people like me can have any say about how the government runs things." (Voting only way.) Positive alternative: "disagree".
2. "Sometimes politics and government seem so complicated that a person like me can't really understand what's going on." (Politics complicated). Positive alternative: "disagree".
3. "I don't think public officials care much what people like me think." (Officials don't care.) Positive alternative: "disagree".
4. "People like me don't have any say about what the government does." (Don't have say). Positive alternative: "disagree".
5. "The way people vote is the main thing that decides how things are run in this country." (Vote main thing.) Positive alternative: "agree".

Because the repeated reference to these items in what follows calls

*This section is a revision of a paper presented at the International Conference on Comparative Electoral Behavior, Ann Arbor (Mich.), April 5–8, 1967, and subsequently published (Mokken, 1969a, 1969b).

for some abbreviation, we have tried to label them (as indicated in parentheses) in a way that suggests their content.

In the Michigan study, this set of items was subjected to a scale analysis based on the Guttman model with some modifications as proposed by Jackson (Jackson, 1949). The procedure required the identification for each item of the response alternative considered to be positive on the dimension being scaled. These alternatives have also been indicated above. As a result of the analysis, item 5 (Vote main thing) was rejected as not fitting the scaling model. The remaining four items showed a satisfactory scale structure according to the criteria used at the time and defined the scale of the "sense of political efficacy". The same scaling model was apparently used without any alterations in the next Michigan study, *The American Voter*, which reported on the voting behavior at the presidential elections of 1956 (Campbell, Converse, Miller and Stokes, 1960, 103–5).

The concept almost immediately proved its usefulness in political research. Janowitz and Marvick, analyzing the same data of the 1952 Michigan study, used this concept under a different name: political self-confidence. Not applying scale analysis, they based it on an index constructed from four items, three of which belonged to the original scale: items 2 (Politics complicated), 3 (Officials don't care) and 4 (Don't have say).

In addition, another item was used which in the Michigan study formed part of a scale measuring the "sense of citizen duty" (Campbell *et al.*, 1954, 194–9). The wording of this item, item 6 in this chapter, is as follows:

6. "So many other people vote in the national elections that it doesn't matter much to me whether I vote or not." (So many voters). Positive alternative: "disagree".

Items 1 (Voting only way) and 5 (Vote main thing) were used by Janowitz and Marvick together with two other items for an index of "self-interest in elections" (Janowitz and Marvick, 1956, 114–7). They do not give any operational reasons for eliminating not only item 5, the one rejected by Campbell *et al.*, but also item 1. The addition of item 6 to their index is not explained either. Apparently they based their indices on purely intuitive considerations.

The original Michigan scale (items 1, 2, 3 and 4) proved to be useful in other investigations and was widely used in later years, though sometimes under different names. As the "sense of political futility", the concept was used by Kornhauser *et al.* (Kornhauser, Sheppard and Mayer, 1956, 155–66). Lane refers to the scale as measuring "political effectiveness" (Lane, 1959, 149–55). Farris introduces the concept as "political anomie" (Farris, 1960), whereas Agger *et al.* prefer the more virile term of "political potency" (Agger, Goldstein and Pearl, 1961; Agger, Goldrich and Swanson, 1964, 755). In all these cases the Michigan four-item scale was used. Douvan and Walker used a related concept, which they also called "political effectiveness" or "competence" (Douvan and Walker, 1956). Elders-veld mentions experiments with six items. He finally used three items which are virtually the same as items 2, 3 and 4, referring to them as a basic dimension called "personal optimism" or "political pessimism" (Eldersveld, 1964, 498, 570–1). Although he does not scale the items, the fact that he does not use items 1 and 5 is inter-esting, as we shall see later in this paper. Dahl refers to the scale under its original name of "political efficacy" and calls it a widely used and well-tested scale (Dahl, 1961b, 286–91). Milbrath gives a review of the research findings concerning the relation of political efficacy to a number of other concepts used in political research (Milbrath, 1965, 56–60, 156–57).*

The concept of the "sense of political efficacy" was originally defined as

"...the feeling that individual political action does have, or can have, an impact upon the political process, *i.e.*, that it is worth-while to perform one's civic duties. It is the feeling that political and social change is possible, and that the individual citizen can play a part in bringing about this change." (Campbell *et al.*, 1954, 187).

Subsequent use of the concept established it as a basic attitudinal variable which was accorded well nigh personality status from the social-psychological point of view of the Michigan school (Campbell *et al.*, 1960, 516–9).

Easton and Dennis (1967) provided evidence in support of this point of view by demonstrating the existence of a factor-analytically defined "efficacy" structure for elementary school children at as early an age as seven years. In doing so they firmly established the theoretical status of this attitudinal concept by relating it to the political culture of a democratic regime: the "sense of political efficacy" embodied the set of expectations held with respect to a regime norm implying responsiveness on the part of the authorities to participating citizens (Easton and Dennis, 1967, 26).

In view of the apparent theoretical importance of the concept and

---

*A more extensive reference can be found in Easton and Dennis (1967).

the widespread use of the scale, it seemed worthwhile to investigate its operationalization for use in Dutch electoral research as being planned at the Institute for Political Science of the University of Amsterdam.

7.1.2 *A new analysis of the efficacy items: Dutch-American comparisons*

In 1965 Daudt and Stapel undertook an exploratory survey of political attitudes on a national sample of Dutch adults (Daudt and Stapel, 1966, 64–70), in which the author participated. The questionnaire of this survey, conducted by the Netherlands Institute for Public Opinion (NIPO), contained a number of variables that were inspired by analogous studies in American voting research. Among them were the six items. As is well known, the American and Dutch political structures differ strongly. The latter has its roots in a society which has been organized around denominational groupings. Its political correlate consists of a multiparty system and a parliament chosen by means of proportional representation. The result is a sequence of coalitions in which either a left-wing socialist party or a right-wing liberal party joins a semi-permanent Christian block with the Catholic People's Party in the center (Daalder, 1955; Daalder, 1966, 188–236; Goudsblom, 1967, 71–127; Lijphart, 1968). These difficulties not only complicated the translation problems involved, but also sometimes necessitated stringent adaptations of the contents of the items to fit appropriate equivalents peculiar to the Dutch system. For the same reasons we thought it wise not to simply adopt the four items of the original scale, but to start with a re-scaling of the larger set of items of the Michigan study of 1952.

At the time of this 1952 study, the method of scale analysis proposed by Guttman had achieved widespread acknowledgement. The full discussion of some drawbacks of this method or, more specifically, the choice of an adequate coefficient of scalability, had only just started. Since that time new insights in unidimensional scaling methods and the formulation and definition of the Guttman model have made some improvements possible. Since 1962 the author of this study has been developing different versions of scale analysis, some of which were reported in chapter 5. A form of the Guttman model has also been used for the construction of a Dutch version of the efficacy scale, starting with the items of the Daudt-Stapel study. The scale definition used in this chapter is that of section 5.1.8, with defining constant 0.30.

The scale procedure used is that of section 5.2.1, according to which the set of items is examined as a whole. Coefficients and tests were computed to enable us to evaluate the whole set of items as a scale.* In the Daudt-Stapel study** this procedure was applied to the Dutch equivalents of the items indicated in this study as items 1 (Voting only way), 2 (Politics complicated), 3 (Officials don't care), 4 (Don't have say) and 5 (Vote main thing). These five items, as we saw above, were the ones that were scale-analyzed in the Michigan study of 1952. It would not be practical to reproduce them here in their exact Dutch wording, but for what follows the reader should be aware of the fact that they were translated very freely and were formulated in such a way as to convey their original meaning within the context of the Dutch political culture (see Daudt and Stapel, 1966, 65–8).

The scale analysis produced some surprising results. Table 7.1 summarizes the results (for the readers familiar with the concept of the coefficient of reproducibility we computed Green's version (Green, 1956), Rep-B, as well).

Table 7.1   The sense of political efficacy (5 items) (Netherlands)

		Netherlands 1965 (786)	
		coeff.	z-score*
Scale	$\hat{H}$	0.18	11.50
	Rep-B	0.88	12.81
Items			
1. Voting only way	$\hat{H}_1$	0.01	0.37
2. Politics complicated	$\hat{H}_2$	0.21	9.38
3. Officials don't care	$\hat{H}_3$	0.27	12.03
4. Don't have say	$\hat{H}_4$	0.27	11.96
5. Vote main thing	$\hat{H}_5$	0.05	1.88

*Standard normal deviate. Critical value (one-sided) at significance level 0.01: $z = 2.33$.

They indicate that in the Netherlands the set of five items did not meet our standards for a scale. Item 5 (Vote main thing) scales badly

*All the computations were carried out on the Dutch Electrologica X-8 computer of the Mathematical Centre in Amsterdam.

**The NIPO survey was based on a probability sample of Dutch families resulting in 786 interviews. The survey was held in the spring of 1965.

and should be rejected, as was done by Cambell *et al.* in 1952. It has a low item scalability ($\hat{H}_5 = 0.05$) which, under the null hypothesis of random response, falls short of reasonable statistical significance as indicated in the column "z-score" (1.88). But another item, one of the items in the original four-item Michigan scale of political efficacy, produced even worse results: item 1 (Voting only way) has an item scalability, 0.01, of no statistical significance whatsoever (z-score: 0.37). Understandably the coefficient of scalability for the whole set of five items ($\hat{H} = 0.18$) was below standard. As a result of our analysis, it was decided that not only item 5 but also item 1 should be rejected from the scale, leaving only the set of items 2 (Politics complicated), 3 (Officials don't care) and 4 (Don't have say) as a possible basis for the scale.*

From the point of view of cross-national comparison, these findings, which seemed at odds with the American scaling results, suggested a further investigation of the cross-national robustness of the scale. A preliminary question might be how the original 1952 data would scale according to our procedure, which deviates from the Guttman analysis originally used in 1952. For the purpose of this secondary analysis it was possible for the author to obtain the necessary data from the archives of the Survey Research Center of the University of Michigan, where they formed part of the Data Repository of the Inter-University Consortium for Political Research.** The data are those of the full pre-election sample from the 1952 SRC-Study.†

The results of the re-analysis of our five items again are interesting. They are given in table 7.2, which includes both the American and the Dutch data to facilitate comparison. Our scaling procedure confirms the bad scaling qualities of item 5 (Vote main thing) which led to the rejection of this item in the original study. Its item scalability (0.08) is low, although, due to the sample size, it reaches significance at the 0.001 level.

But here too item 1 (Voting only way) scales even worse: $\hat{H}_1 = 0.00$ and does not even reach statistical significance (z-score: 0.09). The overall coefficient $\hat{H}$ (0.27) is also below our standards.

In spite of the negative results, these findings increase our hopes of

---

*For the paper of Daudt and Stapel (1966) the scale was extended *ad hoc* with two other items which fitted the scale reasonably well.

**We are grateful to Professor Warren E. Miller and his staff for making the Consortium data available to us.

†For the analysis we used the full pre-election sample of the 1952 study, corrected for western overload. This sample consisted of 1,799 interviews. For details see Cambell *et al.*, (1954, 229–30).

Table 7.2 *The sense of political efficacy (5 items)*
(U.S. and Netherlands)

		Netherlands 1965 (786)		United States 1952 (1799)	
		coeff.	z-score*	coeff.	z-score*
Scale	$\hat{H}$	0.18	11.50	0.27	19.46
	Rep-B	0.88	12.81	0.92	23.43
Items					
1. Voting only way	$\hat{H}_1$	0.01	0.37	0.00	0.09
2. Politics complicated	$\hat{H}_2$	0.21	9.38	0.37	15.52
3. Officials don't care	$\hat{H}_3$	0.27	12.03	0.37	19.69
4. Don't have say	$\hat{H}_1$	0.27	11.96	0.38	20.15
5. Vote main thing	$\hat{H}_5$	0.05	1.88	0.08	3.44

*Standard normal deviate. Critical value (one-sided) at significance level $0.01: z = 2.33$.

constructing a cross-culturally robust scale. The striking similarity of the outcomes for the two countries on the basis of the same measurement models cannot be denied. When scale analyses with thirteen years between them which were performed in two vastly different western political cultures break down in exactly the same way by rejecting the very same items, this may certainly be regarded as a positive result from the comparative point of view.

Thus far we have analyzed the whole set of five items that were originally considered in the 1952 Michigan scale. We will now subject the four items which formed the final scale of political efficacy to a re-analysis based on our criteria.

7.1.3 *The original scale re-analyzed cross-culturally*

The results of our tests, as applied to the four original efficacy items, are given in table 7.3. As was to be expected from the evidence given in the last section, they do not scale very well. For the Netherlands the set does not meet our standards by any means. Item 1 (Voting only way) has too low an item scalability, 0.09, and thus reduces the scalability of the other items to below the lower bound of 0.30. The overall coefficient of scalability ($\hat{H} = 0.25$) is below standard too.

Table 7.3   The original four-item scale

		Netherlands 1965 (786)		United States 1952 (1744)	
		coeff.	z-score*	coeff.	z-score*
Scale	$\hat{H}$	0.25	13.63	0.39	21.92
	Rep-B	0.89	11.30	0.94	21.59
Items					
1. Voting only way	$\hat{H}_1$	0.09	3.07	0.16	5.52
2. Politics complicated	$\hat{H}_2$	0.28	11.69	0.43	16.92
3. Officials don't care	$\hat{H}_3$	0.29	12.08	0.44	19.40
4. Don't have say	$\hat{H}_4$	0.28	11.01	0.44	18.75

*Standard normal deviate. Critical value (one-sided) at significance level $0.01: z = 2.33$.

Nor do the U.S. data, although better than in the former section, form a really good scaling structure. This is due to a too low value of the scalability of item 1 ($\hat{H}_1 = 0.16$), although the overall coefficient $\hat{H} = (0.39)$ in itself is not unsatisfactory. The slight differences between the Netherlands and the United States indicated by the data invite an inquiry into the cross-cultural robustness of this set of items *within* the U.S. population.

The author therefore decided to select some subgroups from the sample of the 1952 study which could be regarded as indicative of certain different sub-cultures. These sub-groups and their definitions and sizes in the 1952 sample were the following:

1. Four regional sub-groups spanning the whole sample:
   (for definitions, see Campbell *et al.*, 1954)
   - North east   (448)
   - Mid west   (618)
   - South   (509)
   - Far west   (224)

2. Sex:
   - Male   (821)
   - Female   (978)

3. Race:
   - White   (1618)
   - Negro   (171)

4. Two educational sub-groups:
   –"Highest" (college level)   (262)
   – "Lowest" (grade-school only)   (712)

5. Two income levels (1952 standards):
   – "Highest" ($ 5,000 or more)   (458)
   – "Lowest" (less than $ 3,000)   (624)

The reader should note that on the last two points we restricted ourselves to two extreme sub-groups. The four efficacy items were scaled within every sub-group, again being followed the procedure of section 5.2.1. (An analysis of the set of five items considered in section 7.1.2 gave the same results in all cases, as reported in that section).

The findings of our analyses are given in table 7.4. Although the overall coefficients of scalability are not too bad, all of them being larger than or equal to the lower bound of 0.30, a close scrutiny of the item scalabilities confirms our suspicions of item 1 (Voting only way). In all the twelve sub-groups its scalability falls below the bound of 0.30. In addition, its wayward behavior over the sub-groups is striking. Its performance is really bad for the mid west ($\hat{H}_1 = 0.08$), the far west (0.04), the negroes (0.06), the lowest educational group (0.04) and the lowest income group (−0.05). On the other hand, its scalability reaches relatively high values for the male sex (0.21), the highest income group (0.29) and in the south (0.25), where this item, which concerns the role of voting as the sole means of political influence, may have other meanings.

We may conclude that the evidence of our cross-cultural analysis supports our inclination to drop item 1 (Voting only way) from the scale. There are, however, other considerations which support this decision.

7.1.4   The non-monotony of item 1 (Voting only way)

There are other, intuitive, reasons for distrusting item 1. Let us consider the original wording of item 1: "Voting is the only way that people like me can have any say about how the government runs things", and the answer "disagree" as the positive response. This positive response should be given by a person with a fairly strong sense of political efficacy. The relatively high scalability coefficients in "efficacious" sub-groups such as the highest income group and the male voters suggest this. On the other hand, we may imagine that a

Table 7.4 The original scale,* United States 1952

		Region				Sex		Race		Education		Income	
		North east (448)	Mid west (618)	South (509)	Far west (224)	Male (821)	Female (978)	White (1618)	Negro (171)	High-est (262)	Low-est (712)	High-est (458)	Low-est (624)
Scale													
	$\hat{H}$	0.35	0.37	0.42	0.33	0.40	0.36	0.36	0.43	0.32	0.35	0.38	0.30
	Rep-B	0.93	0.94	0.94	0.94	0.94	0.94	0.93	0.95	0.94	0.94	0.93	0.93
Items													
1. Voting only way	$\hat{H}_1$	0.18	*0.08*	0.25	*0.04*	0.21	0.11	0.15	*0.06*	*0.16*	*0.04*	0.29	*−0.05*
2. Politics complicated	$\hat{H}_2$	0.43	0.43	0.40	0.39	0.45	0.39	0.41	0.48	0.29	0.40	0.41	0.34
3. Offials don't care	$\hat{H}_3$	0.37	0.45	0.45	0.41	0.43	0.44	0.42	0.46	0.41	0.42	0.40	0.37
4. Don't have say	$\hat{H}_4$	0.37	0.43	0.50	0.42	0.46	0.42	0.42	0.48	0.44	0.41	0.40	0.39

*Coefficients not significant at the 0.01 level are italicized.

respondent with very low political efficacy will even deny that the act of voting is a way in which he can exercise political influence and who is, therefore, more likely to disagree with the statement for reasons of *low* political efficacy. In this case we might suspect that the scale response or "positive" response ("disagree") to item 1 will be given with high probability by respondents with *high* levels of the "sense of political efficacy" as well as by respondents with *low* levels of the "sense of political efficacy".

What does this mean in terms of our scaling theory?

Scaling models of the type under consideration are based on items possessing the property of monotone homogeneity (see section 5.1.2), which means that the probability of a "positive" answer increases accordingly as the position of the respondent on the continuum is higher. Thus a respondent with a very high position on this continuum (or, for that matter, attitude) will most probably give the positive answer, whereas a respondent with a very low position on this continuum will in all likelihood fail to do so. In other words: item 1 may not be a monotone item as defined above, but a sort of *point item* (see section 2.2.2), *i.e.* an item with a response alternative that will be given with high probability by respondents of either *high* or *low* levels of political efficacy. In the case of item 1 this might imply that for respondents with the low level of political self-confidence sketched above, *not the answer "disagree" but the response alternative "agree" would be the "efficacious" alternative.*

To investigate this hypothesis we scaled the original set of four items (1, 2, 3 and 4) for three groupings of well-established low political efficacy (Campbell *et al.*, 1954, 191–2): the negroes, the lowest educational group, and the lowest income group, "inverting" item 1 (Voting only way) by choosing the response alternative "agree" as the positive answer on the efficacy continuum. Our hypothesis of the non-monotony of item 1 would then lead us to expect a somewhat better performance on this item in these cases. The results, as reported in table 7.5, are remarkable. As a matter of fact, they seem to be even better than we had hoped. For the negroes the four items form a strong scale, according to our criteria, and for the lowest income category they form a medium scale. For the lowest educational group the items do not scale, but the item coefficient of item 1 is fairly high, 0.24.

An application of the same reasoning would result in a prediction of a deterioration of the "inverted" item 1 in groupings such as "male"

Table 7.5   The original four-item scale
            (Item 1 "inverted"*)

		Negro (171)	Education lowest (712)	Income lowest (624)
Scale	$\hat{H}$	0.52	0.42	0.43
	Rep-B	0.95	0.95	0.94
Items				
1. Voting only way ("inverted"*)	$\hat{H}_1$	0.46	0.24	0.31
2. Politics complicated	$\hat{H}_2$	0.54	0.47	0.48
3. Officials don't care	$\hat{H}_3$	0.50	0.46	0.43
4. Don't have say	$\hat{H}_4$	0.54	0.44	0.46

*For item 1, the response category "agree" was chosen as the positive alternative.

and "income highest", in which its scalability reached the highest values (see table 7.3). According to our checks this proved to be true. The scalability of the "inverse" item was very low for the grouping "male" 0.09) and for the highest income group (0.08).

7.1.5   A cross-culturally robust scale

The above re-analysis of the original four-item efficacy scale led to the conclusion that the non-monotone item 1 (Voting only way) could not be used in a cumulative scale. This leaves us with the three items 2 (Politics complicated), 3 (Officials don't care) and 4 (Don't have say). As we wanted a scale with more items, we thought it worthwhile to investigate the scaling qualities of item 6:

"So many other people vote in the national elections that it doesn't matter much to me whether I vote or not."

(So many voters; positive alternative: "disagree").

Although this item formed part of a different scale ("sense of citizen duty") in the Michigan study of 1952, we saw in section 7.1.1 that Janowitz and Marvick in their secondary analysis used this item together with the "efficacy" items 2, 3 and 4 for their index of political self-confidence. They gave no clear reason for doing this, but we must admit that the content of item 6 seems to bear a clear relation to the dimension of political efficacy. The results of our scale analysis fully confirm this conjecture for the U.S. data.

In table 7.6 we give the results for the whole U.S. sample. The four items clearly form a "strong" scale ($\hat{H} = 0.59$), which is not very difficult for scales of four items. All the item coefficients are higher than 0.50, the coefficient of the "new" item 6 (So many voters) even attaining 0.71.

Table 7.6. The United States: an improved scale of political efficacy

		United States 1952 (1799)	
		coeff.	z-score*
Scale	$\hat{H}$	0.59	33.05
	Rep-B	0.95	27.54
Items			
2. Politics complicated	$\hat{H}_2$	0.58	17.41
3. Officials don't care	$\hat{H}_3$	0.54	25.80
4. Don't have say	$\hat{H}_4$	0.57	26.85
6. So many voters	$\hat{H}_6$	0.71	23.58

*Standard normal deviate. Critical value (one-sided) at significance level 0.01; $z = 2.33$.

In accordance with the comparative approach of this chapter, we may want to investigate the cross-cultural robustness *within* the United States. This intra-cultural robustness also proved to be good, as can be seen from table 7.7, which gives the results of scale analyses performed on the set of items 2, 3, 4 and 6 in the twelve sub-groups. In all the sub-groups the items form a scale, again according to our criteria. Except for the highest income and education groups, where the set of items can be rated "medium scales", the items form a "strong scale".

Having established a reasonable four-item scale with a possibility of a desirable cross-cultural robustness within the United States, can we expect a reasonable robustness for this scale from a cross-national point of view as well? How do these items scale in the Netherlands?

A positive reply to this question would open many prospects for the utilization in international comparative research of scales and other operational constructs of proven *intra-national* robustness.

Table 7.7. *The improved scale of the sense of political efficacy (U.S. data)*

	Region				Sex		Race		Education		Income	
	North east (448)	Mid west (618)	South (509)	Far west (224)	Male (821)	Female (978)	White (1618)	Negro (171)	Highest (262)	Lowest (712)	Highest (458)	Lowest (624)
Scale												
$\hat{H}$	0.53	0.58	0.59	0.58	0.55	0.60	0.55	0.64	0.48	0.58	0.42	0.58
Rep-B	0.95	0.96	0.95	0.96	0.95	0.95	0.95	0.95	0.97	0.95	0.95	0.95
Items												
2. Politics complicated $\hat{H}_2$	0.57	0.60	0.53	0.54	0.55	0.59	0.56	0.59	0.53	0.52	0.45	0.53
3. Officials don't care $\hat{H}_3$	0.47	0.54	0.55	0.55	0.51	0.56	0.51	0.60	0.45	0.56	0.41	0.42
4. Don't have say $\hat{H}_4$	0.49	0.56	0.58	0.59	0.55	0.57	0.53	0.62	0.46	0.55	0.43	0.57
6. So many voters $\hat{H}_6$	0.70	0.67	0.68	0.74	0.67	0.72	0.66	0.75	*0.55	0.68	0.34	0.70

*This estimate lacks precision because of the extreme marginal (260) of item 6.

A secondary analysis on the Daudt-Stapel data showed that there may be reasons for optimism in this respect! From table 7.8, in which we have given the results for the Netherlands and, for easy comparison, those for the United States too, we can see that the four items are scalable. The Dutch versions of items 2 (Politics complicated), 3 (Officials don't care), 4 (Don't have say) and 6 (So many voters) also form a (medium) scale ($\hat{H} = 0.43$).

Table 7.8   The improved scale of the sense of political efficacy

		Netherlands 1965 (786)		United States 1952 (1799)	
		coeff.	z-score*	coeff.	z-score*
Scale	$\hat{H}$	0.43	19.85	0.59	33.05
	Rep-B	0.91	14.44	0.95	27.54
Items					
2. Politics complicated	$\hat{H}_2$	0.33	12.39	0.58	17.41
3. Officials don't care	$\hat{H}_3$	0.42	15.39	0.54	25.80
4. Don't have say	$\hat{H}_4$	0.43	15.53	0.57	26.85
6. So many voters	H_6	0.63	12.74	0.71	23.58

*Standard normal deviate. Critical value (one-sided) at significance level $0.01 : z = 2.33$.

7.1.6.   *A comparison of the efficacy scale across sub-groups within the Dutch sample*

We may now ask whether the Dutch scale would stand up to a cross-cultural analysis over sub-groups in the Netherlands. The possibilities for such a secondary analysis were rather limited for the Daudt-Stapel data, because a number of the socio-economic attributes were not collected as personal attributes but as attributes of the heads of households. Nevertheless we thought it worthwhile to perform an analysis of this kind, using household attributes as indicators of cultural differences.

The sub-groups, their sizes and definitions were as follows:

1. Four regional sub-groups:
   – North (the provinces Groningen, Friesland and Drente)   (93)

– East (Overijsel, Gelderland and Utrecht)   (186)
– West (Noord-Holland and Zuid-Holland)   (331)
– South (Noord-Brabant and Limburg) *   (148)

2. Sex:
– Male   (455)
– Female   (325)

3. Two educational groups:**
–"Highest", high school or more, (M.O. or more)   (97)
–"Lowest", elementary school only, (at most VGLO)   (517)

4. Two income levels (1965 standards):†
–"Highest" (f10,000 or more)   (185)
–"Lowest" (f7,000 or less)   (517)

5. Four religious groups:
– Roman Catholic   (260)
– Dutch Reformed   (222)
– Dutch Calvinist   (73)
– No religious affiliation   (170)

For these sub-groups we first analyzed the main items of the original scale "sense of political efficacy" (items 1, 2, 3 and 4). The results were very much like those reported in table 7.4. For all the sub-groups except two, item 1 had a value $\hat{H}_1$ which was very low and not significantly different from zero. Only in the south and (not surprisingly) for the Roman Catholic sub-group was $\hat{H}_1$ relatively high (respectively 0.23 and 0.17), though still not high enough for a scale according to the convention we follow.

When we repeated the analysis with inversion of item 1 (Voting only way) for the low efficacy groups "education lowest" and "income lowest", the Dutch data corroborated the findings concerning the non-monotony of item 1 reported for the U.S. in table 7.5: for both groups item 1 proved to scale with coefficients of, respectively, 0.36 and 0.32. The analysis of the improved scale with items 2, 3, 4 and 6 (So many voters) also confirmed the results for the U.S. data given in table 7.7. There are, however, some indications that item 2 (Politics

*We excluded the province of Zeeland to preserve the religious homogeneity of the predominantly Roman-Catholic south.
**Completed education reported for the head of the household.
†Reported annual income of the head of the household.

complicated) may not be a very good item in the Netherlands: in the groups "income highest" and "no religious affiliation" the values of H_2 were 0.24 and 0.23 respectively. We shall see in chapter 8, section 8.4, that there are other signs that this item 2 may not fit too well in the scale "sense of political efficacy"!

7.1.7   *The item marginals in cross-national comparison*

We have not yet compared or even mentioned the marginal frequencies for the positive response categories of the items. We may now investigate their significance for comparative research.

These item marginals give the proportion (or number) of respondents giving the positive response. More precisely: the sample marginal ($\hat{\pi}_i$ or p_i) of item i is an estimate of this proportion (π_i) for the population from which the sample was drawn. In chapter 2, section 2.3, we denoted these proportions as the sample difficulty and the population difficulty of item i respectively. We also described the *item difficulty* (δ_i) as a parameter independent of the population and characteristic of item i. This item difficulty defines the location of the items on the continuum (*i.e.* the attitude) being measured by means of the items. The items may be ordered according to their difficulty in terms of these difficulty parameters. We saw in section 5.1.4 of chapter 5 that for certain models (doubly monotone or holomorph) the order of the *population* difficulties (π_i) will be the same as that of the *item* difficulties. In this sense the sample difficulties are indicators of the location of the items on the continuum to be measured. A difficult item, which will be located higher on the continuum, will tend to show sample marginals smaller than those of a more popular (less difficult) item, which will be located lower on the continuum.

Consequently, a cross-cultural comparison of the sample difficulties of items may serve *two* purposes.

In the *first* place such a comparison may enable us to investigate the difficulty order of items. Because *item* difficulties were defined independently of a specific population we may expect the difficulty order to be the same if equivalent items are compared across cultures or nations. In table 7.9 we give the sample difficulties for the items of the improved scale for the United States and their equivalents for the Netherlands. It will be seen that for all the items the order is practically the same for the two countries. The only exception concerns the pair of items 2 and 3 where the difficulty order may be different.

Table 7.9. The sample difficulties of efficacy items
              (Improved scale)*

	Netherlands 1965 (786) %		United States 1962 (1799) %	
2. Politics complicated	34	(2)	28	(1)
3. Officials don't care	34	(1)	62	(2)
4. Don't have say	40	(3)	66	(3)
6. So many voters	78	(4)	86	(4)

*rank order of items indicated in brackets.

We may now consider the question what implications a change in the difficulty ordering from one culture to another would have for the equivalence of a set of items as instruments for obtaining comparable measurements in these cultures. This problem may have some important consequences for the comparison of linguistically strongly different groups, which is a crucial question in cross-national comparison. If it does, the framework of our scaling theory will enable us to shed some light on the possible effects of the translation of verbal items. When we try to construct an equivalent item in another language by means of a careful translation of a given item, mere literal translation will seldom be sufficient. Often a relatively "free" translation will be necessary. Yet even when more or less literal translation has led to a set of items that seems satisfactory on the basis of content, we may very well find that the difficulty order of their marginals varies between cultures. This gives rise to the question whether such cross-cultural shifts of the marginals for an item may also be a sign of a lack of robustness.

The answer to this question is perhaps that this will frequently be the case, but not always so. The cross-cultural change of the marginal of an item and especially of its relative position in the rank order of the item difficulties may indicate a change of the identity or meaning of the items and its *location* on the continuum. But although its meaning and location change and vary cross-culturally, the item may still be measuring the same dimension, so that the change will not disturb the *(uni)dimensionality* of the scale. We can easily imagine an item which cross-culturally changes its meaning and consequently its position on the continuum (item difficulty) without breaking out of the dimension it measures, thus preserving the property of robustness.

The process of translation will change the nature of the items, so that a direct comparison of their marginals (or, what amounts to the same thing, of their scores) will in general lack validity. But under favorable conditions the process of translation will transform an item, worded in one language, into another, different, item in another language. The difficulty of the item (the location on the continuum) can, and generally will, change in the process. If we are lucky, the *dimension* (the continuum) of the items will be roughly preserved in the process due to the robustness of the scale, the effect of the translation being restricted to a shift of the item difficulty (δ-value) along the continuum.

These considerations suggest that we may slacken considerably the rigid requirements that are traditionally set for translation in cross-national research. We believe that in the case of the cross-national robustness of scales the effects of the process of translation may be mainly restricted to a change in the identity of the items as given by their item difficulties, without affecting the dimension being measured and thus the variable itself.

In section 7.2.1 we shall consider the problem of equivalence in a broader context.

In the *second* place, a cross-cultural comparison of the item marginals may enable us to investigate the *level* of the variable measured by the items for the cultural groups involved in the analysis. For instance, in table 7.9 we see that item 6 (So many voters) was answered positively and "efficaciously" by 78% of the Dutch respondents and by 86% of the United States sample, a result which might lead us to think that the U.S. sample was more "efficacious" than the Dutch one. What we would then be doing is just comparing "efficacy" in terms of items as single indicators. A comparison of the marginals for an efficacy item across certain cultural groups will teach us at the most something about the level of efficacy in those groups. This can, however, be done better and more reliably by comparing the *scores* on the scale. After all the scale is designed for that purpose.* The scale scores in our model will of course only rank order the respondents along the continuum within their own national area. The relation of this rank order to the order of other variables in this area will provide the basis for comparison between these variables. Thus, again quoting Almond and Verba:

"By phrasing the comparison *between* nations in terms of the

*A recent article by Dennis *et al.* (1968) on a cross-national comparison of certain attitudes in children contains such an item-wise comparison of the efficacy items. The authors thus let slip an opportunity of giving a penetrating analysis of the efficacy variable in terms of the scale.

similarities and differences in the patterns of relations *among* variables *within* each country, one controls somewhat for the difference in meaning that these variables may have from one nation to another" (Almond and Verba, 1963, 70).

7.2.   SOME FURTHER POSSIBILITIES

In this chapter we have presented a specific application of scale analysis in the field of cross-national or, more generally speaking, cross-cultural research: the investigation of what we called the cross-cultural robustness of a scale. We will now conclude with some general remarks about the possibilities of this type of investigation for cross-cultural methodology and research in general.

7.2.1.   *Equivalence and comparability: an operational framework*

In the last chapter we mentioned that in the older literature rather strong requirements were set for the cross-cultural equivalence of measurements. Strong definitions of equivalence, however, proved to be untenable, as they resulted in the requirement of virtually identical instruments.

Duijker, in his analysis of comparative research concerning attitudes, stated that

"not the instruments must be the same, but the results obtained with them must be similar enough to be comparable. The instruments must not be identical, but equivalent" (Duijker, 1955, 561). Przeworski and Teune (1966) have recently made an important contribution to the theoretical and methodological development of cross-cultural equivalence. They state that:

"In seeking equivalence in cross-national research one must go beyond the problem of identical stimuli. Single items are rarely sufficient to measure concepts at any level of analysis. The problem of whether a concept can be measured cross-nationally by a set of identical indicators is empirical. Although complete equivalence is probably never possible, attempts can be made to measure equivalence if they are based on a *set* of indicators or observations" (Przeworski and Teune, 1966, 556).

They then go on to develop a theory of cross-cultural equivalence or comparability of instruments and measurements that results in an operational framework that fits the analysis reported in this chapter remarkably well. It may therefore be worthwhile to borrow their ideas, formalizing them a little more and adapting them to our purposes.

We again assume that we want to measure some concept, such as a political attribute, attitude, etc., which we denote as θ, taking on values in a set Θ. Let C be a set of cultures (or nations, for that matter) and let $c \in C$ denote a culture belonging to that set. Our measurement problem is restricted to the set C, *i.e.* only cultures belonging to C $(c \in C)$ are compared in terms of θ. In any culture c we may assume the existence of a great variety of possible indicators of θ, such as items which may be used for the measurement of this variable. For any culture $c \in C$, let this collection of possible indicators be denoted by $I_c(\theta)$ with elements (particular indicators) $i_c(\theta) \in I_c(\theta)$.

We will now assume that it is possible to compare certain elements $i_c(\theta) \in I_c(\theta)$ across C for all $c \in C$. In other words, we assume that it is possible to find some indicators which may be used and compared in *every* culture of the set we are interested in. We will also assume that it is possible by means of this procedure to establish some sort of equivalence across C for some indicators. Identifying these indicators over C, we may now introduce the set

$$I(\theta) = \bigcap_{c \in C} I_c(\theta) \neq 0$$

as the intersection of the sets $I_c(\theta)$ over C, which is not empty by assumption.

$I(\theta)$ may be regarded as the set of indicators common to *all* cultures $c \in C$ for the measurement of θ. It should be stressed that the introduction of $I(\theta)$ presupposes the possibility of imagining a pool of indicators or items, each of which is equivalent cross-culturally in C as an indicator of θ. In this sense the set $I(\theta)$ denotes the common core of indicators of θ valid for our set of cultures C.

We may restrict our definition of this common set still further. Let us denote by $I_H(\theta) \subset I(\theta)$ the set of common indicators, contained in $I(\theta)$, which are homogeneous in an operational sense for all cultures $c \in C$. As an example we may define $I_H(\theta)$ as the set of dichotomous items belonging to $I(\theta)$ which is such that any set of items selected from that set forms a scale for all cultures $c \in C$.

Przeworski and Teune (1966, 557) regard items chosen from $I_H(\theta)$ as cross-culturally *identical*. For this reason they call such items *identities*, a term which seems much too presumptuous in the uncertain field of cross-cultural comparison. We therefore propose to call such items *equivalent* over C, the equivalence depending on the type of homogeneity defining $I_H(\theta)$. Hence, $I_H(\theta)$ may by definition be regarded as the set of possible indicators which are equivalent over C. We will wherever possible sample items from $I_H(\theta)$ when constructing sets of indicators such as scales for cross-culturally comparative measurements of θ. This is not, however, a necessary condition for valid comparative measurement.

Let us consider for any culture $c \in C$ the set $I_c(\theta) - I_H(\theta)$. This set contains the indicators of θ in culture c that are not common to and homogeneous for all other cultures in C. We may call such indicators *culture-specific* within C. We may now define for culture c the set $I_{cH}(\theta) \subset I_c(\theta) - I_H(\theta)$ as the set of items belonging to the culture-specific set $I_c(\theta) - I_H(\theta)$ which is such that any item $i_c(\theta) \in I_{cH}(\theta)$ will be homogeneous with those in $I_H(\theta)$.

Again, we may for our purposes regard $I_{cH}(\theta)$ as the set of items i that will scale in culture c with any k items selected from $I_H(\theta)$.

The items which are homogeneous and culture-specific for culture c are called *equivalent* by Przeworski and Teune, which again seems too strong a term. We prefer to use a term with less strong connotations in this case too and will call the set $I_{cH}(\theta)$ the set of the *comparable* items of culture c adequate for the comparative measurement of θ.

The general idea behind this theory is that for comparative purposes we need not necessarily restrict ourselves to the selection of equivalent items for the measurement of θ. Having selected a set of r *equivalent* items for the set of cultures C as a common core for the measurement of θ, we may add for each culture c another set of, say, $k - r$ *comparable*, culture-specific items to form a k item scale for culture c. These culture-specific *comparable* indicators may derive their cross-national validity as indicators of θ from their homogeneity (association) with the equivalent indicators.*

This theory has the advantage of providing a neat conceptual framework for the problem of the cross-cultural equivalence of measurements. As such it sets much milder requirements than have usually been formulated in the literature, in that culture-specific indicators

---

*Przeworski and Teune (1966, 557–8) introduce the terms "identical cross-national validity" and "equivalent cross-national validity", a distinction which does not seem a very felicitous one to the author. For one thing, it does not make much sense methodologically to split up the major concept of validity according to the particular operational context in which it plays a role. Moreover, the measurement of θ as such should possess validity; we should not suggest that a measuring instrument is valid in one sense and not valid in another.

may be used for comparative measurement under certain conditions. Of course, the full empirical purport of the theory, especially as regards the general cross-national validity of the measurements obtained by it, still requires empirical verification. But the theory gives all the operational possibilities of doing so. The work reported in this chapter in itself may well be regarded as an empirical application of these principles.

For instance C, the set of cultures or nations, consisted in our case of the United States and the Netherlands. In the intra-national analysis, C consisted of a larger group of sub-cultures within the U.S. Cross-cultural robustness of a scale over the set C may be an indication of the *equivalence* over C of the items forming the scale. In section 7.1.5, the items 2, 3, 4 and 6 proved to be such a set of items, belonging to $I_H(\theta)$.

In chapter 8, section 8.1.1, we will see that an extension of the efficacy scale for the Netherlands contains at least one *culture-specific* but *comparable* item. It is an item connected with the compulsory voting in the Netherlands. (See table 8.1, item 7).

7.2.2   The consequences for parametric models

Although we shall not make use of parametric models in this study, a number of the points treated in this chapter seem pertinent to such models; it seems worthwhile to elaborate them to some extent, though such an elaboration must remain theoretical.

In our review of parametric scaling models in chapters 3 and 4 we emphasized the role played by population distributions. Measurement procedures based on the estimation of subject parameters (θ) and item parameters (δ_i) in response functions ($\pi(\theta, \delta_i)$) with given trace lines were shown to depend generally on the population distribution of θ involved in the problem at hand.

This general dependence of the measurements of a variable on its distribution in the particular population for which the measurements were taken is shown to be significant in cross-cultural comparative measurement. There the different populations, corresponding to the different cultures analyzed, are central to the whole field of investigation.

Parametric measurement models possessing certain properties of invariance for changes in the population distribution may therefore well be preferred for cross-cultural analysis to models not possessing such virtues. In chapter 3 (section 3.1.2, theorem 1.2.1), we indicated a general response function of this type which, when it was specialized for dichotomous items, proved to be identical to the model proposed by Rasch (section 3.2.4), which possessed some of these properties. It was possible to measure (estimate) θ independently of the population distribution of the items, *i.e.* independently of the *procedure of item selection*. Analogously, it was possible to estimate the item difficulties (δ_i) independently of the population distribution of the stochastic variable θ (the distribution of subjects). Both these properties are obviously particularly desirable in cross-national or, more generally speaking, cross-cultural research.

It clearly follows from these properties that the items used for different cultures need not be equivalent in the sense of parallel tests. It will be sufficient if at most two items (and only one item if the Rasch model applies) can be considered equivalent cross-culturally in this strong sense. We may then calibrate the scales of measurement in all the cultures in the set C to the same unit and origin (zero point) by choosing the value of, say, 1 for the item difficulty of one of these equivalent items and fixing the difficulty of the other equivalent item at zero in every culture in set C. For Rasch models only one equivalent item i is needed to choose the unit of measurement ($\delta_i = 1$).

In any culture $c \in C$ all the other items may in theory be *comparable* and culture-specific for c.

From these remarks it will be seen that the use of adequate parametric measurement models may give rise to additional possibilities for satisfactory comparative measurement. Although it was shown in section 3.2.4 that the model of Rasch set strong requirements for the data, its desirable properties make it very much worthwhile to investigate its possible empirical application for the benefit of cross-cultural analysis.

It might also be worthwhile to search for sets of items which may be considered to fit the Rasch model. If we can construct our measurement instruments from and around such items, the outlook for valid comparative measurement seems very good indeed.

7.2.3   *The theoretical relevance of scale structure*

In this chapter we have also tried to demonstrate that the type of cross-cultural comparison of the scalability of sets of items proposed by us may have a theoretical significance which will make it more than just an instrument of measurement.

In the development of a scale into such an instrument two stages can be distinguished.

In the first stage we try to find a set of items which forms a scale. Once the *scalability* of the set has been established, this scalability is assumed to be a legitimate basis for using ratings on the scale as measurements of levels on the variable to which the items are related.

In the second stage, therefore, the scale is used solely as an instrument of measurement. When the question of scalability has been solved, the scale no longer plays an important part at this stage. In by far the larger part of the applications of scale analysis, interest has been focused mainly on the second goal: the use of scales as measuring instruments. The problem of scalability was of secondary importance only and was wholly subordinated to the attaining of this goal.

Only very rarely has any attention been paid to the more essential implications of the scalability of sets of items. Yet if the variables we are hoping to find are important ones, the fact that related items scale may well be worth further investigation.

Converse (1964, 207) has introduced the concept of a *belief system* as

"... a configuration of ideas and attitudes in which the elements are bound together by some form of constraint or functional interdependence",

remarking that:

"Constraint must be treated, of course, as a matter of degree, and this degree can be measured quite readily, at least as an average among individuals."*

The scalability of a set of items tapping different attitudinal or cultural elements is simply a very special case of such a belief system.

For instance, the scalability of the efficacy items shows that the different elements (responsiveness of officials, relevance of voting, influence on government, intelligibility of politics) are closely interrelated in a very specific way for a given cultural group. For this reason an attitude such as the "sense of political efficacy" may be thought of as a structure of closely interrelated opinions, feelings and dispositions which may be represented by a one-dimensional attitudinal variable for this group. This tightly constrained set of elements serves as a stable frame of reference by means of which respondents relate their own personalities to certain aspects of the political system.

---

*In an accompanying note Converse suggests that coefficients of scalability are such measures (Converse, 1964, 256, note 4).

The degree of constraint of the set of elements is measured by the coefficients of scalability (H and H_i).

Having established the significance of a concept such as the "sense of political efficacy" as an attitudinal element of a belief system or the political culture of a particular group, we may want to investigate whether this element can be established for other cultural groups as well. We have shown in this chapter that such an analysis may be performed in terms of our scalability coefficients.

Our comparative analysis of the scalability of the "efficacy" items *intra-* and *inter*-nationally may therefore also be interpreted as an investigation of the cross-cultural generality of the existence of this "sense of political efficacy" as a particular, compact attitude structure. We saw, for instance, in section 7.1.4 that the deviant behaviour of item 1 was of substantial interest also because it indicated that this item might have a very different meaning for groups with low or high efficacy. Of course, the point made here is not new. Guttman clearly realized that a set of items may scale for one population and not for a different population at a different time or in a different place, remarking that:

"This would indicate a change in the structuralization of the attitude from many dimensions to one dimension, or that an "unstructured" attitude has become "structured"" (Guttman, 1950a, 82).

We should also explicitly mention "time" as one of the dimensions on which the scalability of a set of items may differ. We can easily imagine situations where a *cross-temporal* analysis of the scalability of a set of items instead of an analysis of the robustness of a scale *cross-culturally* would be of some theoretical interest. Such an analysis may be especially rewarding in cases where *developmental* processes concerning the formation and disintegration of, for instance, attitude structures throughout time are being investigated.

An example, again concerned with "political efficacy", is of the type of problem that was dealt with by Easton and Dennis (1967) in their study of the political socialization of children at elementary school (ages 7–13). A factor analysis of the data revealed that as from grade 3, for every grade in elementary school a factor could be identified which clearly corresponded to the dimension of the "sense of political efficacy".* This finding suggested that at this early age a

*The analysis by Easton and Dennis corroborates the evidence presented in this chapter about item 1 (Voting only way). Their equivalent item 1 "Voting is the only way that people like my mother and father can have any say about how the government runs things", also did not fit into the efficacy factor well. Another item was also a

"sense of political efficacy" has already been formed as an attitudinal structure. Easton and Dennis conclude that this basic attitude is likely to crystallize early in the life of the individual, whereas the development of a specific *level* of efficacy may take place at a later period (Easton and Dennis, 1967, 31). Strong evidence therefore exists that for children in the lowest grades of elementary school the different elements tapped by the efficacy items have already been organized into a consistent attitude complex as the *perceived* political culture of the adults. In terms of our scaling theory we may expect from the findings of Easton and Dennis that their efficacy items would form a scale even in the lowest grades of elementary school.

But would they scale equally well in the lowest grades as in the highest? In other words, would the consistency, the degree of organization of the attitude complex of political efficacy be the same from the lowest grades to the highest ones?

In fact there are no particular theoretical reasons for believing this to be true. It may be more realistic to investigate the possibility that this consistency of an attitude complex, like the interrelationship of the different attitudinal elements which are part of it, is developing from a condition of relatively loose association to a condition of increasingly firmer interdependence throughout the process of socialization. Easton and Dennis did not investigate this phenomenon, nor can we analyze it from their published data.

---

failure, but probably for a different reason than the one mentioned by Easton and Dennis. This item is their equivalent of item 2 (Politics complicated): "Sometimes I can't understand what goes on in the government". According to Easton and Dennis this item did not fit the dimension simply because politics are sometimes incomprehensible to children.

We feel that another reason is more plausible. All the efficacy items except this second item were reformulated by Easton and Dennis to suit their juvenile subjects in such a way that they referred to the world of adults. The only item which referred directly to the child itself, thus requiring clear self-perception of the child, was this equivalent of item 2 (Politics complicated). Because of its relation to the child itself instead of to its parents, the item did not fit into the efficacy factor. This alternative explanation not mentioned by Easton and Dennis is far from trivial, because they tend to interpret their measure of political efficacy as being based on projection. We may therefore stress the point that the deviant behavior of this comprehensibility item may be regarded as important evidence that the other efficacy items are based on the child's *perception* of adult political culture (the expectations and perceived norm), and not on *projection* on the part of the child. (Easton and Dennis, 1967, 29–31).

We may conclude by pointing out that here too we may learn more from the analysis of a set of items than from the cross-cultural (or cross-temporal) comparison of responses to single items.

For scalable attitudes or dispositions such as the sense of political efficacy, the process of socialization would imply a steady increase of scalability with increasing age. We could analyze this development across age groups much more specifically in terms of the scalability of the set of items for the several grades. We may then with the help of criteria H and H_i verify when this scalability starts, as a sign of attitude formation, and how it develops over the grades. If, for instance, we found a coefficient $\hat{H} = 0.30$ for the lowest of three age groups, $\hat{H} = 0.40$ for the middle age group and $\hat{H} = 0.50$ for the highest age group, this would indicate that the degree of attitude organization of the efficacy items is developing from relatively loose to more tight forms with increasing age.

Consequently, *two* types of developmental processes may be considered for these scales:
1. the development of the *level* of the variable over age, *i.e.* the level of efficacy as measured by the *score*;
2. the development of the *degree* of attitude organization or *constraint* of the attitudinal elements, *i.e.* the degree of scalability as measured by the *coefficients of scalability*.

We shall return to this question in section 8.2, where we shall see that there are some signs that such a subsequent development of the second type may even continue throughout adolescence and adult life, *i.e.* throughout the whole life cycle.

CHAPTER 8

An exploration of political efficacy

The last two chapters were devoted to the problems of cross-cultural comparative research and some possible substantial and instrumental contributions to this research that might result from applications of our procedure which may enable us to assess the practical useful-ness of most of the properties proved in chapter 4 and summarized in chapter 5. In the Netherlands our scaling model and the system of programs based on it have already been used in various fields of social research. As far as we know, the results have up to now gener-ally been stisfactory. (Koomen and Winnubst, 1968).

8.1 A DUTCH EXTENSION OF THE EFFICACY SCALE

The applications reported here are mainly drawn from research in the fields of mass communications and political science in which the author participated. Many of the possibilities of the scaling model put forward in this study may be demonstrated with the aid of our further development of the important scale of the "sense of political efficacy". At the time of the Daudt-Stapel study, items 2, 3, 4 and 6 (section 7.1.1) formed the basis of a scale enlarged *ad hoc* with two other items that fitted the scale satisfactorily. Because of their content, however, these two items were not considered desirable components of a defini-tive Dutch version. It was decided to extend the concept and the scale considerably for future use in a long-term research project planned by Daudt, Van der Maesen and the author.

8.1.1 *A nine-item efficacy scale*

In the winter of 1965–1966 the author conducted a study of mass communications and opinion leadership concerning political information with a sample (269 respondents) of the Amsterdam male population of voting age. In this study we experimented with an enlarged version of the efficacy scale consisting of eleven items. Subsequently the same eleven items were used by Van der Maesen in a study of political participation in Amsterdam at the time of the local elections of June 1966. For both studies we primarily used the procedure suggested in section 5.2.4 for the extension of an existing scale. As a result a nine-item (medium) scale was established in both studies. As the sample of 1513 respondents of Van der Maesen's study was drawn from the whole Amsterdam population of voting age and not only from the male part of it, as in the author's special study, we shall present the results for the sample of Van der Maesen (Van der Maesen, 1967).

Table 8.1 gives the items that were selected for the final scale. The items marked with an asterisk indicate the equivalents of the four efficacy items described in section 7.1.5.

Items 4, 5 and 9 are given in the English wording of the original items 4, 2 and 6. Items 1 and 2 are two versions of the original item 3 (Officials don't care). The other new items are translated as literally as possible.

The author also tried to devise new items that would give a better spread of the sample difficulties. Apparently we have been moderately successful in attaining this objective. Items 6 (Shouldn't vote), 7 (Wouldn't go to polls) and 8 (Votes taken into account), with sample difficulties varying from 0.63–0.66, partly fill the gap between the older items 5 (Politics complicated; 0.35) and 9 (So many voters; 0.79). However, there is still a sizable gap in the range of sample difficulties between 5 (0.35) and 6 (0.63).

The two versions of the original item 3 (Officials don't care), items 1 (MPs don't care) and 2 (Cabinet Ministers don't care), as well as item 3 (Parties interested only in my vote), judging by their sample difficulties, are more or less equivalent items 0.25–0.27), which proves that they refer to three distinct but closely related types of authorities at the national level of the Dutch political system.

Originally, we wanted to add two rather difficult items in order to obtain a wide variety of sample difficulties for better discrimination. Literally translated, these items were:

*Table 8.1   A Dutch efficacy scale (9 items)
(Sample taken from Amsterdam electorate) n = 1513*

Items	Sample difficulties	$\hat{H}_i$
1.* Members of Parliament don't care much about the opinions of people like me. (Positive alternative: "disagree")	0.25	0.40
2.* Cabinet Ministers don't care much about the opinions of people like me. (Positive alternative: "disagree")	0.27	0.41
3. The political parties are only interested in my vote and not in my opinion. (Positive alternative: "disagree")	0.27	0.43
4.* People like me don't have any say about what the government does. (Positive alternative: "disagree")	0.31	0.39
5.* Sometimes politics and government seem so complicated that a person like me can't really understand what's going on. (Positive alternative: "disagree")	0.35	0.33
6. Because I know so little about politics, I shouldn't really vote. (Positive alternative: "disagree")	0.63	0.47
7. I wouldn't go to the polls, if I weren't obliged to do so. (Positive alternative: "disagree")**	0.66	0.44
8. In the determination of government policy, the votes of people like me are taken into account. (Positive alternative: "agree")	0.66	0.32
9.* So many other prople vote in the national elections that it doesn't matter much to me whether I vote or not. (Positive alternative: "disagree")	0.79	0.49

Scale coefficient: $\hat{H} = 0.41$; 0.95 confidence interval: $0.38 \leq H \leq 0.43$.

*Equivalents of the older efficacy scale (see section 7.1.5.)

**In the Netherlands, everyone who is qualified to vote is by law obliged to go to a polling station on election day. This legal obligation was abolished in 1970.

> "If I communicated my views to the Cabinet Ministers, they would be taken into account",
> (Positive alternative: "agree"; 0.19);

and

> "If I communicated my views to Members of Parliament, they would be taken into account",
> (Positive alternative: "agree"; 0.27).

The first item did not scale very well and the second item only scaled marginally (in both studies this second item was the last to be added to the scale in the step-wise procedure). Because of their similar content and their doubtful scaling qualities it was decided to drop both from the scale. The scaling properties of the final nine-item scale can be judged from table 8.1. Here, as in all the subsequent scales reported in this study, all the scale and item coefficients differed significantly from zero. For this reason we shall not give the "z-scores" for these tests in the tables. The scale appears to have a good structure: it is a medium scale ($\hat{H} = 0.41$).

A computation of the non-null sampling distribution with the method derived in section 4.3.3* enabled us to obtain an asymptotic 0.95-confidence interval for the population coefficient H: $0.38 \leqslant H \leqslant 0.43$. For the sake of completeness we have also listed the item coefficients of scalability in table 8.1.

With the usual procedures of Guttman scaling and their too stringent criteria, it is in general difficult to set up scales of more than six items. Researchers typically end up with scales of four or five items. Table 8.1 suggests that with our scaling procedure, scales based on sets of ten or more items may easily be produced. Since the time of that study, this suggestion has been borne out by experience.

8.1.2 *A local efficacy scale (8 items)*

Van der Maesen's study, in which the author participated, was focused on the local political system of the city of Amsterdam. To provide some background to the scales forming part of this study and treated in this and the next chapter, we will mention some facts concerning local government in Amsterdam.

These facts hold good for the whole structure of local government in the Netherlands. The remnants of two constitutional principles can be discerned: the principle of a certain degree of *autonomy* on the one hand, and the principle of *self-administration* in the execution of centralized national legislation on the other. More or less in accordance with the first principle, the members of the *city council* are elected in each community every four years by the citizens of that community. In accordance with the latter principle the *mayor* of each community is not elected by the citizens of this community but

*The computations were carried out on the Electrologica X-8 computer of the Mathematical Centre in Amsterdam. The procedure was programmed in ALGOL by programmer Douwe de Jong. The analysis reported here is an example of the second type of evaluation of a scale as described in section 5.2.1.

appointed by the central government as a representative and also a trustee of the national interest.

Every four years municipal elections are held simultaneously in all the communities of the Netherlands to elect the members of the city councils. In all the major cities and towns the national political parties dominate the local political scene. For this reason, local elections are often treated in the campaign as a sort of mid-term elections, by which the national government coalition in power at the time may be judged, rather than as a measure of politics at the local level.

After the elections the new city council chooses its aldermen from the parties represented in the council. Under the chairmanship of the mayor they form the municipal executive board, the Board of Mayor and Aldermen, which is the head of the city administration.

Further details about the local political scene in Amsterdam will be given in a study by Van der Maesen based on the municipal elections of June 1966. In trying to construct a scale for this study, it became clear that it would be necessary not only to use the efficacy scale which refers only to elements at the national level of the Dutch political system, but also to try to develop a local efficacy scale.

The eight items used for the local scale were adapted from the national scale and referred explicitly to elements in the local political system of Amsterdam. In table 8.2 we give a literal translation of these items together with the results for our 1966 sample of 1513 Amsterdam voters.

Three of the items in the national scale ("Parties interested only in vote", "Wouldn't go to polls", and "So many voters") could not very well be transferred to the local scene. We used the procedure of section 5.2.2.

The eight local efficacy items proved to scale equally well as the nine national efficacy items. In table 8.2 it can be seen that the value for $\hat{H}$ (0.41) and the 0.95-confidence interval ($0.38 \leqslant H \leqslant 0.43$) are the same as those given in table 8.1.

The sample difficulties of the local efficacy items seem to overlap those of the national efficacy scale, or rather, to range over a segment 0.30–0.60) not adequately covered by the national scale. We suggest as a possible interpretation that the local efficacy scale measures the same dimension as the national scale, but at some intermediate difficulty level. This will be investigated in section 8.3.

Table 8.2   A local efficacy scale (8 items)
(Sample taken from Amsterdam electorate) n = 1513

Items	Marginals	$\hat{H}_i$
L 1. If I communicate my views to the municipal authorities they will be taken into account. (Positive alternative: "agree")	0.33	0.35
L 2. The municipal authorities don't care much about the opinions of people like me. (Positive alternative: "disagree")	0.34	0.46
L 3. Members of the City Council don't care much about the opinions of people like me. (Positive alternative: "disagree")	0.35	0.44
L 4. People like me don't have any say about what the city government does. (Positive alternative: "disagree")	0.37	0.39
L 5. If I communicate my views to members of the City Council they will be taken into account. (Positive alternative: "agree")	0.37	0.39
L 6. Sometimes city politics and government in Amsterdam seem so complicated that a person like me can't really understand what's going on. (Positive alternative: "disagree")	0.41	0.31
L 7. In the determination of city politics, the votes of people like me are not taken into account. (Positive alternative: "disagree")	0.62	0.47
L 8. Because I known so little about city politics, I shouldn't really vote in municipal elections. (Positive alternative: "disagree")	0.68	0.48

Scale coefficient: $\hat{H} = 0.41$; 0.95 confidence interval: $0.38 \leqslant H \leqslant 0.43$.

8.2   AN ANALYSIS ACROSS SUB-GROUPS

We thought it worthwhile to investigate the robustness of the enlarged efficacy scale along lines similar to those followed in chapter 7. We therefore performed some scale analyses on several sub-groups of our Amsterdam sample. In each sub-group we used the procedure described in section 5.2.1 of chapter 5, i.e. the full sets of items of both the established national efficacy scale and the local efficacy scale were evaluated as scales.

We also used the asymptotic sampling distributions derived in section 4.3.3 of chapter 4 and in particular the χ^2-test of the values of the coefficient of scalability H over the sub-groups.*

This section may therefore also serve as an illustration of the tests suggested in section 4.3.3 and the second method suggested in section 5.2.1. Although we know from our theory of chapter 4 that the value of H will also depend on the population distribution in the sub-groups along the attitude dimension, the equality of H of a set of items across subgroups may nevertheless be taken as a sign of the approximate equal scalability of that set for these groups.**

The results of our comparisons across groups are presented in table 8.3 for both scales and for sub-groups set up according to
– formal education (completed);
– sex;
– age;
– religious denomination;
– annual income of the head of the household (or personal income if the interviewee was self-supporting).

The results for the local efficacy scale show a satisfactory robustness of the scale across groups. In none of the five sub-groups did our statistic $\underline{T}$, distributed approximately as chi-square under the null hypothesis of equal H-value across the groups, reach values which justified the rejection of this null hypothesis. The pooled (weighted) estimates $\bar{H}$ of the overall coefficient H, with values 0.40–0.41, correspond well with the value (0.41) of table 8.2.

The data for the national efficacy scale tell a different story. For two of the criteria, religious denomination and sex, no significant differences in scalability were found between the sub-groups. For income, education and age, however, the national efficacy scale seems to be less robust.

These results may serve as examples of the application of the χ^2-tests derived in theorem 3.3.2 of section 4.3.3. The null hypothesis that for the five sub-populations the coefficient of scalability H will have the same value was tested for the sub-group "income". We proved that the statistic $\underline{T}$, used to test this hypothesis, is distributed

*The computations were carried out on the Electrologica X-8 computer of the Mathematical Centre in Amsterdam.

**When the sub-groups themselves differ in the location of their distribution along the attitude dimension, the H-coefficients may differ. In this case the difference may well be the result only of a difference in population distribution, and not of a difference in the homogeneity of the set of items for the various groups.

approximately as χ_4^2 (with four degrees of freedom, d.f. = 4: the number of sub-groups minus one).

For *income*, $\chi_4^2 = 11.34$, the right-tail probability of which, $P\{\chi_4^2 \geqslant 11.34\}$ is 0.02. Therefore the null hypothesis should be rejected at a level of significance of $\alpha = 0.05$. Judging by the test criterion, the national efficacy items are not robust across income levels: they do not scale to the same degree in terms of approximately equal H-values across these groups.

For *education* too the H-values differ significantly at the significance level $\alpha = 0.05$, according to test-statistic $T = 14.39$ (degrees of freedom, d.f. = 3) with an approximate right-tail probability of 0.002.

In both cases scalability is best in the lowest groups (f 5000, – or less", $\hat{H} = 0.47$; "Grade school only", $\hat{H} = 0.43$) and reaches the lowest values in the highest groups ("f 12,000 or more", $\hat{H} = 0.31$; "College or university", $H = 0.26$).

How are we to interpret these indications of a lack of robustness of the *national* efficacy scale for income and education, when for both these variables the robustness of the *local* efficacy scale is satisfactory? Are there reasons for doubting the qualities of the efficacy scale as such?

In fact these findings may be explained by means of the scaling model itself as developed in chapter 4.

We have stated that according to our theory we would expect H to depend on the population distribution along the attitude continuum, when our set of items forms a scale, *i.e.* when they are monotonely homogeneous on that continuum. Therefore we may expect to find differences in scalability as measured by H when we are comparing two sub-groups or populations which are distributed along different parts of the continuum. How these differences arise can be seen from an inspection of the proof of theorem 1.4.1 of section 4.1.4, which states that any two items in a monotonely homogeneous set will be positively associated. The degree of their correlation (which also determines the value of H) will depend on the way in which the population is distributed.

We have illustrated this in figure 8.1 in what is probably an exaggerated way. We have given the trace lines of two hypothetical items together with the densities of two differently distributed populations.

The distribution of population I covers well that part of the continuum along which the two items show good discrimination. Their correlation will therefore be fairly high for population I. For population II, however, the situation is different: the distribution of this

Table 8.3 An analysis across sub-groups
(Amsterdam sample: n = 1513)

	National efficacy scale		Local efficacy scale
	n	$\hat{H}$	$\hat{H}$
I. Formal education (completed)			
1. Grade school only (LO, VGLO, BLO)*	702	0.43	0.43
2. Lower type of vocational training (LO + lager vakonderwijs)*	352	0.37	0.40
3. High school (MULO, HBS (3j.), Handelsschool (3j.))*	279	0.38	0.40
4. College or university (Middelbaar of hoger vakonderwijs, MO, VHMO, universiteit, hogeschool)*	180	0.26	0.36

National efficacy scale: $\bar{H} = 0.38$, $T = 14.39$, d.f.: 3, $P\{\chi_3^2 \geq 14.39\} = 0.002$

Local efficacy scale: $\bar{H} = 0.41$, $T = 2.32$, d.f.: 3, $P\{\chi_3^2 \geq 2.32\} = 0.51$

	National efficacy scale		Local efficacy scale
	n	$\hat{H}$	$\hat{H}$
II. Sex			
1. Men	725	0.40	0.42
2. Women	788	0.39	0.39

National efficacy scale: $\bar{H} = 0.39$, $T = 0.16$, d.f.: 1, $P\{\chi_1^2 \geq 0.16\} = 0.69$

Local efficacy scale: $\bar{H} = 0.40$, $T = 0.84$, d.f.: 1, $P\{\chi_1^2 \geq 0.84\} = 0.36$

III. Age

1. 26 years and younger (Born April 1940 or later)	166	0.34		0.37	
2. 26–35 years	234	0.35	$\bar{H} = 0.41$	0.42	$\bar{H} = 0.41$
3. 35–45 years	293	0.38	$T = 11.43$	0.36	$T = 5.12$
4. 45–55 years	282	0.42	d.f.: 5	0.44	d.f.: 5
5. 55–65 years	255	0.45		0.41	
6. 65 years and older	283	0.47	$P\{\chi^2_5 \geqslant 11.43\} = 0.04$	0.45	$P\{\chi^2_5 \geqslant 5.12\} = 0.40$

IV. Religious denomination

1. Roman Catholic	311	0.41	$\bar{H} = 0.40$	0.39	$\bar{H} = 0.41$
2. Dutch Reformed	200	0.37		0.39	
3. Dutch Calvinist	62	0.49	$T = 4.38$	0.41	$T = 3.01$
4. Other denominations	118	0.48	d.f.: 4	0.48	d.f.: 4
5. No religious affiliation	818	0.39	$P\{\chi^2_4 \geqslant 4.38\} = 0.36$	0.41	$P\{\chi^2_4 \geqslant 3.01\} = 0.56$

V. Income** (1966 standards)

1. ƒ5,000 or less	233	0.47	$\bar{H} = 0.37$	0.39	$\bar{H} = 0.40$
3. ƒ5,000–ƒ7,000	267	0.39		0.46	
3. ƒ7,000–ƒ9,000	323	0.34	$T = 11.34$	0.37	$T = 4.62$
4. ƒ9,000–ƒ12,000	307	0.38	d.f.: 4	0.39	d.f.: 4
5. ƒ12,000 or more	252	0.31	$P\{\chi^2_4 \geqslant 11.34\} = 0.02$	0.40	$P\{\chi^2_4 \geqslant 4.62\} = 0.32$

* Dutch equivalents.

** Income as reported for the head of the household, or personal income if interviewee was self-supporting.

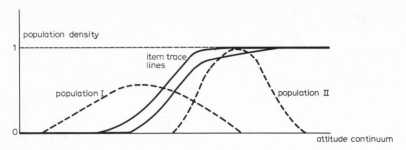

Figure 8.1   Two populations located differently with respect to two item trace lines.

population covers mainly a segment of the continuum which is "diffi-cult" with respect to that part of the continuum along which the trace lines of the items show good discrimination. These trace lines, which approximate unity, run virtually parallel for the segment covered by population II. Consequently their correlation (and therefore H) may be low for population II, in spite of the fact that the items are mono-tonely homogeneous and form a scale.

It is a well-known fact that the "sense of political efficacy" cor-relates highly with indicators of socio-economic status such as income and education (Milbrath, 1965, 57; Campbell *et al.*, 1960, 479). The same was shown to be true for the Netherlands (Daudt and Stapel, 1966; Daudt, Van der Maesen and Mokken, 1968).

The distribution of the income sub-groups will therefore be located along the efficacy continuum. With respect to table 8.1, we noted that as regards their sample difficulties the items of the national efficacy scale fell into roughly two sets. One set (items 1–5) covers a relatively "difficult" part of the continuum (sample difficulties 0.25–0.35), the other set (items 6–9) covers the more "easy" part (sample difficulties 0.63–0.79).

On the basis of our argument concerning figure 8.1, we could expect the scalability of the least difficult items to deteriorate in the highest efficacy groups ("College or university" and "*f* 12,000 or more"). Judging by their item coefficients, this may be true. Item 9 (So many voters) has low values of $\hat{H}_9 = 0.15$ ("College or university") and $H_9 = 0.24$ ("*f* 12,000 or more"). Item 8 (Votes taken into account) also has low values ($H_8 = 0.16$ and 0.19 respectively), but we shall see that it may have doubtful scaling qualities in other sub-groups as well.

We may conclude this analysis by stating that for income and education the lack of robustness may be caused by the relatively high correlation of these variables with the efficacy dimension and not by a lack of monotone homogeneity (scalability) of the items.

We shall see in the next section that there are reasons to regard the local efficacy scale as measuring the same efficacy dimension as the national efficacy scale. Judging by their sample difficulties, the items of the local efficacy scale seem to cover an intermediate part of this dimension. The fact that this local efficacy is robust even for income and education may support our conclusion concerning the robustness of the national scale.

Table 8.4   The sense of political efficacy and age (9-item national scale; Amsterdam sample: n = 1513)

	Level of scale score			
	L (0–3) %	M (4–5) %	H (6–9) %	
Age groups:				
1. 26 years and younger	47	27	26	166 (100%)
2. 26–35 years	39	39	22	234 (100%)
3. 35–45 years	34	33	32	293 (100%)
4. 45–55 years	39	35	26	282 (100%)
5. 55–65 years	35	35	30	255 (100%)
6. 65 years and older	42	31	27	283 (100%)

The results for *age* tell an entirely different story. For the national scale (and for the Amsterdam sample) these results are rather interesting, as they show a definite increase of scalability from the lowest to the highest age group. The values of the scalability coefficient $\hat{H}$ increase monotonically from 0.34 (26 years and younger) to 0.47 (65 years and older). The differences between the $\hat{H}$-values are significant, as indicated by the value of $T = 11.43$, the right-tail probability of which, 0.04, exceeds a significance level of $\alpha = 0.05$.

The argument which was used to explain the variation in H for income and education will not help us here, because there is no clear relation between "sense of political efficacy" and age. Such a relation is not demonstrated in either American research (Campbell *et al.*, 1954, 191; Milbrath, 1965, 58) or Dutch research (Daudt and Stapel, 1966, 71). For the 1966 Amsterdam sample we did not find an appreciable relation between political efficacy and age either, as witnessed by table 8.4.

Summarizing our results, we may conclude that with respect to the *national* scale

　　a. there is no appreciable relation between the *level* of the "sense of political efficacy" and age (table 8.4);

　　b. there is a striking relation between the *scalability* of the "sense of political efficacy" and age (table 8.3).

We will now return to the remarks made at the conclusion of section 7.2.3 with respect to the Easton and Dennis findings concerning children at elementary school. We suggested that it would be worthwhile to investigate the scalability of the efficacy items for the several age groups to make it possible to study the process of attitude formation. We do not know of any study in which the type of analysis of scalability proposed here has been used to investigate processes of attitude formation.

　　That such an analysis may be of considerable theoretical interest is illustrated by the present findings, which show a steady increase of the values of $\hat{H}$ for the national efficacy scale over adult age groups. Although a more or less definitive explanation cannot be given at this stage, these data suggest that the development of the sense of political efficacy as a consistent attitude structure may not be completed in childhood and adolescence but may continue to develop towards greater consistency throughout the life cycle. Against this developmental hypothesis at least one other hypothesis may be put forward as a conceivable explanation of our data.

　　For instance, it may be conjectured that the development of a sense of political efficacy as a consistent attitude structure may be confined to the formative years of the individual. After its completion at some time in childhood or adolescence, this specific attitude organization and its pattern of constraints would then remain stable or constant throughout adult life. In terms of our scaling model, the final degree of internal consistency of the efficacy elements as measured by the scalability coefficient H will be determined by the conditions prevailing in the political system and culture at the time when a particular age group acquires its political culture. After that the coefficient of scalability H would be approximately *constant* for this age group over the life-cycle.

　　If this hypothesis were true, our results for age in table 8.3 would have to be seen in an entirely different light. In this case the results would suggest that for successive age groupings (cohorts) this final degree of attitude organization has been steadily decreasing over the decades. We may then conjecture, for instance, that the rapid development of western industrial society throughout this century towards increasingly more complex structures at the national level may have weakened the internal consistency of central attitude and expectation structures such as the "sense of political efficacy".

In that case our scalability measures would have enabled us to detect phenomena which perhaps characterize age cohorts in terms of Mannheim's concept of a "generation as an actuality":

> "We shall therefore speak of a *generation as an actuality* only where a concrete bond is created between members of a generation by their being exposed to the social and intellectual symptoms of a process of dynamic de-stabilization" (Mannheim, 1953, 303).*

At the present stage it is impossible to verify which of the two hypotheses is most likely to be true: the *developmental* hypothesis mentioned first or the *generational* hypothesis suggested in our later remarks. Our data concern only a fixed point of time (1966) and a given place (Amsterdam). Comparative (cross-national) and longitudinal research based on cohort analysis will be necessary to investigate the possibilities suggested by these results from our survey of the Amsterdam electorate in order to decide which hypothesis is valid.

Of course our results may be valid only for the shifting political structure of the Netherlands in the sixties, or even more specifically, for the politically uproarious year 1966 in the historically and traditionally highly politicized city of Amsterdam (Van der Land *et al.*, 1967, Van der Maesen, 1967; Moerkerk, 1967).

For the local efficacy scale no significant differences in scalability could be found for the different age groups. Table 8.3 (III) does not show a clear trend in scalability either, although the first three age groups seem to have somewhat lower scalability than the last three.

Perhaps the fact that the local efficacy items cover the "middle part" of the efficacy continuum, whereas the national efficacy items cover a relatively "difficult" and a relatively "easy" segment has some connection with this phenomenon. In this case we may surmise that especially the national elements of the political system, as referents of the national scale, play an important role in the trend of the scalability over the age groups.

In concluding our analysis of the results of table 8.3, we may point out that on the whole our T-test of the scalability across groups, as derived in theorem 3.3.2 of section 4.3.3, is not unsatisfactory. It does not seem too severe a test. In the case of the local efficacy items, a difference of some nine percentage points in scalability between the

---

*Daudt (1961, 100–4) has given a critical review of the concept of political generation in relation to the age variable in electoral research. His remarks, which were made along lines suggested by Heberle and Mannheim, are relevant for our problems too.

two income groups did not lead to a value of T large enough to reject the null hypothesis.

The investigation of the cross-cultural robustness of scales may also serve to evaluate the scale performance of individual items. In our analysis across groups we also considered individual items. We shall not report all the item coefficients for all the groups. It will be sufficient to mention the items with low item coefficients of scalability $(\hat{H}_i)$. We shall only mention values below 0.28. In general the items performed well. Nevertheless some exceptions may be noted. The national scale items 5 (Politics complicated) and 8 (Votes taken into account) showed low values several times. $\hat{H}_5$ was 0.26 in the first and second age groups, 0.27 in the second and third income groups, 0.23 in the highest income group, 0.24 in the third educational group and 0.20 in the highest educational group. Furthermore, item 8 had values for $\hat{H}_8$ of 0.25–0.26 in the first three age groups, 0.25 in the third income group and 0.19 in the highest income group. $\hat{H}_8$ was 0.16 in the highest educational group. Apart from the results for the highest educational group and for the items mentioned above, only one other item (4: Don't have say) for only one sub-group, income group 3, attained a low value: $\hat{H}_4 = 0.26$.

For the highest educational group, "College or university", the whole scale deteriorated considerably, as may be judged from the values of the item coefficients lower than 0.28 which we list below:

- item 9 (So many voters) : $\hat{H}_9 = 0.15$
- item 8 (Votes taken into account) : $\hat{H}_8 = 0.16$
- item 5 (Politics complicated) : $\hat{H}_5 = 0.20$
- item 6 (Shouldn't vote) : $\hat{H}_6 = 0.25$
- item 1 (MPs don't care) : $\hat{H}_1 = 0.26$
- item 4 (Don't have say) : $\hat{H}_4 = 0.26$

How can this be explained?

In our discussion of the results of table 8.3 concerning income and education we used figure 8.1 to illustrate how some of these results could be explained, by means of our scaling theory itself, as the effects of a particular distribution of the population along the attitude continuum.

Our scaling theory contains yet another, related, feature, on the basis of which this failure of the scale in the highest educational group might be explained.

We have already mentioned the fact that education is associated rather strongly with the sense of political efficacy. Especially the highest educational group is characterized by a high level of political efficacy. It might therefore be expected that the distribution of this sub-group would be concentrated mainly in a segment of the efficacy continuum with high values. Consequently, this sub-group might be more homogeneous as regards political efficacy than others. A perfectly homogeneous sub-group would contain elements with the same value (θ) of efficacy. In this ideal case one of the central assumptions of our model, that of *local independence* (assumption (1.2.), section 3.1.1, chapter 3), would imply that the responses to items were uncorrelated, so that the coefficient of scalability of items and scale would be zero.

Of course, it is not realistic to expect perfectly homogeneous groups in practice. Yet, if the data fit our scaling theory, we can expect to detect effects of local independence of this type when we investigate populations which are more or less homogeneous on the variable measured by a scale.

For the highest educational group this is precisely what happened in the case of the national efficacy scale: six of its nine items showed drastically lower item coefficients, and consequently the scale coefficient $\hat{H} = 0.26$ was strongly reduced.

For these reasons the results may also be regarded as some evidence in favour of our fundamental hypothesis of local independence.

For the local efficacy scale only item L6 (City politics complicated) had low coefficients in more than one group: in the third age group ($\hat{H}_{L6} = 0.27$), the first (0.27) and fifth (0.22) income groups and the highest educational group (0.22). Item L1 (Views taken into account) had a low value ($\hat{H}_{L1} = 0.27$) in the first income group and item L8 (Shouldn't vote) (municipal elections) ($\hat{H}_{L8} = 0.26$) in the highest educational group. Although the homogeneity of the highest educational group does not seem to be clearly of great impact for the local efficacy items, a slight influence of local independence may perhaps be detected in the fact that only for this group are two items (L6 and L8) clearly below level (0.22 and 0.26), while the overall coefficient of 0.36 is also lower than for the other groups.

We may conclude our analysis with the remark that the results also illustrate the influence which the population distribution of subjects may have on the estimates of scale, test and item parameters. As such the results support the approach of Rasch, referred to in sections 3.2.4 and 7.2.2, of developing models and statistics which are less susceptible to variations in distribution (*population free*).

8.3   A BROADER EFFICACY DIMENSION: A COMBINED SCALE (17 ITEMS)

In their exploration of the efficacy dimension, the original designers of the scale tried to relate it to a more basic underlying general personality dimension which they called "personal effectiveness", stating that:

"The sense of control or mastery over the environment is an important component in modern personality theory" (Campbell *et al.*, 1960, 516; see also Campbell, 1962).

We do not intend to pursue this social-psychological line of investigation in this section, but will restrict our attention to the efficacy dimension as a conceptual element of the culture of any political system.

The two scales we used referred explicitly to two different parts of the Dutch political system: one at the national level, the other at a specific local level, that of the city of Amsterdam, both observed on the same Amsterdam sample.

The political systems that correspond with these two levels may be regarded as affecting their common members in different ways, corresponding to differently defined citizen and subject role sets. According to this line of thought we may expect national and local efficacy to correspond to probably related but different dimensions.

On the other hand we may as well regard the political system of a community with all its interrelated sub-systems as forming one political environment with respect to which its members develop a general sense of political efficacy. The national and local sub-systems are parts of the same political environment perceived from different distances, the sphere of local politics being closer to the average citizen and the national political scene being perceived as further away. It would then be more easy for a person to feel "efficacious" with respect to the relatively near local sub-system than with respect to the more distant national system.

This line of reasoning would lead us to expect a general efficacy dimension along which local items would cover a segment of the efficacy continuum less "difficult" than that covered by the national items. In this case we would expect a close association to exist between the two scales of a special type; this association is the subject of table 8.5 (see also Daudt, Van der Maesen and Mokken, 1968, 293). For the sake of convenience we have grouped the values of the scores on both scales into three classes.

*Table 8.5   The association of the national and local efficacy scales**

Score classes local scale		Score classes national scale			
		Low (0–3) %	Medium (4,5) %	High (6–9) %	
Low %** (0,1)		55 *85*	11 *14*	1 *1*	100% (n = 382)
Medium % (2–4)		35 *34*	57 *48*	26 *18*	100% (n = 603)
High % (5–8)		10 *11*	32 *31*	73 *58*	100% (n = 528)
		100% (n = 585)	100% (n = 510)	100% (n = 418)	N = 1513

*Source: Daudt, Van der Maesen and Mokken (1968, 293).
**Horizontal percentages are given in italics.

The strong association between the two scales is evident in table 8.5. Moreover, it is exactly the type of association one would expect. Respondents scoring high on the *national* scale may be expected to score high on the *local* scale as well: 73% of the respondents who scored "high" on the national scale scored "high" on the local scale. The reverse need not necessarily be true: of the respondents scoring high on the local scale, a smaller percentage (58%) also scored "high" on the national scale. Again, the respondents scoring "low" on the *local* scale would be expected to score "low" on the *national* scale as well. This proved to be true for 85% of the respondents who had a low score on the local scale.

Here too, the reverse need not be true: of the respondents with a low score on the *national* scale a considerably smaller percentage (55%) scored low on the local scale. The results of table 8.5 are therefore well in line with the hypothesis that the local scale simply measures an "easier" segment of the efficacy dimension than the national scale.

We may test this hypothesis directly by means of an application of our scaling procedure to the combined set of national and local efficacy items. Using the step-wise procedure sketched in section 5.2.2, chapter 5, we saw that all the seventeen items formed a scale, as can be seen from table 8.6.

The value of the overall coefficient of scalability $\hat{H} = 0.39$ is not appreciably lower than the values for the smaller constituent scales (both 0.41; see tables 8.1 and 8.2).

Our scaling method has again proved its capacity to isolate large scales. In fact we have enlarged our efficacy scale from some eight or nine items to a near-medium scale of seventeen items without appreciably lowering the value of the scalability coefficient. The item coefficients all satisfy the scale-defining condition of section 5.1.8: they are all at least 0.30.

The results of table 8.6 form evidence in favour of our conjecture that the two scales may be measuring the same efficacy dimension. Table 8.6 again illustrates the previously mentioned fact that, judging by the sample difficulties, the "local" items roughly fill up the "gap" in the middle part of the efficacy scale between items 4 and 6.

8.4 INVESTIGATING THE DOUBLE MONOTONY OF SCALES

Thus far we have analyzed one set of items as scales in terms of *monotone homogeneity* as defined in chapter 4 and section 5.1.2.

Table 8.6 *Efficacy scale (national and local combined: 17 items)*

Items*	Marginals	$\hat{H}_i$
1. MPs don't care	0.25	0.40
2. Cabinet Ministers don't care	0.27	0.41
3. Parties interested only in my vote	0.27	0.40
4. Don't have say	0.31	0.36
L 1. Views taken into account	0.33	0.31
L 2. Authorities don't care	0.34	0.42
5. Politics complicated	0.35	0.30
L 3. City Council don't care	0.35	0.42
L 4. Don't have say	0.37	0.39
L 5. Views taken into account (City Council)	0.37	0.34
L 6. City politics complicated	0.41	0.36
L 7. Votes *not* taken into account (city politics)	0.62	0.42
6. Shouldn't vote	0.63	0.44
7. Wouldn't go to polls	0.66	0.42
8. Votes taken into account	0.66	0.34
L 8. Shouldn't vote (municipal elections)	0.68	0.50
9. So many voters	0.79	0.50

Scale coefficient: $\hat{H} = 0.39$
*Item numbers refer to those used in tables 8.1 and 8.2 respectively.

There we saw that the main feature of such models is that the probability that a subject will give the scale response (or positive response) to any item of the scale will increase with this subject's value on the continuum. To put it briefly: the higher the value on the continuum of the subject, the higher the probability that he will respond positively to any given scale item.

We can specialize this model somewhat further by adding a second very reasonable requirement: the probability of a scale response or positive response should decrease when the difficulty of the items presented to a subject increases. This property of the *double monotony* of item trace lines has been called *holomorphism* by Rasch, who did not investigate it further. In chapter 4 we showed that this simple property has some interesting consequences for our scaling procedures, and we derived some criteria with which to test whether a set of items forming a scale might form a holomorphic scale as well.

Because a holomorphic. or doubly monotone scale* is perhaps the most natural probabilistic model for generalizing the original deterministic Guttman scale, it may be worthwhile to strive at constructing such holomorphic scales.

8.4.1　*Some examples*

We shall investigate the holomorphism of our efficacy scales using our main criterion, which was derived in theorem 1.4.2 of section 4.1.4 and summarized in section 5.1.6. It is based on the inspection of two cells, $(1, 1)$ and $(0, 0)$, of the 2×2-tables for all item pairs as given by the matrices Π and $\Pi^{(0)}$ defined in these sections. In order to illustrate the method we will first investigate a simple example.

Political knowledge. For our study of opinion leaders of 1966, mentioned in section 9.1, we gauged the political knowledge of our *male* respondents with the help of a battery of five questions resembling quiz questions which concerned certain political personalities and membership of the European Common Market. Because of the cumulative nature of such specific knowledge, we might expect a good scale. The data did not disappoint these expectations, as can be seen from table 8.7, which gives a translation of the items as well as the relevant parameters: sample difficulties, item coefficients and coefficients of scalability.

The set of five items forms a strong scale ($\hat{H} = 0.52$) with neatly spaced sample difficulties. Even for our male respondents our test of political knowledge proved to be rather hard, judging from the difficulties of items such as those concerning political personalities as much in the public eye as the French Prime Minister and the West German Foreign Secretary.

For the purpose of judging the holomorphism of the scale we may inspect the matrices given in table 8.8. The $\hat{\Pi}$-matrix gives for every pair of items the estimated proportion of respondents giving the scale response (positive response) to *both* items.

In agreement with the convention of ordering the items according to their estimated population difficulties (sample difficulties), the most difficult item was given the number 1 and the least difficult item the

---

*In section 4.1 we distinguished *holomorphic* and *doubly monotone* sets of items. For the results in this section this theoretically important distinction will not be given too much weight. The general reader may therefore consider the terms as synonymous for all practical purposes.

Table 8.7 Political knowledge (5 items)
(Male sample from Amsterdam electorate, January 1966)
n = 269

Items	Sample difficulties	$\hat{H}_i$
1. Could you name a number of Members of Parliament? (Scale response: at least four correct names)	0·19	0·64
2. Could you name the Prime Minister of France? (Scale response: "Pompidou")	0.26	0.42
3. Could you name the Foreign Secretary of the German Federal Republic? (Scale response: "Schröder")	0.33	0.47
4. Could you name a number of Cabinet Ministers? (Scale response: at least four correct names)	0.37	0.54
5. Do you know which countries form the Common Market? (Scale response: all six countries correct)	0.56	0.55

Scale coefficient $\hat{H} = 0.52$

number 5. From theorem 1.4.2 of section 4.1.4 (see also section 5.1.6), we would expect that in each column (or row, by symmetry) the elements would *increase* monotonically from item 1 to item 5 if the scale is holomorphic. This is exactly the case for the $\hat{\Pi}$-matrix of table 8.8, and very neatly so.

Similarly, the $\hat{\Pi}^{(0)}$-matrix of table 8.8 gives for every pair of items the estimated proportion of respondents giving a non-scale response to *each* item. On the basis of theorem 1.4.2 we would expect the elements of each column of this $\hat{\Pi}^{(0)}$-matrix to *decrease* monotonically from item 1 to item 5. Because of the symmetry of the $\hat{\Pi}^{(0)}$-matrix the same should be true of the elements of the rows.

Again the expected relation is exactly given in table 8.8.

Hence, at least by these two tests, the inspection of the $\hat{\Pi}$- and $\hat{\Pi}^{(0)}$-matrices, there is no reason to doubt the double monotony or holomorphism of this five-item scale of political knowledge.

Before we illustrate the utility of this method with further examples we shall have to make some qualifications.

In the first place this test is mainly a visual one and how strong a criterion it is for the holomorphism of a scale remains a question. Even if the test works in practice we should keep in mind that the trends predicted for the $\hat{\Pi}$- and $\hat{\Pi}^{(0)}$-matrices by theorem 1.4.2 are a necessary and not a sufficient condition for double monotony.

Table 8.8   Holomorphism of the scale of political knowledge

$\hat{\Pi}$-matrix

Item numbers*	1	2	3	4	5
1	–	0.12	0.13	0.17	0.17
2	0.12	–	0.14	0.17	0.19
3	0.13	0.14	–	0.22	0.27
4	0.17	0.17	0.22	–	0.29
5	0.17	0.19	0.27	0.29	–

Sample
difficulties   0.19   0.26   0.33   0.37   0.56

$\hat{\Pi}^{(0)}$-matrix

Item numbers*	1	2	3	4	5
1	–	0.67	0.61	0.61	0.42
2	0.67	–	0.56	0.54	0.37
3	0.61	0.56	–	0.51	0.37
4	0.61	0.54	0.51	–	0.36
5	0.42	0.37	0.37	0.36	–

Sample
difficulties   0.19   0.26   0.33   0.37   0.56

*Item numbers refer to those given in table 8.7.

Secondly, there is no useful statistical theory which will enable us to test these trends for *sample* data. The only thing we can do is to see if the $\hat{\Pi}$- and $\hat{\Pi}^{(0)}$-matrices (as consistent estimators) reflect these trends fairly faithfully for large samples.

To understand the third qualification table 8.8 should be inspected more closely. We should note, for instance, that the proportions in the first column of the $\hat{\Pi}$-matrix cannot exceed 0.19, the sample difficulty of item 1, whereas those of column 2 are less restricted, as they are bounded by the larger item difficulty 0.26 of item 2. For item 3 with its sample difficulty of 0.33 this restriction is less severe. This phenomenon has some consequences for the *rows* of $\hat{\Pi}$: for any row the first element is more restricted in variation than the second element, and so on.

Row elements will therefore tend to reproduce these column restrictions. This is equivalent to saying that row elements will tend to reproduce the difficulty ordering of the items for any set of tables, which is the ordering that we are looking for.

In spite of this undeniable fact, we shall see in what follows that systematic deviations from holomorphism may sometimes be detected.

Finally, the elements of $\hat{\Pi}^{(0)}$ depend partially on those of $\hat{\Pi}$ and the sample difficulties. Nevertheless we have to use *both* matrices to check the full set of conditions given in theorem 1.4.2.

We shall now see how these two tests may help us to evaluate the double monotony of the efficacy scale.

The national efficacy scale. In tables 8.9A and 8.9.B are given respectively the matrices $\hat{\Pi}$ and $\hat{\Pi}^{(0)}$ of the national efficacy scale. Here we are already confronted with some of the difficulties accompanying correct visual inspection. Our first problem is to decide which deviations from the pattern of double monotony should be taken as a sign of the non-holomorphism of the scale.*

We cannot give an adequate statistical criterion on which we may base our test, nor shall we attempt to suggest some "short-and-dirty" statistics that may be helpful. The only way open to us at this stage is simply to suggest some more or less self-evident guide lines which may be of use in the visual inspection of matrices $\hat{\Pi}$ and $\hat{\Pi}^{(0)}$.

Here and in the following examples we shall begin by inspecting the *columns* from top to bottom as our main approach.

If we accept "small" deviations of 0.03 or less as more or less compatible with sampling variation, we cannot find fault with the matrix $\hat{\Pi}^{(0)}$ of table 8.9.B: it neatly shows the downward, decreasing trend when we inspect columns from top to bottom.

Table 8.9A., which gives the $\hat{\Pi}$-matrix of the national scale, just tells a different story. According to theorem 1.4.2 of section 4.1.4, the elements should increase monotonically in a $\hat{\Pi}$-matrix if holomorphism exists.

Noting the deviations in each column, we see that one criterion of a deviation from double monotony could be that:

1. *inspection by columns may isolate a certain row in which deviations of holomorphism are located. This row identifies a probably deviant item*

In table 8.9A we have made bold in each column striking deviations from the expected trend as well as the deviations that are relatively small but similar in trend to the more pronounced ones.

---

*An additional difficulty is the fact that the difficulty order of the items, which is essential for the determination of the trends, is also being estimated from the sample. Consequently, sampling variation may also influence this order.

Table 8.9A **Π̂**-*matrix efficacy scale (9 items)*

Item numbers*	1	2	3	4	5	6	7	8	9
1	–	0.14	0.14	0.14	0.14	0.19	0.20	0.20	0.22
2	0.14	–	0.15	0.15	0.14	0.21	0.23	0.23	0.25
3	0.14	0.15	–	0.15	0.15	0.23	0.23	0.22	0.25
4	0.14	0.15	0.15	–	0.15	0.25	0.25	0.26	0.28
5	0.14	0.14	0.15	0.15	–	0.29	0.28	**0.25**	0.31
6	0.19	0.21	0.23	0.25	0.29	–	0.54	**0.46**	0.57
7	0.20	0.21	0.23	0.25	0.28	0.54	–	**0.48**	0.59
8	0.20	0.23	0.22	0.26	**0.25**	**0.46**	**0.48**	–	**0.57**
9	0.22	0.25	0.25	0.28	0.31	0.57	0.59	**0.57**	–

Sample difficulties.

	0.25	0.27	0.27	0.31	0.35	0.63	0.66	0.66	0.79

Table 8.9B **Π̂**$^{(0)}$-*matrix efficacy scale (9 items)*

Item numbers:	1	2	3	4	5	6	7	8	9
1	–	0.63	0.62	0.58	0.54	0.32	0.30	0.29	0.18
2	0.63	–	0.62	0.58	0.53	0.31	0.29	0.29	0.19
3	0.62	0.62	–	0.57	0.54	0.33	0.30	0.29	0.19
4	0.58	0.58	0.57	–	0.50	0.31	0.28	0.29	0.18
5	0.54	0.53	0.54	0.50	–	0.32	0.27	0.24	0.17
6	0.32	0.31	0.33	0.31	0.32	–	0.25	0.17	0.14
7	0.30	0.29	0.30	0.28	0.27	0.25	–	0.15	0.14
8	0.29	0.29	0.29	0.29	0.24	0.17	0.15	–	0.11
9	0.18	0.19	0.19	0.18	0.17	0.14	0.14	0.11	–

Sample difficulties:

	0.25	0.27	0.27	0.31	0.35	0.63	0.66	0.66	0.79

*Item numbers refer to those used in table 8.1.

For instance, in column 6, element $\pi_{86} = 0.46$ disturbs the upward trend (from $\hat{\pi}_{76} = 0.54$ to $\hat{\pi}_{96} = 0.57$). The elements in row 8 are consistently too low in columns 5, 6, 7 and 9. A related criterion may be derived from a row-wise comparison of approximately *equivalent* items. Equivalent items may here be taken to be items with approximately equal sample difficulties. From theorem 1.4.2 we would expect the columns for equivalent items in the matrices **Π̂** and **Π̂**$^{(0)}$ to be identical.

An example may be given using items 1, 2 and 3 from the national efficacy scale. According to their sample difficulties (0.25 and 0.27), these items are approximately equivalent. When we compare columns

1, 2 and 3 of the matrices $\hat{\Pi}$ and $\hat{\Pi}^{(0)}$ of table 8.9A and 8.9B row-wise, we can conclude that their similarity is satisfactory.

A second criterion for the deviation from holomorphism could therefore be:

2. *a row-wise comparison of the columns of equivalent items may indicate a defective column*

In the national efficacy scale, items 6, 7 and 8 are more or less equivalent (sample difficulties: 0.63, 0.66). A row-wise comparison of their columns shows that the last four values of column 8 may be too low.

Although this second criterion is clearly related to the first one, it is this additional consideration of equivalence which again isolates item 8 as a defective item. The conclusion of our analysis would probably be that item 8 (Votes taken into account) should be eliminated if we want a doubly monotone scale. It may be interesting to note that in the analysis across groups this item was also one of the two suspect items.

The local efficacy scale. In table 8.10.A and 8.10.B are given the matrices $\hat{\Pi}$ and $\hat{\Pi}^{(0)}$. Apart from relatively small deviations ($\leqslant 0.03$) a few conspicuous calls can be located in $\hat{\Pi}$ mainly by applying the above-mentioned criterion 2 again. As L 1, L 2 and L 3 are approximately equivalent (sample difficulties 0.33, 0.34, 0.35), a row-wise inspection of their columns of $\hat{\Pi}$ shows that the elements L 4–L 1 (0.17) and L 6–L 1 (0.16) are probably too low. Again, as L 3, L 4, L 5 are equivalent (sample difficulties 0.35, 0.37, 0.37), a comparison of their elements of the first row indicates that L 1–L 4 (0.17) is the low cell, while the first element L 1–L 6 for the slightly more difficult item L 6 (sample difficulty 0.41) is clearly too low too. Incidentally, a comparison of row L 7 for the more or less equivalent items L 3, L 4 and L 5 shows that the joint probability L 7–L 4 (0.32) is probably too high.*

Which item is the defective one? A third criterion that may be helpful is:

3. *the item whose removal best improves the holomorphism of the scale may be considered defective*

In this case criterion 3 will not be of much help in deciding whether item L 4 or item L 7 should be removed from the scale. The removal

*The element L 1–L 5 (0.24) also seems too high compared with, for instance, L 5–L 6 or L 1–L 7.

Table 8.10A   Π̂*-matrix local efficacy scale (8 items)*

Item numbers*	L 1	L 2	L 3	L 4	L 5	L 6	L 7	L 8
L 1	–	0.20	0.20	**0.17**	*0.24*	**0.16**	0.26	0.27
L 2	0.20	–	0.24	0.23	0.22	0.21	0.29	0.29
L 3	0.20	0.24	–	0.21	0.22	0.22	0.29	0.29
L 4	**0.17**	0.23	0.21	–	0.21	0.21	**0.32**	0.31
L 5	*0.24*	0.22	0.22	0.21	–	0.19	0.28	0.30
L 6	**0.16**	0.21	0.22	0.21	0.19	–	0.32	0.36
L 7	0.26	0.29	0.29	**0.32**	0.28	0.32	–	0.50
L 8	0.27	0.29	0.29	0.31	0.30	0.36	0.50	–
Sample difficulties	0.33	0.34	0.35	0.37	0.37	0.41	0.62	0.68

Table 8.10B   Π̂$^{(0)}$*-matrix local efficacy scale (8 items)*

Item numbers:	L 1	L 2	L 3	L 4	L 5	L 6	L 7	L 8
L 1	–	*0.52*	**0.51**	**0.47**	*0.54*	**0.41**	*0.30*	0.26
L 2	0.52	–	0.55	0.52	0.51	0.45	0.32	0.27
L 3	*0.51*	0.55	–	0.50	0.50	0.46	0.32	0.26
L 4	**0.47**	0.52	0.50	–	0.47	0.43	0.33	0.26
L 5	*0.54*	0.51	0.50	0.47	–	0.41	0.29	0.25
L 6	**0.41**	0.45	0.46	0.43	0.41	–	0.28	0.27
L 7	*0.30*	0.32	0.32	0.33	0.29	0.28	–	0.20
L 8	0.26	0.27	0.26	0.26	0.25	0.27	0.20	–
Sample difficulties	0.33	0.34	0.35	0.37	0.37	0.41	0.62	0.68

*Item numbers refer to those used in table 8.2.

of only one of the two items L 1 and L 4 will lead to the removal of two "defective" cells, so that a third cell remains: cell L 4–L 7 if item L 1 is removed or cell L 1–L 6 if item L 4 is removed. The removal of either L 1 and L 4 or of L 1 and L 7 is necessary if we are to be left with a reasonably doubly monotone or holomorphic set of items. It seems that item L 1 is a certain candidate for removal if we are to obtain a better correspondence with holomorphism.

This finding is corroborated by the additional information supplied by Π̂$^{(0)}$, as we can see in table 8.10.B. There we have made bold conspicuously deviating cells and made italic some smaller deviations which seem to be in line with these cells. A comparison of the columns of the equivalent items L 1, L 2 and L 3 (criterion 2) shows that the elements L 3–L 1 (0.51), L 4–L 1 (0.47) and L 6–L 1 (0.41) are too low. These findings are confirmed by criterion 1: an inspection of the columns of $\hat{\Pi}^{(0)}$ in table 8.10.B. shows that all the elements except one (L 1–L 5) in the first row (L 1) may be bold or italic, as they run counter to the trend expected on the basis of theorem 1.4.2.

Therefore the combined evidence of matrix $\hat{\Pi}$ and $\hat{\Pi}^{(0)}$ leads us to suspect that item L 1 disturbs the holomorphism of our scale. Hence removal of this item would improve the double monotony of the scale. We have formulated a fourth criterion, necessary according to theorem 1.4.2.:

4. *combination of the evidence based on* $\hat{\Pi}$ *and* $\hat{\Pi}^{(0)}$ *may show which items disturb the holomorphism of the scale*
Criterion 4 will not help us to find out which of the two items L 4 and L 7 is responsible for the high value of their common cell in $\hat{\Pi}$: for $\hat{\Pi}^{(0)}$ the pair L 4–L 7 does not disturb the holomorphism of the scale. We shall see that in this particular example, the combined efficacy scale enabled us to reach a conclusion concerning items L 4 and L 7.

The combined efficacy scale. We will now investigate the holomorphism of the larger seventeen-item efficacy scale that was shown to exist in section 8.3. This investigation will serve two purposes.

In the first place, the establishment of a reasonable fit of the set of national and local items to holomorphism may be considered additional evidence in favour of a common dimension.

Secondly, our analysis may illustrate that here too, a large set of items will enable us to determine more clearly which items disturb the holomorphism than a smaller number of items will.

The matrices $\hat{\Pi}$ and $\hat{\Pi}^{(0)}$ are given in tables 8.11A and 8.11B. Again we have made bold the conspicuously deviating items, italicizing those showing smaller but corresponding deviations.

In the $\hat{\Pi}$-matrix we of course find the same defective cells concerning item 8 of the national scale in table 8.9A and item L 1 of the local scale in table 8.10A, but additional information is now supplied. For instance, items L 1, L 2, 5 and L 3 are approximately equivalent (sample difficulties 0.33–0.35). Following criterion 2, a row-wise comparison of columns L 1, L 2 and L 3 shows that, for example, the element 4–L 1 (0.14) may be too small compared with the value 0.18 of the elements 4–L 2 and 4–L 3.

Again, a similar comparison of the equivalent items 7, 8 and L 8 (sample difficulties: 0.66–0.68) shows that L 6–8 (0.30) may be too low compared with L 6–7 (0.34) and L 6–8 (0.36). We may therefore

Table 8.11A   **Π̂-matrix efficacy scale (national and local: 17 items)**

Item numbers:*	1	2	3	4	L1	L2	5	L3	L4	L5	L6	L7	6	7	8	L8	9
1	–	0.14	0.14	0.14	0.13	0.15	0.14	0.17	0.16	0.14	0.15	0.20	0.19	0.20	0.20	0.20	0.22
2	0.14	–	0.15	0.15	0.15	0.18	0.14	0.18	0.17	0.16	0.16	0.22	0.21	0.21	0.23	0.22	0.25
3	0.14	0.15	–	0.15	0.14	0.16	0.15	0.17	0.16	0.15	0.17	0.22	0.23	0.23	0.22	0.22	0.25
4	0.14	0.15	0.15	–	0.14	0.18	0.15	0.18	0.21	0.17	0.18	0.25	0.25	0.25	0.26	0.26	0.28
L 1	0.13	0.15	0.14	0.14	–	0.20	0.13	0.20	0.17	0.24	0.16	0.26	0.25	0.26	0.27	0.27	0.29
L 2	0.15	0.18	0.16	0.18	0.20	–	0.16	0.24	0.23	0.22	0.21	0.29	0.26	0.27	0.28	0.29	0.31
5	0.14	0.14	0.15	0.15	0.13	0.16	–	0.17	0.17	0.15	0.29	0.25	0.29	0.28	0.25	0.30	0.31
L 3	0.17	0.18	0.17	0.18	0.20	0.24	0.17	–	0.21	0.22	0.22	0.29	0.27	0.28	0.28	0.29	0.32
L 4	0.16	0.17	0.16	0.21	0.17	0.23	0.17	0.21	–	0.21	0.21	0.32	0.29	0.30	0.30	0.31	0.33
L 5	0.14	0.16	0.15	0.17	0.24	0.22	0.15	0.22	0.21	–	0.19	0.28	0.27	0.29	0.30	0.30	0.32
L 6	0.15	0.16	0.17	0.18	0.16	0.21	0.29	0.22	0.21	0.19	–	0.32	0.34	0.34	0.30	0.36	0.37
L 7	0.20	0.22	0.22	0.25	0.26	0.29	0.25	0.29	0.32	0.28	0.32	–	0.45	0.47	0.49	0.50	0.57
6	0.19	0.21	0.23	0.25	0.25	0.26	0.29	0.27	0.29	0.27	0.34	0.45	–	0.54	0.46	0.58	0.57
7	0.20	0.21	0.23	0.25	0.26	0.27	0.28	0.28	0.30	0.29	0.34	0.47	0.54	–	0.48	0.57	0.59
8	0.20	0.23	0.22	0.26	0.27	0.28	0.25	0.28	0.30	0.30	0.30	0.49	0.46	0.48	–	0.50	0.57
L 8	0.20	0.22	0.22	0.26	0.27	0.29	0.30	0.29	0.31	0.30	0.36	0.50	0.58	0.57	0.50	–	0.61
9	0.22	0.25	0.25	0.28	0.29	0.31	0.31	0.32	0.33	0.32	0.37	0.57	0.57	0.59	0.57	0.61	–
Sample difficulties:	0.25	0.27	0.27	0.31	0.33	0.34	0.35	0.35	0.37	0.37	0.41	0.62	0.63	0.66	0.66	0.68	0.79

Table 8.11B II^(o)*-matrix efficacy scale (national and local: 17 items)*

Item numbers:	1	2	3	4	L1	L2	5	L3	L4	L5	L6	L7	6	7	8	L8	9
1	–	0.63	0.62	0.58	0.55	0.57	0.54	0.57	0.54	0.52	0.49	0.33	0.32	0.30	0.29	0.28	0.18
2	0.63	–	0.62	0.58	0.55	0.57	0.53	0.56	0.53	0.53	0.48	0.33	0.31	0.29	0.29	0.28	0.19
3	0.62	0.62	–	0.57	0.54	0.55	0.54	0.55	0.52	0.51	0.48	0.32	0.33	0.30	0.29	0.28	0.19
4	0.58	0.58	0.57	–	0.50	0.53	0.50	0.52	0.53	0.49	0.45	0.32	0.31	0.28	0.29	0.27	0.18
L 1	*0.55*	*0.55*	*0.54*	*0.50*	–	*0.52*	**0.45**	*0.51*	*0.47*	**0.54**	*0.41*	*0.30*	0.28	0.26	0.28	0.26	*0.16*
L 2	0.57	0.57	0.55	0.53	0.52	–	**0.48**	0.55	0.52	0.51	0.45	0.32	0.29	0.27	0.27	0.27	0.18
5	*0.54*	*0.53*	*0.54*	*0.50*	**0.45**	**0.48**	–	*0.48*	**0.46**	**0.44**	**0.53**	**0.28**	**0.32**	0.27	0.24	0.27	0.17
L 3	0.57	0.56	0.55	0.52	*0.51*	*0.55*	*0.48*	–	0.50	0.50	0.46	0.32	0.29	0.27	0.26	0.26	0.18
L 4	0.54	0.53	0.52	0.53	**0.47**	0.52	**0.46**	0.50	–	0.47	0.43	0.33	0.29	0.27	0.27	0.26	0.18
L 5	0.52	0.53	0.51	0.49	**0.54**	0.51	**0.44**	0.50	0.47	–	0.41	0.29	0.27	0.26	0.26	0.25	0.16
L 6	0.49	0.48	0.48	0.45	**0.41**	0.45	**0.53**	0.46	0.43	0.41	–	0.28	0.29	0.26	**0.22**	0.27	0.17
L 7	0.33	0.33	0.32	0.32	*0.30*	0.32	**0.28**	0.32	0.33	0.29	0.28	–	**0.20**	**0.19**	0.20	**0.20**	0.15
6	0.32	0.31	0.33	0.31	0.28	0.29	**0.32**	0.29	0.29	0.27	0.29	**0.20**	–	0.25	**0.17**	0.27	0.14
7	0.30	0.29	0.30	0.28	0.26	0.27	0.27	0.27	0.27	0.26	0.26	**0.19**	0.25	–	**0.15**	0.23	0.14
8	0.29	0.29	0.29	0.29	0.28	0.27	0.24	0.26	0.27	0.26	**0.22**	0.20	**0.17**	**0.15**	–	**0.15**	*0.11*
L 8	0.28	0.28	0.28	0.27	0.26	0.27	0.27	0.26	0.26	0.25	0.27	**0.20**	0.27	0.23	**0.15**	–	0.14
9	0.18	0.19	0.19	0.18	*0.16*	0.18	0.17	0.18	0.18	0.16	0.17	0.15	0.14	0.14	*0.11*	0.14	–
Sample difficulties:	0.25	0.27	0.27	0.31	0.33	0.34	0.35	0.35	0.37	0.37	0.41	0.62	0.63	0.66	0.66	0.68	0.79

* Item numbers refer to those used in tables 8.1 and 8.2.

again conclude that items L 1 and 8 disturb the double monotony of the overall scale.

We shall not deal with every deviation marked in these tables. The reader should by now be able to carry out the investigation of double monotony on his own. We shall merely point out some interesting features in tables 8.11.A and 8.11.B.

The application of criterion 1 only, inspecting all the columns from top to bottom, shows that not only the two items L 1 and 8 but also item 5 very clearly disturbs the trend towards holomorphism. For instance, an investigation of columns L 5 and L 6 shows strongly deviant values: 5–L 5 is too low (0.15) and 5–L 6 is too high (0.29).

As items L 2, 5, and L 3 are equivalent (sample difficulties 0.34–0.35) a row-wise comparison of their columns (criterion 2) confirms our suspicions about item 5. For instance, in row 2 the element 2–5 (0.14) seems too low in comparison with the elements 2–L 2 and 2–L 3 (both 0.18).

All these results are supported by the data for the $\hat{\Pi}^{(0)}$-matrix of table 8.11.B, where items L 1, 5 and 8 are clearly distinct from the rest as probably defective in a holomorphic model. The reader will now be able to verify this fact by an application of our criteria to $\hat{\Pi}^{(0)}$.

A combination of the results for $\hat{\Pi}$ and $\hat{\Pi}^{(0)}$ (criterion 4) will reveal that a fourth item, L 7, probably disturbs the double monotony of the set. Inspection of the columns of $\hat{\Pi}^{(0)}$ according to criterion 1 will show that in row L 7 some elements are probably too low. An additional application of criterion 2 to the columns of the approximately equivalent items L 7, 6 and 7 suggests that the $\hat{\Pi}^{(0)}$-elements 6-L7 (0.20), 7-L7 (0.19), and also L8-L7 (0.20) may be too low. Similar observations may be made for these same cells in matrix $\hat{\Pi}$, where other irregularities may be observed in row L 7 for columns L 2, L 3 and L 4. A comparison of columns L 7, 6 and 7 of $\hat{\Pi}$ suggests that elements L2–L7, L3–L7 and L4–L7 tend to be too high.

We may therefore conclude our analysis by remarking that the following four items seem to disturb the double monotony of the scale:

from the national scale:
   -item 5 (Politics complicated);
   - item 8 (Votes taken into account);
from the local scale:
   -item L 1 (Views taken into account);
   -item L 7 (Votes *not* taken into account–(city politics)).

If we remove these four items from the scale, the remaining set of thirteen items shows much more satisfactory agreement with our requirement of holomorphism.

The only conspicuous cells in the $\hat{\Pi}$ matrix are 4–L 4 (0.21) and L2–L3 (0.24). These values are probably too high. In $\hat{\Pi}^{(0)}$, L2–L3 (0.55) again may be somewhat too high. Effects like this for the pair of items 4–L 4 have an interesting explanation that may concern the pair L 2–L 3 also. Item 4 (Don't have say) and L 4 (Don't have say) are so much alike in wording that due to memory or learning effects, local independence, which is the basic assumption of our model, may be replaced by a certain degree of local dependence. This local dependence may account for a rise in the value of $\hat{\pi}_{4,L4}$ which may disturb the trend expected for holomorphism. Apart from these relatively slight deviations, the thirteen-item scale contains no evidence to make us doubt the double monotony of the set. Its coefficient of scalability, $\hat{H} = 0.43$, characterizes it as a medium scale, all the item coefficients attaining values of at least 0.33.

Our analysis of the holomorphism of the combined efficacy scale therefore forms additional evidence that both scales measure a common variable.

With respect to the four deviant items some remarks may be made.

In the first place we may stress the point that the combination of the two sub-scales, the national and the local efficacy scales, into a larger scale allowed us to detect clearly two defective items, 5 (politics complicated) and L 7 (Votes not taken into account – city politics) which we were not able to spot in the analysis of the sub-scales. Moreover, our analysis confirmed some of the evidence concerning the items mentioned in other sections. Items 5 and 8 were indicated in the analysis across groups (section 8.2) as items adversely effecting the robustness of the national scale. For the local items this was less clearly the case: in the analysis across groups, only item L 6 (City politics complicated) gave rise to some suspicions. There were no clear indications against items L 1 or L 7.

Another way of evaluating the items may be mentioned here: by considering the order in which the items were added to the scale in our step-wise procedure (sketched in section 5.2.2). As this procedure in each step selects the best item from the remaining set of items and adds it to the scale as it has been formed up to that moment, we may expect the last items added to the scale to be the ones most to be suspected. This may be reflected in the analysis of the cross-cultural robustness and of the holomorphism of the scale.

There is some evidence that this holds good on our case: the last two items selected for the national scale were 8 and 5. Item 5 was selected in the last step. For the local scale, item L 1 was selected in the last step after L 6. Item L 7 was, however, selected in the first step in the pair L 4 (Have no say)–L 7! For the whole seventeen-item scale the order of selection was less clearly related to our results concerning holomorphism: L 1 was selected as the last and seventeenth item, 8 as the fifteenth item and L 7 as the twelfth item. But item 5 was selected as the third item, with 6 (Shouldn't vote) and L 8 (Shouldn't vote–municipal elections).

We may round off our analysis by stating that the investigation of the holomorphism of the scale partly tends to confirm other indications concerning items that may not fit the scale. Especially item 5 (Politics complicated) should probably be eliminated from the efficacy scale. Eldersveld has already made this suggestion with regard to this item on the basis of its content: "Sometimes politics and government seem so complicated that a person like me can't really understand what's going on".

He remarked that:

"... it has become a glib standardized reaction of even the sophisticated, and thus is probably a poor test of the level of the public's confidence in its own role" (Eldersveld, 1964, 498).

Concerning the content of the four items, (5, 8, L 1, L 7) suggested for elimination, we may note that two of them had "agree" as their scale response. These items are:

8. "In the determination of government policy, the votes of people like me are taken into account."

and

L 1. "If I communicate my views to the municipal authorities they will be taken into account."

In the remaining overall scale of thirteen items, only one item, L 5 (Views taken into account – City Council) will have "agree" as the positive response, while the other twelve items will have "disagree" as their scale alternative. We may therefore ask whether some (acquiescence) response set may have affected our scale results and the results concerning double monotony. This, however, need not be the case, as we can see from the scale results themselves. If such a response set effect only was responsible for the deviation of item 8 we might have expected that a negative formulation of the item, with "disagree" as the scale alternative, would have scaled well under the operation of the same response set effect.

The nearest anologue to such a negative formulation is the local counterpart (L 7) of item 8:

"In the determination of city politics, the votes of people like me are not taken into account."
Although its scale alternative is "disagree" L7 is the fourth item singled out for elimination by our analysis, as was item 8. This suggests that the similar content of items 8 and L 7 may be responsible for their non-scale behavior rather than a specific response set effect.

8.4.2 Conclusions

In section 8.4 we investigated the empirical consequences of our theory of holomorphic (doubly monotone) models. This investigation was of particular interest because of the fact that these doubly monotone models seem a fairly natural and general alternative for the deterministic cumulative model originally advocated by Guttman.

The criterion proposed in theorem 1.4.2 of section 4.1.4 provided a reasonable test for evaluating scales. In fact it enabled us to isolate items whose elimination would result in scales with a better appearance of holomorphism.

This fact suggests at the same time that our scaling model and the procedures derived from it may generally lead to approximately holomorphic scales. Further experiences with many other scales support this claim.

Although the evaluation of double monotony is mainly based on a visual inspection of matrices $\hat{\Pi}$ and $\hat{\Pi}^{(0)}$, we formulated some criteria to guide this visual evaluation. They were:
1. column-by-column inspection may reveal rows which hold deviations of double monotony, identifying deviant items;
2. row-wise comparison of the columns of equivalent items may indicate defective items;
3. the removal of an item which will best reduce the number of deviations and improve the holomorphism of the scale;
4. combination of the information of $\hat{\Pi}$ and $\hat{\Pi}^{(0)}$ may indicate deviant items.

Apart from these visual criteria for the double monotony of a scale, some other controls were suggested for the evaluation of individual items.

In chapter 7 and 8 we saw that a (cross-cultural) analysis across groups of the robustness of a scale may point to defective items.

The order in which items are added to the scale in the step-wise procedure described in section 5.2.2 may occasionally give us similar information. Particularly the items that were added last to the scale may be less robust, or may disturb the double monotony of the scale. Our explorations in this chapter suggest that all the different criteria listed here may often coincide partially in the determination of defective items.

Last but not least, we want to stress the point that item *content* and its theoretical relevance should also be studied carefully as a criterion in itself for evaluating and if necessary eliminating items. In fact a recurrent theme in this study is the necessity of not relying solely on the output of mathematically defined or other analytical or mechanical procedures, in spite of all their possible sophistication. No creative researcher can do without the sound, critical and theoretical assessment of the results of such procedures, for which no computerized system can be substituted.

8.5　THE RELIABILITY OF DOUBLY MONOTONE SCALES

In chapter 4, section 4.2.2, it was possible to derive for doubly monotone sets of items methods for estimating the reliability coefficient of the simple scale score s. These methods, for which we refer the reader to section 4.2.2, are based on the estimation of the otherwise non-estimable diagonal cells of the $\hat{\Pi}$-matrix and made possible by the property of double monotony of a scale.

The methods compare favorably with other, equally crude, methods such as the split-half method, in that they do not require the assumption of equivalent items or randomized halves. Nor are corrections for the reduced length of the separate parts necessary, as the coefficients can be calculated for the scale at its original length. All the assumptions concerning these length corrections which belong to the usual Spearman-Brown formula for the split-half method can therefore be disregarded too. The only assumption is that of the double monotony of the set, which, as we saw in the last section, is open to empirical verification to some extent.

Having established those sets of items for the national, local and combined scales of the "sense of political efficacy" that may be considered reasonably doubly monotone, we may apply our methods and compute reliability coefficients for each of the scales. In view of the requirement of double monotony we omitted items 5 (Politics complicated) and 8 (Votes taken into account) from the national scale, and items L 1 (Views taken into account) and L7 (Votes *not* taken into account – city politics) from the local scale.

Consequently, reliability coefficients were computed for a six-item local scale, a seven-item national scale and a combined scale of thirteen items. The results are given in table 8.12.

Table 8.12 Reliability coefficients of efficacy scales*

Scales	Method I** $\hat{\rho}(s)$	Method II** $\hat{\rho}(s)$
Local scale (6 items)	0.77	0.77
National scale (7 items)	0.80	0.79
Combined scale (13 items)	0.87	0.87

*The computations were carried out on the Electrologica X-8 computer at the Mathematical Centre in Amsterdam.
**For details see section 4.2.2, chapter 4.

As far as our examples go, the two methods do not lead to very different results: in fact they seem to lead to virtually the same estimates. Table 8.12 clearly demonstrates the well-known fact that reliability coefficients increase as test length (the number of items in the scale) increases. The values of the estimated reliabilities seem rather high. This may be due to the requirement of double monotony. In general, the application of our method of estimation seems rather satisfactory.

CHAPTER 9

Applications of multiple scaling

Thus far we have only considered situations in which essentially one known dimension, political efficacy, could be discovered by means of our technique with a scale of adequately chosen items. Such neat uni-dimensional cases do not abound in social research. We often have to face the possibility that more dimensions may be involved with respect to a given set of items. In section 5.2.3 we mentioned that our set of procedures included a version of multiple scaling,* by which a given set of items may be divided up into a number of clusters, each of which forms a scale. In this chapter we shall report some research concerning the possibility of multiple scales and applying the method described in section 5.2.3.

9.1 SCALING OPINION LEADERSHIP

Our first example concerns our efforts to develop an adequate opera-tionalization of political opinion leadership as a multi-dimensional concept in a survey held in Amsterdam in 1966. We shall see that more or less contrary to our expectations our procedure did not result in more than one scale. Instead, our scaling technique suggested that the political communication behavior measured by the various "political opinion leadership" items may well be scalable as a one-dimensional variable.

---

*'In section 5.2.3 we used the term "multiple scaling" to distinguish the procedure of step-wise scale formation from conventional (metric or non-metric) multidimensional scaling procedures such as factor analysis or methods of the Shepard–Kruskal–Guttman–Lingoes variety.

9.1.1 *Opinion leadership: the concept*

One of the important results in early voting research was the discovery that the opinion leader was a key figure in the conveying of political information (Rossi, 1959, 20). The concept of the opinion leader was introduced and defined in *The People's Choice* as follows:

"Common observation and many community studies show that in every area and for every public issue there are certain people who are most concerned about the issue as well as most articulate about it. We call them the 'opinion leaders'". (Lazarsfeld *et al.*, 1948, 49).

It was found that these opinion leaders play a prominent role in the diffusion of political information and the accompanying process of interpersonal persuasion. They are not identical with the socially prominent people in a community and can be found in approximately equal proportions in all the occupation groups. They talk politics much more than other people (their followers), are more interested in politics and respond more strongly to campaign events. The finding that opinion leaders, more than their "followers", reported that mass media are more effective than personal relationships, suggested the well-known hypothesis of "the two-step flow of communications": ". . . that ideas often flow *from* radio and print *to* the opinion leaders and *from* them to the less active sections of the population" (Lazarsfeld *et al.*, 1948, 151). In this respect the concept of the "opinion leader" suggested a revision of a more elementary theory held in mass communications research, according to which:

"Until very recently, the image of society in the minds of most students of communication was of atomized individuals, connected with the mass media but not with one another" (Katz, 1960, 436).

Informal, interpersonal relations were considered irrelevant to the institutions of modern society.

Another important finding was that "opinion leadership" should not be regarded as a generalized leadership trait which enables certain specific individuals to influence the distribution and diffusion of knowledge as well as the opinion formation in every subject or opinion area and in every social group within their reach. Instead, opinion leadership behavior proved to change with a change in subject area: opinion leaders with respect to politics are other people than opinion leaders in the field of consumer behavior. They can be characterized by a special interest and involvement in a given field, and their social radius of influence also varies from group to group.

Perhaps because of the implications for mass communication of the concept of the "opinion leader", the further elaboration of these research findings did not take place in the field of political research proper, but in that of mass communications research (Katz and Lazarsfeld, 1955; Katz, 1957; Klapper, 1960).

After a while, this branch of research combined with at least two other important and independently developed branches of social research: early studies of the diffusion of cultural traits and innovations of cultural anthropologists and diffusion studies in rural sociology, which were very numerous (Katz, Levin and Hamilton, 1963). Especially the contributions of the rural sociologists with their studies of the diffusion of innovation in the field of farming. (Lionberger, 1960; Rogers, 1962; Van den Ban, 1963) formed a valuable addition to the diffusion studies originating in communications research. In both fields, empirical evidence underlined the special position in the structure of interpersonal communication which is occupied by "adoption leaders" or "opinion leaders" and their mediating roles in the simultaneous processes of information dissemination and the exercise of personal influence and persuasion. The findings covered such diverse processes as the adoption of new techniques such as the use of hybrid seed corn (Ryan and Gross, 1943) or new drugs (Coleman, Katz and Menzel, 1966), the buying of new products in the field of consumer behavior, as well as the diffusion of opinions, ideas, attitudes and the preference for particular policies and new parties.

In political theory, the influential individuals involved in these processes earned a place as "opinion leaders", or "diffuse or popular gatekeepers" in the terminology of Easton (1965, 93–5) (see also Lewin, 1947, 333). Yet, despite the importance of this concept in theories of political behavior, not much has been made of it in political research since the Erie county study.

Rossi (1959, 26) in his evaluation of voting research remarked:

> "Surprisingly, no serious attempt was made to extend the prior concern with opinion leadership, the two relevant items in the Elmira questionnaires being little improvement over the items in the earlier study."

The American Voter, another hallmark of electoral research, contains just a few references to the informal "opinion leader" and his mediating role in connecting or relating the politically inactive or even alienated subjects with the political life of their community (Campbell *et al.*, 1960, 271).

Despite the voluminous empirical evidence accumulated in other fields of diffusion research, the important concept of the opinion leader as an agent of diffusion of political information and influence has still not been fully incorporated into political research.

We may add that its importance as a key concept may even exceed that implied by these diffusion studies. The processes studied in diffusion research were unidirectional. The common feature of these studies is always a process whereby an item (a culture trait, practice, idea or opinion) is introduced from "outside" into a social environment in which informal and interpersonal face-to-face communication assumes an important role (a rural community in rural sociology or family groups, peer groups or work groups in communications research). The "outside" sources are agricultural agencies promoting new farming practices or mass media diffusing new political issues and ideas.

This process has been characterized by Katz *et al.* (1963, 240) as ". . . the (1) *acceptance*, (2) over *time*, (3) of some specific *item*–an idea or practice, (4) by individuals, groups or other *adopting units*, linked (5) to specific *channels* of communication, (6) to a *social structure*, and (7) to a given system of values, or *culture*."

One common finding of these studies has stressed the important role played by "opinion leaders" corresponding to their strategic position in the interpersonal communication network of the social units mentioned sub (4) and their special relation to the channels of communication mentioned sub (5) and the larger social structure sub (6) (Rogers, 1962, Chapter VIII, 208–52).

But this particular role may not be confined to the one-way diffusion process which is the object of all these studies. The importance of these findings may well be that the role of the opinion leader will prove to be just as important when *the direction of the processes studied is reversed*: that is when we study processes by which ideas and opinions etc. originating within the smaller units mentioned sub (4) are diffused through specific channels of communications (5) to a social structure (6) with consequences for a given political system and its culture (7).

Processes such as the perception and formulation of wants and the subsequent conversion of these wants into demands, the generation and formulation of issues, the channeling of (negative or positive) support (see Easton, 1965,) are the kind of processes in which we may well expect the same opinion leader to assume new roles in the more informal social units that seem to be extremely important for the theory of political participation.

For these reasons we began a new study with the purpose of investigating more closely the role of the opinion leader, starting with a definition of this concept of a broader scope than that used in *The People's Choice*.

9.1.2   *A scale of opinion leadership*

In trying to design measures of opinion leadership for use in the Netherlands we were faced with a number of problems concerning the concept itself.

The original definition in *The People's Choice* was based on just two questions (Lazarsfeld *et al.*, 1948, 50):
- "Have you tried to convince anyone of your political ideas recently?"
- "Has anyone asked your advice on a political question recently?"

"Opinion leaders" were defined as the respondents who gave the answer "yes" to either one or both of these two questions, while the other respondents were classified as "followers". In at least two respects this early operational definition probably had great influence on the subsequent theoretical development of the concept of the opinion leader in empirical research.

In the *first* place the introduction of the concept of the opinion leader in a "leader-follower" dichotomy as a *type* instead of a variable or graded classification may have had the effect of focussing further study on the single opinion leader. Yet there has never been any indication in empirical evidence concerning opinion leaderhip which precluded the possibility that communication behavior of the "opinion leadership" type could be observed in *degrees*. In fact, recent research strongly suggests that in an improved theoretical framework it might be possible to distinguish several grades of "opinion leadership".

This primitive "opinion leadership" typology, containing just one opinion leader type, may also have been responsible for a too literal interpretation of the hypothesis of a "two-step" flow of communication (Katz, 1957): are just two steps (from the mass media to *the* opinion leaders, from *the* opinion leaders to the public) sufficient to account for the dispersion of mass media ideas?

Other researchers have advocated a more modified view allowing interpersonal communication between opinion leaders (Rogers, 1962, 214; Van den Ban, 1964). Their point of view implies a more general theory of a multi-step flow of information involving interpersonal communication between different levels of opinion leadership.

In our opinion this is a discussion about trivialities. What is really at stake here is the degree of precision with which we want to distinguish grades of "opinion leadership" and intermediate stages in the flow of interpersonal communication and influence.

It seems to us that the development of the concept of the classic "opinion leader" is a perfect example of a process in which highly inadequate concept formation and correspondinly inferior operationalizations may have seriously hindered the development of empirical theory. We prefer to use a more refined measurement of the communication behavior indicated by the term "opinion leadership". In other words, we shall try to *scale* the "opinion leadership" variable(s).

In the *second* place the original definition contained the assumption of a "leader-follower" relation in the diffusion of information and influence. For this reason the *persuasive* and *advisory* role of the opinion leader was stressed in the original items quoted above. The study that further elaborated these findings, the Decatur study (Katz and Lazarsfeld, 1955) also underlined the advisory role of the opinion leader. The items used in this study were

– "Have you recently been asked your advice about . . . (marketing, fashion, etc.)?" and

– "Compared with other women in your circle of acquaintances, are you more or less likely than any of them to be asked your advice on . . . (marketing, fashion, etc.)?" (Katz and Lazarsfeld, 1955, 374).

Another, highly important, role aspect was added to the definition of the opinion leader in the Elmira study reported in *Voting* (Berelson, Lazarsfeld and McPhee, 1954): *participation in discussions* about politics.

The two items used in *Voting* (Berelson, *et al.*, 1954, 377) were the following:

– "Compared with people you know, are you more or less likely than any of them to be asked your views about politics?"

– "Have you talked politics with anyone recently?"

Although the "discussion" item was studied in *Voting* as a separate variable as well (Berelson *et al.*, 101–9), it was combined with the other item into an index of opinion leadership, defining "opinion leaders" as follows:

". . . (1) all respondents who answered that they were 'more' likely to be asked their views on politics plus (2) all those who answered 'same' *and* had talked politics recently". (Berelson *et al.*, 1954, 377).

Subsequent research in other fields has borne out that this third aspect, participation in discussions, is the one most characteristic for the set of opinion leadership roles. It is this participation in the communication and sharing of information and opinions of those involved and interested in a special subject area that is the real basis for the diffusion of interpersonal influence in social systems.

In accordance with this finding, the original importance of specifically the advisory or persuasive roles has somewhat diminished. Although consequently the older term "opinion leader" is not very satisfactory to indicated the type of specific communication behavior we have in mind, (see also Brouwer, 1967; 1968, 34–45) we shall in this study continue to use this term.

In the two examples given above we can discern a more or less tacit assumption that opinion leadership may be a more or less homogeneous or unidimensional trait: in both cases, responses to questions tapping different qualities, *relative competence* ("being sought for advice"), *persuasion* ("convincing people") and *participation in discussions,* were combined into a simple typology. However, we may well wonder whether such a unidimensional conceptualization is feasible and supported by empirical evidence. It is conceivable that the different aspects of the opinion leadership role set correspond to different dimensions. If this is so, opinion leadership should be seen as a multidimensional rather than a unidimensional phenomenon so that multidimensional or multiple scaling techniques are needed in the first place.

Another important problem is how to find opinion leaders in actual research.

In actual practice three methods have been used to measure opinion leadership (Rogers, 1962, 228–30). Two of these have been used primarily in rural communities, where it may be assumed that interpersonal face-to-face relationships of community members cover the whole community.

One of these techniques is the *sociometric* technique, in which respondents indicate the people who give them advice and information about the issue concerned. This method, though involving a great amount of field-work, may be used as a snowball sampling technique in survey research.

The second technique is a variant of the well-known reputation method: the *key informants* in a community are asked to indicate the opinion leaders.

A third method, the most suitable one for survey research, is based on *self-designation:* respondents are asked a set of questions, the answers to which enable the researcher to estimate the degree of opinion leadership of the respondents.

We saw above that the original definitions of opinion leaders in *The People's Choice* and *Voting* were simple examples of this method of self-designation. This technique was used together with the sociometric technique in the Decatur study. The comparative evidence collected in this study (Katz and Lazarsfeld, 1955, 149–61), as well as the results reported by Rogers (1962, 230–2) suggest a reasonable correspondence between the ratings obtained with the other two methods.

For a study of political opinion leadership on a sample of male citizens of Amsterdam of voting age, we also used the self-designating technique. We conceived of opinion leadership as a variable, *i.e.* we decided to admit different levels or degrees of opinion leadership. The authors of *Voting* had already envisaged such a conceptualization, remarking that

"... one might properly speak less of leaders than of a complex web of opinion-leading relationships"; and that

"... we are reminded again that in practice there must be unending circuits of leadership relationships running through the community, like a nerve system through the body" (Berelson *et al.*, 1954, 109, 110).

We thus thought it desirable to allow for the possibility of multidimensionality of the opinion leadership variable.

We saw above that at least three aspects or dimensions seem to dominate in any assessment that has been made of the political opinion leadership role set:
1. *participation* in discussions about politics;
2. some status among friends and acquaintances as a politically interested and informed person: the political *"expert"* or *adviser;*
3. some aptitude for *political persuasion* of friends and acquaintances.

We formulated and pre-tested three questions for each aspect. The final versions were the following.* The translation is as literal as possible.

*1. Participation in discussions about politics***
OL 3. When in company, do you like to start a discussion about politics, or do you prefer to leave that to other people?

---

*For the Dutch version we refer the reader to the appendix.

**The numbering of the items follows the observed difficulty level of the items (see table 9.1).

(Scale alternative: "like to start most of the time"; or "sometimes, it depends").

OL 8. Have you been discussing politics with acquaintances lately? (Scale alternative: "yes").

OL 9. When you are in company, and a discussion about politics is going on, what do you like best: to join the discussion or just listen, or don't you listen, aren't you interested? (Scale alternative: "(usually) join the discussion").

II. Expert status among friends

OL 2. Suppose some of your acquaintances want to know something about politics; are they likely to consult you or somebody else? (Scale alternative: "likely to be consulted").

OL 4. Have you ever been asked by any acquaintances what party they should vote for? (Scale alternative: "yes").

OL 5. Do you believe that your acquaintances regard you as somebody with a good understanding of what goes on in politics? (Scale alternative: probably").

III. Persuasiveness

OL 1. Have you ever advised acquaintances what party to vote for? (Scale alternative: "yes").

OL 6. Have you ever tried to convince an acquaintance on a political matter? (Scale alternative: "yes").

OL 7. Do you occasionally try to give your acquaintances information concerning some political matter? (Scale alternative: "yes").

These questions formed part of a questionnaire used in a study of opinion leadership in Amsterdam, based on a sample of 269 male respondents of 21 years and older derived from an original random sample of 371 adresses.*

*The research reported in this section is part of a survey conducted during the univeristy year 1965–1966 by students of political science as part of their course in mass communications at the Institute of Mass Communications ("Instituut voor Perswetenschap") of the University of Amsterdam. It was directed and supervised by Drs. F. Bergsma and the author. The interviews took place mainly in January 1966. From the original sample of 371 addresses the response of 72% (269 male respondents) was the results of at least one initial visit and two more calls at the addresses of non-respondents. For details of the sampling design see the appendix.

In our analysis we decided to investigate the dimensionality of these nine items using the multiple scaling procedure sketched in section 5.2.3. This procedure however, produced a single scale, as shown in table 9.1.

Table 9.1   A scale of political opinion leadership (8 items)
(Sample of male Amsterdam voters; n = 269)

Item:	Sample difficulties	Item coefficient
OL 1. Advises party vote	0.17	0.37
OL 2. Likely to be consulted	0.19	0.41
OL 3. Starts discussion	0.22	0.47
OL 4. Has been consulted*	0.22	0.29
OL 5. Believed to have good understanding	0.22	0.39
OL 6. Tried to convince	0.31	0.50
OL 7. Tries to inform	0.31	0.54
OL 8. Has discussed politics lately	0.40	0.52
OL 9. Joins discussions	0.56	0.68

Coefficient of scalability: $\hat{H} = 0.49$
*Non-scale item

One item, OL 4 (Has been consulted) was excluded: its coefficient of 0.29 was slightly lower than the value of our minimum bound $c = 0.30$. Of course we might add it to the scale (the resulting overall coefficient of scalability would then be 0.44), but inspection of the $\hat{\Pi}$ and $\hat{\Pi}^{(0)}$-matrix suggested that the picture of double monotony would be slightly improved if OL 4 was excluded. For the other eight items the corresponding $\hat{\Pi}$ and $\hat{\Pi}^{(0)}$-matrix contained no serious deviations from the trends expected for holomorphism, considering the relatively small size of the sample.

The value for the pair OL 8 (Has discussed politics lately) – OL 3 (Starts discussion) seemed a bit too high. Evidently the people who like to initiate discussions about politics have a better chance of reporting recent political discussions.

Apart from this irregularity, we may well regard the trait of opinion leadership as a more or less unidimensional phenomenon. This result seems to confirm the experience of Rogers (1962, 231), who used the more conventional and less reliable procedures of Guttman scaling with all their possible defects to construct from a similar set of items a six-item scale of opinion leadership with respect to the diffusion of new ideas on farming in rural communities.

9.2   THE SENSE OF CIVIC COMPETENCE AND THE SENSE OF POLITICAL EFFICACY

In section 8.3 we found that two related sets of items which concerned national and local efficacy, in fact formed one scale. We concluded from this result that the two sets may well be measuring the same general variable of the sense of political efficacy.

A similar problem arises with respect to a second important variable that has recently been introduced in electoral research: the sense of civic competence.

The concept of competence was introduced by Almond and Verba in their cross-national study *The Civic Culture* (Almond and Verba, 1963). Unfortunately, their discussion of the various competence concepts they introduce lacks the theoretical rigor necessary for a penetrating analysis and they apparently leave it to the reader to derive a clear and consistent set of competence concepts. We shall not describe such a process here, as the full theoretical implications of the different types of competence will be treated elsewhere (Van der Maesen,–). We shall restrict ourselves to the definition of civic competence.

This concept refers to the possibilities for individuals to influence officials as decision makers and the outcomes of decision processes at the various levels of government.

"If the individual can exert such influence, we shall consider him to be *politically comptetent*; or if he *believes* he can exert such influence, he will be *subjectively competent"* (Almond and Verba, 1963, 181).

The actual potential of the individual to exert political influence in various areas of government may therefore be defined as *political competence* (Almond and Verba, 1963, 181, 215), or *civic competence* (ibid., 187) or *citizen competence* (ibid., 204, 217).

The consciousness or belief of an individual that he is able to exert such influence if necessary was defined by Almond and Verba as the *sense of civic competence* (ibid., 187) or *subjective political competence* (ibid., 231).

In order to simplify the terminology we shall propose to restrict ourselves to the terms "civic competence" and, correspondingly, "sense of civic competence" in this study.*

Almond and Verba measured the "sense of civic competence" in

---

*Van der Maesen (–) will suggest the term "personal political effectiveness".

their survey by asking respondents what they could do if a harmful or unjust (local or national) regulation was to be passed, whether they were likely actually to take action in such a case, and whether they expected success from such action.

In constructing a scale of "subjective political competence" they added two other items. One was of the "sense of political efficacy" type and concerned the comprehensibility of local issues. The other item asked respondents whether they ever had done anything to influence a local regulation. This last item does not seem appropriate for the scale as it concerns not the sense of competence but actual competent behavior in the past. (See also Van der Maesen, −). Nevertheless, this theoretically somewhat inconsistent set of items was found to form a scale of the conventional Guttman type (Almond and Verba, 1963, 231–6).*

Matthews and Prothro have recently aptly summarized this concept as introduced by Almond and Verba with the statement that:

"It consists of (1) a belief that public officials can be and are influenced by ordinary citizens, (2) some knowledge about how to proceed in making this influence felt, and (3) sufficient self-confidence to try to put this knowledge to work at appropriate times and places."

Matthews and Prothro (1966, 526) used a set of items to measure the "sense of civic competence" based on the following technique.

Respondents were presented with hypothetical local and neighborhood problems and were then asked whether they would do anything about them. Matthews and Prothro combined the number of positive answers to form an index of subjective competence. Apparently they did not investigate the scalability of these responses

In her study of local political participation at the time of the local elections of 1966 Van der Maesen independently used a similar approach to measure the sense of civic competence.

The questionnaire contained a section, the purpose of which was to obtain an inventory of the possible means of action mentioned by respondents with respect to several hypothetical neighborhood problems. The respondents were then asked whether for such problems they expected any results or success from certain types of personal

---

*In fact the scale analysis Almond and Verba report is a good example of the conventional, somewhat fortuitous type of Guttman scaling procedure which we have surveyed critically in chapter 2. For instance, coefficients of type S_1, were used, so that deviations from random response were not covered (see section 2.5.2.) and 'imperfect' patterns were allocated to 'perfect' ones (see sections 2.4. and 2.6.2.).

action such as seeking contact with specific local authorities and municipal officials, or taking certain collective courses of action. Their responses to these last questions were assumed to measure their "sense of civic competence". We thought it worthwhile to investigate the scalability of the set, the items of which (in a more or less literal translation) were as follows:

C.1. Do you think you could achieve something by approaching the mayor?
(Mayor: positive alternative: "yes").
C.2. Do you think you could achieve something by urging a political party to do something about it?
(Political party: positive alternative: "yes").
C.3. Do you think you could achieve something by approaching the members of the City Council?
(Members Council: positive alternative: "yes").
C.4. Do you think you could achieve something by approaching an official of the appropriate municipal service?
(Official: positive alternative: "yes").
C.5. Do you think you could achieve something by approaching the Alderman responsible?
(Alderman: positive alternative: "yes").
C.6. You could urge an association or organization that is active in this problem area to do something about it. Do you think you could achieve something in this way?
(Association: positive alternative: "yes").
C.7. Do you think you could achieve something by trying to do something about it together with other people?
(People: positive alternative: "yes").

An application of our procedure showed that five of the seven items formed a near-medium scale, as may be judged from the results given in table 9.2 ($\hat{H} = 0.38$).

From the order of the sample difficulties we see that in the resulting five-item scale, "approaching the mayor" (C.1.) is the most "difficult" item in the scale: 39% of the respondents expected results from such a course of action. The two items concerning types of collective action, (C.6.), urging an association to take action (78%), or (C.7.), undertaking actions together with other people (81%), are the "easiest" items on the competence dimension.

Evidently one need not have a high sense of civic competence to expect success from these approaches in the case of neighborhood problems. What is striking, however, is that one course of action of a more or less collective nature, trying to involve a political party in such problems (C.2.), is rated much more difficult (40%) than the

Table 9.2 A scale of the "sense of civic competence" (5 items) (Sample taken from Amsterdam electorate; n = 1513)

Item:		Sample difficulty	Item coefficient $\hat{H}_i$
C.1.	Mayor	0.39	0.39
C.3.	Members Council	0.53	0.36
C.5.	Alderman	0.55	0.42
C.6.	Association	0.78	0.36
C.7.	People	0.81	0.38
Non-scale items:*			
C.2.	Political party	0.40	0.27
C.4.	Official	0.54	0.20

Coefficient of scalability: $\hat{H} = 0.38$
*Item coefficient: resulting value when item is added to five-item scale.

other "collective" items, almost as difficult as approaching the mayor. Still more striking is the fact that this item (C.2.: Political party) did not scale very well: its item coefficient ($\hat{H}_{C2} = 0.27$) was below our lower bound ($c = 0.30$), so that it was excluded from the scale.

In fact we had some problems which form a good illustration of our remark in section 5.2.8 that the final scale produced by our scaling procedure may sometimes depend on the order of item selection and particularly on the first pair of items selected. In this case our step-wise procedure started with an obviously highly correlated pair C.1.–C.5. (Mayor-Alderman). In view of the relatively high value (0.27) of the item coefficient of "Political party", we decided to re-run the program using the procedure of section 5.2.4 and choosing the next highest correlated pair C.2. (Political party)–C.6. (Association) as the first pair of items.

Again a five-item scale was the result, with a scalability coefficient of 0.37. Item C.1. (Mayor) was excluded ($\hat{H}_{C1} = 0.29$) as well as C.4. Inspection of the matrix of $\hat{H}_{ij}$-coefficients for item pairs showed that in fact the items "Political party" and "Mayor" were uncorrelated.

We may conjecture that the different ways of choosing the representatives of these institutions may have something to do with this phenomenon: in Amsterdam (as in all Dutch municipalities) the mayor is appointed by the central government, whereas the political parties, of course, are of immediate importance in an electoral system.

However, in other scale analyses (see also section 9.3) items concerning political parties also diverged strikingly from our expectations.

One reason may be that in Amsterdam, and probably in many other communities in the Netherlands as well, the political parties perhaps have an ambivalent political significance in the eyes of the public as regards *local* politics.

In section 8.1.2. we gave some background information concerning local government in cities such as Amsterdam. We saw that the same parties which compete on the national level, also compete on the local scene. Their role in the field of local politics is far less comprehensible to the local citizen and is far less publicized than their activities in national politics. During the campaign period the municipal elections are interpreted by the parties as well as in the mass media more as by-elections and indications of the support of the inhabitants for the national coalitions in power than as a straight fight on local issues. For these reasons it may well be that the political parties are seen by the respondents as institutions of immediate importance on the national level and of less direct relevance for local problems of the type indicated in our questionnaire. Consequently, we finally chose for our scale of the "sense of civic competence" the five items listed in table 9.2.

An investigation of the holomorphism of the set showed that in both the $\hat{\Pi}$ and $\hat{\Pi}^{(0)}$-matrices the pair C.1.–C.5. (Mayor-Alderman) had values that were slightly too high. Although their difficulties differ, the obvious explanation of this special association is that the Board of Mayor and Aldermen forms the executive branch in Dutch communities.

Having established our scale of the "sense of civic competence" we may remind the reader of the summary of Mathews and Prothro referred to above. There the concept of civic competence involved the belief that public officials can be influenced by ordinary citizens, some knowledge about how to exercise this influence and a sufficient degree of self-confidence. This definition suggests that this concept bears a rather close relation to the concept of the "sense of political efficacy", which was not used in the Almond-Verba study nor in the survey by Mathews and Prothro. As concepts they are rather alike, so that we may wonder whether the two sets of items, the sense of civic competence and the sense of political efficacy, are not measuring the same subjective competence-efficacy dimension. We have seen that the actual scale of "subjective political competence" which was used by Almond and Verba (1963, 231–6) was composed of both efficacy and competence items. Dennis *et al.* (1968, 79) seem to identify the two concepts *subjective competence* and *sense of efficacy* for the purpose of cross-national comparison.

In this case we may expect the same results as were found in section 8.3 concerning the common dimensionality of the "sense of local and national efficacy": these two sets of items, the "sense of (local) civic competence" and the "sense of (local) political efficacy" may form just one single overall scale.

In terms of the scaling procedures sketched in section 5.2 of chapter 5, our problem may be investigated in several ways.

One way would be to use the procedure of section 5.2.1 and at once test the combined set of *local* efficacy and competence items as one scale. This procedure would lead simply to the rejection or acceptance of this full set of items and the evaluation of the scalability of the single items with respect to this set as illustrated by our analysis of the original efficacy items in section 7.1.2.

Another way would be to use the method of section 5.2.4, taking as our initial scale the set of local efficacy items and using the procedure to find out whether this initial scale can be extended with the competence items. Such a result would also demonstrate the common scalability of the local efficacy and competence items.

A third way would be to use the procedure of sections 5.2.2–5.2.3, our procedure of multiple scaling, as we did in section 8.3 to find the overall "sense of political efficacy" scale and in section 9.1.2 to find just one scale of "opinion leadership". This procedure starts with a best pair of items for the first scale, adding items step-wise and repeating the procedure to find other scales after completion of the first one. We chose this procedure of multiple scaling because it does not impose any restrictions on the formation of scales, and thus allows for the possibility, that several scales may be formed, each consisting of items from both the efficacy and competence sets.

This procedure resulted in two scales which coincided exactly with the local scale of the "sense of political efficacy" and the scale of the "sense of civic competence". The two scales are probably moderately correlated: the item coefficients of the competence items with respect to the local efficacy scale were all in the neighborhood of 0.25. Had we chosen the value 0.25 for our lower bound c, then the two scales might well have formed one scale.

In the present sample, at any rate, our procedure of multiple scaling produced strong evidence that the scales of the "sense of civic competence" and "sense of political efficacy" may be considered to measure associated but different variables.* This suggests that Almond and Verba (1963) and Dennis *et al.* (1968) should probably not have identified these concepts in their studies.

9.3   INFLUENCE STEREOTYPES

Among the many scale analyses we performed for Van der Maesen's study was an interesting case of multiple scales which concerned a set of items that was used to find out how the citizens of Amsterdam perceived the degree of influence exercised on important political decisions in Amsterdam by various authorities, organisations and groups.

The general question was (translated as literally as possible):

"I have here a list of various people and groups. Do you think that the following people or groups have much, little or no say at all in important decisions in Amsterdam?"

The items presented on the list were given in the same order as on the questionnaire:

- The trade unions;
- The Aldermen;
- The Chamber of Commerce;
- The City Council;
- The Mayor;
- The inhabitants of the city;
- The national government;
- The political parties;
- Big concerns;
- The employers' associations;
- High municipal officials;
- The newspapers.

Such questions concerning the perceived influence of certain pressure

*Here we may raise a point which plays a part in most types of cluster analysis. The number of scales formed in our procedure of multiple scaling may partly depend on the value we use for our lower bound c. A high value (*e.g.* $c = 0.40$) may lead to a greater number of scales, each consisting of a smaller number of items, whereas a low value (*e.g.* $c = 0.25$) may lead to a smaller number of weaker scales containing more items. We are not able to give an "optimal" value for c. In our experience, the value of $c = 0.30$ has performed reasonably well.

groups, organizations and authorities are very common in electoral research. Up to now no attempts at scaling such data have been reported. One reason may be that applications of scale analysis in electoral research have been restricted mainly to data within the framework of conventional attitude scaling. There are, however, no methodological or theoretical reasons to prevent us from applying such formal measurement models and to profit from their analytical strength in other problem areas as well.

As we had no particular theoretically (or empirically) founded reasons to expect scalability of the set of items concerning influence perception, we again used the multiple scaling procedure of sections 5.2.2–5.2.3, using as scale alternative the rating "much influence".

The results, as reported in table 9.3, are rather interesting. The set of twelve items fell apart in two scales and a set of three non-scale items. The first (weak) scale contained five items ($\hat{H} = 0.35$) and the second (medium) scale contained four items ($\hat{H} = 0.40$). Although the

Table 9.3   Scales of influence stereotypes (2 scales) (Sample of Amsterdam electorate; n = 1513)

Items	Sample difficulty	Item coefficient $\hat{H}_i$
Scale 1: Pressure groups (5 items)		
Coefficient of scalability: $\hat{H} = 0.35$*		
PG 1 Employers' associations	0.52	0.43
PG 2 Chamber of Commerce	0.55	0.32
PG 3 Trade unions	0.58	0.29
PG 4 Big concerns	0.65	0.38
PG 5 National government	0.78	0.33
Scale 2: Local authorities (4 items)		
Coefficient of scalability: $\hat{H} = 0.40$		
LA 1 High municipal authorities	0.49	0.45
LA 2 Mayor	0.77	0.34
LA 3 Aldermen	0.79	0.38
LA 4 City Council	0.87	0.46
Non-scale items		
1. Inhabitants of the city	0.23	
2. Newspapers	0.44	
3. Political parties	0.63	

*For scale 1 without the "trade unions" item: $\hat{H} = 0.40$

overall coefficients of scalability are not very high, in view of the small number of items in each of the two scales, they rather neatly suggest two different dimensions along which influence on major local policy decisions is perceived by the respondents in terms of the items presented.

In the first place a common source of influence is located *in the city administration itself*. The images or stereotypes which respondents have with respect to the influence exercised by officials and allotted to offices within this administration can be scaled along one dimension. This is suggested by scale 2 (Local authorities), which contains all the local authorities that were represented on our list.

The most "difficult" item, *i.e.* the people rated influential by the smallest percentage of respondents, is "high municipal officials" (LA 1:49%). The "easiest" item, or the body rated influential by the highest percentage (LA 4: 87%) of the respondents, is the city council. In between and more or less *ex aequo* are rated the mayor (LA 2: 77%) and the Aldermen (LA 3: 79%).

A second dimension along which influence on local political decisions is perceived seems to concern organisations and groups operating outside the sphere of the local government itself.

The first scale given in table 9.3 contains items of this type. The order of the sample difficulties gives the order of the items along this dimension, which may measure perceived *pressure group influence*. This order is interesting too. The most "difficult" items are "employers' associations" (PG 1: 52%) and the "Chamber of Commerce" (PG 2: 55%). Yet they were perceived as influential by more than half the respondents. Incidentally, their "difficulty" (or perceived influence) seems slightly to exceed that of the "high municipal officials", (LA 1), the most difficult item on the "local authorities" dimension. The trade unions may also belong to this dimension. In fact, the item was excluded from the scale, as its item coefficient with the other four items ($\hat{H}_{PG3} = 0.29$) just failed to reach our lower bound of 0.30. Because this value of $c = 0.30$ was chosen rather arbitrarily and because the "trade unions" item fits the pressure groups dimension very well on theoretical grounds too, we decided to add this item to scale 1.

The trade unions are perceived as slightly more influential (PG 3: 58%) in local decisions than the last two items mentioned. Appreciably higher is the influence allotted to big business by our respondents: two thirds of them (PG 4: 65%) thought that big concerns had much influence on important local decisions.

A most interesting result concerns the role which the national government is believed to take on in exerting its influence on local decisions. In terms of the two dimensions detected by our scaling procedure it does so *as a pressure group* and the most influential at that. Its "difficulty" (PG 5: 0.78) on the pressure group dimension is about as high as that of the mayor (LA 2: 0.77) and aldermen (LA 3: 0.79) on the local authorities dimension. In view of the circumstance that in the Netherlands, the cities, as all other municipalities, are completely dependent on the national government for their financial resources and that all their major projects also require the consent of the central authorities, this allocation of the "national government" to the influence dimension of "outside" pressure group influence certainly seems highly realistic.

As a consequence of these results, the respondents may be measured in terms of each of the two influence dimensions by means of the score on each of the two scales. Respondents are by these two scores characterized for the influence perception items in terms of two variables: the degree to which they perceive *pressure group* influence and the degree to which they are perceiving influence of the *local authorities*.

In their criticism of multiple scale analysis as a multidimensional technique, Alker and Russett (1965, 28–30) mention as a major drawback the fact that items are allocated to just one scale and cannot be evaluated with respect to other scales resulting from the analysis. In contrast to this, factor analysis, the technique they use in their analysis of roll calls in the General Assembly of the United Nations, gives one the opportunity of evaluating each item on each of the factors produced in the analysis.

We have indicated in section 5.2.3 that our procedure of multiple scaling is free of the defects mentioned by Alker and Russett. The item coefficient H_i enables us to evaluate the scalability of any item with respect to any given scale. Consequently, after the completion of the multiple scale analysis it is possible to find for any item belonging to a given scale the value of its item coefficient with respect to any other scale. For non-scale items the item coefficients are given with respect to each of the scales produced in the scale analysis. We may illustrate this with examples taken from our analysis of the influence stereotypes.

It may be interesting to note that the "city-council" item (LA 4) has some significance for the dimension of *pressure group influence*: its item coefficient with respect to scale 1 is 0.29. Similarly, the "Chamber of Commerce" item (PG 2) has an item coefficient of 0.28 with scale 2 measuring the *local authorities* dimension.

The results concerning the *non-scale* items are interesting too. Especially the items concerning the inhabitants of the city are striking: not only are the citizens perceived as the least influential of all (only 23% of the respondents thought they had much influence), they also do not fit the two dimensions.

Consequently, it seems reasonable from these results to suggest as a hypothesis that respondents hold the highly realistic view that immediate and significant influence on political decisions in large local political systems such as that of Amsterdam is exercised mainly through the institutionalized channels originating *within* the authority structure of local government ("local authorities") or *outside* that structure ("pressure groups").*

More or less similar remarks may be made with respect to the *newspapers*: their perceived influence is relatively low, as is shown by the percentage of respondents who say it is low. With 44% the newspapers are considered slightly less influential than "high municipal officials" (LA 1) (49%) on the local authorities dimension. The influence of the newspapers is clearly not perceived along either one of the two dimensions defined by the two scales in table 9.3.

For the *political parties* we again observe the deviating behavior that was noted and tentatively explained in section 9.2. Their perceived influence (sample difficulty: 63% of the respondents) is considerable and of the same magnitude as that of the "big concerns" (PG 4: 65%) along the pressure group dimension. But the influence of political parties is not clearly seen as exercised in terms of one of the two dimensions of table 9.3.

It may well be possible that yet other dimensions, not tapped by the set of items of table 9.3, may be involved in the perception of influence on major political decisions at the local level, dimensions into which items such as "citizens", "newspapers" or "political parties" may fit. On the other hand it may just as well be possible that no such dimensions can be found because the influence of the groups mentioned in such items is perceived as being exercised along not just one, but several dimensions at once. To investigate this possibility we may with the help of our item coefficients determine to which of the two

---

*Since 1966, when this study was held, the city of Amsterdam has known an extremely interesting case in which spontaneous civic action prevented the authorities from permitting a chemical industry (Progil) to be set up in the new industrial area west of the city. Under the mounting pressure of civic protest, the municipal council decided in May 1969 to refuse permission for setting up this industry. It would be highly interesting to investigate whether such successful action on the part of citizens would result in a higher perceived influence on their part!

dimensions (or scales) these non-scale items are most closely related. For instance, for the inhabitants of the city we might expect that their small influence would be more important along the local authority dimensions than along the pressure group dimension.

In correspondence with this expectation we may remark that the item coefficient (0.22) of (1) "inhabitants of the city" with scale 2 (local authorities) is higher than with scale 1 (pressure groups) (0.12). Inversely, the newspapers may be more closely related to the pressure group dimension than to the local authority dimension. This is reflected by a higher value of the item coefficient with scale 1 (0.22) than that with scale 2 (0.14). We should, however, take into account that the Amsterdam newspapers cannot be considered *local* newspapers. All of them clearly belong to the *national* press. We may therefore wonder whether in other communities the genuinely local press would show a much better fit to the "pressure group influence" scale.

For "political parties" the item coefficients with scale 1 (0.21) and with scale 2 (0.24) were approximately equal. Here, though admittedly on a low level, we have an illustration of our statement that influence may be perceived as being exercised along several dimensions at a time. There are some signs that the influence of the political parties is seen as operating more or less equally through the pressure group and through the local authorities channels. Again, we may wonder whether, in view of the *national* significance of the political parties, a similar analysis of perceived influence at the national level would show that they fitted the *authorities* dimension more clearly.

We argued in section 5.2.8 that the order of selection may sometimes determine not only the shape of the final scales but also the number of scales that are produced, because in our program of multiple scaling items are added step-wise and consecutively to the scales. The order in which the various scales are produced from a set of items is therefore important too. For instance, items that were admitted to scale 1 in our example of table 9.3 were automatically excluded from scale 2 which was constructed after scale 1 from the remaining items. Yet some of the items of the first scale might well have been selected at some stage for scale 2, if they had still been available. If we had started the whole procedure with the formation of scale 2, these items belonging to scale 1 would have been added to scale 2, so that we would have obtained different scales in the end.

One way to control for such a contingency is given by the procedure sketched in section 5.2.4. We may start by using a given sub-set of scale 2 as the initial scale, and extend this scale with items from the remaining set of items by means of multiple scaling. In the case of the influence stereotypes, such a reversal in the order of scale formation resulted in the same scales.

We shall see in section 9.4.2 that a close analysis of item coefficients between scales may teach us a good deal about other possible scales different to those produced by a particular run of the procedure.

As far as could be judged with such small numbers of items, the double monotony or holomorphism of each of the two scales was not contradicted by the Π and $\Pi^{(0)}$-matrices.

9.4   SCALING POLITICAL PARTICIPATION

Thus far we have reported instances in which our method resulted in one or more reasonably neat scales. In all these cases, the sets of items apparently divided up into one or two homogeneous sets of items, with a residual of a few non-scale items.

The results of our method, however, are not always as clear cut as that. To illustrate the type of difficulties which will be dealt with in this section, we will introduce a hypothetical example.

Let us suppose that we have four sets of five items each and let each set of items prove to be a scale when tested in terms of the procedure given in section 5.2.1. Each set may therefore be thought to measure a certain variable. Let us suppose furthermore that the four scales measure *different* but *interrelated* variables. Because of this relation between the variables, items from different scales will sometimes show a high degree of correlation. What would happen if we combined the items of all four scales and applied the multiple scaling procedure of sections 5.2.2–5.2.3?

It may well be that this procedure, which uses highly intercorrelated pairs of items and adds other correlated items, would start with the selection of a number of interrelated items taken from *different* scales, adding other items from the rest of the scales. This procedure would therefore break up the original scales, form one first large scale of, say, twelve items, and subsequently produce four different two-item scales as the residuals of the hypothetical original five-item scales.

Using the item coefficients of the items that were selected in the first overall scale with respect to the other four two-item scales, however, we may hope to be able to more or less rediscover the original four scales.

Of course, in this case one may well argue that we should choose the model of one scale of twelve items, as the intercorrelation of the original four scales may well be interpreted as evidence of a single common dimension tapped by the four sets. The crucial point here is that the decision of which model to choose, one dimension measured by the set of twelve items, or four interrelated dimensions measured by four scales, cannot be made by the scaling procedure and the computer. It must be made by the researcher himself with the aid of a careful consideration of the content of the items and scales guided by a good theoretical framework and the available systematic empirical evidence.

Summarizing our example, we may state that when our procedure is applied to a large and heterogeneous set of items containing clusters that may be considered to measure different but highly intercorrelated variables, it may be that one compound scale is formed of items taken from each cluster, leaving a large residual of items that splits up into a number of two-item or three-item scales, which may well be remnants of better scales.

We apparently had some problems of this kind when we investigated the scalability of a large set of items concerning political participation in the 1966 Amsterdam study.

9.4.1   *The dimensionality of political participation*

The full discussion of the theoretical relevance of our indices of political participation will be published elsewhere (Van der Maesen,—). We shall therefore not venture to give an elaborate analysis of this concept. As it is, a great variety of types of political behavior have already been brought together under the heading of political participation. In general, the concept seems to have been restricted more to activities than to dispositions and attitudes.

In a recent review, Milbrath (1965, 16–22) presents a list containing a hierarchy of types of political activity from inactivity (apathetics) and "spectator" activities (such as exposing oneself to political stimuli and voting) *via* "transitional" activities (*e.g.* contacting a public official or a political leader) to "gladiatorial" activities like giving one's time to a political campaign and holding public and party offices.

The theoretical importance of the concept of political participation necessitates a serious investigation of the dimensions involved. Such investigations, however important they are, for the conceptualization of political participation, seem to be extremely rare. Students usually seem to be satisfied with indices, and take the homogeneity of these indices for granted.

In our introductory chapter, section 1.2, we referred to the indices used by Dahl in his study of New Haven. One index measured campaign participation on the basis of voting and a number of campaign activities. Another index was related to non-campaign participation by such activities as talking about politics with friends, getting in touch with local officials or politicians on an issue, taking some active part in a local issue or problem, and reporting any contact with political or governmental officials in the past year. Apparently taking the homogeneity or dimensionality of these types of behavior for granted, Dahl combined the levels on these two indices into a single index of local action.

In his survey and summary of the available empirical evidence concerning political participation, Milbrath (1965, 16-7) suggests a hierarchical ranking of types of behavior, remarking that:

"Political participation is often spoken of as being cumulative; persons who engage in one political action often engage in others as well".

Yet his survey reflects the virtual neglection of a thorough empirical investigation of the dimensions of political participation. He also uses an index based mainly on a number of campaign activities (Milbrath, 1965, 155-6), again obviously taking their homogeneity for granted. Recently Matthews and Prothro, applying the traditional methods of Guttman scaling, investigated the scalability of a set of participation items. With respect to the Guttman model they remark:

"If the facts conform to this logical scheme or model, then we have reason to believe that all these actions probably are different forms of the same thing – political participation. If the facts conflict with this model, we can be certain that no single concept such as 'political participation' underlies all the behavior we have described so far" (Matthews and Prothro, 1966, 53-4).

Their results are positive, as they report a four-item scale of political participation based on the following types of political behavior:

– talking politics with friends, community leaders, etc.;
– voting;
– participation in campaigns (attending meetings and rallies, working for candidates, giving money, buying tickets);
– belonging to political associations or holding party or public office.

Their results (Matthews and Prothro, 1966, 523-5) can be summarized as follows:

Coefficient of scalability	Negro	White
Rep	0.95	0.98
Rep_{min}	0.75	0.81
Rep_I	0.92	0.96

Although Matthews and Prothro mention the difficulties usually associated with Rep coefficients in general, their evaluation of the scalability of the items is in terms of Rep and leads to the suggestion that about equal scalability of the set of items exists for the samples of both negroes and whites. However, the fact that they report Rep_{min} and Rep_I (the value of Rep in the case of random response with given sample difficulties) enables us to transform the Rep coefficients into the better coefficients of type S_2 (see section 2.5.2), if we accept the above values as being correct.
The results are the following:

$$\text{Negro: } S_2 = \frac{Rep - Rep_I}{1 - Rep_I} = \frac{0.03}{0.08} = 0.38$$

$$\text{White: } S_2 = \frac{Rep - Rep_I}{1 - Rep_I} = \frac{0.02}{0.04} = 0.50$$

They illustrate clearly the superiority of S_2 coefficients in comparison with the insensitive Rep coefficients. The scalability of the four participation items is much better for whites than for the negro sample in the south. We may wonder whether the scalability of the voting item can be good, taking into account the restrictions on voting for negroes as a means of ensuring minimal political participation on the part of the negroes.* With this limited set of four items, however, Matthews and Prothro concluded that it seemed legitimate to postulate a *single* dimension of political participation. Our results for the Amsterdam sample were less encouraging.

9.4.2   *Scales of political participation*

In our analysis of political participation, a total set of twenty-one items was involved in the numerous attempts at scale analysis which we

---

*We suspect that if we applied our method of scale analysis, using item coefficients, the voting item would prove non-scalable. We again refer the reader to sections 7.1.3 and 7.1.4, and in particular to the results concerning item 1 (Voting the only way) for the negro population.

made, and which we shall not try to describe fully here. We will restrict the discussion to the results of the multiple scale analysis of the whole set and to the most important scales that we finally decided to use.

The twenty-one items covered a wide variety of types of behavior that may well fall under the general heading of political participation. For reasons of space we shall not reproduce their exact form and wording in the questionnaire, and refer the reader to Van der Maesen's forthcoming dissertation (Van der Maesen, -).

A sub-set of four items referred to activities within a political party:

1. membership of a party (9% of the 1513 respondents);
2. has attended party meetings (5%);
3. has spoken at party meetings (2%);
4. has served on a committee of a party (1%).

Another set of items referred to local activities of a participatory nature.

5. often or occassionally discusses Amsterdam problems with other people (64%);
6. has approached a municipal office about some Amsterdam problem (17%);
7. has joined in at least one of the following types of *collective* action concerning some problem (17%);
   – has tried to do something about it together with other people;
   – has visited some special meeting;
   – has helped to organize a special meeting;
   – has collected signatures for a petition;
8. has performed at least one of the following types of (*institutional*) action (8%):
   – has urged a political party to do something about a problem;
   – has asked for action in some association of which he is a member;
   – has become a member of an association that deals with such special problems;
9. has approached a member of the city council (8%);
10. has sent letters to the editor concerning local problems (5%).

Two of the items concerned two highly publicized issues of Amsterdam local politics: the decision to grant permission for the setting up of a new Mobil Oil refinery in the vicinity of Amsterdam and the actions of the police during the turbulent spring of 1966.*

11. has joined in discussions or other actions concerning possible air pollution resulting from the Mobil Oil refinery (26%).

*See Van der Land *et al.* (1967).

12. has joined in discussions or other actions concerning the police activities in Amsterdam (49%).
Some items concerned the elections and the campaign:
13. has cast a valid vote (93%)*;
14. has read pamphlets of political parties (27%);
15. has joined discussions about the elections (27%);
16. has advised or discouraged other people, family members, friends or associates to vote for a particular party or list (10%);
17. has joined in activities for the promotion of a party during the campaign (6%):
   – contributing money;
   – attending campaign meetings;
   – displaying pamphlets in windows or on walls;
   – distributing pamphlets for a political party;
   – helping to organize campaign meetings;
   – other types of campaign activities.
Other items concerned exposure to political information from the mass media:
18. frequently watches news programs and general news reports on television (59%);
19. frequently listens to news programs and general news reports on the radio (27%);
20. regularly reads one or more Dutch or foreign opinion weeklies (13%);
21. regularly reads one or more party papers (2%).

As we were quite prepared for the possibility that political participation would have to be conceptualized as a multi-dimensional phenomenon, it seemed a good idea to apply the multiple scaling procedure of sections 5.2.2–5.2.3 to the full set of twenty-one participation items. The application of our procedure of multiple scaling resulted in *one* medium scale of eleven items, *four* two-item scales and *two* non-scale items.
The *first* scale of eleven items consisted of the following items:
I   1. party membership;
     2. attended party meetings;
     3. spoken at party meetings;
     4. served on committee of a party;
     5. discussed local problems;

---

*In the Netherlands voters were at that time obliged by law to appear at a polling station.

     7. collective action;

     8. institutional action;

    13. cast valid vote;

    15. discussed elections;

    16. advised others re vote;

    17. campaign activities.

The four two-item scales, in the order in which they were produced by our program, were:

II   11. discussed Mobil Oil;

     12. discussed police activities;

III 18. frequently watched T.V.;

     19. frequently listens to radio;

IV   6. approached municipal office;

     9. approached member City Council;

 V 20. regularly reads opinion weeklies;

     21. regularly reads party papers.

The two *non-scale* items were:

    10. sent letters to the editor;

    14. read pamphlets of political parties.

How should these results be interpreted?

At a first glance, they seemed to give some support to the hypothesis concerning one general dimension of political participation. The four two-item scales also seemed to be particularly suggestive of possible other dimensions. But after a close scrutiny of the results and the nature of the items that formed the large scale, compared to those that formed the other scales or did not fit into a scale, we hesitated to accept these results.

From the example in the introduction to this section we know that when procedures of multiple scaling are applied to a large, hetero-geneously composed set of items, the outcomes may be doubtful in the case of several intercorrelated variates, each of which may be measured by a scalable sub-set of items. In this case the procedure may well result in one big scale because certain appropriate items from each of the intercorrelated sub-sets are chosen. The remaining items may then be split up into a number of small scales, which may at best be investigated as remnants of the underlying scales.

This is what may have happened in our analysis of political partici-pation.

To find out whether this did occur, we may apply three types of controls.

The *first* control is an analysis of the content of the items selected in the first overall scale of eleven items.

The *second* control is based on a close scrutiny of the four two-item scales in order to find residuals of possible other scales from which items were selected in the compound eleven-item scale I.

The *third* control makes use of the method of comparing item coefficients between scales that was proposed in section 5.2.3 and used in section 9.3. With this method we may compare the item coefficients of items assigned to scale I with their coefficients in the other scales, in order to ascertain whether they might also form scales with one of the other scales.

An application of the first control showed that the composition of the eleven-item scale seemed to be rather heterogeneous from a theoretical point of view. Its items covered related but rather different sets of participative behavior.

One set concerned a number of activities directed at support for specific political parties (items 1, 2, 3, 4, 17). This area of participation may be called *party participation*. Outside of scale I, no other items of this type can be found, among the other scales and among the non-scale items.

Another set of items in scale I (5, 7 and 8) concerned activities directed at the solving of local problems. Activities of this type fall under the heading of *local participation*. Other items of this type (6, 9, 10, 11 and 12) were not adopted in the overall eleven-item scale I. These items (the *second* control) divided up into two two-item scales and one non-scale item: scales II (11 and 12) and IV (6 and 9) and item 10.

Two of the other items of scale I (15 and 16) are related to opinion leadership with respect to the elections and campaigns. Item 5 (discussed local problems), which has been mentioned above, is also of this type with respect to local problems.

The theoretical implications of item 13 (cast valid vote) were hard to assess in view of the legal obligations concerning voting. Our first control therefore leads to the conclusion that two separate sets of items may be distinguished: one concerning *party participation* (items 1, 2, 3, 4, 17) and one concerning *local participation* (items 5, 6, 7, 8, 9, 10, 11, 12).

Within the scope of our *second* control we may now investigate scales II, III, IV and V and the two non-scale items.

In the first place we may single out scales III and V, which concern exposure to general political information as diffused by the mass media. These results confirmed findings of former research by the author in the field of mass communications, according to which exposure to news programs and local political information on the *audio-*

visual mass media television and radio could not be scaled together with exposure to such information in the *printed* mass media. Here too different scales were formed. Scale III (items 18 and 19) measures exposure to television and radio, while scale V (items 20 and 21) concerns the regular reading of opinion weeklies and party papers. These exposure scales should therefore be regarded as different variables which should be distinguished from other possible dimensions of political participation.

The other two (two-item) scales, scale II (11 and 12) and scale IV (6 and 9) have been mentioned in our discussion of scale I. They were shown to be related to local participation, together with the three items 5, 7 and 8 of scale I and the non-scale item 10.

What was the likelihood of this set of items (5, 6, 7, 8, 9, 10, 11 and 12) forming a scale as well?

With regard to this question our *third* control, based on a comparison of the item coefficients between scales, may be useful. Applying this control we found that from the first scale items 5 (discussions of local problems), 7 (collective local action) and 8 (institutional local action) might well have formed a scale with items 6 and 9 too. For each of these items the item coefficient with respect to scale IV (items 6 and 9), was above 0.30 (the value of our scale defining constant *c*).* Such a scale may be regarded as measuring *local participation*, as we will see from table 9.4.

From other analyses we found that the two items 11 (discussed Mobil Oil) and 12 (discussed police activities) of scale II tended to stand apart from the other items concerning local participation, in the same way that they formed a scale which differed from scale IV, items 6 and 9. The reasons for this are not yet very clear. One possible explanation may be that items 11 and 12 concerned *general local issues* of a broad scope at the municipal level, whereas the type of local problem-solving activities tapped by the other items concerning local participation may well have referred to *personal* or *specific neighborhood demands* of the respondents. If this were true, it might be necessary to distinguish these different demand and issue areas in research in the field of local politics.

We may now summarize the results of our three controls. One set of items (1, 2, 3, 4, 17) could just as well produce a scale of

---

*The item coefficients with respect to scale IV were also above 0.30 for items 3 and 4 ("spoken at party meetings" and "served on a party committee") of scale I. We preferred, however, to include these, together with items (1,2,17) of scale I, in a scale of specific *party participation*, for reasons given below.

party participation containing items concerning specific party-orientated activities. These items all formed part of scale I.

Another set of items (5, 6, 7, 8, 9, 10), taken from scales I, II and the non-scale items, present some prospects of scalability for measuring *local participation*.

Two other items of scale I (15 and 16) could just as well form a seperate two-item scale of *opinion leadership* or face-to-face communication with respect to local elections and *campaigns*.

Scale III (items 18 and 19) may be regarded as measuring *exposure* to general political information on the *audio-visual mass media* television and radio.

The different but related items of scale V (items 20 and 21) may be regarded as measuring *exposure* to general political information as given by the *printed mass media*.

Scale II (items 11 and 12) can probably be regarded as a scale of *opinion leadership* or face-to-face communication with respect to *general local issues*.

The remaining item 13 of scale I (cast valid vote), if used at all, had best be used as a separate index.

With respect to the remaining *non-scale* item 14 (has read pamphlets of political parties) we can suggest an interesting explanation for its non-scalability. Participation in the form of the reading of campaign material and pamphlets of political parties is not solely a (monotone) function of the individual citizen's interest; it also depends strongly on the campaign activity of the parties in his neighborhood. After all, even a politically involved citizen must be contacted by party activists who give him pamphlets or must find pamphlets in his letter-box before he can read them. These types of "exposure" items, which are very popular in electoral surveys, generally seem to be bad indicators of individual political involvement, as they need not be monotonically related to the variables they are supposed to measure.

Our analysis as summarized above led us not to choose one compound scale of political participation (scale I), but to follow the line of reasoning given above. Consequently, we investigated the scalability of the two sets of items concerning *party participation* and *local participation*.

The results indicated that two scales may indeed be formed, as may be judged from table 9.4.

The scale of *party participation* is a strong scale ($\hat{H} = 0.77$) but scales a very "difficult" segment of such a dimension. In terms of the sample difficulties defined for the whole population party membership

Table 9.4   Scales of political participation (2 scales)

(Sample of Amsterdam electorate; n = 1513)

Items	Sample difficulty	Item coefficient $\hat{H}_i$
Scale of party participation (5 items)		
Coefficient of scalability: $\hat{H} = 0.77$		
4. Has served on party committees	0.01	0.88
3. Has spoken at party meetings	0.02	0.90
2. Has attended party meetings	0.05	0.80
17. Campaign activities	0.06	0.60
1. Party member	0.09	0.81
Scale of local participation (6 items)		
Coefficient of scalability: $\hat{H} = 0.35$		
10. Has sent letters to the editor	0.05	0.27
9. Has approached member City Council	0.08	0.33
8. "Institutional" action	0.08	0.36
6. Has approached municipal office	0.17	0.31
7. "Collective" action	0.17	0.38
5. Has discussed local problems	0.64	0.46

is the "easiest" item (9%). In future investigations it may be worthwhile to look for still easier items. For instance, we may expect
milder forms of party orientation, such as regular voting for the same
party and considering becoming a member, to fit a scale of this type.
The scale of *local participation* is a weak scale ($\hat{H} = 0.35$). We
included item 10 (letters to the editor), a non-scale item in the multiple
scaling procedure, because its item coefficient ($\hat{H} = 0.27$) was relatively high but fell just below our lower bound of 0.30. Yet its content
seemed to be related reasonably well to the "universe of content"
covered by our items of local participation.

The two scales are correlated with each other and with the other,
smaller, scales mentioned above.

One other reason, finally, to doubt the appropriateness of the eleven-
item scale I described above, was that the double monotony proper-
ties were not satisfactory in the $\hat{\Pi}$- and $\hat{\Pi}^{(0)}$-matrices for this scale.
For the two scales of *party* and *local participation,* each admittedly

based on a smaller number of items, the holomorphism was not contradicted by the data.

To return to the example given in the introduction to this section, section 9.4, the results concerning the two scales of party and local participation give us an opportunity of re-interpreting the original outcome of the multiple scale analysis. According to this new interpretation, the two related scales, which measured intercorrelated variables, failed to materialize because the procedure selected highly intercorrelated items and items from other related scales to form just one compound eleven-item scale. We have demonstrated that it is extremely important and desirable that procedures of multidimensional or multiple scaling should provide opportunities of controlling for contingencies such as these. In fact, we have reconstructed the case of our introductory example to explain the failure of our multiple scaling program to produce neatly a number of intercorrelated sub-sets of items, each forming a scale for measuring interrelated variables.

We may nevertheless ask why the original product of one compound eleven-item scale and the corresponding model of one underlying general variable or factor should not be chosen as a good representation of the data. The answer we suggest is that such a choice (one general factor and one large scale, or several, probably intercorrelated, factors and correspondingly smaller scales), should not be made according to a mathematically defined, computerized procedure only, however sophisticated this procedure may be. The final choice should be made by the researcher on the basis of the content of the items, a good theoretical point of view and earlier empirical evidence.

The ultimate test, of course, is the empirical evidence concerning the different nature of the several scales which is produced when these scales are applied in relation to other variables in research. If, for instance, these applications always lead to similar results, we may well regard the scales as measuring the same variable, and revert to the model of one general variable.

In the case discussed here, however, Van der Maesen has produced some evidence that the two related scales of local party participation do behave differently when they are related to other constructs (Van der Maesen, –).

CHAPTER 10

Conclusion

In this study we have attempted to give a critical analysis and reappraisal of the assumptions associated with the deterministic measurement model underlying some highly popular and useful techniques of scale analysis. As a result of the formulation of a general measurement model of a probabilistic nature, we obtained a more appropriate basis for the cumulative Guttman scale. This enabled us to develop a set of scaling procedures which do not suffer from the many defects which are inherent to the conventional procedures of Guttman scaling.

The *first part* of this book contains the development of theory, model and procedures, which starts in *chapter 2* with an investigation of the main features of the traditional methods of Guttman scaling. We restricted ourselves mainly to the properties, problems and criteria which seemed to be most conspicuously the result of inadequate deterministic assumptions and most relevant for our task of trying to develop and evaluate scaling procedures from a stochastic point of view.

We restricted ourselves to dichotomous response data, a restriction which did not seem too severe in view of the prevalence of such data in social research.

In our discussion we emphasized the consequences of the necessity of admitting, as *error,* the deviations from the deterministic model which may be served in practical applications.

A consequence of major importance was the inadequate definition of the main criterion of scalability; *the coefficient of scalability.* In our review of the various coefficients that are actually used, we developed a simple typology of coefficients which covered most of them. We distinguished coefficients of reproducibility (Rep), coefficients of type S_1, and coefficients of type S_2, and showed that type S_2 did not have the defects of the other two types. In our study we accumulated evidence that Loevinger's coefficient of homogeneity (Loevinger, 1947), which is of type S_2 is a good criterion of scalability.

Another consequence of the deterministic background of Guttman scaling was an exaggerated emphasis on the *perfect* patterns which were to be expected. This led to strange definitions of "error" based on the comparison of the "imperfect" patterns with the "perfect" patterns which were the "best" approximations according to some criterion. Sometimes such "error" definitions gave rise to unsound practices. For instance, respondents producing "imperfect" response patterns were given a scale score that was based on some related "perfect" pattern instead of on the actual response pattern that they had produced.

As a consequence of the many difficulties which resulted from the fundamental necessity of introducing a concept of "error" which did not form part of the (deterministic) model itself, practical scaling procedures usually had a great number of criteria of scalability of an unsatisfactory and often arbitrary nature. Consequently, it was difficult to construct scales of more than four or five items which satisfied all these criteria. We finally showed in chapter 2 that Guttman's concept of a quasi-scale, in which random non-systematic deviations from the perfect patterns are allowed, in fact implies a departure from the deterministic model which necessitates a theory incorporating such random variation. This can best be done explicitly in terms of an appropriately general stochastic measurement model based on probabilistic response, treated in the mathematical chapters 3 and 4.

The preparations for the developing of this type of model were made in *chapter 3,* in which we gave a generalization of Lazarsfeld's latent structure model (Lazarsfeld, 1959) to multivariate response variables and multidimensional subject and item parameters. This enabled us to treat in terms of this general model the special requirements imposed by a measurement theory developed by Rasch (1961) which led to models in which *item parameters* were estimated independently of the population distribution (or selection) of subjects (*population free estimation*), and in which *subjects* are measured (estimated) independently of the particular selection of items (*item selection free*). This specific importance of the population distribution for measurement procedures was brought to the general attention by Rasch.

A subsequent specialization of the general latent structure model to our dichotomized data enabled us to illustrate these ideas by means of some specific parametric models such as the normal ogive and logistic curves models.

In *chapter 4,* which is central to our study, we began the investigation of a simple model containing one subject and one item difficulty parameter of a very general form. We introduced the concept of *monotone homogeneity* for models in which the probability of a positive response *increases* monotonically with the subject parameter. We also introduced the concepts of *double monotony* and *holomorphism* for monotonely homogeneous models in which the probability of a positive response is also monotonically *decreasing* in the item difficulty parameter.

These appropriately general models seem quite natural formulations of the cumulative quasi-scale, without assuming a special parametric form (*e.g.* a normal ogive or logistic form). In this sense the scaling theory of chapter 4 is non-parametric. We then derived a number of *observable* properties which are population-free in the sense that they are valid for marginal *manifest* response distributions obtained by an integration over the full (population) distribution of the *latent* subject parameter. From these observable properties, appropriate scaling procedures may then be derived.

The results of chapter 4 gave us the opportunity of evaluating the traditional criteria of Guttman scaling analyzed in chapter 2. We found that for monotonely homogeneous models, responses to pairs of items are associated positively, which corresponds with the requirement of small "error" probabilities in the traditional methods. Items can be ordered in terms of their difficulties if double monotony is assumed. From the responses to pairs of items, it was possible to derive certain controls of double monotony. Assuming double monotony, we produced a new method of estimating the reliability coefficient of the test or scale based on its own length, which seems to offer some advantages compared with conventional methods. Loevinger's coefficient of scalability (H) was derived in several ways, proving its good qualities as a coefficient of scalability and its relation to the variance of the scale score s. We also defined a new item coefficient of scalability (H_i) for a given scale. This item coefficient bears a clear relation to H, which can be derived as a weighted combination of the item coefficients H_i. We were able to give the asymptotic distributions of the sample estimate $\hat{H}$ for the null case of random response ($H = 0$) and for the non-null case ($H > 0$). We also derived a χ^2_{p-1}-test to test the equal scalability of a set of items for samples from p populations. It was also possible to demonstrate that there was no reason to emphasize the "perfect" patterns, as in probabilistic models the "imperfect" patterns also provide information about the dimension being measured.

Finally, we were able to demonstrate that the simple score s of the actual response pattern was in this model a reasonable (ordinal) measure of the respondent's position on the scale.

In *chapter 5* we developed from the results a set of scaling procedures based on the simple model investigated in chapter 4. The mild assumptions of this model correspond well with the low level of knowledge concerning variables and related items which is characteristic for most social research concerned with explorative analysis.

Only if, in later, more advanced stages of social research, variables are well defined and accumulated knowledge about the items to measure them has led to available pools of items from which scales may be constructed, may more sophisticated models be used. In this situation, which is probably characteristic of the field of mental and achievement testing, specific parametric models may profitably be used.

Procedures which are derived from the monotonely homogeneous or doubly monotone models of chapter 4 may therefore be useful in early and explorative stages of research in finding and defining variables and selecting the items that can be used to measure them. In subsequent stages of accumulated research concerning the nature of good items, specific parametric models, as discussed in chapter 3, which are special cases of the general model of chapter 4, may then be useful in obtaining more precise measurements.

The scaling procedures of chapter 5 were based on a simple definition of a scale in terms of the item coefficients H_i as the only criterion of scalability. The overall coefficient of scalability H indicated the general quality of the scale. We proposed a considerable relaxation of the usually too strong requirements for H, allowing values of 0.30 or higher.

The set of procedures held the following possibilities:
- the evaluation and testing of a given set of items as one scale (section 5.2.1);
- the step-wise construction of a scale from a pool of items (section 5.2.2);
- the consecutive construction of several scales: multiple scaling section 5.2.3);
- the extension of a given scale by means of the step-wise addition of new items (section 5.2.4);
- the investigation of double monotony (section 5.2.6);
- the computation of reliability coefficients, assuming double monotony (section 5.2.7).

In *part II* of this study we presented a number of applications of our methods taken from the author's studies in the fields of electoral research and mass communications research.

Chapters 6 and 7 dealt with an important problem in cross-cultural research: the detection and verification of cross-nationally common dimensions and variables.

In *chapter 6* some results were given with regard to the common dimensions of readership interest in types of newspaper contents found by factor analyses of interest ratings in two studies made in American communities and one made by the author in the Netherlands. In section 6.6 some evidence was given that dimensions found by factor analysis may sometimes prove to be scalable too.

In *chapter 7* the cross-cultural investigation of common dimensions was pursued in terms of our scaling model. We introduced the concept of *cross-cultural robustness* of scales as a relatively mild but probably sufficient criterion of *cross-cultural comparability* of scales. We gave a comparative analysis for the United States and the Netherlands of the common scalability of the well-known scale of the "sense of political efficacy". The application of our model showed that the usual American scale contains one defective item, which does not scale in the Netherlands either. We also found a striking correspondence between the results for the two countries, which demonstrated the cross-national robustness of the efficacy scale. Other results suggested that *intra*-cultural robustness of a scale across sub-groups may also result in *cross*-cultural robustness.

In chapter 7 we also developed a formal theory of the cross-cultural equivalence of indicators as suggested by Przeworski and Teune (1966). The analysis of chapter 7 concerning the concept of cross-cultural robustness of scales and our scaling model itself proved to be suitable applications of this theory.

We then showed in chapter 7 (and subsequently in chapter 8) that the scalability of a set of items and its measure H had a significance which extended further than just the definition of measuring instruments. The scalability of a set of attitude items, for instance, indicates a specific development and organization of the attitude elements as tapped by the items, into a typical (cumulative) attitude or belief system. The degree of constraint (Converse, 1964) is measured by the overall coefficient H, the relation of a specific element (item) to the system by the item coefficient H_i.

In *chapter 8* we continued our investigations of the sense of political efficacy with the extension of the original four-item scale by means of the addition of new items to a nine-item scale. We also developed an eight-item scale of the sense of political efficacy concerning local affairs. A further analysis proved that both scales formed one satisfactory seventeen-item scale, which supported our supposition that the sense of political efficacy is just one dimension along which a subject measures himself in relation to any part, national or local, of the political system. At the same time these results showed that our scaling method was capable of producing large scales.

We investigated, in section 8.4, the double monotony of the scales of the "sense of political efficacy". This analysis showed that our method, although based only on visual inspection of the appropriate matrices, gave reasonable clues concerning defective items and that our scales could be improved by rejecting such items. Of course, further evidence will be necessary in order to assess the general significance of the concept of double monotony. At the present stage of research, doubly monotone scales seem to us to be quite natural probabilistic counterparts of the original deterministic Guttman scale.

In *chapter 9*, finally, we reported some applications of multiple scaling. In our first example we saw how, for a set of items concerning informal political communication, for which we imagined that the possibility of more than one dimension might exist, such an application of our method yielded just one single scale of political opinion leadership. We were more successful in our analysis of two sets of items, one of which concerned the "sense of political efficacy", the other relating to the "sense of civic competence". Thus far these two concepts have not been distinguished clearly in the literature on political participation (Almond and Verba, 1963) and sometimes they have even been considered to define more or less the same variable (Dennis *et al.*, 1968, 79). An application of our procedure of multiple scaling showed that they clearly formed two separate scales, so that the "sense of political efficacy" and the "sense of civic competence" may be considered *different* political attitudes.

Similarly, we formed two scales concerning the perceived influence of certain persons, authorities and groups on local decision making. One scale concerned "outside" pressure group influence and the other the influence of local authorities.

Our last example concerned our efforts to scale a great number of items in the field of political participation. We saw that there was reason to distrust the original output of our procedure, which resulted in one large scale and a number of two-item scales. In fact we found that we could also construct two separate scales, one concerning *party participation* and the other measuring *local participation*. We chose the latter solution instead of the former, which was based on one large scale, because it seemed more in correspondence with the content of the items concerned and because it suited our theoretical purposes much better.

This particular example illustrated the necessity of always investigating critically the results of such scaling procedures and not depending solely on mathematically defined procedures and the computer for the definition of our variables. A close analysis of item content as well as a good theoretical perspective and relevant evidence should be our major guide lines in the interpretation of the results of scale analysis.

The illustrations given in these chapters may suffice to give the reader some guidance in the application of our technique of scale analysis. Their general significance will ultimately depend also on their usefulness in other fields than those studied by the author. As far as our own experiences go, such applications of our methods have led to reasonable and useful scales.*

We nevertheless hope that we have also demonstrated that these methods do not automatically warrant good scales. In fact such foolproof methods do not exist in research.

Therefore a further evaluation of the resulting scales will generally be necessary, starting, as we have seen before, with an analysis of the content of the items and the theoretical significance of the scales. Other methods of evaluation are necessary too.

For these reasons we will summarize the major points made in this study concerning possible ways of performing such an evaluation.

We remarked in section 5.2.8 that our step-wise procedure of scale construction, as is always the case in step-wise "maximization" procedures in multivariate analysis, does not necessarily produce an *optimal* scale, although it may be expected to produce reasonable ones. For instance, the order in which items are added to a scale from a given set in the process of scale construction, is determined by the definition of our scaling procedure. Consequently, the set may contain other and better scales which may not be reached by the step-wise sequence of the procedure. In particular the first pair of items selected by the procedure may sometimes determine the resulting scale to a high degree. In such a case, we may try to start with another pair of items by an application of the procedure mentioned in section 5.2.4.

---

*A colleague recently reported on a scale concerning Jewish customs and consisting of twenty-two items with a scalability coefficient of $\hat{H} = 0.64$ (F. Lange, personal communication).

An example of this approach was given in section 9.2. The particular order in which items are added to the scale may in itself be an indication of their homogeneity.

These considerations may be of particular importance when the procedure of multiple scaling (see section 5.2.3) is used. We saw in section 9.4.2 that the outcome may sometimes be regarded as a result of the construction of one scale out of several sets of items, each of which may be seen as forming scales for different, though related variables. A careful inspection of the results may reveal such a situation. The fact that in our version of the procedure the item coefficients with a given scale are also computed for items allotted to other scales may be helpful for such an investigation. If as a result of this inspection another cluster of items is thought to scale, the procedure of multiple scaling may be started along the lines of section 5.2.4, beginning with this particular cluster of items.

Then the choice of the scale defining constant c (see section 5.1.8) will still be rather arbitrary. Nevertheless it has some obvious consequences. The choice of a higher value will lead to stronger scales of shorter length, containing a smaller number of items. In the case of multiple scales, such a higher value may lead to a larger number of (shorter) scales. As far as our limited experiences go, a value as low as $c = 0.30$, which has been used by us, seems to be not unsatisfactory. Only further empirical evidence derived from the use of such scales may provide good criteria for choosing a proper value for lower bound c.

Sometimes additional criteria of evaluation can be obtained from the investigation of the intra-cultural robustness of a scale across different sub-groups, as we saw in section 8.2.

The analysis of the double monotony (holomorphism) of a set of items may also provide such criteria, as was shown in section 8.4.

But the ultimate importance of a scale can come only from construct validation: the theoretical and explanatory evidence gained from its use in empirical research in relation to other variables (Cronbach and Meehl, 1955; De Groot, 1961, 1969).

Once we have succeeded in constructing adequate scales from larger sets of items, and acquired some knowledge concerning the nature of the items required for particular important scales, more refined parametric measurement models, as discussed in chapter 3, may be used for what will probably be more precise and better measurements. Because such specific parametric models are simply special cases of the general model that led to our scaling procedure, there is some hope that our procedure may select items which are well adapted to such more sophisticated techniques.

The mathematical treatment of our general model has underlined the importance of the population distribution governing the selection of subjects to which the scales will be applied. By symmetry, the methods of item selection will have equally important impact. It may well be wortwhile to investigate the importance for *comparative* measurement of the strong models constructed by Rasch (see sections 3.1.2 and 3.2.4), which are "population distribution free", *i.e.* which incorporate certain invariance properties with respect to the selection of both subjects and items.

Appendix

1. SAMPLING DESIGNS

For the studies reported in sections 6.4.1, 6.5.1, 6.6 and 9.1.2, a two-stage probability sample was used. The population consisted of persons of 23 years of age or more (male persons of 21 years or more in the study reported in sections 6.6 and 9.1.2) listed in the electoral register and living in the non-agrarian part of Amsterdam. In order to limit interviewing costs and efforts, the relatively small northern part of the city, north of the harbour, was also excluded. For the same reasons of convenience, a two-stage technique of sampling was chosen.

For the study referred to in section 6.4.1, in the *first* stage a simple random sample of 42 electoral districts was chosen, each forming a cluster of approximately equal size (1,000 voters). In the second stage a simple random sample of 7 persons was drawn from each sampled district. Elimination of 11 addresses which were clearly wrong or outside the population definition, gave the ultimate sample size of 283. The response of 70% was obtained on the basis of at least one initial visit, followed by two more calls at non-response addresses. In some cases an even higher number of calls was made. This resulted in 199 completed interviews.

For the study reported in section 6.5.1 (the '65-study), the population definition and sampling procedure were exactly the same. Here 234 completed interviews were collected from an initial start of 288 regular addresses. The higher response percentage (81%) may partly be due to a procedure which involved considerably more calls than two after the initial visit.

For the study referred to in sections 6.6 and 9.1.2, a simple random sample of 129 electoral districts was used in the first stage. In the second stage, a simple random sample of 7 persons was drawn from each sampled district. Elimination of women and 37 addresses which fell outside the population definition, led to our ultimate sample of 371 *male* respondents, for the informal political communication study. Again the resulting response of 72% was effected on the basis of at least one initial visit and two subsequent calls at non-response addresses.

The sample for the study of the 1966 municipal elections, from which the other results of this study were obtained, was a simple random sample drawn from the electoral register (registered population of 21 years and over) as prepared for the municipal elections. The initial sample of 2776 individuals eventually produced 1513 interviews. The low response rate (55%) was due to the period in which the field work was done, which was June, the start of the holiday season. Here two calls were also made in the case of not-at-homes, after the initial visit.

We owe much to the kind cooperation of Dr. P. Bakker, director of the Registration Office and Bureau of Elections of the city of Amsterdam, and his staff.

2. THE DUTCH TEXT OF THE SCALES

For easy reference we give here the Dutch text of the most important scales reported on in this study. The text of the participation items will be given in the study of Van der Maesen (-).

2.1 *Politiek zelfvertrouwen; nationaal niveau*
(Sense of political efficacy; national level)

'Hier heb ik een blad met uitspraken over de Tweede Kamer en Regering. Wilt u mij die één voor één hardop voorlezen en steeds bij elke uitspraak zeggen of dit volgens u zo is of niet zo is?'

*Uitspraken over Tweede Kamer en Regering**
**Als ik ministers mijn opvattingen laat weten, dan zullen zij daar rekening mee houden.
(Scale alternative: 'Is zo').

*Numbering of statements follows the order in the questionnaire. Numbering of items is that of section 8.1.1.
**Non-scale items.

7. Als er geen opkomstplicht was, zou ik niet stemmen.
(Scale alternative: 'Is niet zo').
5. Voor mensen zoals ik, is de Nederlandse politiek te ingewikkeld.
(Scale alternative: 'Is niet zo').
1. Kamerleden bekommeren zich niet veel om de mening van mensen zoals ik.
(Scale alternative: 'Is niet zo').
3. De polieke partijen zijn aleen maar geinteresseerd in mijn stem en niet in mijn mening.
(Scaling alternative: 'Is niet zo').
8. Bij de bepaling van de Regeringspolitiek tellen de stemmen van mensen zoals ik mee.
(Scale alternative: 'Is zo').
6. Omdat ik zo weinig van politiek afweet, zou ik eigenlijk niet moeten stemmen.
(Scale alternative: 'Is niet zo').
*Als ik Kamerleden mijn opvattingen laat weten, dan zullen zij daar rekening mee houden. (Scale alternative: 'Is zo').
4. Mensen zoals ik hebben geen enkele invloed op de regeringspolitiek.
(Scale alternative: 'Is niet zo').
9. Er stemmen zoveel mensen bij verkiezingen dat mijn stem er niet toe doet.
(Scale alternative: 'Is niet zo').
2. Ministers bekommeren zich niet veel om de mening van mensen zoals ik.
(Scale alternative: 'Is niet zo').

2.2 Politiek zelfvertrouwen; lokaal niveau
(Sense of political efficacy; local level)

'Hier heb ik nog zo'n blad met uitspraken, maar het gaat nu over Amsterdam. Wilt u mij die uitspraken één voor één hardop voorlezen en steeds bij elke uitspraak zeggen of het volgens u zo is of niet zo is?'

*Uitspraken over Amsterdam***
L 1. Als ik het Gemeentebestuur mijn opvattingen laat weten, dan zullen zij daar rekening mee houden.
(Scale alternative: 'Is zo').

*Non-scale items.
**Numbering of statements follows the order in the questionnaire. Numbering of items is that of section 8.1.2.

L 6. Voor mensen zoals ik, is de Amsterdamse gemeentepolitiek te ingewikkeld.
(Scale alternative: 'Is niet zo').
L 3. Gemeenteraadsleden bekommeren zich niet veel om de mening van mensen zoals ik.
(Scale alternative: 'Is niet zo').
L 7. Bij de bepaling van de gemeentepolitiek tellen de stemmen van mensen zoals ik niet mee.
(Scale alternative: 'Is niet zo').
L 5. Als ik gemeenteraadsleden mijn opvattingen laat weten, dan zullen zij daar rekening mee houden.
(Scale alternative: 'Is zo').
L 4. Mensen zoals ik hebben geen enkele invloed op de gemeentepolitiek.
(Scale alternative: 'Is niet zo').
L 2. Het Gemeentebestuur bekommert zich niet veel om de mening van mensen zoals ik.
(Scale alternative: 'Is niet zo').
L 8. Omdat ik zo weinig van de politiek in de gemeente Amsterdam afweet, zou ik eigenlijk niet moeten stemmen in gemeenteraadsverkiezingen.
(Scale alternative: 'Is niet zo').

2.3   *Informele politieke communicatie*
      *(Opinion leadership)**

OL 3. Begint u in gezelschap zelf graag over politiek of laat u dat liever aan anderen over?
(Scale alternative: "begint meestal zelf; soms, dat hangt er van af").
OL 8. Heeft u de laatste tijd met bekenden over politiek gesproken?
(Scale alternative: "ja").
OL 9. Als er in gezelschap over politiek wordt gesproken, wat doet u dan het liefst: meedoen met het gesprek of alleen maar luisteren, of luistert u niet, heeft u geen belangstelling?
(Scale alternative: (meestal) meedoen met het gesprek).
OL 2. Stel, dat uw kennissen iets over politiek willen weten, is er dan een goede kans, dat zij dat aan u vragen, of eerder aan iemand anders?
(Scale alternative: "wordt geraadpleegd").

*Numbering of statements follows that of the questionnaire. Item numbering is that of section 9.1.2.

OL 4. *Hebben kennissen u wel eens gevraagd op welke partij zij zouden moeten stemmen?
(Scale alternative: "ja").
OL 5. Gelooft u dat uw kennissen u beschouwen als iemand die een goede kijk heeft op wat er in de politiek gebeurt?
(Scale alternative: "lijkt me wel").
OL 1. Heeft u kennissen wel eens aangeraden op welke partij zij zouden moeten stemmen?
(Scale alternative: 'ja').
OL 6. Heeft u op politiek gebied wel eens getracht een kennis te overtuigen?
(Scale alternative: 'ja').
OL 7. Probeert u wel eens kennissen op politiek gebied iets bij te brengen?
(Scale alternative: 'ja').

2.4 *Verwachting van persoonlijke politieke effectiviteit*
   *(Sense of civic competence)***

'Nu we het toch over problemen hebben, waar onder meer de gemeente iets aan zou kunnen doen, wou ik nog een paar mogelijkheden noemen.'
C 1. Denkt u dat u bij de burgemeester iets zou bereiken?
(Scale alternative: 'ja').
C 5. Denkt u dat u iets zou bereiken bij de wethouder?
(Scale alternative: 'ja').
C 3. Denkt u dat u iets zou bereiken bij de leden van de gemeenteraad?
(Scale alternative: 'ja').
C 4. *Denkt u dat u iets zou bereiken bij een ambtenaar van de betreffende gemeentedienst?
(Scale alternative: 'ja').

'Ik kom nu terug op een paar andere mogelijkheden. Het gaat over problemen, waar onder meer de gemeente iets aan zou kunnen doen.'

C 7. Denkt u dat u iets bereiken zou door te proberen er met andere mensen iets aan te doen?
(Scale alternative: 'ja').

  *Non-scale item.
  **Numbering of statements follows that of the questionnaire. Item numbering is that of section 9.2.

C 6. U zou er bij een vereniging of organisatie, die zich met dit soort problemen bezighoudt op aan kunnen dringen, dat zij er iets aan doen. Denkt u dat u daarmee iets zou bereiken?
(Scale alternative: 'ja').
C 2.** Denkt u dat u iets zou bereiken door er bij een politieke partij op aan te dringen dat zij er iets aan doen?
(Scale alternative: 'ja').

2.5 *Invloedsstereotypen*
*(Influence stereotypes)**

'Hier heb ik een blad met personen en groepen. Denkt u dat de volgende personen of groepen bij belangrijke beslissingen in Amsterdam, veel, weinig, of helemaal niets te zeggen hebben?'
(Scale alternative: 'veel').

PG 3. De Vakbonden
LA 3. De Wethouders
PG 2. De Kamer van Koophandel
LA 4. De Gemeenteraad
LA 2. De Burgemeester
1.** De Inwoners van de stad
PG 5. De Regering
3.** De Politieke Partijen
PG 4. Grote Ondernemingen
PG 1. De Werkgevers-organisaties
LA 1. Hoge Gemeente-ambtenaren
2.** De Kranten

*Numbering of statements follows that of the questionnaire. Item numbering is that of section 9.3.
**Non-scale item.

References

AGGER, R. E., GOLDSTEIN, M. N., and PEARL, S. A. (1961). Political cynicism: measurement and meaning. *Journal of politics, 23*, 477–505.

AGGER, R. E., GOLDRICH, D., and SWANSON, B. E. (1964). *The rulers and the ruled.* New York: Wiley.

AHMAVARAA, Y. (1954). The mathematical theory of factorial invariance under selection. *Psychometrika, 19*, 27–38.

ALGER, C. F. (1966). Interaction in a committee of the United Nations General Assembly. *Midwest journal of political science, 10*, 411–47.

ALKER, H. R. JR. (1964). Dimensions of conflict in the General Assembly. *The Americal political science review, 58*, 642–57.

ALKER, H. R. JR. (1966). Causal inference and political analysis. In: Bernd, J. L. (ed.). *Mathematical applications in political science. II.* Dallas (Tex.): Southern Methodist University Press, 7–43.

ALKER, H. R. JR. and RUSSETT, B. M. (1965). *World politics in the General Assembly.* New Haven (Conn.): Yale University Press.

ALMOND, G. A., and VERBA, S. (1963). *The civic culture.* Princeton (N.J.): Princeton University Press.

ANAST, P. (1961). Attitude toward the press as a function of interests. *Journalism quarterly, 38*, 376–80.

ANDERSEN, E. B. (1967). *Asymptotic properties of conditional maximum likelihood estimators.* Copenhagen: Technical report no. 1. Copenhagen School of Economics and Business Administration.

ANDERSEN, E. B. (1968). *Posterior analysis of individual parameters in item analysis.* Copenhagen: Technical report no. 4. Copenhagen School of Economics and Business Administration.

ANDERSEN, E. B. (1969). *The numerical solution of a set of conditional estimation equations.* Copenhagen: Technical report no. 5. Copenhagen School of Economics and Business Administration.

ANDERSON, L. F., WATTS, M. W. JR., and WILCOX, A. R. (1966). *Legislative roll-call analysis.* Evanston (Ill.): Northwestern University Press.

ANDERSON, T. W. and GOODMAN, L. A. (1957). Statistical inference about Markov chains. *The annals of mathematical statistics, 28*, 89–110.

340 *References*

ANDERSON, T. W. (1959). Some scaling models and estimation procedures in the latent class model. In: Grenander, U. (ed.), *Probability and statistics.* (The Harald Cramér Volume). Stockholm: Almqvist and Wiksell.

BAN, VAN DEN, A. W. (1963). *Boer en landbouwvoorlichting* (in Dutch). Wageningen: Centrum voor Landbouwpublikaties en Landbouwdokumentatie.

BAN, VAN DEN, A. W. (1964). A revision of the two-step flow of communications hypothesis. *Gazette, X,* 237–49.

BERELSON, B. R., LAZARSFELD, P. F., and McPHEE, W. N. (1954). *Voting.* Chicago (Ill.): University of Chicago Press.

BERKSON, J. (1953). A statistically precise and relatively simple method of estimating the bio-assay with quantal response, based on the logistic function. *Journal of the American Statistical Association, 48,* 565–99.

BERTING, J. (1962). Enige bezwaren tegen scalogram-analyse als toets voor uni-dimensionaliteit (In Dutch). *Sociologische gids, 9,* 2–15.

BERRIEN, F. K. (1967). Methodological and related problems in cross-cultural research. *International journal of psychology, 2,* 33–43.

BIRNBAUM, A. (1965). *Some latent trait models and their use in inferring an examinee's ability.* Princeton (N.J.): Educational Testing Service.

BIRNBAUM, A. (1968). Some latent trait models and their use in inferring an examinee's ability. In: Lord and Novick, 397–479.

BLALOCK, H. M. JR. (1961). *Causal inferences in nonexperimental research.* Chapel Hill. (N.C.): The University of North Carolina Press.

BOUDON, R. (1966). Analyse hiérarchique et indice de transitivé. In: Michelat, G. et Thomas, J-P, H. *Dimensions du nationalisme.* Paris: Armand Colin, 171–6.

BOUDON, R. (1967). *L'analyse mathematique des faits sociaux.* Paris: Librairie Plon.

BORGATTA, E. F. (1955). An error ratio for scalogram analysis. *Public opinion quarterly, 19,* 96–100.

BRADLEY, R. A. and TERRY, M. E. (1952). Rank analysis of incomplete block designs, I. The method of paired comparisons. *Biometrika, 39,* 324–45.

BROUWER, M: (1967). Prolegomena to a theory of mass communication. In: Thayer, L. (ed.) *Communication-concepts and perspectives.* Washington: Spartan Books, 227–39.

BROUWER, M. (1968). *Stereotypen als folklore.* Vinkeveen: Fringilla.

CAMPBELL, E. Q. and KERCKHOFF, A. C. (1957). A critique of the concept "universe of attributes". *Public opinion quarterly, 21,* 295–303.

CAMPBELL, N. R. (1928). *An account of the principles of measurements and calculations,* London; Longmans, Green.

CAMPBELL, A. (1962). The passive citizen. *Acta sociologica, VI,* 9–21.

CAMPBELL, A., GURIN, G. and MILLER, W. E. (1954). *The voter decides.* Evanston (Ill.): Row, Peterson.

CAMPBELL, A., CONVERSE, P. E., MILLER, W. E. and STOKES, D. E. (1960). *The American voter.* New York: Wiley.

CARTER, R. E. JR. and CLARKE, P. (1963). Suburbanites, city residents and local news. *Journalism quarterly, 40,* 548–58.

COLEMAN, J. S., KATZ, E. and MENZEL, H. (1966). *Medical innovation. A diffusion study,* New York: Bobbs Merrill.

CONVERSE, PH. E. (1964). The nature of belief systems in mass publics. In: Apter. David E. (ed.), *Ideology and discontent,* New York: Free Press of Glencoe, 206–61.

CONVERSE, PH. E. (1966). The problem of party distances in models of voting change. In: M. K. Jennings and L. H. Zeigler, (eds.) *The electoral process.* Englewood Cliffs (N.J.): Prentice-Hall, 175–207.

CNUDDE, C. F. and McCRONE, D. J. (1966). The linkage between constituency attitudes and Congressional voting behavior: a causal model. *The American political science review, 60,* 66–72.

COOMBS, C. H. (1950). Psychological scaling without a unit of measurement. *Psychological review, 57,* 145–58.

COOMBS, C. H. (1953). The theory and methods of social measurement. In: L. Festinger and D. Katz (eds.) *Research methods in the behavioral sciences.* New York: Dryden Press, 471–535.

COOMBS, C. H. (1964). *A theory of data.* New York: Wiley.

CRONBACH, L. J. and MEEHL, P. E. (1955). Construct validity in psychological tests. *Psychological bulletin, 52,* 281–302.

DAALDER, H. (1955). Parties and politics in the Netherlands, *Political studies, III,* 1–16.

DAALDER, H. (1966). The Netherlands: opposition in a segmented society. In Dahl, R. A. *et al., Political oppositions in Western democracies.* New Haven (Conn.): Yale University Press.

DANIELSON, W. A. (1957). A data reduction method for scaling dichotomous items. *Public opinion quarterly, 21,* 377–9.

DAUDT, H. (1961). *Floating voters and the floating vote.* Leiden: Stenfert Kroese.

DAUDT, H., and STAPEL, J. (1966). Parliament, politics and the voter: results of an opinion-survey (in Dutch). *Acta Politica, I,* 46–76.

DAUDT, H., MAESEN, VAN DER, C. E., and MOKKEN, R. J. (1968). Political efficacy: a further exploration. *Acta politica, III,* 286–307.

DAVID, H. (1963). *The method of paired comparisons.* London: Griffin.

DAHL, R. A. (1961a). The behavioral approach in political science: epitaph for a monument to a succesful protest. *The American political science review, 55,* 763–72.

DAHL, R. A. (1961b). *Who governs?* New Haven (Conn.): Yale University Press.

DENNIS, J., LINDBERG, L., McCRONE, D. and STIEFBOLD, R. (1968). Political socialization to democratic orientations in four Western systems. *Comparative political studies, I,* 71–101.

DOORNBOS, R. (1966). *Slippage tests,* Mathematical Centre Tracts 15. Amsterdam: Matematisch Centrum.

DOUVAN, E., and WALKER, A. M. (1956). The sense of effectiveness in public affairs. *Psychological monographs, 70,* no. 32.

DUIJKER, H. C. J. and ROKKAN, S. (1954). Organizational aspects of cross-national social research. *Journal of social issues, X,* 8–24.

DUIJKER, H. C. J. (1955). Comparative research in social science with special reference to attitude research. *International social science bulletin, VII,* 555–66.

DUIJKER, H. C. J. and FRIJDA, N. H. (1960). *National character and national stereotypes.* (Confluence, Vol. I) Amsterdam: North-Holland Publishing Company.

DYNKIN, E. B. (1951). Necessary and sufficient statistics for a family of probability distributions. In: *Selected translations in mathematical statistics and probability, 1961, 1,* 23–41.

EASTON, D. (1965). *A systems analysis of political life.* New York: Wiley.

EASTON, D. and DENNIS, J. (1967). The child's acquisition of regime norms: political efficacy. *The American political science review, 61,* 25–38.

EDWARDS, A. L. (1957). *Techniques of attitude scale construction.* New York: Appleton – Century – Crofts.

EDWARDS, A. L. and KILPATRICK, F. P. (1948). Scale analysis and the measurement of social attitudes, *Psychometrika, 13,* 99–114.

EEDEN, VAN, C. and RUNNENBURG, J. TH. (1960). Conditional limit-distributions for the entries in a 2×2-table. *Statistica neerlandica, 14,* 111–26.

ELDERSVELD, S. J. (1964). *Political parties.* Chicago (Ill.): Rand McNally.

ERVIN, S. and BOWER, R. T. (1952). Translation problems in international surveys. *Public opinion quarterly, 16,* 595–604.

FARRIS, C. D. (1960). Selected attitudes on foreign affairs as correlates of authoritarianism and political anomy. *Journal of politics, 22,* 50–67.

FESTINGER, L. (1947). The treatment of qualitative data by "scale analysis". *Psychological bulletin, 44,* 149–61.

FINNEY, D. J. (1952). *Probit analysis.* London: Cambridge University Press.

FORD, R. N. (1950). A rapid scoring procedure for scaling attitude questions. *Public opinion quarterly, 14,* 507–32.

FRASER, D. A. S. (1957). *Nonparametric methods in statistics.* New York: Wiley.

FRASER, D. A. S. (1966). Sufficiency for regular models. *Sankyā, (Series A), 28,* 137–44.

FRIJDA, N. and JAHODA, G. (1966). On the scope and methods of cross-cultural research. *International journal of psychology, 1,* 109–27.

GALTUNG, J. (1967). *Theory and methods of social research.* Oslo: Universitetsforlaget.

GIBSON, W. A. (1959). Three multivariate models: factor analysis, latent structure analysis, and latent profile analysis. *Psychometrika, 24,* 229–52.

GIBSON, W. A. (1967). A latent structure for the simplex. *Psychometrika, 32,* 35–46.

GOLDBERG, A. S. (1966). Discerning a causal pattern among data on voting behavior. *The American political science review, 60,* 913–22.

GOODENOUGH, W. M. (1944). A technique for scale analysis. *Journal of educational and psychological measurement, 4,* 179–90.

GOODMAN, L. A. (1959). Simple statistical methods for scalogram analysis. *Psychometrika, 24,* 29–43.

GOODMAN, L. A. and KRUSKAL, W. H. (1954). Measures of association for cross classifications. *Journal of the American Statistical Association, 49,* 732–64.

GOODMAN, L. A. and KRUSKAL, W. H. (1959). Measures of association for cross classifications. II: Further discussion and references. *Journal of the American Statistical Association, 54,* 132–63.

GOODMAN, L. A. and KRUSKAL, W. H. (1963). Measures of association for cross classifications. III: Approximate sampling theory. *Journal of the American Statistical Association, 58,* 310–64.

GOUDSBLOM, J. (1967). *Dutch society.* New York: Random House.

GREEN, B. F. (1954). Attitude measurement. In: G. Lindzey (ed.), *Handbook of social psychology, volume I.* Cambridge (Mass.): Addison-Wesley. 335–69.

GREEN, B. F. (1956). A method of scalogram analysis using summary statistics, *Psychometrika, 21,* 79–88.

GROOT, DE, A. D. (1969). Methodology. The Hague: Mouton.

GULLIKSEN, H. (1950). *Theory of mental tests.* New York: Wiley.

GUTTMAN, L. (1947). The Cornell technique for scale and intensity analysis. *Educational and psychological measurement, 7,* 247–80.

GUTTMAN, L. (1950a). The basis for scalogram analysis. In: Stouffer *et al.* 60–90.

GUTTMAN, L. (1950b). Problems of reliability. In Stouffer *et al.* 277–311.

GUTTMAN, L. (1950c). Relation of scalogram analysis to other techniques. In: Stouffer *et al,* 172–212.

GUTTMAN, L. (1954a). A new approach to factor analysis: the radex. In: Lazarsfeld, P. F. (ed.). *Mathematical thinking in the social sciences,* Glencoe, (Ill.): The Free Press, 258–348.

GUTTMAN, L. (1954b). The Israel alpha technique for scale analysis. In: Riley *et al.*

GUTTMAN, L. (1968). A general nonmetric technique for finding the smallest coordinate space for a configuration of points. *Psychometrika, 33,* 469–506.

HALEY, D. C. (1952). Estimation of the dosage mortality relationship when the dose is subject to error. *Technical Report No. 15.* Stanford (Cal.): Applied mathematics and statistics laboratory, Stanford University.

HARDY, G. H., LITTLEWOOD, J. E. and PÓLYA, G. (1934). *Inequalities.* Cambridge: Cambridge University Press.

HEMELRIJK, J. (1965). *A priori* distributions in industry, or conditional and unconditional moments. *Report SP 86, Dept. of Mathematical Statistics.* Amsterdam: Mathematical Centre.

HENRY, A. F. (1952). A method of classifying non-scale response patterns in a Guttman scale. *Public opinion quarterly, 16,* 94–106.

HOFSTETTER, R., BOYD, R. W. and VAN HOUWELING, D. (1967). A Fortran 3400/3600 program for computing multiple-scale Guttman scalogram analysis. *Behavioral science, 12,* 500–1.

JACKSON, J. M. (1949). A simple and more rigorous technique for scale analysis. In: *A manual of scale analysis,* Part II. Toronto: McGill University, Mimeo.

JACOBSON, E. (1954). Methods used for producing comparable data in the OCSR seven-nation attitude study. *Journal of social issues, X,* 40–51.

JACOBSON, E., KUMATA, H. and GULLAHORN, J. E. (1960). Cross-cultural contributions to attitude research. *Public opinion quarterly, 24,* 205–23.

JAKOBOVITS, L. A. (1966). Comparative psycholinguistics in the study of cultures. *International journal of psychology, 1,* 15–37.

JANOWITZ, M. (1952). *The community press in an urban setting.* Glencoe (Ill.): The Free Press.

JANOWITZ, M. and MARVICK, D. (1956). *Competitive pressure and democratic consent.* Ann Arbor (Mich.): Bureau of Government, Institute of Public Administration, University of Michigan.

KAHN, L. A. and BODINE, A. J. (1951). Guttman scale analysis by means of IBM equipment. *Educational and psychological measurement, 11,* 298–314.

KATZ, E., and LAZARSFELD, P. F. (1955). *Personal influence.* Glencoe (Ill.): The Free Press.

KATZ, E. (1957). The two-step flow of communication: an up-to-date report on an hypothesis. *Public opinion quarterly, 21,* 61–78.

KATZ, E. (1960). Communication research and the image of society. Convergence of two traditions. *The American journal of sociology, LXV,* 435–40.

KATZ, E., LEVIN, M. L. and HAMILTON, H. (1963). Traditions of research on the diffusion of innovation. *The American sociological review, 28,* 237–52.

KLAPPER, J. T. (1960). *The effects of mass communication.* New York: The Free Press.

KOOMEN, W. and WINNUBST, J. A. M. (1968). Onder en boven de Moerdijk (In Dutch). *Sociologische gids, 15,* 299–308.

KORNHAUSER, A., SHEPPARD, H. L., and MAYER, A. J. (1956). *When Labor votes.* New York: University Books.

KRANTZ, DAVID H. (1967). *A Survey of measurement theory.* Michigan Mathematical Psychology Program, MMPP 67–4. Ann Arbor (Mich.): University of Michigan.

KRUSKAL, J. B. (1964a). Multidimensional scaling by optimizing goodness of fit to a nonmetric hypothesis. *Psychometrika, 29,* 1–27.

KRUSKAL, J. B. (1964b). Nonmetric multidimensional scaling: a numerical method. *Psychometrika, 29,* 115–30.

LAND, VAN DER, L. (ed.) (1967). *Provo-issue of Delta* (a review of arts, life and thought in the Netherlands) *X,* no. 3.

LANE, R. (1959). *Political life.* Glencoe (Ill.): The Free Press.

LAZARSFELD, P. F., BERELSON, B. and GAUDET, H. (1948). *The people's choice,* second edition, New York: Columbia University Press.

LAZARSFELD, P. F. (1950). The logical and mathematical foundation of latent structure analysis. In: Stouffer *et al.,* 362–412.

LAZARSFELD, P. F. (1959a). Latent structure analysis. In: Koch, S. (ed.). *Psychology: a study of a science, Vol. 3.* New York: McGraw-Hill.

LAZARSFELD, P. F. (1959b). Evidence and inference in social research. In: Lerner, D. *Evidence and inference,* Glencoe (Ill.): The Free Press, 107–38.

LEHMANN, E. L. (1959). *Testing statistical hypotheses.* New York: Wiley.

LEWIN, K. (1947). Group decision and social change. In: Newcomb, T. H. and Hartley, E. L. Eds.), *Readings in social psychology.* New York: Henry Holt, 330–44.

LIONBERGER, H. F. (1960). *Adoption of new ideas and practices.* Ames (Iowa): Iowa State University Press.

LOEVINGER, J. (1947). A systematic approach to the construction and evaluation of tests of ability. *Psychological monographs, 61,* no. 4

LOEVINGER, J. (1948). The technic of homogeneous tests compared with some aspects of "scale analysis" and factor analysis. *Psychological bulletin, 45,* 507–30.

LORD, F. M. (1953). An application of confidence intervals and of maximum likelihood to the estimation of an examinee's ability. *Psychometrika, 18,* 57–77.

LORD, F. M. and NOVICK, M. R. (1968). *Statistical theories of mental test scores.* Reading (Mass.) Addison-Wesley.

LUCE, R. D. (1959). *Individual choice behavior.* New York, Wiley.

LIJPHART, A. (1968). *The politics of accomodation.* Berkeley and Los Angeles: University of California Press.

MacRae, D. Jr. (1958). *Dimensions of congressional voting.* Berkeley (Cal.): University of California Press.

Maesen, van der, C. E. (1967). Kiezers op drift (in Dutch) *Acta Politica, II,* 169–200.

Maesen, van der, C. E. *Dissertation* in preparation.

Mannheim, K. (1953). *Essays on the sociology of knowledge.* New York: Oxford University Press.

Marder, E. (1952). Linear segments: a technique for scalogram analysis. *Public opinion quarterly, 16,* 417–31.

Matalon, B. (1965). *L'analyse hiérarchique.* Paris: Gauthier-Villars; Mouton.

Matthews, D. R. and Prothro, J. W. (1966). *Negroes and the new Southern politics.* New York: Harcourt, Brace and World.

McDonald, R. P. (1962). A note on the derivation of the general latent class model. *Psychometrika, 27,* 203–206.

Menzel, H. (1953). A new coefficient for scalogram-analysis. *Public opinion quarterly, 17,* 268–80.

Meredith, W. (1964a). Notes on factorial invariance. *Psychometrika, 29,* 177–85.

Meredith, W. (1964b). Rotation to achieve factorial invariance. *Psychometrika, 29,* 187–206.

Meredith, W. (1965). Some results based on a general stochastic model for mental tests. *Psychometrika, 30,* 419–40.

Milbrath, L. W. (1965). *Political participation.* Chicago (Ill.): Rand McNally.

Miller, W. E. and Stokes D. E. (1963). Constituency influence in Congress. *The American political science review, 57,* 45–56.

Moerkerk, J. H. (1967). De gemeenteraadsverkiezingen van 1966 in Amsterdam: campagne, voorkeurstemmen en absenteïsme (in Dutch). *Acta politica, II,* 201–19.

Mokken, R. J. (1969a). Dutch-American comparisons of the 'sense of political efficacy': some remarks on cross-cultural 'robustness' of scales. *Acta politica, IV,* 425–48.

Mokken, R. J. (1969b). Dutch-American comparisons of the 'sense of political efficacy'. *Quality & quantity, European journal of methodology, 3,* 125–52.

Moscovici, S. et Durain, G. (1956). Quelques applications de la théorie de l'information á la construction des échelles d'attitudes. *L'année psychologique, 56,* 47–57.

Noland, E. W. (1945). Worker attitude and industrial absenteeism: a statistical appraisal. *American sociological review, 10,* 503–10.

Mosteller, F. (1949). A theory of scalogram analysis, using noncumulative types of items: a new approach to Thurstone's method of scaling attitudes. *Report no. 9,* Lab. of Soc. Relations, Harvard University.

Osgood, C. E., Suci, G. and Tannenbaum, P. (1957). *The measurement of meaning.* Urbana (Ill.): University of Illinois Press.

Osgood, C. E. (1964). Semantic differential technique in the comparative study of cultures. *American anthropologist, 66,* 171–200.

Pearson, R. G. (1957). Plus percentage ratio and the coefficient of scalability. *Public opinion quarterly, 21,* 379–80.

Pfanzagl, J. (1968). *Theory of measurement.* Würzburg: Physica-Verlag.

Pinneau, S. R. and Newhouse, A. (1964). Measures of invariance and comparability in factor analysis for fixed variables. *Psychometrika, 29,* 271–81.

PRZEWORSKI, A. and TEUNE, H. (1966). Equivalence in cross-national research. *Public opinion quarterly, 30,* 551–68.

RASCH, G. (1960). *Probabilistic models for some intelligence and attainment tests.* (Studies in mathematical psychology I). Copenhagen: Nielsen and Lydiche (for Danmarks Paedagogiske Institut).

RASCH, G. (1961). On general laws and the meaning of measurement in psychology. In: *Proceedings of the Fourth Berkeley Symposium on mathematical statistics and probability, Vol. IV,* Berkeley: University of California Press, 321–33.

RASCH, G. (1966). An individualistic approach to item analysis. In: Lazarsfeld, P. F. and Henry, N. W. *Readings in mathematical social science.* Chicago: (Ill.): Science Research Associates, Inc. 89–108.

RASCH, G. and LEUNBACH, G. (1966). Population–free item analysis. In: IBM-Symposium. *Computers in psychological research.* Paris: Gauthiers-Villars, 193 – 214.

RASCH, G. (1967a). An informal report on a theory of objectivity in comparisons. In: *Psychological measurement theory.* (Proceedings of the NUFFIC international summer session in science at "Het Oude Hof", The Hague, July 14–28, 1966). Leiden: Psychological Institute of the University of Leiden).

RASCH, G. (1967b). An individual-centered approach to item analysis with two categories of answers. In: *Psychological measurement theory.* (Proceedings of the NUFFIC international summer session in science at "Het Oude Hof", The Hague, July 14–28, 1966). Leiden: Psychological Institute of the University of Leiden.

RIESELBACH, L. N. (1960). Quantitative techniques for studying voting behavior in the UN General Assembly. *International organization, 14,* 291–306.

RILEY, M. W., RILEY, J. W. and TOBY, J. (1954). *Sociological studies in scale analysis.* New Brunswick (N.J.): Rutgers University Press.

ROGERS, E. M. (1962). *Diffusion of innovations.* New York: Free Press of Glencoe.

ROSKAM, E. E. CH. I. (1968). *Metric analysis of ordinal data in psychology.* Dissertation University of Leiden. Leiden: University of Leiden.

ROSS, J. (1966). An empirical study of a logistic mental test model. *Psychometrika, 31,* 325–40.

ROSSI, P. H. (1959). Four landmarks in voting research. In: Burdick, E., and Brodbeck, A. J. (eds). *American voting behavior.* Glencoe (Ill.): The Free Press. 5–54.

RYAN, B. and GROSS, N. (1943). The diffusion of hybrid seed corn in two Iowa communities. *Rural sociology, 7,* 15–24.

SAGI, P. C. (1959). A statistical test for the significance of a coefficient of reproducibility. *Psychometrika, 24,* 19–27.

SCOTT, D. and SUPPES, P. (1958). Foundational aspects of theories of measurement. *Journal of symbolic logic, 23,* 113–28.

SHAPIRO, G. (1948). Mydral's definition of the 'South'; A methodological note. *American sociological review, 13,* 619–21.

SHEPARD, R. H. (1962a). The analysis of proximities: multidimensional scaling with an unknown distance function I. *Psychometrika, 27,* 125–40.

SHEPARD, R. H. (1962b). The analysis of proximities: multidimensional scaling with an unknown distance function II. *Psychometrika, 27,* 219–46.

SIXTL, F. (1967). *Messmethoden der Psychologie.* Weinheim: Julius Beltz.

SMOLENAARS, A. J. (1968). *Kerkelijkheid en persoonlijkheidskenmerken in twee Zuider-zeepolders.* (In Dutch, with English summary). Amsterdam: Stichting voor het bevolkingsonderzoek in de drooggelegde Zuiderzeepolders.

STEVENS, S. S. (1951). Mathematics, measurement and psychophysics. In: S. S. Stevens (ed.) *Handbook of experimental psychology.* New York: Wiley.

STEVENS, S. S. (1959). Measurement, psychophysics, and utility. In: Churchman, C. W. and Ratoosh, P. (ed). *Measurement: definitions and theory.* New York: Wiley, 18–63.

STOKES, D. E. (1963). Spatial models of party competition. *The American political science review, 57,* 368–77.

STOUFFER, S. A. GUTTMAN, L., SUCHMAN, E. A., LAZARSFELD, P. F., STAR, S. A. and CLAUSEN, J. A. (1950). *Measurement and prediction. Studies in social psychology in World War II, Volume IV.* Princeton, (N.J.): Princeton University Press.

STOUFFER, S. A., BORGATTA, E. F., HAYS, D. G. and HENRY, A. F. (1952). A technique for improving cumulative scales. *Public opinion quarterly, 16,* 273–91.

STOUTHARD, PH. C. (1965). *Data Modellen.* (In Dutch: English summary). Tilburg: Catholic School of Economics.

SUCHMAN, E. A. (1950a). The scalogram board technique for scale analysis. In: Stouffer *et al.,* 91–121.

SUCHMAN, E. A. (1950b). The utility of scalogram analysis. In: Stouffer *et al.,* 122–71.

SUPPES, P. and ZINNES, J. L. (1963). Basic measurement theory. In: R. D. Luce, R. R. Bush and E. Galanter, (eds.) *Handbook of mathematical psychology,* New York: Wiley, 1–76.

TANTER, R. (1967). Toward a theory of political development. *Midwest journal of political science, 11,* 145–72.

THURSTONE, L. L. (1927). A law of comparative judgment. *Psychological review, 34,* 273–86.

TOBY, J. and TOBY, M. L. (1954). A method of selecting dichotomous items by cross-tabulation. In: Riley *et al.,* 339–55.

TORGERSON, W. S. (1958). *Theory and methods of scaling.* New York: Wiley.

TUCKER, L. R. (1952). A level of proficiency scale for a unidimensional skill. *American psychologist, 7,* 408.

ULMER, S. S. (1966). Sub-group formation in the constitutional convention. *Midwest journal of political science, 10,* 288–303.

VERBA, S., BRODY, R. A., PARKER, E. B., NIE, N. H., POLSBY, N. W., EKMAN, P., BLACK, G. S. (1968). Public opinion and the war in Vietnam. *The American political science review, 61,* 317–33.

WHITE, B. W. and SALTZ, E. (1957). Measurement of reproducibility. *Psychological bulletin, 54,* 81–99.

WHITING, J. W. M. (1954). The cross-cultural method. In: *G. Lindzey (Ed.), Handbook of social psychology, Volume I.* Cambridge (Mass.): Addison-Wesley, 523–31.

ZEHNA, P. W. (1966). Invariance of maximum likelihood estimates. *The annals of mathematical statistics, 37,* 744.

Index

other techniques, 62
 examples in political research, 3
 H-technique (Stouffer), 67
 multidimensional, 12–13, 195
 score, *s.* SCORE

SCORE
of non-scale patterns, 34, 68–69, 185
optimal linear–, 104, 141, 186
 and sufficiency, 34
simple–(test, scale), 34, 69, 109, 177
 correlation with latent variate, 140
 local discrimination, 139, 186
 optimal linear, 141, 186
 Rasch's model, 109–110, 141, 156, 186
 relation to H, 151
 reliability, 145
 sufficiency, 34, 110, 156, 186
 trace line, 139, 179

SIMPLEX
perfect–, 137
quasi–, 137

TRACE LINE
holomorph–, 106
item–, 28, 94
monotonely homogeneous–, 118
specific objectivity, 108
trace function, 93

UNITED NATIONS
Sixteenth General Assembly, 13

VALIDATION
construct–, 6, 194, 331